General Business in Our Modern Society

Charles R. Hopkins University of Minnesota

Thomas B. Duff University of Minnesota, Duluth

Robert E. Gades University of Nebraska

Dennis C. Lytle Bowling Green State University

Glencoe Publishing Co., Inc.
Encino, California

Glencoe Publishing Co., Inc.
17337 Ventura Boulevard
Encino, California 91316
Collier Macmillan Canada, Ltd.

Library of Congress Catalog Card Number: 77-73296

ISBN 0-02-472860-8

 2 3 4 5 6 7 8 9   83 82 81 80

Preface

The private enterprise system can only be truly effective when all its participants are sufficiently informed to make intelligent decisions. In the private enterprise system, all sectors of the economy—business, labor, consumer, and government—have specific, interrelated roles and responsibilities. How each of these sectors operates affects not only the total economy, but each of the other sectors as well. Consumer decisions affect business decisions and are affected by business decisions. Business decisions influence government decisions and are influenced by government decisions. The actions of each sector often depend on the actions of the other sectors. Consequently, in order to make intelligent decisions, it is essential that all people have an understanding of the nature of these relationships and of the operation and scope of each economic sector.

OBJECTIVES

The primary objective of *General Business in Our Modern Society* is to help students understand our private enterprise system and their relationship to it as citizens, consumers, and workers. After completing their study of this text, students should be able to demonstrate an understanding of the following:

- How intelligent decision making contributes to the general welfare of all.
- How business firms operate within the private enterprise system.
- How consumer demand affects what and how much goods and services are provided by the business and government sectors of the economy.
- How to develop and assert individual responsibility.
- How to develop personal economic competence.
- How to develop and use career decision making skills and job seeking skills.

ORGANIZATION

General Business in Our Modern Society is organized into five major parts, each of which may be presented in whatever sequence best fits individual instructional needs. Part I examines the nature of our private enterprise system and the role business plays in it. Part II covers money, banking, and consumer credit. Part III focuses on consumer decision making and the management of personal finances. Part IV discusses methods of building financial security. And Part V points out job opportunities and suggests ways in which students may prepare for specific careers.

Each chapter is preceded by objectives that clearly identify student learning goals. The end-of-chapter activities have been constructed to measure student attainment of these goals as well as to reinforce the student's understanding of material presented in the chapter. Within the chapter itself, student comprehension is constantly challenged. New topics are introduced in small learning segments, and each of these segments is immediately followed by one or more thought questions. These questions require the student to consider what they have just read by relating it to personal attitudes and experiences. And in the classroom, the questions provide a stepping-off point for individual expression.

SPECIAL FEATURES

General Business in Our Modern Society is based on classroom teaching experience and on extensive research that includes the study "Measurement of Personal Economic Understandings Developed in Basic Business," for which Dr. Thomas B. Duff received the Robert E. Slaughter Research Award. The contents of the text have been thoroughly tested to provide maximum benefit to both student and teacher.

For example, special attention was given to the reading level of *General Business in Our Modern Society*. Professional Resources Associates, Inc., computer-analyzed the text for reading difficulty. As a result of the analysis, difficult nontechnical terms, unnecessary technical terms, and complex sentence structures were adjusted. Technical terms that may be new to students but which are commonly used in business are defined at their first point of use and printed in color for quick reference.

Consistent with its primary objective of helping students understand our private enterprise system and their relationship to it as citizens, consumers, and workers, *General Business in Our Modern Society* places particular emphasis on career awareness and preparation. Individual chapters are devoted to such topics as career opportunities, career self-assessment, career preparation, and finding and keeping a job.

SUPPORTING MATERIALS

General Business in Our Modern Society is by itself a self-contained instructional system. It is also the major component of a more comprehensive system that includes two student activity guides and a teacher's manual and key. Student Activity Guide I correlates with Chapters 1 through 22 of the textbook, and Student Activity Guide 2 correlates with Chapters 23 through 46. Each guide contains working papers for all text activities as well as supplemental activities for each chapter. The guides also contain integrated end-of-part projects that use mini-simulations, role playing, record keeping, budgeting, and career planning to reinforce student understanding of the major topics covered in each of the parts.

The fourth component of the system, the teacher's manual and key, contains a general methodology section, specific chapter-by-chapter teaching suggestions, recommended sources of additional information, transparency/duplicating masters, and a series of achievement tests, which can be either duplicated in whole or used as a bank from which individual tests can be constructed.

ACKNOWLEDGMENTS

In researching and preparing the manuscript for *General Business in Our Modern Society*, the authors enlisted the counsel of hundreds of teachers, administrators, and business-people. Although we cannot individually acknowledge here each of these contributions, we are deeply grateful for the guidance they provided. Special recognition, however, must be made to Gary R. Seiler, Chairperson, Department of Business Administration, College of St. Catherine, St. Paul, Minnesota, for his assistance with the end-of-part activities, as well as for his exhaustive review of the entire manuscript.

We would also like to acknowledge the help of certain individuals, business firms, organizations, and government agencies in reviewing specific portions of the manuscript for technical accuracy. Among these are Joseph G. Bonnice, Insurance Information Institute; James H. Hammil, Federal Reserve Bank of Minneapolis; American Council of Life Insurance; Credit Union National Association; and The New York Stock Exchange.

Charles R. Hopkins
Thomas B. Duff
Robert E. Gades
Dennis C. Lytle

Contents

Part One

THE PRIVATE ENTERPRISE ECONOMY– BUSINESS AND GOVERNMENT

Chapter 1

What Is Economics?

Objectives

After completing your study of this chapter, you will be able to do the following:

1. Define the word *economics*.

2. Identify and discuss the basic economic problem.

3. Give examples of goods and services and know the difference between the two.

4. Define and discuss what is meant by economizing.

5. Define and describe the economic activities of production, distribution, and consumption.

When you hear the word *economics,* what does it bring to mind? Do you think of long, confusing definitions and hard-to-follow formulas? You shouldn't, because economics is part of your everyday life. It is concerned with all of the things related to how people go about getting what they need and want. Let's take a typical example. Suppose you want a new pair of shoes. First you find a store that carries the kind you want, and then you decide to buy them. It seems simple enough. But you might ask yourself the following questions:

- Where did the materials from which the shoes were made come from?

- How were the shoes made? By whom?

- Why did the manufacturer choose to make this particular shoe?

- How were size, color, and style decided?

- How did the shoes get from the factory to the store?

- Why did the shoes cost as much as they did?

- Where did you get the money to buy the shoes?

Can you supply complete answers to these questions and others like them? If you can, you know quite a lot about economics already. Look at each question again. Note that the answer to each question involves people. In every case, somebody did something. You are able to buy the shoes you want because someone designed them and made them. Someone packaged them, shipped them, delivered them, and priced them. And, finally, someone sold the shoes to you. *Economics,* then, is the study of how people produce, distribute, and consume the things that satisfy their wants.

THE BASIC ECONOMIC PROBLEM

What are wants? *Wants* are the desires for all types of things that people feel will make life better for them. Every person has wants. Suppose you were to list the wants of every man, woman, and child in the nation. You would realize quickly that people have more wants than it is possible to satisfy. That is, there are not enough resources available to satisfy everyone's wants. Economists usually refer to this as the *basic economic problem*.

Do you think you could ever prepare a *complete* list of wants for yourself? Explain your answer. Do you think you could ever satisfy all your wants? Why?

Unlimited Wants

If you were to examine your list of wants carefully, you would realize that you could continue to add wants each time you looked at the list. Your wants are unlimited and never-ending. As you satisfy some wants, new wants take their place or the same wants occur again. Your wants for food, clothing, and medical care are examples of wants that occur again and again. New wants can take various forms. As you grow older, you will have wants that differ from those you have today. New products are developed, and changes are made in products already on the market. When your grandparents were your age, they did not want electronic calculators, color televisions, or ten-speed bicycles. Nor did they want the services needed to maintain these things, because these things were not available. As more and different kinds of products become available, wants change. As the overall population of the world expands, there are more people who have wants to satisfy. People have unlimited economic wants. Therefore, they must organize ways and means to carry on economic activities and make economic decisions so that they can best satisfy their wants.

Why do you think different persons have different wants? What factors determine or affect the type of wants a person has?

Goods and Services   Economic wants are satisfied by goods and services. *Goods* are material things that people are willing to pay for. They include such things as clothes, cars, records, skis, books, pencils, city water, soap, food, houses, and candy. People are willing to pay for them because they can be used to satisfy their wants.

Some things such as the air you breathe, the heat of the sun, and the water of a mountain stream also satisfy your wants for material things. But they would not be thought of as goods because you don't have to pay for them.

 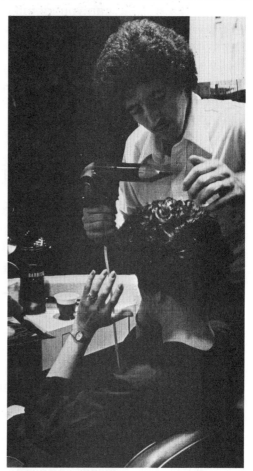

Our economic wants are satisfied by goods and services. (Monkmeyer; Lejeune/Stockmarket, Los Angeles)

Services are the nonmaterial things for which people are willing to pay. They include work done by doctors, dentists, lawyers, teachers, actors, street cleaners, bus drivers, and the like. Secretaries, salespersons, teachers, social workers, police, and fire fighters also provide services. These people do not make products or goods. They provide services, and other people are willing to pay for these services to satisfy their wants.

What kinds of goods and services other than those listed above can you identify?

ECONOMIC ACTIVITIES

In our definition of economics we said there are three kinds of activities: production, distribution, and consumption. Let's now examine each of these activities.

Production

The process of providing goods and services to satisfy human wants is called *production.* All activity, whether physical or mental, that is required to produce goods and services is part of production. To produce goods and services, certain productive resources, called the *factors of production,* are required. These are natural resources, labor, and capital goods.

Natural Resources   All the things provided by nature are *natural resources.* Minerals, forests, oil, fertile land, and water are all natural resources. Natural resources are needed for the production of all goods. This is true of even the so-called synthetics, which are made by combining or breaking down natural resources. The amount and kind of natural resources owned or available to an individual, business, or nation is very important.

Labor   All forms of physical and mental effort are defined as *labor.* Labor is the human element that goes into the production of goods and services. The farmer plowing wheatfields, the secretary typing letters, the auto mechanic installing new spark plugs, the scientist doing medical research—all are forms of labor. Without labor, natural resources are of little value. Therefore many people feel that labor is the most valuable of the resources. There are, of course, degrees of skill and knowledge in labor. The more skilled the labor force is in a country, the more goods and services that country produces.

Natural resources, labor, and capital goods are required to produce all goods and services. (Pennzoil, Sunkist, IT&T)

Capital Goods   All the machinery, buildings, equipment, and so forth, that are used to produce goods and services are called *capital goods*. Examples are a steel plant, an office calculator, and farm machinery. Capital goods do not satisfy our wants directly. They are used by individuals, businesses, and government to produce the goods and services that do satisfy our wants. (Note that capital goods and capital are *not* the same. *Capital* usually means the money that a person needs to start a business.)

Distribution

The process of directing the flow of goods and services from the producer to the consumer is called *distribution*. Your local grocer or druggist is part of distribution. The person who delivers pizza or a newspaper to your front door is involved in distribution too. These people are sometimes called middlemen. *Middlemen* are the

What kind of economic activity is being performed here? (Santa Fe Railway)

people who provide the productive services of distributing goods and services. In an economic system, there must be a link that connects the producer and consumer. Those people who get goods and services from the producer to the consumer are this link. The link is called distribution.

What other types of businesses and individuals would be considered to be part of distribution?

Consumption

The process of buying or using goods and services is *consumption*. All the people who buy or use (consume) goods and services are called *consumers.*

You consume many goods each day. This textbook will be consumed by you and other students over a period of months or years. The food you eat is consumed over a shorter period of time; it is consumed very quickly by most teenagers. Depending upon the fabric and quality of workmanship, clothing may be consumed over months or years. A car is consumed over a period of years. A home is consumed over an even longer period of time.

You also consume a number of services each day. Bus drivers, custodians, cooks, and teachers in your school district provide services you use often, if not daily. In addition to these services, you may use the services of doctors, lab technicians, police, fire fighters, librarians and libraries, waitresses, gas station attendants, baseball players, entertainers, and ministers or priests. You, and all other individuals in our society, consume many kinds of economic services while satisfying your wants. As a matter of fact, in our society the consumption of services is growing at a much faster rate than is the consumption of economic goods. You and others like you are asking for more and more services.

ECONOMIZING

Economic resources are not always available in a large enough supply to produce all the goods and services that people want. This shortage of resources available to produce all the goods and services people want is referred to as *scarcity.* There may not be

Wise use of scarce resources reduces the impact of shortages. (Marshall Licht)

enough oil to make products to both heat homes and fuel cars. There may not be enough skilled workers to make both planes and bicycles. Or there may not be enough good farming land to raise both corn and wheat. The amount and kind of economic resources available to an individual, family, business, or nation is very important.

When a shortage of economic resources, or *scarcity,* exists, economic choices have to be made. The process of deciding how to use the available resources to satisfy as many wants as possible is known as *economizing*. Economists often call decisions of this type decisions on how to allocate resources.

All of us—individuals, businesses, and governments—have to make decisions on how to use resources. You are economizing when you decide to use a certain half hour studying for a quiz rather than to use it watching television or talking with a friend. An automaker is economizing when it decides to produce compact cars rather than full-size cars. And a local government is economizing when it decides to use certain land to build a park rather than a parking lot.

Learning Activities

Increasing Your Business Vocabulary

You should become familiar with each of the terms shown below. On a sheet of paper write the numbers 1 through 11. Then write alongside each number the term that best matches each of the numbered definitions.

capital goods / consumers / economics / economizing / goods / labor / natural resources / production / scarcity / services / wants

1. Material things for which people are willing to pay.

2. The desires for all types of things that people feel will make life better for them.

3. The process of deciding how to use the available resources to satisfy as many wants as possible.

4. The study of how people produce, distribute, and consume the things that satisfy their wants.

5. The nonmaterial things for which people are willing to pay.

6. The process of providing goods and services to satisfy human wants.

7. All the machinery, buildings, equipment, and so forth, that are used to produce goods and services.

8. The shortage of resources available to produce all the goods and services people want.

9. All forms of physical and mental effort.

10. All the things provided by nature.

11. All the people who buy or use goods and services.

Understanding
Business

1. What is the basic economic problem?

2. Explain what is meant by the statement "People have unlimited wants."

3. Why must people organize ways and means to carry on economic activities?

4. Explain the difference between goods and services.

5. List three types of productive resources.

6. Give some examples of natural resources.

7. Why are natural resources so important?

8. Who makes decisions on using resources?

9. Why is labor an important factor of production?

10. What is the difference between capital goods and capital?

Business Problems
and Projects

1. On a form similar to the one shown below, list ten of your most important wants. Place a check in the appropriate column to indicate whether the want is a good or a service.

	Want	Good	Service
Example	Jeans	✓	
Example	Hair styling		✓

2. Individuals, businesses, and governments have to make decisions on how to use resources. Prepare a list of three examples of economizing for each of the three categories.

Chapter 2

The Nature of
Economic Systems

Objectives

After completing your study of this chapter, you will be able to do the following:

1. Identify and describe the major purpose of an economic system.

2. Identify and discuss the specific questions that must be answered for a society by its economic system.

3. Define the terms *market economy, centralized economy,* and *mixed economy.*

4. Compare and contrast the principal features of the communist, socialist, and capitalist economic systems.

The problem of scarcity has affected every society throughout history. If all the goods and services wanted cannot be produced, which ones should be produced? Which of the limited productive resources and how much of each should be used? How should the productive resources be combined to produce goods and services? If only part of the goods and services wanted are produced, which members of the society get what is produced? Deciding which goods and services to produce and deciding how to use the productive resources available are, in fact, what economizing is all about. In order to have a systematic way to answer these questions, societies develop an economic system.

WHAT IS AN ECONOMIC SYSTEM?

An economic system has no size or weight or color. It is, therefore, difficult to describe or picture. Generally, an *economic system* is a system for supplying daily answers to basic economic questions. It provides answers to the questions that result from a scarcity of productive resources. It helps to answer the questions of what to produce, how to produce, and how to distribute what is produced.

The basic economic problem and the decisions that must be made regarding economic choices are the same for all nations. It doesn't matter where the nation is located. The United States, the Soviet Union, Chile, Saudi Arabia, Indonesia, China, Nigeria—in short, all nations—face the same problem.

Look at the problem on a personal level. You have a limited amount of money with which to buy the things you want. You therefore find it necessary to choose from among the many things you would like to have. Societies must make the same kinds of choices. Their economic systems help them to make these choices.

Write a letter to a friend who is not familiar with economics, explaining why nations have economic systems and generally what the economic system should do.

QUESTIONS ANSWERED
BY ALL ECONOMIC SYSTEMS

The economic systems of all nations are designed to answer the same questions. These questions are *what to produce, how to produce,* and *for whom to produce.* In this section you will examine each of these questions to see in more detail what is involved.

What to Produce?

The first decision that a nation must make is the one involving *what* goods and services to produce. To do this, it must determine what goods and services its consumer population is demanding.

Someone has to decide whether to use land to produce cattle or computers.
(USDA, IBM)

Because there are limited productive resources to meet so many human wants, choices must be made. For example, land can be used for only one thing at a time. If an acre of land is used for growing corn, it cannot be used for a public park. If it is used for a home, it cannot be used for a manufacturing plant. Should steel be used to make a spacecraft, a drill press, or a refrigerator? Should oil be used to heat homes, to make electricity, or to power automobiles? Choices must be made to determine how a resource should be used. A resource can be used to produce a good for all members of society (a park). It can be used to produce a capital good (machinery). Or it can be used to produce a consumer good (a car). The economic system of a nation determines how these complex decisions are made.

List some examples of choices that must be made regarding the use of two productive resources: (1) labor and (2) capital goods.

How to Produce?

Once the choice of *what* to produce is made, it must then be determined *how* to produce the goods and services in the most efficient way. The productive resources available to a nation can be

Fabrics can be woven either by handlooms or highly mechanized looms. (Burlington Industries, Laurie Gottlieb)

combined in many different ways. For example, a million bushels of corn may be produced using large amounts of land and labor and small amounts of fertilizer and machinery. The same quantity of corn may also be produced using smaller amounts of land and labor with larger amounts of fertilizer and machinery. Because goods can be produced using different combinations of productive resources, decisions must be made about how to combine productive resources. A nation's economic system must make these complex decisions on the basis of productive resources available.

Developing nations, such as many of those in Asia and Africa, usually rely heavily on human labor but use little machinery and equipment to produce goods. Industrialized nations, such as the United States, the Soviet Union, Japan, and West Germany, rely more on machines and equipment and much less labor to produce similar goods. In industrialized nations, labor is highly trained and skilled. With the use of machines and equipment, skilled labor produces a great quantity of goods and services.

For Whom to Produce?

Another economic question faced by each nation is who gets the goods and services that are produced. This is really a question of how to distribute income in a society, since income is needed to buy goods and services. Should each person share the income equally? Must one work in order to get a share of the income? Does the type of work a person does affect his or her share of the income? A nation's economic system determines how income is to be shared; thereby, determining *for whom* goods and services will be produced.

TYPES OF ECONOMIC SYSTEMS

The nations of the world do not all go about making economic decisions in the same way. People of different nations and societies have developed and used different economic systems to do this. Each system, however, is designed specifically to help make basic economic decisions.

Economists classify economic systems in a variety of ways. Among these systems, the most common are a market economy, a centralized economy, or a mixture of market and centralized.

In a *market economy* decisions are made by individuals and businesses operating in what is called the marketplace. Many people participate in making these economic decisions. The American economic system today is market-oriented but not completely a market economy. In a *centralized economy,* decisions are made by one leader or a small group of leaders for all the members of the society. These decisions are handed down to others to carry out. China and the Soviet Union are examples of countries that are considered to have centralized economies.

Today few, if any, economic systems fit into a single category. Modern economies are almost always mixed economies. In a *mixed economy* decisions are made partly by individuals and businesses operating in the marketplace and partly by a centralized authority. What differs in the economies is the degree to which they are market or centralized.

Why do almost all nations in the world have mixed economies?

Compare the variety of car models available to the American consumer with those available to the Soviet consumer. (Ford, Sovfoto)

Communist Economic System

The economic systems of most communist nations are centralized. *Communism* is an economic system in which the productive resources—natural resources, labor, and capital goods—are owned or controlled by the government. And most economic decisions are made by the government. The government in these countries may consist of one person. However, it usually is made up of a small group of people who are leaders in the Communist Party. Under this type of economic system, government has almost complete control of what will be produced, how it will be produced, and who will get what is produced. It has this control because it owns almost all the natural resources, directs the use of capital goods, and decides what type of work people will do.

Some characteristics of a communist economic system include the following: People can choose what goods and services they want to buy. However, they can obtain only what the government decides to produce. The amount and variety of goods available to people are quite limited in a communist economy. Most workers belong to unions, but wages, hours, and working conditions are controlled by the government. Many public services such as education and medical care are free to everyone.

Socialist Economic System

Socialism is an economic system in which both individuals and the government own productive resources. Both make the economic decisions for the society. Many of the important economic decisions are made by government agencies. They can do this because they own and operate some of the most important industries. In Great Britain, for example, airlines and railroads, television and radio, hospitals and the post office are run by the government.

But consumers and businesses also make important economic decisions. Many businesses are privately owned and operated. A private individual can start a business so long as it is not of the same type as one of those owned and operated by the government. People can buy the goods and services they want. But the amount is limited in some cases to what the government, because of its control of certain industries, produces. In Western Europe, Sweden and Great Britain are the best-known examples of nations with socialist economic systems.

The different socialist nations have different amounts of centralized authority. In some, such as Sweden, government has a great deal of control. In others, such as Mexico, individuals and businesses control large amounts and varieties of productive resources. None of the socialistic nations, however, has as much government control as the centralized communist economies.

List several nations that have socialist economic systems.

Capitalist Economic System

Capitalism is an economic system in which productive resources are owned by individuals and businesses. Economic decisions are made by these groups operating in the marketplace. Under capitalism the government owns and controls some productive resources. The vast majority, however, are privately owned. Individuals and businesses jointly make most of the major economic decisions. Individuals are more involved in decision making in a capitalist economy than in either a communist or socialist economy. In capitalist economies, the role of government is to act more as a watchdog or referee than as a producer or decision maker. Government, therefore, indirectly influences economic activities under capitalism.

The economic system of the United States is generally described as capitalism. Americans are relatively free to use the productive resources as they wish. They also seek to have major influence in deciding what to produce, how to produce, and for whom to produce. In the next chapter you will study the economy of our nation in detail. You will see how our particular form of capitalism works.

Give examples of nations other than the United States that have capitalist economic systems.

Learning Activities

Increasing Your Business Vocabulary

You should become familiar with each of the terms shown below. On a sheet of paper write the numbers 1 through 7. Then write alongside each number the term that best matches each of the numbered definitions.

capitalism / centralized economy / communism / economic system / market economy / mixed economy / socialism

1. An economy in which decisions are made by individuals and businesses operating in what is called the marketplace.

2. An economy in which decisions are made by one leader or a small group of leaders for all the members of the society.

3. An economic system in which productive resources are owned by individuals and businesses.

4. An economy in which decisions are made partly by individuals and businesses operating in the marketplace and partly by a centralized authority.

5. A system for supplying daily answers to basic economic questions.

6. A system in which the productive resources are owned or controlled by the state.

7. A system in which both individuals and the government own the productive resources.

Understanding Business

1. Why do societies develop an economic system?

2. What are the three major questions that must be answered by an economic system?

3. Explain why economic choices must be made.

4. Give an example of how productive resources available to a nation can be combined in different ways.

5. How does an economic system determine for whom goods and services will be produced?

6. Explain how economic decisions are made in the following:

    a. market economy.

    b. centralized economy.

    c. mixed economy.

7. Describe the principal features of the following:

    a. communist economic system.

    b. socialist economic system.

    c. capitalist economic system.

8. Why is the American economic system generally described as capitalism?

Business Problems and Projects

1. The choice of products that a country produces is often determined by the skill of its labor force. For each of the

products listed below, determine whether a skilled or un-skilled labor force is required.

	Product	Type of Labor Force
Example	Automobiles	Skilled
	a. Rice	
	b. Watches	
	c. Hand-made crafts	
	d. Raw rubber	
	e. Airplanes	
	f. Precision tools	
	g. Coffee beans	

2. Indicate which of the statements listed below apply to a capitalistic economic system and which apply to a communistic economic system.

   a. Decisions regarding the economy are made by a central authority.

   b. Almost all productive resources are privately owned.

   c. Government acts as a watchdog rather than as the major decision maker.

   d. The amount and variety of goods and services available to individuals is limited.

   e. Almost all productive resources are owned by government.

   f. Government decides what type of labor individuals will perform.

   g. Most economic decisions are made by individuals and business firms in the marketplace.

Chapter 3

Features of Our Private Enterprise Economy

Objectives

After completing your study of this chapter, you will be able to do the following:

1. Identify the four basic features of our economy and discuss why it is called a private enterprise economy.

2. Describe the difference between private and public property and explain why private property is one of the basic features of our private enterprise economy.

3. Define the word *competition* and identify the role it plays in our economy.

4. Explain the market system and its role in our economic system.

5. Discuss the meaning of the term *profit motive* and show how it acts as an incentive in our private enterprise economy.

Citizens attending this town meeting in New Hampshire are exercising two of their most precious rights: the right of peaceful assembly and the right of free speech. (UPI)

"The basic test of freedom is perhaps less in what we are free to do than in what we are free not to do." This statement was made by Eric Hoffer, an American worker-philosopher of our day. It is an appropriate way to begin a general discussion of the economic system of our nation.

Individuals and businesses are much more involved in making economic decisions in a capitalist economic system than in a socialist or communist system. They have a wide degree of freedom in choosing what things they want to do and what things they do not want to do. They do not have complete freedom in making these decisions, however.

When they choose to do certain things, they are at the same time choosing not to do other things. In this chapter you will study the basic features of our economic system. As you examine the roles freedom and private rights play in our system, you will see why it has been described as a private enterprise economy.

FREEDOM IN OUR SOCIETY

The United States has a free, democratic political system. Citizens use the secret ballot to elect officials to school boards, city councils, state legislatures, and Congress. They also elect mayors, sheriffs, judges, governors, and the President and Vice President.

All persons who have reached voting age are free to take part in electing these leaders. These leaders then make decisions affecting all members of the society. Most people do not take part directly in making decisions in our society. They do, however, enjoy political freedom because they are free to elect and, in certain cases, recall the decision makers.

Along with their political freedom, individuals in our society have a number of civil rights. These rights are guaranteed to citizens under the Constitution. Civil rights include the right of free speech, the right to worship as one chooses, and the right to trial by jury. Civil rights enable a person to do almost anything that person wishes. However, there are limits. For example, you cannot deny someone else the right of free speech. American citizens have always been concerned about their freedom. They have worked for freedom since the first American colonies were founded.

List some civil rights or liberties that were not included in the paragraph above.

Economic Freedom

Members of our society enjoy one other group of freedoms. These are the economic freedoms. Individual freedom of choice is basic in

These consumers have the economic freedom to spend their money as they wish. (Monkmeyer)

our system. As you study the main features of our economy, you will see how decisions are made. You will see what freedom *does* and *does not* mean. And you will see how our economy functions with relative stability even though individuals are free to make individual economic decisions.

In our economy, individual consumers are almost completely free to spend their money as they wish. They are free to use their resources as they see fit. A person can choose to go into almost any type of business he or she pleases. There is much more economic freedom in our nation than in most others today. These freedoms, however, are limited. For example, laws that protect the people and nation in general limit economic freedoms. Individuals and businesses are not free to break agreements or to be untruthful about what they sell.

Why do you think there are more economic controls on business than on individuals?

PRIVATE PROPERTY

Things of value that are owned by an individual or business are called *private property*. Private property includes such things as buildings, land, machines, money, or the like. People generally have the right to do as they please with their property. The right to own and use property as one sees fit encourages people to start business firms of their own. *Business firms* are individuals who have organized to produce goods and services in the hope of making a profit. Almost all business firms are privately owned. Thus, individuals own almost all property that is used to produce goods and services.

Some property is not owned by private individuals. Property owned by local, state, or federal government is called *public property*. Public property includes streets, highways, schools, post offices, and all government facilities.

There are two important results of the right to own property. Individuals directly (or indirectly through businesses) decide what will be produced with the resources and how it will be produced.

This is very different from an economy in which government owns the productive resources and makes these decisions. Ownership of private property and the right to use such property to earn income enables individuals to gain and build up *wealth*, which is the dollar value of all property owned at a given time. As the value of a person's private property increases, his or her wealth increases.

List some examples of private property owned by your family.

COMPETITION

Consumers have a choice as to what they will buy. Most of the time they also can choose from whom they will buy. For example, several different firms each manufacturing their own brand of detergent will try to get consumers to buy their brand. The efforts of two or more business firms trying to sell to the same consumer is called *competition*. Competition exists among businesses to sell their goods and services. It also exists among individuals to sell their skills and abilities.

Competing motels in this resort community provide travelers with a choice of accommodations and prices. (Monkmeyer)

In perfect competition there are many sellers of the same product. However, competition in our economy is seldom perfect. In some industries there is little or no competition at all. Telephone and utility companies are good examples. In your community is there more than one company that supplies telephone service? Do consumers have a choice when they buy electrical service? A situation in which there is only one producer of a good or service is called a *monopoly*. Consumers have no choice. They either buy from that firm or they do not buy at all.

Monopolies limit the choice that consumers have. For this reason they are not desirable. In certain cases, however, it is not practical for two or more companies to compete in the same area. For example, most communities are served by only one telephone company, one electric company, and one gas company. To protect consumers, government controls the rates these companies may charge the consumer.

In all other businesses, competition exists to varying degrees. Most people agree that competition is a good thing. For our economic system to work well, it is a necessity. Both consumers and producers benefit from competition. From a consumer's point of view, there are two important advantages:

1. Competition drives prices down to the lowest possible level.

2. Competition causes producers to do their best to provide goods or services of top quality.

In our society today, there are forms of competition besides price and quality. For example, business firms compete by offering more or better service on goods sold. They compete by providing guarantees on their products. They compete by making improved products. And, of course, business firms compete through the use of advertising. All of these things are done to get you, the consumer, to buy a company's goods and services.

Select any product that you buy regularly. List as many business firms as you can that make the product. Is one business firm more successful at selling the product than the others? Why?

Just as businesses compete to sell their goods or services, individuals compete to sell their labor. You need not look far to see examples of competition among individuals in our society. Once you leave school, you will discover how competitive life is in the world of work. Competition for jobs is very strong. People are paid for the skills, abilities, or special talents that they have. If an individual has special skills or abilities, business firms will compete with each other to hire that person—probably offering higher salaries. Competition among individuals is as important to our private enterprise economy as is business competition.

A MARKET SYSTEM

Have you ever attended an auction sale? If you have, you know how an auction works. Goods to be offered for sale are brought to one place. Buyers and would-be buyers gather around. The auctioneer selects an item and asks the buyers to make an offer, or bid. The person who makes the highest bid gets the item.

Places or ways in which individuals are brought together for the purpose of buying and selling goods and services are called *markets*. The buyers and sellers in a market do not necessarily have to gather in one place as they do in an auction. They carry on these activities in person, by phone, or by letter. For example, a buyer for ladies' dresses, or children's toys, or for raw materials like cotton, steel, or paper may place bids in markets thousands of miles away.

Because of the many markets in our economy, our economic system is sometimes called a market system. There are markets for every good or service that is produced. There are markets for wheat, coal, and steel. There are markets for teachers, entertainers, and athletes. All these markets provide an orderly way for buyers and sellers to get together to exchange goods and services.

Supply and Demand

In the summer people eat a lot more ice cream than at any other time of the year. As a result, the demand for ice cream increases. For any good or service, the total amount that consumers are willing and able to buy at any given time is the *demand*. Consumers express demand for all types of goods and services. To meet these demands producers create an available supply of the goods and services that people want. *Supply* is the total amount of a good or service that is available for sale at a given time.

Price

Supply and demand interact with each other in the market. In this way the price of a good or service is determined. *Price* is the amount of money exchanged between buyer and seller when goods or services are bought or sold. If the demand is higher than supply, the price tends to go up. If supply is higher than demand, the price tends to go down.

Think back to the discussion of the auction sale. Sometimes there are a lot of buyers who all want the same item. As buyers bid against each other, they cause the price of an item to go up. Eventually the price gets so high that some buyers stop bidding.

SUPPLY AND DEMAND

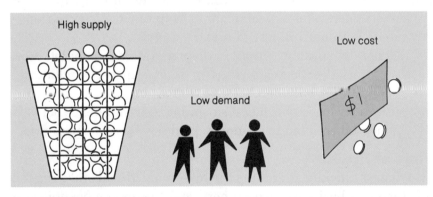

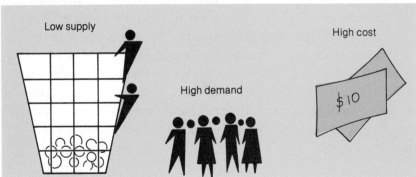

When there are no further bids, the item is sold to the last (and highest) bidder. On other occasions the opposite is true. If not enough buyers are interested in an item, the item may be sold to the first person who makes a bid. If there are no bids at all, the auctioneer may lower the asking price to encourage the sale. Lack of demand, then, causes the price of an item to fall. The price that can be obtained for a good or service determines whether productive resources will be used to produce it. Thus, prices, based on supply and demand, play a major role in seeing that we get the goods and services that we want most from our scarce resources.

List some products that you buy that show a change in price in response to supply and demand.

PROFIT MOTIVE

Many people feel that the opportunity to make a profit, or the so-called profit motive, is the most important feature of capitalism. When foreigners refer to Americans as "capitalists," they normally are referring to our interest in making a profit.

Generally speaking, *profit* is the amount of money left from income after all expenses have been paid. Expenses include the cost of materials, labor, rent, taxes, and all other costs related to operating a business. One might say profit is the difference between the money taken in and the money paid out by a business firm.

Role of Profits

The hope of making a profit is the reason individuals take the risk of starting a business. As used here, *risk* means the possibility of loss. Whenever a business is formed to produce goods or services, there is always the possibility that the business may lose money.

People who start a business believe that the chance of making a profit from a particular good or service is greater than the chance of incurring a loss. Profits, therefore, determine what kinds of businesses will be started. Profits also determine if a business will continue to operate. A business that does not make a profit will close its doors.

Decisions on how to produce are also influenced by the profit motive. Remember, profit is the amount of money left after expenses have been paid. A business that can reduce its expenses will increase its profits. For that reason business firms use the most efficient production methods available.

What usually happens when businesses producing a certain good or service earn very high profits for a period of years?

THE PRIVATE ENTERPRISE ECONOMY

Our economy is a mixed economy. It has been called a market economy by some, a free enterprise economy by others. In fact, it is not truly a market or free enterprise economy because the economy does not operate freely. You will see later that there is control of the free operation of the economy in various ways. Government limits the economic freedom of individuals and businesses.

Our economy is a unique form of mixed economy. Because it is not completely a free economy, it has been called a *private enterprise economy* in this chapter. This term indicates that private individuals and businesses play the major role in making economic decisions. Private property, competition, the market system, and profit motive are the most important features of our economy. They all enable individuals to take part in making economic decisions. Private individuals compete in our market system to earn a profit. By doing so, these individuals make most of the major economic decisions. Thus, the words *private enterprise* are an accurate description of our economic system. Other names are often used to describe our system, but we will use private enterprise economy throughout this book.

What are some other terms or words you have seen or heard used to describe the economic system of the United States?

Learning Activities

Increasing Your Business Vocabulary

You should become familiar with each of the terms shown below. On a sheet of paper write the numbers 1 through 10. Then write alongside each number the term that best matches each of the numbered definitions.

business firms / competition / demand / markets / monopoly / price / profit / public property / supply / wealth

1. The amount of money exchanged between buyer and seller when goods or services are bought or sold.

2. The total amount of a good or service that consumers are able and willing to buy at a given time.

3. The efforts of two or more business firms trying to sell to the same consumer.

4. Individuals who have organized to produce goods and services in the hope of making a profit.

5. Property owned by the local, state, or federal government.

6. The total amount of a good or service that is available for sale at a given time.

7. The amount of money left from income after all expenses have been paid.

8. The situation that exists when there is only one producer of a good or service.

9. The dollar value of all property owned at a given time.

10. Places or ways in which individuals are brought together for the purpose of buying and selling goods and services.

Understanding Business

1. List some examples of private property. Of public property.
2. In the United States, who owns most of the property that is used to produce goods and services?
3. Who decides how productive resources will be used in our society?
4. What are two advantages to consumers when businesses compete?
5. Why is our economic system sometimes called a market system?
6. Describe how prices are determined in our economy.
7. Explain how price determines what will be produced.
8. Why do people take the risks involved in organizing and operating a business firm?
9. How do profits determine what will be produced in our economy?
10. It is often said that the American economy is a private enterprise economy. Why?

Business Problems and Projects

1. In their advertisements, some companies today openly compare their products with those of the competition. List five examples of such advertisers as well as the competing products mentioned in their ads.
2. The following article recently appeared in a daily newspaper. After reading the article, answer the questions that follow.

GREATER FARMER PRODUCTIVITY SPELLS LOWER INCOME FOR THE FARMER

Derby, Kansas—Tom Moos, a local wheat farmer, and many of his colleagues are not jumping for joy over the bumper crop of grain. The reason is that for many of these farmers record-breaking crops this year may result in a lower income. The larger crops mean greater supply and, unless demand increases significantly, lower prices. Tom and other farmers are hoping that international grain sales by the United States will push prices up to last year's level, a record year. The chief foreign markets for grain are Japan, China, the Soviet Union, and India.

Despite the anticipated record crops, consumers should not look forward to a decrease in the price of grain-fed beef, poultry, dairy products, or cereals. Consumers will bear some of the additional costs added on by the middlemen who contribute labor, transportation, and other services before the product eventually reaches the market. As a result, it looks like Tom and the consumer will face a tighter squeeze on income.

a. Does it look like Tom's income will be higher or lower than last year's income? Why?

b. What could cause grain prices to rise to last year's level?

c. What are the chief foreign markets for American grain?

d. Name the products that will not decrease in price despite the predicted record crops. Why won't the prices for these products decrease?

Chapter 4

How Decisions Are Made in Our Private Enterprise Economy

Objectives

After completing your study of this chapter, you will be able to do the following:

1. Name and describe the three major sectors of our private enterprise economy.

2. Identify and discuss the major flows among the sectors of our economy.

3. Describe how our private enterprise economy decides what goods and services to produce.

4. Explain the process by which our private enterprise economy decides how to produce goods and services.

5. Discuss the factors that determine for whom goods and services are produced in our private enterprise economy.

In our economy, economic decisions are made by three different groups, or *sectors*: consumers, business firms, and government. Consumers make economic decisions every day. They decide what products or services they will buy. They decide when to buy and how much to buy. Sometimes consumers decide not to buy. This, too, is an economic decision. They also decide to work or not to work. And they decide for whom they will work. In order to operate, business firms must make a number of economic decisions each day. They have to decide what kinds of goods or services to provide—in the hope that consumers will buy them. If a good or service does not sell as well as expected, they must decide whether to continue it or try something different. The firm might decide to do more advertising. It may change the product—redesign it, repackage it, or reduce its price. These decisions, taken individually, may not seem too important. But when the decisions of all business firms are taken together, they have a great effect on consumers and government alike.

Federal, state, and local governments all make economic decisions. They decide what kinds of taxes consumers and businesses will pay, determine how much money to spend, and establish standards under which businesses and consumers can operate. These decisions, in turn, affect the economic decisions made by consumers and business firms. In fact, all economic decisions—whether made by consumers, businesses, or governments—have an effect on each other. Taken together, they determine how well our economic system works. Understanding how each of these sectors works with the others will help you see how the entire economic system works.

CONSUMER SECTOR

The consumer sector includes private individuals like you, your parents, your friends, and so on. Look ahead at Figure 4-1, on page 44. Note that the consumer sector plays two primary roles in our economy. The *consumer sector* is the group within our economy that supplies productive resources and buys goods and services. These two roles are closely related. To buy goods and services, consumers must have money. They obtain money by selling their

Every purchase you make involves some kind of an economic decision.

productive resources to business and government. For example, they can earn income by selling their labor, a natural resource such as their corn crop, or a capital good such as land. The money that consumers receive for the sale of their productive resources is in turn used to buy goods and services produced by business and government.

BUSINESS SECTOR

The business sector includes all the business firms in our economy. Some of these firms are large manufacturers like General Motors, U.S. Steel, and International Business Machines (IBM). Some are service firms such as banks, savings and loan associations, and insurance companies. Some are business firms owned and operated by one individual such as a law office, a restaurant, or a hardware store. The *business sector* is the group within our economy that produces goods and services and buys productive resources. These two roles, producing and buying, are closely related. A business firm will buy productive resources only if it feels they can be used to produce something that can be sold. If the business firm does not sell the good or service produced, it will stop buying the productive resources. Further, the business firm will try to buy productive resources at a price low enough to allow a profit from the production of the goods or services. The business sector sells its goods and services not only to consumers and government but also to other firms within the business sector.

Decision making in business firms is accomplished through both formal and informal means. (TRW)

GOVERNMENT SECTOR

The government sector is that part of our economy made up of various levels of government—federal, state, and local. Government does, in a small way, take part in both the consumer and business sectors of our economy. Stated another way, government is both a producer and consumer of productive resources in our economy. Government sometimes acts as part of the business sector. It buys productive resources and uses them to produce public goods and services such as highways and fire protection. Government sometimes also acts as part of the consumer sector. It

State legislatures daily make decisions that can have an important effect on individuals and business firms. (State of Oregon)

buys goods and services such as food for school lunch programs or health insurance for its employees.

As can be seen from Figure 4-1, government plays two other important roles in our economy. First, government acts as a transfer agent. In this role it collects money in the form of taxes from those who are able to pay and gives, or transfers, some of this money to needy individuals in the form of transfer payments. *Transfer payments* are payments made by a government agency for which the government currently receives no goods, services, or productive resources in return. Social security payments to the aged and disabled are an example. Unemployment payments to those out of work and welfare payments are other examples. Money is also transferred to businesses in the form of subsidies. A *subsidy* is financial aid given to business firms by government. Airlines, railroads, and farms are examples of business firms that receive subsidies from the government.

A second role of the government sector is to protect the business and consumer sectors. Some government agencies protect business firms from illegal actions by other business firms or individuals. The Federal Trade Commission, the Interstate Commerce Commission, and the Bureau of Standards are examples. Other government agencies protect individuals in the consumer sector. The Food and Drug Administration and the Office of Consumer Affairs are examples. They protect consumers from illegal activities of other consumers or business firms. In summary, the *government sector* produces and buys goods and services while it acts as a transfer agent and protective agency in our economy.

HOW OUR ECONOMY WORKS

You have studied the three major sectors in our economy. Now you will learn how these sectors work with each other. Look at Figure 4-1. It shows the general flow of productive resources, goods and services, and money in our economic system.

FLOWS IN OUR ECONOMIC SYSTEM

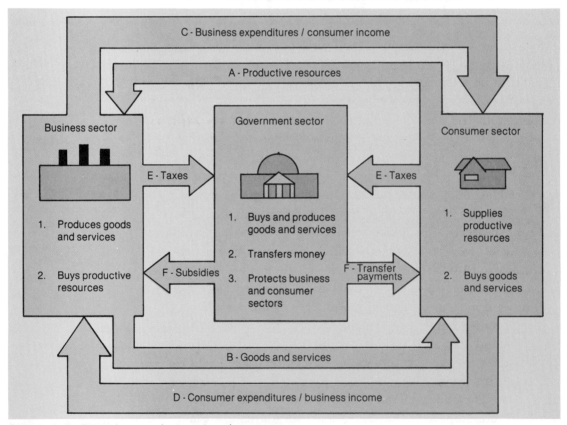

Figure 4-1. Flows in our private enterprise economy.

Consumer and Business Sectors

The most important flows of resources are shown as A and B. The flow of productive resources (labor, capital, and natural resources) from individuals in the consumer sector to business firms in the business sector is shown as A. To complete this circular flow, follow line B. This shows the flow of goods and services from business firms to the consumer sector.

Let us now look at the circular flow of money between the consumer and business sectors. The flow of money from the business firms to individuals in the consumer sector is represented by the top flow, shown as C. This flow represents an expenditure of money for business firms. For consumers, however, it represents income. The income is in the form of rent, wages, interest, and profit. *Rent* is the payment received by those who supply property for others to use. *Wages* (and *salaries*) are the payment received by those who supply labor. *Interest* is the payment made for the use of someone else's money. As you learned earlier, profit is the amount of money left after all expenses have been paid. To complete the flow of money, look at the bottom of the illustration where the other half of the flow is shown as D. This flow represents an expenditure to consumers. They spend the money to buy goods and services. The flow represents income to the business firms who produce the goods and services.

There is another way to look at the flows between the business and consumer sectors. In the two top flows (A and C) note the exchange of productive resources for income. Consumers exchange their productive resources with business and receive income. The bottom two flows (B and D) show another exchange. Consumers exchange part of their income for goods and services produced by business firms.

Government and Other Sectors

Governments are involved in exchanges with both the consumer and business sectors. In Figure 4-1 you can see that government receives payments from both business firms and individuals in the form of taxes (line E). Government uses some of the tax money for transfer payments and subsidies. It provides, therefore, income for some members of both the consumer and business sectors, shown as *F*. Government operates in all the major sectors of our economy.

BASIC ECONOMIC DECISIONS IN OUR ECONOMY

In the discussion of our economic system thus far, it has been emphasized that freedom of choice is most important. As long as individuals and business firms act within the law, they are free to do as they please. You have seen that individuals are free to buy whatever economic goods and services they desire. Business firms are free to produce whatever goods and services they desire. And owners of productive resources are free to make their resources available however they wish. How can our private enterprise economy work as well as it does with this much freedom of choice? How can this economic system make the basic decisions that must be made by all economies under these conditions? In the remaining sections of this chapter you will see that there are some limits put on the choices of the various sectors of our economy.

What to Produce

To understand why businesses decide to produce what they produce, you must first recall that all businesses seek to make a profit. They can only make a profit, however, by satisfying the wants of consumers. In a sense, consumers choosing goods and services can be compared to voters choosing political leaders. Consumers cast "dollar votes" in the marketplace for various goods and services. There must be enough voters for a good or service so that the business can make a profit by producing it. If the consumers fail to vote for a product, the product will not make a profit. And the business will then stop producing that good or service. Thus, business firms are influenced by the votes, or demand, of consumers. In other words businesses produce what the consumers want, not what they themselves want to produce.

The same holds true for the use of productive resources. The business sector will buy productive resources only if they can be used to produce the goods or services that consumers want. If consumers stop buying cars, for example, automakers will stop buying steel, rubber, assembly line labor, and so on.

Do business firms influence consumers in their choice of goods and services? How is this done?

How to Produce

Competition plays the major role in determining how goods and services will be produced in our economy. Business firms are forced to produce in the most efficient way if they are to continue to earn a profit. If they are not efficient, other firms may provide better products at a lower cost to consumers. In order to compete, the less efficient firm must lower its prices and eventually lose its profits.

This refuse-to-energy plant is an example of how new technology can be used to solve existing problems. (Department of Energy)

Because of competition, business firms constantly look for better ways to use productive resources. In our economy this has led to advances in *technology*, the scientific use of knowledge in business and industry. As a result of this technology, new machines and processes have been created to produce goods and services at lower cost. Firms that cannot keep up with changes in technology are forced out of business because they cannot operate at a profit.

Describe a recent invention that has made some business firms change their methods of production.

For Whom to Produce

How does our economic system decide which individuals in the consumer sector will get what is produced? Goods and services are offered for sale to everyone. But they are available only to those who are willing and able to pay the market price for them. Those who have more money are able to buy more than those who have less. In other words, those people who have more productive resources and who use them wisely are able to get a larger share of the total production of the economy.

Some people have criticized our economic system because of the way in which it answers the question for whom to produce. If carried to the full extreme, those with no money or income would not be able to share at all in the production of the economy. Recognizing this problem, governments make transfer payments to individuals who cannot earn enough for themselves to survive. Most people agree that this help should be provided to those who are unable to support themselves. There is disagreement, however, over how to decide when a person is unable to earn income. There is also disagreement over how much income should be provided by government.

Identify some things not listed above that will affect the amount of goods and services an individual will get in our private enterprise economy.

Learning Activities

Increasing Your Business Vocabulary

You should become familiar with each of the terms shown below. On a sheet of paper write the numbers 1 through 9. Then write alongside each number the term that best matches each of the numbered definitions.

business sector / consumer sector / government sector / interest / rent / subsidy / technology / transfer payment / wages

1. Supplies productive resources and buys goods and services in the economy.

2. A payment by a government agency for which the government currently receives no goods, services, or productive resources in return.

3. The payment made for the use of someone else's money.

4. The payment received by those who supply labor.

5. Produces and buys goods and services while it acts as a transfer agent and protective agency in our economy.

6. Produces goods and services and buys productive resources in the economy.

7. Financial aid given to business firms by government.

8. The scientific use of knowledge in business and industry.

9. The payment received by those who supply property for others to use.

Understanding Business

1. List the major sectors of our private enterprise economy.

2. What two roles does the consumer sector play in our economy? Explain how these roles are closely related.

3. What two roles does the business sector play in our economy? Explain how these roles are closely related.

4. Explain how government acts as part of the business sector.

5. List some examples of how the government sector operates as a transfer agent.

6. Describe the flow of productive resources from the consumer sector to the business sector and the flow of goods and services from the business sector to the consumer sector.

7. What effect do dollar votes have on the production of goods and services?

8. In a private enterprise economy, who decides *what* goods and services will be produced? Explain how they do this.

9. In our economy, what plays the major role in determining *how* goods and services will be produced? Why?

10. What determines how an individual shares in the total production of our private enterprise economy? Explain.

Business Problems and Projects

1. The article below is similar to one that appeared recently in daily newspapers across the country. After reading the article, answer the questions that follow it.

PERSONAL INCOME AND ITS SOURCES

LINCOLN—Personal income for last year totaled $1,150.4 billion. This was up $95.4 billion from the previous year, a gain of 9 percent. As in previous years, wages and salaries continued to be the largest source of personal income. Income from wages and salaries was $802.5 billion, while income from rent and interest combined was only $163 billion. It is interesting to note that income from transfer payments, $139.8 billion, made up the third largest source of personal income.

Transfer payments included benefit payments made under social security, unemployment, and veterans' programs. Proprietors' income, $93 billion, was the only income source to show a decrease from the previous year. Personal contributions for social insurance were up 11.9 percent to $47.9 billion. Since these contributions are deducted in the calculation of personal income their more rapid increase tends to reduce the increase in personal income.

a. What was the total amount of personal income for last year?

h. Was this amount up or down from the previous year? How much? What was the percent of increase or decrease over the previous year?

c. What source accounted for the largest amount of personal income? What was the amount for that source?

d. How much income was received from rent and interest?

e. What was the third largest source of personal income? What types of programs were included in this personal income source?

f. Was there any source of personal income for which the amount was lower last year than the previous year? If yes, which one?

Chapter 5

The Economy: Performance and Problems

Objectives

After completing your study of this chapter, you will be able to do the following:

1. Explain why our private enterprise economy is a successful economic system.

2. Name and define three important measures of economic activity.

3. Describe some of the major economic problems that exist in our economic system today.

4. Identify some causes for, and persons affected by, the major economic problems in our economy.

The success of an economic system can be determined by measuring the economic output; that is, the amount of goods and services that the system produces. In this chapter you will take a brief look at how the economic system of the United States compares with other systems on the basis of the amount of economic output.

Our private enterprise economy has been very successful by any measure. However, it is not without problems. In the last part of this chapter some of those problems will be looked at.

MEASURING ECONOMIC PERFORMANCE

The success of any economic system is hard to measure. The reason is that the goal of satisfying all the wants of people can never be reached. Nevertheless, it is possible to measure the performance of an economy. To do this, we will use the same methods or yardsticks used by economists.

Economic performance is measured in terms of production and distribution of goods and services. Goods and services are a good measure of economic performance because they represent the results of all economic activities. Comparing the output of goods and services from one year to another, or from one country to another, makes it possible to make judgments about how well (or badly) any economy is performing.

What measures other than economic performance would you use to judge how well a society is meeting the needs of its individual citizens?

Gross National Product (GNP)

One of the most important and most common yardsticks used to measure economic performance is called gross national product (GNP). *Gross national product* (GNP) is the total dollar value of all goods and services produced in a nation in a given year. Our government and the governments of most other nations regularly measure and report GNP. The methods involved in computing the GNP are beyond the scope of this book. But you should know that it is computed the same way from year to year. And thus the total amount of output for a nation can be compared from year to year. GNP figures are also computed in the same way from nation to nation. It is therefore possible to compare the economic growth of the various countries. Table 5-1 shows that there has been a rapid increase in the level of GNP for our nation during the last 25 years.

TABLE 5-1   GROSS NATIONAL PRODUCT OF THE UNITED STATES (for selected years—in current dollars)

Year	GNP (in billions of dollars)
1950	$ 284.8
1955	398.0
1960	503.7
1965	684.9
1970	976.5
1975	1,516.0
1976	1,692.0

Source: Statistical Abstract of the United States, 1977

There are at least two cautions one must take when using GNP figures to judge economic activity. First, GNP is always reported as the total dollar amount, or as prices, of all the goods and services produced and distributed. As you well know, prices of goods and services do not remain the same from year to year. If prices increase, the GNP figure will increase. For example, a nation could produce the same amount of goods and services two successive years in a row. But suppose the prices of all the goods and services doubled during the second year. Then the GNP would be doubled for the second year. Therefore, one must look at price increases as well as at increases in GNP to determine true increases in output. Second, the population of a nation usually does not remain the same from year to year. When population increases, there are then more people to share the total output of the economy. To allow for price increases and population increases, economists adjust GNP figures so they are more meaningful. Adjusted GNP figures provide two additional measures: real GNP and per capita GNP.

Real GNP   To get a truer GNP figure for various years, an adjustment must be made to allow for price increases. The total dollar value of the GNP is adjusted by subtracting the amount of the change in GNP caused only by increases in the prices of goods and services. Suppose, for example, that the GNP for a given year was $200 but that prices had increased an average of 5 percent over the previous year. To get a truer GNP figure for the year, $10 ($200 × 5 percent) would be subtracted from the total GNP ($200). The real GNP is therefore $190. The total value of all goods and services produced in a nation in a given year, adjusted for price increases or decreases, is called *real gross national product*. By looking at real GNP figures for various years, such as shown in Table 5-2, one gets a picture of the true increase in output in the economy. The increases for the American economy are considerably less than the increases shown in Table 5-1.

TABLE 5-2   REAL GROSS NATIONAL PRODUCT OF THE UNITED STATES (for selected years—in 1972 dollars)

Year	(in billions of dollars)
1950	$ 534
1955	655
1960	737
1965	926
1970	723
1975	1,192

Source: Statistical Abstract of the United States, 1977.

What are some reasons for the steady increase in real production in our economy?

Per Capita GNP   The GNP figures should also be adjusted to reflect the total population of a country. This is done on a per person, or per capita, basis. The *per capita GNP* is obtained by dividing the total GNP by the total population figure. The per capita adjustment is an important one. Suppose one looks only at GNP or real GNP totals for nations throughout the world. As you might expect, the nations with the largest populations tend to rank the highest, and the nations with the smallest populations tend to rank the lowest. But this is misleading because it doesn't reflect the different standards of living in the different nations. The per capita GNP adjusts GNP for population and enables one to compare

TABLE 5-3   TOTAL GNP, POPULATION, AND PER CAPITA GNP FOR SELECTED NATIONS OF THE WORLD

Nation	GNP Total ($ in millions)	Population Mid-1975 (in millions)	GNP Per Capita (in dollars)
Kuwait	13,900	1.0	13,900
United States	1,516,300	213.6	7,098
Sweden	60,910	8.2	7,428
Switzerland	44,640	6.4	6,975
Canada	145,250	22.8	6,362
France	303,560	52.9	5,737
Saudi Arabia	31,000	5.6	5,536
Australia	73,280	13.5	5,424
Japan	483,506	111.0	4,358
Israel	11,850	3.4	3,516
U.S.S.R.	786,700	254.5	3,088
Venezuela	27,300	12.0	2,277
Spain	73,780	35.5	2,080
Argentina	39,810	25.4	1,569
Mexico	64,360	60.2	1,070
Brazil	97,810	107.1	913
Nigeria	26,000	62.9	413
India	94,220	598.3	158
Vietnam	4,500	44.0	102
Ethiopia	2,770	28.0	99

Source: CBS News Almanac, 1978.

levels among nations. As you can see in Table 5-3, some small nations such as Switzerland and Sweden have higher per capita GNPs than some larger nations such as Brazil and India. The per capita GNP of the United States is among the highest in the world. Our private enterprise economy continues to keep our standard of living above that of most other nations.

Give some reasons for the extreme differences in real per capita GNP among the nations listed in Table 5-3.

How Well Does Our System Work?

The American economy is, by any economic measure, one of the most successful economic systems in the world. Americans enjoy one of the highest per capita real GNPs in the world. The United States produces and consumes in much greater quantities than any other nation in the world. Our real GNP has increased steadily during the first 200 years of our history. Most Americans consider automobiles, refrigerators, stoves, washers, dryers, and televisions to be necessities. Almost every family or household owns at least one of each of these items. Yet the majority of families or households in the world today would have no idea how to operate any one of these items. Our economic system has made us an affluent society.

What do you think is meant by the term "affluent society"?

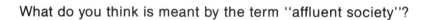

PROBLEMS IN OUR ECONOMIC SYSTEM

The American economic system is very successful. But, not everyone in the United States enjoys a high standard of living. In fact, many Americans are poor. It is said that a fourth of our nation lives at the poverty level. In recent years, the problem of rising prices throughout the economy has hurt millions of Americans, especially the elderly. Another serious problem is pollution, which affects everyone. And lastly there is the energy crisis, which is already causing changes in our way of living. These four economic problems—inflation, poverty, pollution, and the energy crisis—will now be looked at more carefully.

Inflation

One of the most constant problems faced by all sectors of the economy is the continuous increase in prices. If you think that it takes more and more money to buy the same goods or services each year, you are right. Prices are said to be inflated when more and more money is needed to buy the same goods and services. This problem, when referred to in economic terms, is called inflation. *Inflation,* then, is a general increase in the level of prices. Not all prices rise during inflation. Some may remain the same, and others may even fall. But when prices in general go up from year to year, or month to month, or even day to day, the economy is troubled with inflation. Inflation is the most discussed problem in our economy in recent years.

Most economists believe that inflation comes about when there is too much money in relation to the amount of goods and services. Those who have a lot of money bid up prices to get what they want. As a result, everyone must then pay more. Once started,

Inflation affects all consumers, but its impact is particularly felt by those on fixed incomes. (Stock, Boston)

inflation tends to feed on itself. For example, a price increase in one good often leads to a price increase in another. As prices rise, workers demand higher wages. This in turn encourages producers to raise prices even further. If not brought under control, inflation eventually destroys the value of money.

Who is Affected?   A general rise in prices does not immediately affect people whose incomes are increasing. For many years most Americans had incomes that increased rapidly enough so that some inflation did not really hurt them. In recent years, continued inflation has affected almost everyone—individuals, business firms, and government. The people hurt most by inflation are those living on fixed incomes. Their incomes remain the same while the general price level is rising. Examples of such people are those living on pensions, social security, welfare, or interest income. They can buy fewer and fewer goods and services as prices continue to rise.

Inflation usually helps those who are in debt. A *debtor* is someone who borrows money or buys on credit. If a debtor's income increases during the period of inflation, a smaller percentage of the debtor's income is needed to repay the debt. Though inflation helps the debtor, it hurts the creditor. A *creditor* is someone who lends money or sells on credit. The creditor is hurt because the money being paid back is worth less than when the loan was first made. Inflation also hurts those who save. As price levels go up during periods of inflation, the amount of money one has saved will buy fewer and fewer goods and services. As inflation continues, the savings become less and less valuable.

Identify some things that you think can be done to prevent, or at least slow down, inflation in our economy.

Pollution

From an economic point of view, the basic problem of pollution is the damage it causes to productive resources. Air pollution affects the health of people, and it damages forests and buildings. Water pollution in rivers and lakes kills fish and disrupts fishing industries. It makes water resources unfit for human use and endangers recreational facilities for swimming and boating. It has often created a threat to public health. Another problem is the disposal of refuse. Every community, large or small, faces this problem.

Pollution of our environment was not widely recognized as a national problem until the 1960s. By that time, the situation had become serious. The federal government took action and passed a number of new laws designed to reduce pollution. The chief targets were industries that pollute the air and water. Producers were required to change their production methods and install new equipment that would limit pollution.

The early detection of possible air pollutants allows communities to set up emergency controls. (ERDA)

Both producers and consumers must bear part of the responsibility for our present environmental problems. Consumers demand more and more goods and services at the least possible cost. They have had little or no concern for the effects of the use and disposal of these products on the environment. Producers have used the least expensive means in production so that they can earn the most profit. Like consumers, they haven't cared how their production methods affect the environment. Everyone feels he or she has a right to use the environment as each person pleases. As the environment is polluted with materials in the air, in the water, and on land, a major economic problem results. The effect is that usefulness of polluted productive resources is decreased.

Who Is Affected?   Pollution affects some people more directly than others. All of us are affected indirectly, however. Persons living near a polluted river or in a city with a major air pollution problem are directly affected. Industrial workers who are laid off because their employer will not conform to antipollution laws are affected. Farmers who can no longer use DDT to kill harmful insects because of the effects of DDT on birds, fish, and other animals are directly affected. It must be kept in mind, however, that the general decline in the quality of the environment affects all of us. Our health and our economic activities are affected by the actions of those who pollute and destroy our environment.

Briefly describe two or three specific pollution problems that have developed in your city or community in the past two years.

Poverty

The number of people considered to be poor in our society ranges from 25 to 30 million. Between 10 and 15 percent of our population falls into this category. In an economy that is said to be one of the percent of our population. In an economy that is said to be one of the most successful in the world, these figures may be surprising. The major problems faced by these poor people are a direct result of their lack of income. They eat inadequate food. They wear inadequate clothing. They live in inadequate housing, and they get inadequate medical care. The poverty problem is an economic problem for our entire society. It is not just a problem for those who are poor. Money for programs to aid the poor is raised by taxing other individuals and businesses. Each of us, therefore, pays a share of the costs involved.

Why does poverty exist in our society? It is difficult to identify all of the reasons. Individuals from low-income families most often

Some relief for poverty-level families is provided through the distribution of surplus government food. (Monkmeyer)

do not receive an adequate education. They lack the training that they must have to get a job in today's job market. When they do find jobs, they are almost always the first to be laid off when the economy slows down. Racial discrimination has played a large part in keeping minority groups in the poverty category. In the past, minority people were denied the opportunity to obtain education or training. As a result, they could not raise themselves out of the cycle of poverty.

Another cause of poverty is the fact that social security payments and pension plans have not kept up with the increase in the cost of living. For many old or disabled people this means living in poverty and doing without.

Who Is Affected?   Some clues as to the groups directly affected by poverty were given above. Families that have serious health problems are usually poor. Families in which unemployment or part-time employment is a frequent occurrence are often poor. Families in which the head of the household lacks the education or training needed in the job market are likely to be poor. A fairly large number of minority-group members and elderly persons live in poverty. All, however, of us are affected in an economic sense by the problem of poverty.

Suggest some solutions for the poverty problem in our society.

Energy Crisis

In the early 1970s Americans recognized that our nation faced an energy crisis. Experts warned that the crisis would grow worse. However, many people felt that the shortage of petroleum and natural gas was being exaggerated. Surely the most productive nation in the world could not be caught with a short supply of energy! In the last few years, it has become obvious that the warning was true. Our major sources of energy, gas and oil were found to be in short supply. The United States must depend on foreign sources of supply to make up the shortage. Depending on foreign suppliers for something so necessary as petroleum has worried many government leaders. It places the nation in a very uncertain position. Efforts are being made, therefore, to find other sources of energy. Our supply of coal is one of the largest in the world. But the use of coal decreased rapidly after the passage of the Clean Air Act of 1970. This act restricted the amount of smoke and dust particles that could be put into the air and caused many coal-burning plants to change to oil. Thus an action designed to help solve the problem of air pollution added to another problem—the energy crisis.

The cause of the energy crisis has been, like the cause of most major problems, difficult to identify. The wasteful use of energy by many consumers and business firms is one cause. Government control of prices of natural gas and oil is another cause. Because prices were kept low, many producers felt it was not profitable enough to spend money exploring for new sources of gas and oil. Thus, the gas and oil from available wells continued to be used up without developing new ones. Energy was wasted in literally hundreds of little ways. Driving cars at high speeds and driving cars that use too much gas wasted energy. Heating homes and businesses to high temperatures both day and night wasted energy. And leaving lights on even though they were not being used wasted energy.

But wasteful use was not the only cause. Groups concerned with the quality of the environment were also involved. They fought the tapping of new sources of energy. Where producers did want to drill for new energy supplies, these groups were often able to stop them because of possible damage that would be done to the environment. As you can see, responsibility cannot be placed on any one group. The combination of a variety of actions by many different individuals, businesses, and levels of government brought about the energy crisis.

Who Is Affected?   Naturally, in energy shortages such as that of the early 1970s, some individuals and business firms are affected more directly than others. Many gasoline service stations across the nation were closed while gasoline was in short supply. The people who owned or operated these stations were surely affected. So were the people who could not get gasoline for their cars or who had to wait in long lines. The automobile industry cut back the production of large automobiles. It changed to the production of smaller cars with better gas mileage. Other businesses changed production methods. They shortened hours of business, and tried out other methods of saving energy. Soon, unemployment began to spread in several oil-related industries.

The shortages of goods and services related to the gas and oil industries, in general, have affected and will continue to affect almost all Americans in some way. For example, the energy crisis resulted in higher prices for gas and oil. These higher prices cause an increase in prices for any good or service that is dependent on petroleum or petroleum products. In today's world that means almost everything, including food, clothing, and housing.

Describe some changes that your family has made because of the energy crisis.

Learning Activities

Increasing Your Business Vocabulary

You should become familiar with each of the terms shown below. On a sheet of paper write the numbers 1 through 6. Then write alongside each number the term that best matches each of the numbered definitions.

creditor / debtor / gross national product (GNP) / inflation / per capita gross national product / real gross national product

1. A general increase in the level of prices.

2. The dollar amount of GNP divided by the population of the nation.

3. Someone who borrows money or buys on credit.

4. Someone who lends money or sells on credit.

5. The total dollar value of all goods and services produced in a nation in a given year, adjusted for price increases or decreases.

6. The total dollar value of all goods and services produced in a nation in a given year.

Understanding Business

1. Why is it important to compute gross national product (GNP) the same way from year to year and the same way in all nations?

2. Explain the difference between gross national product and real gross national product.

3. Why should per capita figures be used when comparing GNP for nations throughout the world?

4. Why is it said that the United States' economy is one of the most successful economic systems in the world?

5. Inflation is said to be the most discussed problem in our economy in recent years. What generally is said to be the cause?

6. What groups of people does inflation hurt most? Why?

7. Explain how inflation helps debtors and hurts creditors.

8. From an economic point of view, what is the basic problem of pollution?

9. Explain why poverty is an economic problem for our entire society.

10. The United States faces an energy crisis. List some things that cause this crisis.

Business Problems and Projects

1. Read the following newspaper article and answer the questions that follow it.

CLOSING 10 STEEL FURNACES THREATENS HAMPTON AREA

Hampton—The decision of Kluth Steel Company to close 10 open-hearth furnaces at its Hampton Works because they pollute the air threatens the economy of the entire Hampton area, one of the most industrialized regions in the country. The decision to close the facility, rather than pay a fine of $2,300 a day for violating federal clean-air laws, will have several immodiate effects.

- Closure will cause the layoff of 2,500 Hampton Works employees and the loss of at least 1,500 jobs in steel related or steel-dependent industries in the area.

- Closure will reduce by 80,000 tons a month production from the nation's largest steel plant.

- Closure will cause economic trouble for an area that until now was able to keep unemployment down, industrial expansion up, and business income at a reasonable level.

- Closure will endanger the truce between environmentalists and industrialists, which in recent months has allowed the start of air- and water-pollution control programs in the steel-oil manufacturing center of Hampton, Villard, and Lake Henry.

a. What decision has been made by the Kluth Steel Company?

b. Why is the company being fined? How much is the fine per day?

c. How many employees of Hampton Works are to be laid off? Are other jobs in the area expected to be lost? If so, what type of jobs?

d. As a result of the closure, how much less steel production will there be in one year?

e. What effect will the closure most likely have on unemployment in the area? On industrial expansion?

f. Would you recommend that the daily fine be removed or that the facility be closed if you were (1.) an employee of the Kluth Steel Company, (2.) a home-owner in Hampton who operates an automobile dealership there, or (3.) an individual who doesn't live in Hampton and is not directly affected by the decision.

2. The graph below shows the GNP growth rate from 1966 to 1975 in terms of the value of the 1972 dollar. Study the graph and answer the questions that follow.

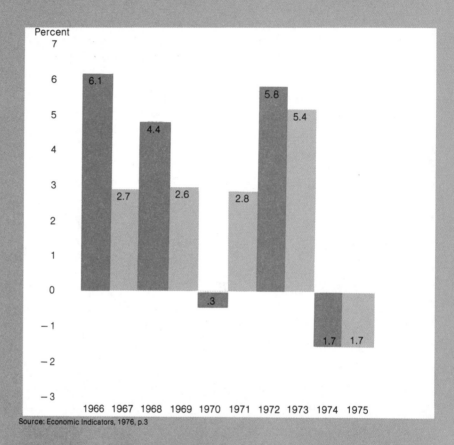

Source: Economic Indicators, 1976, p.3

a. In which year was the economic growth rate highest?

b. In which year(s) was there a negative growth rate?

c. In which year(s) was the economic growth rate lower than the previous year?

d. How much higher was the growth rate in 1972 than in 1971?

Chapter 6

The Nature of Business

Objectives

After completing your study of this chapter, you will be able to do the following:

1. Define the term *business* and identify several examples of activities that business firms carry out in our economic system.

2. Discuss why business firms are organized and operate in our economic system.

3. Classify a business firm by industry and by activity.

4. Indicate whether business activity is increasing or decreasing.

The United States has an effective, relatively successful economic system. Although not perfect, it is one of the best systems yet devised to provide people with the goods and services they want. It offers more opportunity to more people and has resulted in a higher standard of living than almost any other economic system. Much of the credit for this success should be given to the people and business firms that make up the business sector of the economy. The major purpose of this unit is to make you more familiar with this important sector.

Before starting your study of business, write down your own definition of *business.* What do you think business is and what do you think it includes?

WHAT IS BUSINESS?

If you tried to answer the question above, you probably found it difficult. Business is a hard term to define because it is used in so many different ways. Compare your definition with those suggested by your classmates. You will probably find that no one of you is in complete agreement with another. There may be as many definitions as there are students in your class. The reason is that business includes such a wide range of activities.

The definition of business that will be used in this book draws upon your earlier study of economics in this book. In its broadest sense, *business* is the organized activities designed to satisfy people's wants for goods and services. Most of these activities are performed by business firms that are owned by private individuals who are seeking to make a profit.

KINDS OF BUSINESS ACTIVITIES

Business firms engage in many different kinds of activities. They are organized in many different ways, and they produce a tremendous variety of goods and services. They are located in places as different as the coastline of the Gulf of Mexico and the foothills of the Rocky Mountains. They may be found on the Avenue of the

Americas in New York City or the corn fields of Iowa. They may be as small as a one-person local barber shop or grocery. Or they may be as large as Exxon Corporation, General Electric, and American Telephone and Telegraph Company. There are vast differences among business firms. Because of this, it is impossible to describe a typical business firm. Yet all businesses do have some things in common. Their activities generally fit into one of these five categories: producing raw goods, processing raw goods, manufacturing goods, distributing goods, and providing services.

List some things that you think all business firms may have in common. Be prepared to explain your answers.

Producing Raw Goods

Much of the business activity in our economy involves producing raw goods. *Raw goods* are things of value grown on or taken from the earth. Almost all of these goods, sometimes called *commodities,* need to be processed in some way before they are used by the final consumer. Farmers who grow wheat, corn, fruits, and vegetables are producers of raw goods. Mining firms that remove iron ore, copper, and other minerals from the earth are producers of raw goods. The fishing industry taking fish from the Atlantic and Pacific Oceans or the Great Lakes is a producer of raw goods. Wood taken from forests and crude oil pumped from the earth are two other types of raw economic goods that business firms produce.

Farmers grow crops that are used for food and crops that are not used for food. List as many nonfood farm crops as you can.

Processing Raw Goods

Most raw goods are not very useful in their natural form. Wheat, cotton, crude oil, iron ore, and most other raw goods need to be processed before they are useful. *Processing* involves the activities that change a raw good into a usable form. Wheat, for example, is ground into flour. Logs are sawed to make lumber. Crude oil is

Because iron ore is not generally usable in its original form, it must be processed into steel. (American Iron & Steel Institute, American Iron & Steel Institute)

The steel can then be used to manufacture automobiles, which will be shipped to the ultimate consumer. (Marshall Licht/Stockmarket, Los Angeles; Santa Fe Railway)

refined into gasoline, motor oils, and other products. These activities are processing activities.

Some processed goods, because they are ready to be used, are purchased by consumers. Flour, for example, is in a useful form after the wheat has been milled. Fruits and vegetables are ready for consumers after they have been cleaned or canned or frozen. Other processed goods are purchased by business firms. They are used to produce other kinds of goods. Iron ore, for example, may be first processed into steel rods or sheets. The steel, in the form of rods or sheets, is then used to make fenders for cars or beams for skyscrapers.

In some cases the firm that produces the raw goods may also do some or all of the processing. Giant oil companies are good examples. They not only produce crude oil but they also refine it into gasoline. Farmers, on the other hand, who grow wheat, corn, fruits, cotton, and other commodities seldom process their goods into finished form. Other business firms take these products and process them into usable goods for other processing companies or for consumers.

What is the difference between raw goods and processed goods? Using milk as an example, when would you consider it to be a raw good? A processed good?

Manufacturing Goods

Manufacturing refers to the activities involved in combining raw goods or processed goods to produce other goods. Radios, lawnmowers, ballpoint pens, typewriters, paper bags, and clothing are just a few examples of manufactured goods. Thousands of business firms are formed for the sole purpose of manufacturing goods. These firms rely on other business firms to supply them with the materials they need to make finished products.

Name some manufactured goods other than those listed above that you use. What raw and processed goods were used to manufacture the items you listed?

Distributing Goods

You will recall that *distribution* is the link between the producer and the consumer. Distribution is the function of business firms that sell products to consumers. Some examples with which you are familiar include supermarkets, department stores, gasoline stations, and drugstores. Many other business firms also engage in distributing goods. Freight and transportation companies, for example, move goods from the places where they are produced to the stores where consumers buy them. Advertising firms prepare radio or television commercials that tell consumers what goods are available and where they can be purchased. Banks that extend credit for a purchase also help to distribute economic goods and services. Each business firm depends, to some degree, on the activities performed by others to get its goods to the consumer.

What types of business firms other than those listed above are involved in distributing economic goods?

Providing Services

Providing services is one of the fastest growing areas of business activity in the United States. Almost every consumer and every

Services like those provided by automotive mechanics represent an increasingly important economic activity.
(Maria Karras)

business firm relies on one or another of the services provided by business. Among the services provided by privately owned business firms are telephone service, all types of insurance, banking, communications (radio, television, newspapers), hotels and motels, cleaning and repair services, and transportation. Many of these business firms are one-owner firms. Lawyers, doctors, veterinarians, insurance agents, beauticians, barbers, and repair technicians often individually own and operate a business. If our standard of living continues to increase, people will want more of these services than is now available. They will also demand additional services as well. It appears that business firms providing services will continue to account for much of the business activity in the economy.

List the names of some service businesses that are located in your city or community.

WHY BUSINESS FIRMS ARE ORGANIZED

In earlier chapters it was explained that there are two major reasons why business firms are organized. First, all business firms organize and operate to make a profit. Second, business firms organize to produce goods and services.

Earning a Profit

You will recall that profit is the amount of money left from income after all expenses have been paid. The goods or services being produced must be sold at a price that will cover the costs of production and provide a fair profit. There must be enough profit so that the owner of a business is willing to continue to take the risk of operating it. If this is not true, the business firm will most likely go out of business.

Judging from the above definition, profit seems to be a rather easy term to understand. But you need to get a clearer notion of what profit means for a business firm. To do so, one must be aware of what things are included in both income and expenses for a business firm. Money received from sales of goods or services is the major source of income for a business firm. Most people, however, are not aware of all the costs that go into production. Some of the major business costs that go into production include the cost of raw goods, rent, wages and salaries, and interest.

After paying production costs, there must be something left to pay the owner, or owners, for the risk of operating the firm. This is a major purpose of profit. The profit of a firm is usually reported in relation to the dollar amount of sales of the firm. A firm with $10,000 of sales and $300 of profit would, for example, have a 3 percent profit. A firm with $10,000 of sales and $900 of profit would have profit of 9 percent. The percent of profit based on the dollar amount of sales varies a great deal among business firms. The average profit of business firms in our country today is 5 to 6 percent of sales.

Should government limit the amount of profit a firm can earn? Why or why not?

Satisfying Human Wants

Business firms organize to produce and distribute the goods and services that people want. Most of the goods and services produced in our economy are used here in the United States. However, some of the things that are produced are sold to other nations. In our economic system, individual consumers have a considerable influence on what kinds of things are produced by business firms. A business firm must produce goods or services that are in demand. If it does not, it will not be able to continue operating. Suppose the goods or services made by a business firm are no longer purchased. The business firm will have to produce something else or it will have to close its doors. No business firm can continue to operate very long if it cannot sell the goods or services it produces.

What are some goods or services that were produced in the past but are not being produced now? Why are the items you listed no longer produced?

MAJOR INDUSTRY GROUPS

Information about business firms is usually reported under the categories of industry shown in Table 6-1. These categories are very broad, and each contains several industries in the usual meaning of the word. An *industry* is a group of business firms producing the same or similar goods or services. There would be several different industries in the broad category of "manufacturing." All the automobile industry manufacturers and all the clothing industry manufacturers, for example, would be included in this broad category.

TABLE 6-1   NUMBER AND PERCENTAGE OF BUSINESS FIRMS IN EACH INDUSTRY

Industry	Number (in thousands)	Percent of Total Business Firms
Agricultural, forestry, and fisheries	3,561	25.6
Mining	87	0.6
Construction	1,145	8.2
Manufacturing	456	3.3
Transportation, communication, and public utilities	454	3.3
Wholesale and retail trades	2,998	21.6
Finance, insurance, and real estate	1,594	11.5
Services	3,524	25.3
Other	83	0.6
Total business firms	13,902	100.0

Source: Statistical Abstract of the United States, 1977.

Classifying by Activity

Although Table 6-1 does not show it, business firms can be classified by major activity such as production or distribution. For example, business firms that specialize in producing and processing raw goods and in manufacturing are said to be production businesses. In Table 6-1 these business firms are found under the headings of agriculture, forestry, and fisheries; mining; construction; and manufacturing. There are also business firms that specialize in distribution. In Table 6-1 these business firms are under the heading of transportation, communication, and public utilities. The last group is made up of those specializing in services. Included in this group are finance, insurance, real estate, and service industries.

ANALYZING BUSINESS ACTIVITY

Privately owned business firms produce most of the goods and services in this country. They employ most of the people in the labor force. Although there are more than 12 million business firms nationwide, almost three-fourths of our gross national product comes from only 500 firms. Judging the level of business activity by

TABLE 6–2 NUMBER EMPLOYED AND PERCENT OF TOTAL EMPLOYED BY EACH INDUSTRY

Industry	1960		1977	
	Number (in thousands)	Percent of Total	Number (in thousands)	Percent of Total
Agriculture, forestry, and fisheries	5,723	9.5	3,298	3.9
Mining	712	1.2	820	1.0
Construction	2,885	4.8	3,394	4.1
Manufacturing	16,796	28.0	19,118	22.9
Transportation, communication, and public utilities	4,004	6.7	4,512	5.4
Wholesale and retail trades	11,391	19.0	17,810	21.3
Finance, insurance, and real estate	2,669	4.5	4,410	5.3
Services	7,423	12.4	14,957	17.9
Government	8,353	13.9	15,229	18.2

Source: *Statistical Abstract of the United States,* 1977.

comparing how much is produced and by whom is only one way of looking at business. You could also look at employment figures. What industries employ the most people? Or you could look at sales volumes. What industries account for the greatest dollar sales? Or you could look at profits. Which companies or industries earned the greatest dollar profits. Tables 6-2 through 6-4 provide some interesting data that answer some of these questions.

Employment

Employment data tells us something about business activity. If a lot of people are employed in one industry, that industry can be considered important because so many depend on it for earning their living. Any major problem in that industry could mean unemployment for large numbers of workers. Look at Table 6-2. It shows, for example, a considerable decline in the percentage of persons employed in production businesses such as agriculture. In 1960 about 43.5 percent of all people employed worked in production industries. In 1977 the percentage had decreased to 34 percent. More and more people are working in the service industries and

TABLE 6-3 EMPLOYMENT FOR GROUPED INDUSTRIES— GOODS-RELATED AND SERVICE-RELATED

Industries	1950		1960		1977	
	Number (in thousands)	Percent of Total	Number (in thousands)	Percent of Total	Number (in thousands)	Percent of Total
Goods-related	18,475	40.9	20,393	37.6	23,331	29.1
Service-related and other	26,747	59.1	33,840	62.4	56,921	70.9

Source: Statistical Abstract of the United States, 1977.

government. Employment in service industries and government increased from about 31 percent to 41 percent of all people employed from 1960 to 1970. Table 6-3 shows the shift even more dramatically. The percentage of persons employed in goods-related industries decreased from about 41 percent in 1950 to about 29 percent in 1977. Employment in service-related and other areas went up from less than 60 percent to more than 70 percent in the same period.

Receipts and Profits

Total receipts and total net profits of all business firms add up to figures so large they are hard to grasp. Table 6-4 lists data on the percent or portion of total receipts and total net profits earned by

TABLE 6-4   PERCENT OF BUSINESS RECEIPTS AND NET PROFIT BY INDUSTRY—1974

Industry	Percent of Total Dollars of Business Receipts	Percent of Total Dollars of Business Net Profit
Agriculture, forestry, and fisheries	2.9	4.5
Mining	2.0	12.6
Construction	5.2	3.6
Manufacturing	36.6	37.1
Transportation, communication, and public utilities	6.5	5.0
Wholesale and retail trades	31.5	17.7
Finance, insurance, and real estate	9.9	5.7
Services	5.4	13.3

Source: *Statistical Abstract of the United States,* 1977.

business firms in various industries. Note that business firms in manufacturing and wholesale and retail trades accounted for over 68 percent of the total business recepts for 1974. Business firms in the wholesale and retail trades earned a considerably smaller percentage of the net profits than they did of the receipts. The business firms in the service category, on the other hand, accounted for only 5.4 percent of the receipts. But they earned over 13 percent of the net profit.

Learning Activities

Increasing Your Business Vocabulary

You should become familiar with each of the terms shown below. On a sheet of paper write the numbers 1 through 5. Then write alongside each number the term that best matches each of the numbered definitions.

business / industry / manufacturing / processing / raw goods

1. The activities that change a raw good into a usable form.
2. A group of business firms producing the same or similar goods or services.
3. The activities involved in combining raw goods or processed goods to produce other goods.
4. Things of value grown on or taken from the earth.
5. The organized activities designed to satisfy people's wants for goods and services.

Understanding Business

1. Why is the term *business* so hard to define?
2. Who purchases the processed goods in our economy? For what purpose do business firms use these goods?
3. List several goods produced by manufacturing firms.
4. Give examples of business firms that are organized to distribute economic goods.

5. What is one of the fastest growing areas of business activity in the United States?

6. What are the two major reasons why all business firms are organized?

7. What is usually the major source of income for a business firm?

8. List some of the major business costs that go into production.

9. Who uses most of the goods and services produced in our nation?

10. Give some examples of production businesses. Of distribution businesses. Of service businesses.

Business Problems and Projects

1. On a form similar to the one shown below, list the names of ten business firms in your local community. In the second column, indicate whether the firm is engaged primarily in production, distribution, or a service. In the third column, classify each of the firms according to the industry classification given in Table 6-1 on page 77.

	Name of Firm	Type of Activity	Industry Classification
Example	Trenton China	Production	Manufacturing

2. Most of the goods and services produced in our economy are used in the United States. However, some of the goods are sent to other nations, and other nations produce goods and send them to us. Products shipped from the United States for consumption in other countries are known as *exports*. Prod-

ucts made in foreign countries and brought into this country to be sold are known as *imports*. Study the table below and answer the questions that follow.

U.S. EXPORTS AND IMPORTS BY BROAD END-USE CLASS
(in millions of dollars)

Item	Exports			Imports		
	1973	1974	1975	1973	1974	1975
Foods, feeds, and beverages	15,185	18,608	19,221	9,129	10,585	9,684
Industrial supplies and materials	20,036	30,648	30,779	28,211	54,689	51,371
Capital goods, except auto-mobiles	21,848	30,410	35,831	8,132	9,544	9,686
Automobile vehicles, parts, and engines	6,878	8,625	10,628	10,319	12,079	11,848
Consumer goods (nonfood, except automobiles)	4,791	6,382	6,547	13,218	14,786	13,739
All others	2,672	3,637	4,127	1,490	1,996	1,822
Total	71,410	98,310	107,133	70,499	103,679	98,150

Source: *Statistical Abstract of the United States*, 1976.

a. What was the total amount of United States exports in 1973?

b. What was the total amount of imports to the United States in 1975?

c. Was there any year(s) in which imports were less than exports?

d. Which item accounted for the largest amount of exports in 1973? The smallest?

Chapter 7

How Business Firms Are Organized

Objectives

After completing your study of this chapter, you will be able to do the following:

1. Name the legal forms by which business firms are organized.

2. Describe and compare the general characteristics of each of the major types of business organizations.

3. Describe and compare the advantages and disadvantages of a sole proprietorship.

4. Describe and compare the advantages and disadvantages of a partnership.

5. Describe and compare the advantages and disadvantages of a corporation.

A business firm may be organized by one person, two persons, or several people. The number of owners of a business firm is often related to the size of the business and the kind of activities it specializes in. A shoe repair shop, for example, would probably have only one owner. There are several reasons for this. First, the nature of the business depends on the skills of one person. Because the business is small, the owner fills many roles—salesperson, manager, accountant, and custodian. In other words, one person can perform all the duties connected with the operation of the business. A telephone company, on the other hand, would probably have many owners. To provide telephone service requires huge amounts of capital for equipment. Very few individuals could start a telephone company because so much capital is needed. To provide such service would also require a large number of workers.

Because of differences in size and the nature of their activities, business firms are organized as sole proprietorships, partnerships, corporations, or cooperatives. Business owners choose a particular form of organization to best meet their objectives.

Where would you go in your community to get information that would be helpful in deciding how to organize a business firm? Identify as many sources as possible.

SOLE PROPRIETORSHIPS

A *sole proprietorship* is a business firm organized and owned by one person. It is the oldest and simplest form of business organization. It is also the easiest form of business to organize and start. The owner simply gets the materials and equipment needed and begins to produce goods or services. Any type of good or service can be produced as long as the operation is not against the law. For some businesses, however, licenses or permits may be necessary. An example would be a real estate office or a barber shop. The sole proprietorship is generally a one-person or one-family operation, but there may be many employees involved.

As can be seen from Table 7-1, the number of sole proprietorships is greater than the number of other forms of business

TABLE 7-1   PROPRIETORSHIPS, PARTNERSHIPS, AND CORPORATIONS: NUMBER (in thousands) AND PERCENT BY INDUSTRY—1973

Industry	Proprietorships		Partnerships		Corporations		Total Firms
	Number	Percent of Total	Number	Percent of Total	Number	Percent of Total	
Agriculture, forestry and fisheries	3,415	95.2	124	3.5	47	1.3	3,586
Mining	58	67.4	15	17.5	13	15.1	86
Construction	857	78.0	66	6.0	176	16.0	1,099
Manufacturing	210	46.8	30	6.7	209	46.5	449
Transportation, communication, and public utilities	341	78.6	16	3.7	77	17.7	434
Wholesale and retail trade	2,164	73.4	199	6.8	582	19.8	2,945
Finance, insurance, and real estate	739	46.9	410	26.0	427	27.1	1,576
Services	2,821	83.8	178	5.3	368	10.9	3,367
Total	10,605	78.3	1,038	7.6	1,899	14.1	13,542

Source: Statistical Abstract of the United States, 1976.

organization in every industry. Most sole proprietorships, however, are small business firms. While their number is large, they account for only a small percentage of the total business receipts in our economy (see Table 7-2.) The large number of sole proprietorships is often cited as proof of the economic freedom available to individuals in our society. Except when a license or permit is required, individuals do not have to ask for governmental permission to go into business. Anyone who is ambitious and who has initiative can start a business.

Write down the names of several business firms in your community that are organized as sole proprietorships.

PARTNERSHIPS

Sometimes the sole owner of a business decides to expand the business. This is often done when there is a need for more capital or more management know-how. To do this, a partnership may be formed. A *partnership* is a business firm owned by two or more persons who share the profit or the loss. A written agreement called the *articles of copartnership* is usually drawn up when creating a business firm as a partnership. The articles of copartner-

TABLE 7-2 BUSINESS RECEIPTS—1974
(by industry and legal form of organization—amounts in billions of dollars)

Industry	Proprietorships		Partnerships		Corporations		Total Receipts
	Receipts	Percent of Total	Receipts	Percent of Total	Receipts	Percent of Total	
Agriculture, forestry, and fisheries	66.9	64.6	12.5	12.1	24.2	23.4	103.6
Mining	3.0	4.3	3.5	5.0	62.9	90.7	69.4
Construction	32.7	18.4	11.4	6.4	133.7	75.2	177.8
Manufacturing	9.1	.7	7.5	.6	1,252.4	98.7	1,269.0
Transportation communication, and public utilities	9.6	11.6	19.0	34.8	30.0	35.0	
	10.3	4.6	2.1	.9	214.2	94.5	226.6
Wholesale and retail trade	142.3	13.0	43.4	4.0	906.9	83.0	1,092.6
Finance, insurance, and real estate	11.6	3.4	29.1	8.5	303.2	88.1	343.9
Services	51.3	27.2	27.1	14.3	110.5	58.5	188.9
Totals	328.3	9.5	136.7	3.9	3,008.8	86.6	3,471.8

Source: Statistical Abstract of the United States, 1977.

ship should spell out the amount of capital each partner provides, the duties of each partner, and how profits are to be divided among partners. All owners can share equally, but other arrangements can be made. One partner may put up a larger share of money than the others. That partner may then be given a larger share of the profits. Sometimes, one partner may provide all the capital but have no job responsibility in the firm. The other partner may be responsible for managing the firm. If these two partners agree, the partnership can be set up so that each shares equally in any profits earned by the firm. Partners can arrange to share profits and responsibilities in any way they wish.

There are about 1 million partnerships in the United States (see Table 7-1.) There are more than ten times more sole proprietorships. Yet the partnerships have net receipts equal to almost half of those of sole proprietorships (see Table 7-2.) In other words, the average partnership does a greater volume of business than does the average sole proprietorship. Since partnerships often grow out of sole proprietorships, it would seem natural that partnerships would receive a greater amount of the total figure for business receipts.

Name some business firms in your community that are organized as partnerships. Do these business firms have anything in common? If so, what?

CORPORATIONS

A *corporation* is a business firm that is created by law to have the same legal status as a person. It can buy resources, own property and equipment, produce and market goods and services. It can borrow money and become liable for debts, extend credit, sue and be sued. In other words, it can carry on all the activities of a sole proprietorship or partnership. The main difference is that a corporation carries out all its activities in its own name, not in the name of its owners. It is organized under a charter. A *charter* is written authority from a state or the federal government to organize and operate a business firm as a corporation.

In a sole proprietorship or partnership, the owners directly own the business. In a corporation the owners own stock in the business. The stock may be divided into thousands or millions of shares. People who own stock in a corporation are known as *stockholders.* They receive a *stock certificate* that states the

More people own this particular stock then any other stock offered. (AT&T)

number of shares of stock a person owns in a corporation. The more shares of stock a person owns in a corporation, the greater is that person's share of the total ownership. Two corporations that have very large numbers of stockholders are American Telephone and Telegraph Company and General Motors. The first has over 3 million stockholders and the second about 1.5 million stockholders.

Why do you suppose this business firm is organized as a corporation and not as a partnership? (Maria Karras)

Most stockholders in a corporation do not work in the business. They do, however, vote at an annual meeting to elect a board of directors. The *board of directors* is a group that serves as the decision-making body of the corporation. The members may be actively involved in managing the business or they may select other people to manage it. At regular intervals the board of directors examines the overall operation and profit. If profits are sufficient they declare a dividend to be paid for each share of stock. A *dividend* is payment of a portion of a corporation's profits to its stockholders.

Do you or any member of your immediate family own stock in a corporation? If so, in what corporation or corporations?

A look at Table 7-1 reveals that less than 15 percent of the business firms in the United States are organized as corporations. Almost half of the manufacturing firms are corporations, and about one-third of the financial, insurance, and real estate firms are corporations. In the other industries a relatively small percentage of the business firms are incorporated. Table 7-2 shows that corporations received over half the business receipts for every industry except agriculture. Indeed, they received more than three-fourths of the business receipts in all industries other than agriculture and services. When measured by dollar volume of business activity, the corporation is truly the major form of business firm in our society today.

What are the names of some business firms in your community that are organized as corporations?

COOPERATIVES

A *cooperative* is a business firm organized, owned, and operated for the mutual benefit of its members. An example would be Sunkist growers. It is owned by a group of citrus growers who use their cooperative to market their products. Many dairies also use this form of organization.

As the definition indicates, a cooperative is owned by a number of people. The owners of a cooperative are called members or shareholders. An individual becomes a member by depositing a sum of money or buying a share of stock. Also, the individual must be associated with or belong to the group of persons for whom the benefits of the cooperative are intended. A cooperative is organized and operated to best serve its members' needs. It helps its members get a lower price when they buy goods or services. It also helps them get a better price when they sell products.

Each of the members attending this shareholders meeting has an equal voice in the operation of the cooperative. (Sunkist)

The cooperative form is similar to the corporation. A cooperative has the legal status of a person and can do all the things that were mentioned above concerning a corporation. To establish a cooperative, a charter must also be obtained from the state or federal government.

There are several different types of cooperatives. Credit unions and consumer, producer, and grower cooperatives are found throughout the nation. Credit unions are by far the most popular type of cooperative. They account for approximately half of all cooperatives. Cooperative business firms, except for credit unions, are more common in rural and agricultural business areas. Consumer cooperatives of all types, including food, housing, insurance, medical care, and medical supplies, have become more common in urban areas in recent years, however.

Is any member of your family a member of a consumer cooperative or a credit union? If so, what is the name of the cooperative or credit union?

When members of a cooperative elect a board of directors, each member has only one vote. This is true no matter how many shares the person owns. This is a major difference between a cooperative and a corporation. A second major difference is in the manner of distributing dividends. Like a corporation, a cooperative usually determines its earnings at the end of each year. Most of the cooperative's earnings are refunded to the owners at the end of the year in the form of a patronage dividend. A *patronage dividend* is a payment of a portion of the earnings of a cooperative to its members based on the amount of business each member has done with the cooperative. The more active a member is in dealings with the cooperative, the greater will be the amount of the patronage dividend. Cooperatives are not organized and operated to make a profit. Therefore, they are taxed under laws that are different from those that apply to other types of business firms.

Name some business firms in your community that are organized as cooperatives.

COMPARING THE THREE MAJOR TYPES OF BUSINESS ORGANIZATIONS

Why do some business owners choose to organize their business firm as a sole proprietorship? Why not a partnership or a corporation? There can be many different reasons for choosing one form over another. In some cases, there may be a tax advantage to the owner by organizing as a sole proprietorship. In other cases, there may be a tax advantage by organizing as a corporation.

In the following section different features of each form of organization will be examined. These features will help you understand why some businesses are organized as corporations or partnerships while others are organized as sole proprietorships.

Advantages of a Sole Proprietorship

As you know, the sole proprietorship form of business firm is often a one-person operation. This is a real advantage to the owner because he or she is his or her own boss. Sole proprietorships, therefore, are ideal for very small businesses that can be run by one person.

A sole proprietorship is the easiest form of business firm to organize. All one needs to do is to acquire the necessary skills and capital. There are no legal papers unless a license is necessary. In a sole proprietorship, the business and the owner are one and the same. Business profits, therefore, are taxed as personal income. For most sole proprietorships this usually means a lower tax rate than that paid by corporations. But if a sole proprietorship has very high profits, say over $50,000, the owner may be better off to form a corporation to take advantage of a more favorable tax rate. Finally, in a sole proprietorship there is a relatively close relationship between the firm's owner and its employees and customers. This makes it well suited to businesses in which personal service is important. The owner often knows all the employees and customers personally because the business is small. In large corporations, this is seldom possible.

Disadvantages of a Sole Proprietorship

Sole proprietorships also have some disadvantages. One of the most unfavorable features is that the owner is personally responsible for all debts the business may incur. If the business fails, the owner may lose not only the business, but also his or her personal property and life's savings. In other words, the liability of the owner is unlimited. This is not the case when a business is organized as a corporation. Another disadvantage of a sole pro-

Why are sole proprietorships the most popular form of business organization? (Robert Rubinstein)

prietorship is that capital for growth or expansion may be difficult to obtain. Banks are often unwilling to risk large sums of money in small businesses. Another bad feature of a sole proprietorship is that the owner must make decisions in all areas of management. Few, if any, individuals can be expert in selling, accounting, advertising, personnel, and all other areas. Yet the owner must be prepared to make decisions in all areas. Finally, sickness or death of the single owner may disrupt the business firm's operations or force it to close completely.

Prepare a list of some other things that might be considered as good features or bad features of a sole proprietorship.

Advantages of a Partnership

The partnership form of organization avoids some of the unfavorable features of the sole proprietorship. It does, however, have some bad features of its own.

Like the sole proprietorship, a partnership is relatively easy to organize. Because there is more than one owner, a partnership can have more specialization and ideas in the operation of the firm.

Two or more partners usually have more capital to put into a business. In addition, they often find it easier to obtain additional money when it is needed. Like the sole proprietorship, profits are usually taxed as personal income for each partner. This means the rate of tax will usually be less than the tax rate on profits paid by corporations. The partnership, then, keeps some of the good features of the sole proprietorship. It has some additional advantages because there are two or more owners involved.

By successfully pooling managerial and technical skills, partnerships can overcome some of the disadvantages of sole proprietorship. (Maria Karras)

Disadvantages of a Partnership

A partnership, however, does not overcome many of the disadvantages of the sole proprietorship. Moreover, a partnership creates some additional problems that sole proprietorships do not have. Because there is more than one owner, disagreements can arise. If one of the partners is irresponsible, the others may suffer. Each partner is individually responsible for all the debts of the business, even if another partner acted without the consent of the others. Because of these disadvantages, the number of partners in a partnership is often small. Often there are only two or three. Like the sole proprietorship, a partnership has unlimited liability. If the firm fails, each partner stands to lose not only the money invested in the business but all of his or her personal property as well.

Long-term illness or the death of one of the partners can harm the firm. If one of the partners is disabled or dies, the firm may break up completely. When a partner is not ill but simply wants to sell his or her share of the firm, it may be difficult to do so. Each of the partners may have to approve the sale of ownership by any of the other partners. This could make it extremely hard for a partner to dispose of his or her share of the business. If the business had to be sold in a short period of time, a difficult situation could result.

List some other advantages and disadvantages of the partnership form of business organization.

Advantages of a Corporation

Corporations account for most of the business conducted in the United States today. The corporate form of organization is well suited to large business firms. All corporations, however, are not large and some can in fact be quite small. Several well-known corporations such as Ford Motor Company and U.S. Steel were originally organized as sole proprietorships or partnerships. To overcome some of their disadvantage and to provide a means in which a business could more easily grow and expand, the corporation was developed.

Perhaps the most important advantage of a corporation is its limited liability. In the eyes of the law, it is an individual person apart from its owners. If the corporation fails, the personal property of its owners cannot be touched. Shareholders, therefore, have limited liability. They can lose no more than what they invested in the stock of the corporation. A corporation can usually raise additional capital more easily than can a sole proprietorship or partnership. It can sell additional stock or borrow money by selling bonds. In addition, bank credit is often more readily available to corporations than it is to other types of business firms. Banks consider corporations less risky because they usually have managers who are well trained in running a business. Since a corporation is a legal person separate from its owners, usually the firm will continue to operate smoothly regardless of what happens to the owners. Owners can generally transfer shares of stock without approval of other owners. Such a transfer normally does not affect the activities of the business firm. Business firms organized as corporations generally hire specialized and efficient management teams. They make the operating decisions for the firm.

Disadvantages of a Corporation

There are some disadvantages, however. In order to form a corporation, the prospective owners must be willing to meet certain legal requirements. For example, they must pay legal fees to get the charter they need. In some instances the charter may restrict the activities of the business firm. Corporations must pay income tax on their profits. Their tax rate, however, is not the same as that for individuals. Dividends paid to shareholders are taxed as personal income. Shareholders have criticized this system of taxation as being unfair because the income tax on dividends is paid twice— once by the corporation, and again by the stockholder. Another undesirable feature of the corporation is that stockholders have little direct relationship to the business firm. As a result, they have little or no influence on management decisions. In contrast to the close relationship of owner, employee, and customer under the sole proprietorship, the corporation may seem cold and impersonal to employees and customers alike.

Prepare a list of some other advantages and disadvantages of business firms organized as corporations.

Learning Activities

Increasing Your Business Vocabulary

You should become familiar with each of the terms shown below. On a sheet of paper write the numbers 1 through 10. Then write alongside each number the term that best matches each of the numbered definitions.

board of directors / charter / cooperative / corporation / dividend / partnership / patronage dividend / sole proprietorship / stock certificate / stockholders

1. A business firm organized and owned by one person.

2. A business firm owned by two or more persons who share the profit or the loss.

3. Payment of a portion of a corporation's profits to its stockholders.

4. Written authority from a state or the federal government to organize and operate a business firm as a corporation.

5. People who own stock in a corporation.

6. A piece of paper that states the number of shares of stock a person owns in a corporation.

7. A business firm created by law to have the same legal status as a person.

8. A business firm organized, owned, and operated for the mutual benefit of its members.

9. Payment of a portion of the earnings of a cooperative to its members based on the amount of business each member has done with the cooperative.

10. The decision-making body of a corporation.

Understanding Business

1. What are the three legal forms of business organization?

2. Is the number of businesses organized as sole proprietorships large or small? Do they account for a large or small percentage of total business receipts?

3. Are there more or fewer partnerships than sole proprietorships? Do partnerships generally receive more or less income than sole proprietorships?

4. As a corporation, the business firm has the same legal status as a person. List the types of activities it can therefore carry on.

5. Approximately what percent of businesses are organized as corporations? What fraction of the total business receipts are received by corporations?

6. List some common types of cooperatives. Which is the most popular type?

7. List the major differences between a corporation and a cooperative.

8. What are the major advantages of a proprietorship? The major disadvantages?

9. What are the most important advantages of a partnership? The most important disadvantages?

10. What are the major advantages of a corporation? The major disadvantages?

Business Problems and Projects

1. The Fall River Corporation, a manufacturer of electronic equipment, has a total of 100,000 shares held publicly by stockholders. The stock sells for $30 per share. The corporation recently declared a 6 percent annual dividend, with dividends paid quarterly.

   a. How much would the company pay in dividends for one year?

   b. How much would a stockholder holding 150 shares receive in dividends each quarter?

2. Corporations provide annual reports to those who have invested in them. One part of the annual report is the consolidated statement of earnings. This statement gives a financial accounting of the corporation's performance in terms of revenue, expenses, and profit or loss. Use the statement shown on the facing page to answer the questions that follow.

   a. What is the name of the corporation?

   b. What years does the report cover?

   c. What were the two sources of revenue?

   d. How much larger was the total revenue in 1979 than in 1978?

   e. For which item(s) in the Costs and expenses section of the report was the amount larger in 1978 than in 1979?

   f. Did the corporation make a profit or suffer a loss in 1978?

   g. How much larger was the profit in 1979 than in 1978?

   h. How much was the net earnings per share in 1978? In 1979?

The Rogers Corporation
Consolidated Statement of Earnings
Years Ended November 30, 1978 and 1979

	1978	1979
Revenues:		
Net sales	$177,892,000	$139,426,000
Interest income	216,000	96,000
Total Revenue	178,108,000	139,522,000
Costs and expenses:		
Cost of sales	125,398,000	99,285,000
Selling, general, and		
administrative expenses	40,360,000	31,177,000
Other operating expenses	1,554,000	1,814,000
Total costs and expenses	167,312,000	132,276,000
Earnings before tax profit	10,796,000	7,246,000
Taxes (federal and state)	5,622,000	3,527,000
Net Earnings	$ 5,174,000	$ 3,710,000
Net earnings per common share	$2.32	$1.66

3. Refer back to Table 7-1, "Proprietorships, Partnerships and Corporations," shown on page 87. Using the data in the table, answer the following questions.

a. What industry has the largest number of sole proprietorships? How many sole proprietorships are there in this industry?

b. What industry has the largest number of partnerships? What percent of all business firms in this industry are partnerships?

c. What industry has the largest number of corporations? How many corporations are there in this industry?

d. Which industries have more partnerships than corporations?

e. What was the total number of business firms in 1973?

Chapter 8

The Production Function of Business

Objectives

After completing your study of this chapter, you will be able to do the following:

1. List the four main types of utility created by production.

2. Discuss the importance of each of the four types of utility.

3. Define the term *specialization* as it relates to production.

4. Identify and describe the major advantages of specialized production.

5. Identify and describe the major disadvantages of specialized production.

Almost everything you, your friends, and members of your family use is made by some other person. Suppose you made a list of the things you have used so far today. Your list would probably include such things as pens, pencils, paper, and books. It would also include the food you eat, the clothes you wear, your bike or your car, and the house or apartment you live in. All of these things were most likely made by people you do not know. Everyone in our society uses many goods every day that are produced in other parts of this country or in foreign countries throughout the world. The reasons for this will be made clearer in this chapter.

ECONOMIC DEFINITION OF PRODUCTION

In Chapter 1 *production* was defined as the process of providing goods and services to satisfy human wants. This broad definition of production included all activity, whether physical or mental, required to produce goods or services. Thus, all the activities of business firms are considered to be production. Producing, processing, manufacturing, and distributing goods and providing services are major areas of production.

Which activities of business firms or their employees would be considered as production activities that do not directly satisfy consumer wants?

CREATION OF UTILITY

The ability of a good or service to satisfy human wants is called *utility*. The utility, or usefulness, of goods and services depends upon many things. Iron ore beneath the surface of the earth in Minnesota does little to satisfy a consumer's desire for a new car. In order to satisfy that particular want, the ore first must be mined. It must be shipped by rail to the Lake Superior port of Duluth, and transported by ship down the Great Lakes to the steel mills of Pittsburgh. The ore must be processed into steel and sent to Detroit. There it is used to manufacture the automobile. The automobile must be transported by rail or truck to a dealer. The dealer must have the car available and ready at the time the consumer wants to take possession of it.

From this one example, notice that several things must happen to goods or services before they are able to satisfy human wants:

1. Raw goods must be processed and changed in physical *form*.

2. Goods and services must be moved to the *place* where they are needed.

3. Goods and services must be available at the right *time*.

4. Goods and services must be put in *possession* of the consumer who wants them.

These four requirements represent different types of utility— form, place, time, and possession. They must be present in both goods and services. Persons such as doctors, lawyers, bus drivers, appliance repairers, and teachers perform *useful* services, which are part of production. All workers make goods or services useful to consumers by adding some type of utility.

Think of what would be involved in creating baseball bats from trees growing in a forest. Give examples of how workers would add utility of form, place, time, and possession.

Form Utility

Most of the goods that people use have been changed in physical form. Fresh fruits and vegetables are two notable exceptions. The usefulness that a good has because of its physical properties is called *form utility*. The purpose of processing and manufacturing is to change raw goods into a form that can satisfy a human want. This involves combining raw or processed goods to create other goods in the shape, size, and color desired by consumers. For example, steel, rubber, plastic, and paint are processed goods which, when combined properly, can produce a motorcycle. The consumer who wants a motorcycle requires that these goods be in the form of a motorcycle and not in their raw or processed states. Goods must possess the physical characteristics (form utility) wanted by the consumer.

Once it has been bent into shape, this sheet of steel possesses the desired form utility. (Westinghouse)

Place Utility

Making sure that economic goods have the proper form is only one purpose of production. Steel, rubber, and other materials will never become a motorcycle until they are brought together at some place where motorcycles are made. Also, all the motorcycles produced and for sale in Japan, England, or New York are of no use to the buyer in Illinois or Florida. They have to be shipped to a dealer near the buyer. Similarly, an apple in an orchard in Washington State cannot satisfy the hunger of a student in Baltimore. It must be picked and shipped across the country. The transportation industry of a nation consists of its railroads, trucks, buses, airplanes, and ships. Transportation creates place utility by moving raw, processed, and finished goods to places where they can be used. *Place utility* is the usefulness that a good or service has because of its location.

List business firms in your community that are involved in making goods useful by moving them to certain locations.

Transporting strawberries from the farm to the retail market creates place utility. (Flying Tigers)

Time Utility

Suppose materials are brought together and combined to form a product that is shipped to a local dealer. The wants of consumers have not yet been satisfied. In order to satisfy consumers' wants, goods and services must be available when the consumer wants them. *Time utility* is the usefulness that a good or service has because it is available when it is wanted. Many goods are more

Would this ski shop possess the same usefulness if it were located on a Florida Beach? (Michael Phillip Manheim)

useful at one time of the year than they are at another. In Montana, for example, a motorcycle is much more likely to be wanted for transportation in summer than in winter. Skis and skiing equipment, on the other hand, would be wanted during the winter months. Many food products become available in large quantities at one particular time of the year. However, people want them throughout the year. These products are stored or processed in some way so that they are available during the entire year. Having goods and services available when they are needed and wanted is another of the activities performed by business firms.

What are some examples of goods, other than those listed above, that are more popular at one time of the year than at another time of the year? List the good, indicate which time of the year it is most popular, and tell why this is true.

Possession Utility

The ultimate goal of all production is to satisfy human wants. Goods and services must be purchased by consumers if this satisfaction is to take place. A good may be in the right form and the right place at the right time. Yet it doesn't satisfy the consumer until it is physically in the consumer's possession. A good or service that can satisfy a person's want is still lacking in utility if the person who wants it is unable to obtain it. *Possession utility* is the usefulness gained by owning a good or receiving a service. It is satisfied when the consumer has enough money to purchase the desired good or service. The use of credit allows people to take possession of goods or to use services at a time when they do not have enough money to pay for them. Banks that lend money to consumers for buying new automobiles, for example, are helping to create possession utility. Without the loan from the bank, the consumer probably would not be able to purchase the new automobile at the time the consumer wants it.

What are some goods other than automobiles that consumers often purchase on credit?

Possession utility occurs when the consumer is actually able to purchase the good or service. (Stock, Boston)

BUSINESS DEFINITION OF PRODUCTION

Utility is created by changing the physical form of some good. It is also created by changing its location and by making it available at a particular time. Finally, utility is created by providing for possession of a good by the final consumer. In economics, all of these activities are included in the broad definition of production. In business, however, most people think of production as only those activities involved in creating form utility. These would include processing and manufacturing activities. The activities involved in creating place, time, and possession utility are then considered to be marketing activities. These marketing activities will be examined in the next chapter.

HOW PRODUCTION HAS CHANGED

In colonial times, the limited needs of people were taken care of largely by goods made at home. Farming was the occupation of most people. Things began to change around 1750. The invention of the steam engine and other machines brought changes to the business world. Small workshops where skilled craftspersons worked together developed. Business firms made use of new machines, equipment, and processes as they organized the factory system of production. *Mass production,* the use of machines and

Mass production of these circuit-breaker handles greatly lowers the cost of each unit. (Westinghouse)

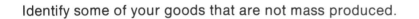

processes to produce large quantities of the same goods, was made possible by the use of machinery. The power to run the machinery came from water, steam, and, later, electricity. Mass production reduced the cost of each unit produced. It also made more and more goods and services available to larger numbers of people. All of this led to greater specialization in the work activities of individual people.

Identify some of your goods that are not mass produced.

SPECIALIZATION IN PRODUCTION

Few people in the United States today produce more than a tiny fraction of the goods and services that they actually consume.

Most people produce only one thing and rely on the production of others to satisfy their wants. In other words, people specialize. In production, *specialization* is a system in which each person produces or helps in the production of only one or a small number of products. The term *division of labor* is another way to describe specialization. It refers to situations in which a job can be broken down into small steps, each performed by different people.

In our society some people may spend their working hours installing single parts on an automobile on an assembly line. At the same time, they may buy an automobile made by another firm. Few households seriously consider producing much of their own food, clothing, and shelter. Dairy farmers sell their milk to a local dairy. In turn, they buy pasteurized milk, butter, and ice cream from the local dairy store. Even the most primitive societies had specialized jobs such as hunting, crop gathering, food preparation, and the like. Humanity learned long ago that when people try to satisfy most of their wants by themselves, they do a relatively poor job of it. Societies such as ours have become extremely specialized. This has greatly increased our capacity to satisfy as many of the people's wants as possible.

Talk with some member of your family or someone else who works where people specialize. Is the person content or happy with the work? Why or why not?

Advantages of Specialization

All the advanced nations of the world use specialization to produce goods and services. The major benefit of specialization is that it increases efficiency. It has been said that the jack-of-all-trades is the master of none. It is almost impossible for the person who performs a variety of tasks to be as efficient at any one of them as the person who performs only one. Specialization allows people to take advantage of individual differences that exist in their abilities and skills. Even if abilities are the same, it may be advantageous to have people specialize in work tasks. People who devote full time to a single task are more likely to develop skill in doing it. In specializing they are more likely to discover better ways of doing things. From your own experience, you know that you become good at a particular task by doing it over and over again. As a worker changes from one job to another, the tools, equipment, and materials being used must be put away. The tools, equipment, and materials for the next job must be found and organized. The worker may have to change work locations. All of this takes time. Specialization avoids this loss of time in shifting from one job to another. It results, therefore, in greater efficiency in the use of human resources.

Specialization by geographical area is also important. It enables us to increase the total amount of goods and services produced in the world. In agriculture, for example, certain areas of the country or the world may be ideal for growing certain crops. Thus Florida produces more oranges than wheat because its climate is perfect for growing oranges. At the same time, wheat can be grown in some states, but oranges cannot. The coastal areas of California are well suited to growing winter vegetables. By specializing in these crops, one area is able to supply most of the nation with lettuce, celery, and other greens when they cannot be grown elsewhere. Without specialization, each area would be dependent on its own production.

Geographical specialization also results from the location of natural resources. Much of the nation's coal is located in the Appalachian Mountain region. Large oil deposits are found in Texas and Oklahoma. Vast forests still cover much of the Northwest. Many of the human and capital resources of these areas are used in getting these natural resources from the earth. Specialization permits each area to produce those goods that its resources can most efficiently produce. By specializing, we become efficient in the use of all the resources of a nation. This applies to the use of the world's resources as well.

Explain how professional football teams use the principle of specialization with players on their teams. Ask a friend who is familiar with professional football to help you if you are not a football fan.

Disadvantages of Specialization

The advantages of specialization generally outweigh the disadvantages. However, there are some important disadvantages to geographical and work specialization that you should understand. The monotony of specialized work is well known. This problem has been widely discussed over the years by management and employees alike. It is not hard to understand why a person who works only at installing bumpers on an automobile becomes bored with the job. Imagine yourself performing such a task for 40 hours every week year after year. No doubt, you would become bored. To relieve boredom for assembly-line workers, some manufacturers are experimenting with rotating workers from one job to another.

Another disadvantage of specialization is that individuals, regions, and nations become dependent upon others to provide vital goods and services. Crop failures in one part of the world can have direct and disastrous effects on the food supply in other parts of the world. A few nations may produce most of the supply of a relatively scarce natural resource such as oil. If they band together to limit production or to raise prices on the vital resource, all other nations in the world are affected. Transportation strikes can create problems when one area depends on goods produced in another area. Because of the specialization in the world, people depend more and more on the output of others. This can lead to serious problems if one group fails to produce what others depended on. Severe shortages can develop almost overnight. There is a limit to how specialized we can afford to become.

What are some good things that have occurred because nations are more specialized today than they were 100 years ago?

Learning Activities

Increasing Your Business Vocabulary

You should become familiar with each of the terms shown below. On a sheet of paper write the numbers 1 through 7. Then write alongside each number the term that best matches each of the numbered definitions.

form utility / mass production / place utility / possession utility / specialization / time utility / utility

1. Usefulness that a good or service has because it is available when it is wanted.

2. The use of machines and processes to produce large quantities of the same goods.

3. Usefulness gained by owning a good or receiving a service.

4. Usefulness that a good has because of its physical properties.

5. Ability of a good or service to satisfy human wants.

6. A system in which each person produces or helps in the production of only one or a small number of products.

7. Usefulness that a good or service has because of its location.

Understanding Business

1. What are the things that must happen to goods or services for utility or usefulness to be achieved?

2. List the four types of utility.

3. What activities are designed specifically to change raw materials into a form that is desired and usable by the consumer?

4. Give an example of place utility.

5. Provide two examples of time utility.

6. How do banks help to create possession utility?

7. Explain what is meant by the term division of labor.

8. What has been the major reason for the move to specialization in production?

9. Give several examples of geographical specialization.

10. List several disadvantages of both geographical and human specialization.

 # Business Problems and Projects

1. On a form similar to the one shown below, list ten goods, their changed forms, and the names of local or national businesses that produce the changed form of the good.

			Business That Changed the Form
Example	Oats	Oatmeal	Quaker Oats Company

2. When organizing a manufacturing firm, initial investment is high. Moreover, manufacturing firms spend a great deal of money each year improving plant facilities and equipment. Examine the table below and answer the questions that follow it.

CAPITAL INVESTED PER EMPLOYEE IN MANUFACTURING

Industry	Capital Invested Per Employee (in thousands)	Total Employees	Capital Invested Per Production Worker (in thousands)	Production Workers
Petroleum	204	140,000	313	98,000
Tobacco	89	66,000	108	57,000
Motor vehicles and equipment	61	808,000	78	669,000
Chemicals and chemical products	51	837,000	89	525,000
Nonelectrical machinery	31	1,828,000	46	1,267,000
Electrical machinery	29	1,662,000	42	1,161,000
Food and food products	28	1,569,000	42	1,085,000
Instruments	23	454,000	38	292,000
Printing and publishing	18	1,056,000	30	637,000
Leather products	12	273,000	14	240,000
Apparel and related products	11	1,368,000	12	1,198,000
Furniture and fixtures	10	462,000	12	384,000
Total Manufacturing	32	19,029,000	40	13,528,000

Source: Statistical Abstract of the United States, 1975

a. Which of the industries listed had the largest number of employees? Did this industry employ the largest number of production workers?

b. Which industry had the greatest amount of capital invested per employee? Per production worker?

c. Which industry had the smallest amount of capital invested per employee? Per production worker?

d. Which industries employed over 1 million workers?

e. How many industries employed over 1 million production workers? What were they?

Chapter 9

The Marketing Function of Business

Objectives

After completing your study of this chapter, you will be able to do the following:

1. List the principal marketing activities business firms.

2. Describe marketing functions such as buying and selling, transportation and storage.

3. Explain what is meant by the *channel of distribution* for an economic good or service.

4. Identify and describe the main channels of distribution.

5. Discuss the two major steps involved in developing a marketing strategy.

"Production is important, but it is marketing that really makes the Unites States' economic system effective." This opinion is held by many economists.

When people produce more than they consume or when they find that they can produce things wanted by other people, the exchange of goods and services becomes possible and important. A marketing system must then be developed in order to bring about the exchange of goods and services. Marketing plays a very important role in maintaining a high standard of living for Americans. Without an effective marketing system the economy would not function as well as it does.

MARKETING—A SPECIAL KIND OF PRODUCTION

Marketing is considered to be a special part of production. It is those activities involved in getting goods and services from the producer to the consumer.

Remember that for goods and services to be useful, they must be where they are wanted, when they are wanted. And they must be physically in the consumer's possession. It is marketing that creates these utilities of place, time, and possession. An effective marketing system permits people to specialize in their work. Individuals, business firms, and geographical regions can specialize in producing certain goods because they know they will be able to exchange their goods for money or other goods.

Check to see if your high school offers a distributive education program. Find out what courses are offered. How do these courses relate to our discussion of marketing?

MARKETING ACTIVITIES

Marketing covers a wide range of activities. Most of these activities fall within one of the following nine functions:

1. Buying
2. Selling
3. Transportation
4. Storage

5. Standardization and grading

6. Pricing

7. Financing

8. Risk bearing

9. Market research

Each of these functions is necessary if goods and services are to reach large numbers of consumers. Consider, for example, the textbook that you are using. Marketing activities began before the authors started to write. Someone had to determine the need for this book. Before the book was printed, someone had to make sure that the book met certain standards of size, paper, binding, and so forth. After the books were printed, they were shipped to the publisher's warehouse. They were stored there until orders came in from customers. The publisher employed salespeople to visit teachers in an effort to sell the book. Teachers had to spend time examining the book before deciding to buy it. The publisher may have extended credit in selling books, thus helping to finance the buyer's purchase. Even while all of these marketing activities were happening, the publisher had to keep informed of changes in the market. Changes in the market continually affect what the publisher produces. For example, subject matter changes, enrollments in courses change, and new teaching methods are introduced.

Buying and Selling Functions

Buying and selling are two of the basic marketing functions. Buying is done by all business firms. But before a business firm can buy, certain activities must be undertaken. The firm must try to predict what it thinks its customers will want. It must also try to predict how much its customers will want to buy. On the basis of these predictions, it must decide what materials it will need. It must then find a supplier that can provide the materials needed. The firm must also negotiate a satisfactory price and arrange for delivery of the materials.

Selling is also done by all business firms. In order to sell, a business firm must first locate potential customers, either consumers or other business firms. It must motivate these potential

Product knowledge and awareness of the consumer's needs make this retail salesperson a vital contribution to the marketing activity. (Michael D. Sullivan)

customers to buy. It does this by setting prices that are comparable to those offered by other firms selling the same or similar goods and services. It also may do this through such activities as advertising, giving free samples, and special sales.

List some of the common names of the occupations of persons who perform the exchange activities of buying and selling for business firms.

Transportation and Storage Functions

Almost all goods are transported in some way from the producer to the consumer. A business firm must find the best way to ship its goods. Should it use water, air, rail, or truck transportation? The type of good and where it is being shipped affects this decision. In addition, the firm must be aware of time schedules and know the cost of using the various methods of transportation. Not all goods that are produced are sold immediately. All business firms must keep stocks of goods on hand so that they will be available when customers ask for them. Goods must often be stored in warehouses.

Storing grain in silos such as these enables the producer to take advantage of favorable market conditions.
(Becky Roller)

This happens when goods are produced far in advance of the time that they will be needed. This also occurs when goods are shipped in large quantities and must be broken down into smaller lots before being marketed. Storage is extremely important in our marketing system. Goods and services must be at the right place, at the right time, and in the right amount. The purpose of transporting and storage activities is to make sure that the goods do get to the right place at the right time.

Give some examples of goods that need to be stored. Explain why these particular goods need to be stored.

Other Marketing Functions

Establishing standards and grades, pricing, financing, risk-bearing, and market research are activities that support the basic buying, selling, storage, and transportation activities. These activities involve creating a demand for new products, seeking ways to improve products, setting competitive prices, and providing credit.

Various industries have established standards for the economic goods produced by business firms in the industry. Federal government agencies such as the Department of Agriculture have developed grades and standards for a variety of goods, especially food products. These agencies inspect goods to make sure that they meet the minimum standards. Banks and financial institutions of all types help business firms and consumers to obtain funds and credit. Many business firms employ individuals to do marketing research and develop market information for the goods produced by the firm. Some business firms today specialize in providing this service for other business firms. For a fee, a business firm can hire marketing experts from a market research firm. These experts help the firm develop ideas for marketing new goods and services.

It is important to realize that each marketing function has a specific purpose and cannot be omitted. To reduce marketing costs, business firms sometimes shift the functions to someone else. For example, suppose a business firm sells products on a cash-and-carry basis. By selling this way, the firm reduces its financing and delivery costs. These functions, however, have not been done away with. They have only been shifted to the consumer.

Give some examples of goods you or your family have bought whore ono or more of the marketing functions have been shifted.

HOW GOODS REACH CONSUMERS

Not all business firms market their products in the same way. Some firms sell the goods they produce directly to consumers. And some firms sell their products to other firms that in turn sell them to consumers. Sometimes a product may pass through several middlemen before it reaches the hands of the consumer. The route that a good takes from the producer to the consumer is called the *channel of distribution*

Direct Marketing

In *direct marketing,* goods or services move from the producer to the final consumer without going through a middleman. Direct

Some business firms only market their products through door-to-door selling. (Stock, Boston)

marketing is the shortest, most direct channel of distribution. Direct marketing takes place in several forms. Selling by mail is one method. Selling at the place of production, such as roadside stands for vegetables, is another example. Selling through door-to-door salespersons and selling through a producer's store are two other types of direct marketing. The firm that chooses to market its product nationwide directly to the consumer needs a large personal sales force. Some business firms, such as Fuller Brush and Avon Products, have selected this method of marketing. A producer with limited capital resources and a limited product line will probably not have enough resources to market directly. Relatively few goods are marketed directly in our economy. In contrast, however, almost all services are marketed directly.

List some of the services that are marketed directly from the producer to the consumer.

Indirect Marketing

While most services are marketed directly, most goods are marketed indirectly. *Indirect marketing* occurs when goods or services move from the producer to the final consumer through one or more middlemen. Producers with limited capital and a limited product line often have to hire an agent or use some other middlemen to sell their goods. The most common indirect channel of distribution for consumer goods is the producer-wholesaler-retailer-consumer channel. *Retailers* are business firms that sell directly to consumers. Business firms that buy goods in large quantities and sell them to retailers in small quantities are *wholesalers.* While the indirect channel is the most common, it is not the most efficient. At each

Indirect marketing through retail stores such as these is the most common channel of distribution. (Stockmarket, Los Angeles)

point in the channel, the producer loses some control over the product. Today many business firms are choosing to market their own products through channels of distribution different from those used 10, 20, or 30 years ago. Procter and Gamble, for instance, markets its products directly to the retailer. As a result of the growth of chain stores, supermarkets, and discount stores, there has been a tendency to eliminate the wholesaler in many product lines. Still, indirect marketing accounts for approximately 45 percent of all wholesale trade in consumer goods.

Four channels of distribution are shown in the illustration below. Notice that the number of middlemen decreases from three at the right to none at the left. Regardless of which channel of distribution a firm chooses, all of the marketing functions will still be performed. If certain middlemen are eliminated, their functions will be performed by someone else. Usually, business firms find it most profitable to use only one channel of distribution. In order to get the greatest distribution of its products, however, a business firm may distribute through several channels at the same time.

CHANNELS OF DISTRIBUTION

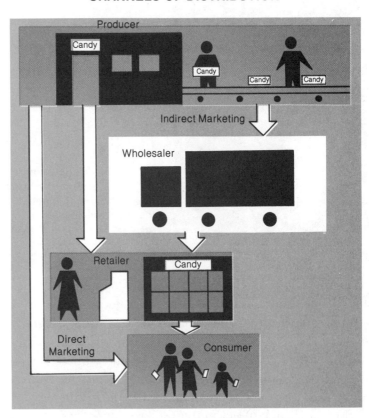

MARKETING STRATEGY

The ways in which management decides to carry out marketing functions is called *marketing strategy*. Most corporations employ people who have special training and skills in marketing goods and services. These people select a market and develop a marketing mix for a particular good or service.

Selecting a Market

There is no such thing as one single national market in the United States. Marketing experts believe that the United States consists, instead, of many smaller markets. For example, there is the teenage market and the senior citizens market. There is the rural market, the urban market, and many others. A business firm must first identify each market and study its needs. Then it can develop a plan for selling a good or service to that market. It must consider a variety of factors such as age, nationality, income, and educational level. The geographic location is also important. The business firm must decide what goods and services best meet the needs of that market. And it must analyze the firm's ability to meet these needs.

Determining a Marketing Mix

After a market has been identified, the business firm has to identify (1) the product to be sold, (2) the price to be charged, (3) the methods to be used to promote the product, and (4) the channel of distribution to be used. The combination of these elements is called the *marketing mix*. The marketing mix that a firm chooses will affect the success of its marketing program. If all the elements do not blend together in the right way, the marketing program will fail. According to marketing experts, there is no one best marketing mix. Markets and firms are always changing. This means that the marketing mix must also change to meet changing conditions. Ongoing consumer research is required if a business firm is to be successful in offering its best marketing mix in its markets.

What marketing mix would you choose to market a new device that people can use in their own home to exercise and stay fit? Assume it costs you $2.00 to make each unit.

Learning Activities

Increasing Your Business Vocabulary

You should become familiar with each of the terms shown below. On a sheet of paper write the numbers 1 through 5. Then write alongside each number the term that best matches each of the numbered definitions.

channel of distribution / direct marketing / indirect marketing / retailers / wholesalers

1. The movement of goods or services from the producer to the final consumer without going through a middleman.
2. The route that a good takes from the producer to the consumer.
3. The movement of goods or services from the producer to the final consumer through one or more middlemen.
4. Business firms that buy goods in large quantities and sell them to retailers in smaller quantities.
5. Business firms that sell directly to consumers.

Understanding Business

1. What types of utility does marketing create?
2. List the nine activities of marketing.
3. What activities are included in the buying function? In the selling function?

4. When is it necessary to store goods?

5. What are the major purposes of the transporting and storing activities?

6. List the activities that support the basic buying, selling, storage, and transportation activities?

7. Can the marketing functions be eliminated? Explain your answer.

8. Are most goods marketed directly or indirectly? Are most services marketed directly or indirectly?

9. List several factors to consider when selecting a market.

10. When determining the marketing mix, what four areas must the business firm identify?

Business Problems and Projects

1. Reexamine the chart on page 124 showing the channels of distribution. On a form similar to the one shown below, indicate which channel of distribution each of the listed products might follow to reach the consumer and whether the channel is direct or indirect.

   a. Encyclopedias
   b. Automobiles
   c. Cereal
   d. Life insurance
   e. Wheat to be used for cereal
   f. Motorcycles

	Produce	Channel	Direct	Indirect
Example	Candy bar	Producer–Wholesaler–Retailer–Consumer		

2. Marketers have to be aware of changes in consumer's buying behavior. The table shown below indicates five trends that will shape tomorrow's life-styles. Examine the table and then answer the questions that follow.

TRENDS IN TOMORROW's LIFE-STYLES

	1975	1985 (estimated)	Change
Median family income	$13,600	$18,000	+32%
Average workweek	36 hours	34 hours	−6%
College enrollment	10,200,000	11,400,000	+12%
Spending for leisure activities	$130 billion	$280 billion	+115%
Workers producing services	54.3 million	68.6 million	+26%

a. Is college enrollment likely to increase or decrease by 1985?

b. How much was the median family income in 1975?

c. How much will the median family income be in 1985?

d. What percent change is estimated from 1975 to 1985 in the number of hours the average person works?

e. How much more will be spent on leisure activities in 1985 than in 1975?

f. If you were going into business for yourself, based on the 1985 projections what kinds of goods or services might you want to produce?

Chapter 10

Government-Business Relationships

Objectives

After completing your study of this chapter, you will be able to do the following:

1. Discuss how government acts to regulate business activities.

2. Explain how government promotes economic growth.

3. Identify some of the activities used by government to promote a stable business environment.

4. Identify some of the protections government provides for business.

5. Form an opinion on how much influence and control government should have on business activity.

In this text, the term *private enterprise* rather than *free enterprise* has been chosen in describing our economy. One reason is that our economy is not free of government influence and control. It is difficult, if not impossible, to find an area of business activity that is not affected by local, state, or federal government.

Government makes the laws that bring order to our society. It sets the rules that individuals and business firms follow in conducting their affairs. By enforcing such laws, government regulates business activity. It sets limits to what firms may or may not do. Making and enforcing such laws also protects the rights of individuals and business firms.

Government also tries to maintain an environment that is favorable to business. It may do this in a number of ways. It may pass laws that encourage new business firms to develop. Taxes may be lowered. It may provide special training for jobs in which workers are needed. Or it may provide direct assistance to individuals or firms in certain industries. The federal government, especially, can influence the general economic picture. It does this by the policies it adopts with respect to spending, taxing, money supply, and interest rates.

REGULATE BUSINESS ACTIVITIES

Laws have been passed by local, state, and federal governments to regulate individuals and business firms. These laws and their enforcement by the courts are intended to prevent some activities from occurring. They are also intended to make certain that other activities do occur. This regulation of activities is designed to protect certain rights of individuals and business firms.

Monopolies

Competition among business firms is one of the most important aspects in our economy. Our economic system relies heavily upon competition for its success and for the high level of living enjoyed by our citizens. An important government function, therefore, is to guarantee that fair competition can and does exist at all times. Early in our country's history there were no laws to control business practices that result in monopoly. A business firm that had a monopoly could keep the price of a good or service high. Consumers could do nothing about it. In 1890, the federal government took the first step in regulating monopoly business practices by passing the Sherman Anti-Trust Act. This law, and others that followed, made it illegal for business firms to form monopolies. These laws are enforced by the Justice Department and other government agencies such as the Federal Trade Commission. Frequent headlines in the news media attest to the fact that these anti-trust laws are still used.

The activities of some business firms such as airlines, are closely regulated by government. (Monkmeyer)

In spite of these government actions, many people feel that some big business firms still hold monopoly powers in certain industries. At what point a firm actually gains monopoly power in an industry is not easy to decide. It is up to the courts to determine if a firm actually holds a monopoly. Such decisions have been made. In 1911, for example, the Standard Oil Company was forced, through court order, to break up into a number of smaller companies.

By encouraging competition, government brings incentive to the production of goods and services of high quality at reasonable prices. Competition helps to lessen the inefficient and wasteful use of limited productive resources.

Do you think government should prevent monopoly business firms? Why or why not?

Public Utilities

Some privately owned business firms are allowed to operate as monopolies—but under government regulation. The best examples of such firms are electric, telephone, and natural gas companies. They provide essential services to the general public and are called *public utility companies.* If you want telephone service, for example, you have no choice but to buy the service from the one company that provides it in your area. What would happen if several competing business firms were to start putting in telephone, gas, or electric lines in a community? Confusion would soon result. The air and ground would be a mass of wires, pipes, and poles. Therefore, government chooses one business firm to supply the service. It decides what services the firm must provide. And it regulates the prices charged for the service. A public utility company may want to increase its rates or change the service it provides. To do this, the company must obtain permission to do so from the government commission that regulates utility companies. The Federal Trade Commission, state public service commissions, and local planning commissions are some examples of government commissions.

Patents

Monopolies are also permitted for inventions protected by the patent laws. A *patent* is a grant made by a government assuring an inventor the sole right to make, use, or sell an invention for a specific period of time. In the United States, the period is 17 years.

The research required to produce new goods or ways of providing services is costly and risky. Our patent laws protect those who have developed their ideas into new types of goods or services. No one else may make or sell the product unless the inventor grants permission.

Some people feel that the period of patent protection is too long. Granting a patent usually means granting a monopoly in production of the patented item. The inventor has 17 years to perfect or refine the product. Thus, competitors find it almost impossible to compete successfully. In addition, patent rights may be renewed by developing improved models of the original invention. This makes it even more difficult for competitors.

Do you feel the patent laws should be changed? If your answer is yes, how should the laws be changed and why should these changes be made? If your answer is no, why should there be no changes in the present patent laws?

PROMOTE ECONOMIC GROWTH

Government acts to affect the overall performance of our economy. Most people believe that government has a responsibility to do whatever is necessary to make sure that there is continued growth in our economy. Economic growth, of course, means a general increase in the level of living for everyone in the nation. This idea became law in the Employment Act of 1946. This law requires the federal government to work toward providing maximum employment, production, and purchasing power for all Americans. To do this, government acts in rather complex ways in some cases. These acts affect not only business activity but all other economic activity as well. They affect the economy in general. And they affect you and your family as well as the business firms in your community. Some of the ways the government achieves this goal are raising or lowering tax rates and increasing or decreasing interest rates. Other examples are expanding or contracting the money supply, increasing or decreasing spending, and borrowing more or borrowing less. Through actions such as these, govern-

Through projects that bring water to desert areas, government can spur the growth of whole regions. (Ameron)

ments try to make gradual changes in the level of economic activity. This approach is used because it is felt that it is easier for individuals and business firms to react and adjust to gradual rather than abrupt changes.

Explain what is meant when it is stated that it is easier for individuals and business firms to react and adjust to gradual rather than abrupt changes in the level of economic activity.

PROMOTE A STABLE BUSINESS ENVIRONMENT

The actions taken by government to promote economic growth also help to promote a stable business environment. There are other important ways government promotes a stable business environment.

Provide Information for Decision Making

Government collects and publishes a wealth of facts and statistics on various topics. Business firms and farmers make many decisions based on data provided by government agencies. Management attempts to collect as much data as possible on an issue before making its final decision. Government provides a very valuable aid to management in this respect by gathering, compiling, and distributing data on payrolls, wages, employment, prices, volume of production, finance, costs, and other aspects of business. Data is collected and published by agencies such as the Department of Commerce, the Bureau of Labor Statistics, the Federal Reserve Board, and many others. Similar information is provided for farmers and those in agricultural marketing. The U.S. Department of Agriculture and state and county agricultural agencies and agents provide the information.

The National Bureau of Standards serves business and agriculture by setting up standards of all types—weights and measures, in particular. It is responsible for overseeing the change from the traditional system of measurement to the metric. It also does a considerable amount of testing in a variety of areas. Private business firms are thereby saved the cost of testing. Many of the divisions of the Departments of Interior, Agriculture, and Transportation primarily serve producers and distributors of goods and services. Again, the number of services is very large. Many of these services are often overlooked or taken for granted. Something as common as the weather reports by the U.S. Weather Bureau in all parts of the country are very important to farmers and some business firms.

Give some examples, other than those used above, of government services that help business firms and farmers. Try to identify which government agency provides each of the services you list.

Educate and Train Workers

Another way government promotes a sound business environment is to educate and train workers. Today there is an increased emphasis on vocational education. *Vocational education* is training designed to prepare a person for an occupation. State and federal governments pay some of the costs of vocational education programs in many high schools. In addition, government provides cooperative work programs in which students receive classroom credit for related work experience. Agriculture, office, health,

Statistics gathered by census takers provides a valuable source of information to business firms. (Michael D. Sullivan)

homemaking, distributive, and industrial education are some of the programs supported by government funding.

Government has also been actively involved in providing money for postsecondary programs. Most states have some form of postsecondary vocational schools. The schools may be known by different names, but their goal of training people for specific occupations is similar. Students under a certain age may be eligible to attend such schools tuition free in their state. The funds for these schools come from local, state, and federal governments. Graduates are usually able to move into jobs for which they have been trained with little or no additional training from the employer. The employer, therefore, has little or no direct expense in training these employees.

Adult vocational education programs in local communities are financed in part by funds from the state and federal governments. One purpose of these programs is to upgrade or update skills of workers. Another purpose is to provide new skills that will enable workers to move to new jobs. These programs, plus many others, aid business and agriculture by preparing well-trained and well-educated workers.

Government also runs employment service offices throughout the nation. An *employment service office* is a government office that helps unemployed persons find jobs. Business firms list job openings and employee needs with the service. Unemployed people go to the service to seek help in finding a job. The employment service then attempts to match the skills of the employee and the employee needs of a business firm.

What are some programs in your school and your community that prepare individuals for employment in specific occupations?

PROTECT BUSINESS

While performing its role as a regulator of business, government acts as a protector of business firms. As you learned earlier, by regulating monopolies government protects business firms from practices that would destroy competition. This right to competition and other rights of business firms must be protected just as individual rights must be protected.

Preserve Property Rights

As indicated in Chapter 3, the concept of private ownership of property is essential to the private enterprise economy. Business firms as well as individuals have the right to ownership of property. A business firm can do as it wishes with its property as long as it does not infringe on the rights of others. The firm can thus be involved in any kind of activity it wants as long as the activity is legal. Of special interest to individuals and business firms are the patent and copyright laws. These are examples of how government acts to protect property rights. Copyright laws are very similar to patent laws except that they apply to printed material. Written materials, such as books and magazines, can be copyrighted to protect an individual or a business firm from having others copy the material. A *copyright* is a right granted by government, assuring an author, composer, playwright, publisher, or distributor the sole right to publish, sell, or distribute a literary, musical, drama, or artistic work. In the United States a copyright lasts for 28 years and may be renewed for 47 years. Government also protects the rights of business firms to certain brand names. trademarks, slogans, and other things used in advertising.

Identify some slogans or jingles used by business firms. Name the product or products the business firm is trying to sell with each of the slogans or jingles.

Enforce Legal Contracts

Government protects business by enforcing agreements between business firms. When two or more business firms enter into a legal contract, each of the firms must carry out its part of the contract. A *contract* is a legally enforceable agreement between two or more parties. Government, through the court system, enforces contracts to make sure that those involved do whatever they have agreed to do. The contract lists the terms of the agreement.

Government also enforces contracts between business firms and individual consumers. The individual consumer has a right to expect a business firm to live up to the terms of a contract. Likewise, the firm has a right to expect the same from the consumer. It is wrong for a business firm to attempt to do less than required under a contract. It is just as wrong for a consumer to attempt to do less than required under the terms of the contract. Because business firms can count on the government to assist in enforcing contracts, they can make plans for their future activities. With a contract the firm is assured that it will receive the requested amount of raw material. It is assured that its goods will be delivered to a certain place by a certain time. Likewise, it knows it will receive a payment of so much money and that it must pay out a specified amount of money. Without enforcement of contracts, little or no planning could occur.

HOW MUCH GOVERNMENT?

The question of how much influence and control government should have on business activity remains an issue of debate and disagreement. There are two basic opinions. One group holds that the forces of supply and demand, operating freely in the market-oriented economy, should dominate business activity. This group believes that competition and the profit motive should determine what and how goods are produced and distributed. They feel there should be little government influence and control. A second group holds that there should be at least the current level of government control and influence. This group believes that it would be impossible to keep present levels of business and economic activity without government assistance. They also believe that government influence and control is needed to balance the power of private consumers and some of the giant corporations. There is no absolute answer to this issue.

The debate over the role of government in business and economic activity will continue. At the present time, it appears that a majority of citizens recognize the value of our mixed economy. It is an economy in which business and economic activity is controlled in many ways. The decisions are made partly by individuals and business firms operating in the market. They are made partly by a centralized authority such as our government. We have attained our present high level of living by the delicate mixture of these two forces in our society.

What is your opinion regarding government influence and control in business activity in our economy? Should it be decreased, increased, or remain about as it is? Why do you feel this way?

Learning Activities

Increasing Your Business Vocabulary

You should become familiar with each of the terms shown below. On a sheet of paper write the numbers 1 through 5. Then write alongside each number the term that best matches each of the numbered definitions.

contract / copyright / employment service office / patent / vocational education

1. A grant made by a government, assuring an inventor the sole right to make, use, or sell an invention for a specific period of time.
2. Education designed to prepare a person for an occupation.
3. A right granted by government, assuring an author, composer, playwright, publisher, or distributor the sole right to publish, sell, or distribute a literary, musical, or dramatic work.
4. A legally enforceable agreement between two or more parties.
5. A government office that helps unemployed persons find jobs.

Understanding Business

1. What is one reason why the term *private enterprise* is more correct than the term *free enterprise* when describing our economy?

2. When did the federal government take the first step to regulate monopoly business practice? What did it do?

3. Give some examples of business firms allowed to operate as monopolies. What are they called?

4. What people do patent laws protect?

5. What does the Employment Act of 1946 require the federal government to do?

6. How does the government promote economic growth?

7. Name at least four agencies that gather and distribute data and information valuable in business and agricultural decision making.

8. How do copyright laws protect individuals and businesses?

9. Why is the government's right to enforce contracts important to business firms?

10. What are the two views on the amount of control and influence government should have on business activity?

Business Problems and Projects

1. The federal government enacts laws to protect the property rights of firms and individuals. On a form similar to the one shown below, list five items that are protected by each of the three types of laws indicated in the column heads.

	Copyright Laws	Patent Laws	Registered Trademark Laws
Example	The novel *Roots*	A Polaroid camera	The word *Kleenex*

2. One of the tools that the federal government can use to influence the economy is taxes. Read the article below and then answer the questions that follow.

PRESIDENT ASKS BONUS TAX CUT, MORE JOBS

The President proposed a $10 billion bonus tax cut effective July 1. The tax cut is designed to put jobless Americans back to work as quickly as possible. The new proposal would add a new tax reduction of $10 billion to the $18 billion already approved by congress last month. The new tax cut would reduce by $227 the taxes paid for a family of four making $15,000 a year.

The President also called for congress to enact legislation that would encourage plant expansion and equipment purchases by businesses in depressed areas. He hopes that such expansion incentives will put more Americans back to work and aid the economic recovery. The unemployment rate last month was 8.3 percent. The President asked that these job creation tax incentives be applied in areas where unemployment exceeds 7 percent. He feels that the tax cut and the additional tax incentives given to industries in high unemployment areas will help produce more jobs.

a. What is the President asking for? When would it take effect?

b. Why is this considered to be a bonus?

c. By how much would the bonus tax cut reduce the taxes for the family mentioned in the article. What are the characteristics of this family?

d. Was this article written during a time of prosperity or a time of recession? Explain your answer.

e. To whom would the new tax incentives go?

f. What is the hoped for effect of the tax cut and the tax incentive program?

g. What is the average unemployment rate?

Chapter 11

Government Services

Objectives

After completing your study of this chapter, you will be able to do the following:

1. Define and discuss the term *social goods.*

2. Give examples of some government services that are provided by each of the three levels of government—local, state, and national.

3. Name the sources from which government obtains revenue to pay for the cost of the services it provides.

More than 100 years ago one of the most popular Presidents of this nation said: "It is the function of the government to do for the people what they wish to have done but cannot do as well or at all in their individual capacities." Today most Americans would agree with these words of Abraham Lincoln. Americans depend on private business firms for most of the goods and services they use. But they also look to government for many services. This chapter will examine some of the goods and services that government provides.

GOVERNMENT PROVIDES SOCIAL GOODS

The goods and services provided by all levels of government are directed toward serving people as groups. The city library, the county sheriff, the state parks, and the interstate highway system

Braille tags on elevators and mandatory ramps are just two of the many services government provides for individuals with special needs. (Aerospace Corporation, Maria Karras)

are all examples of services provided for society at large. Other examples are police and fire protection, ramps for the handicapped, schools, playgrounds, and airports. These goods and services benefit all citizens, either directly or indirectly. And all citizens, either directly or indirectly, have a voice in whether they should be provided. Goods and services provided by government on the basis of group choice are called *social goods*

Because of their special characteristics, it is not profitable for private business firms to produce social goods. People therefore look to government to provide them. Each level of government tries to provide social goods for the people within its area of authority. A city government looks after the social needs of the people in its city. A state government concerns itself with social goods that benefit everyone in the state. And the federal government is concerned with social goods that benefit the nation as a whole. These three levels of government are distinctly separate from one another, but they often overlap or join forces in providing some social goods. The kinds of services provided by each of the three levels of government are discussed in the following sections.

Give some examples of situations, other than school bond elections, where individuals decide directly by their yes or no vote whether or not they want a social good.

Services of Local Governments

There are almost 100,000 units of local government throughout the nation. These include the governments of cities, towns, townships, counties, and school districts. Local governments provide a means of group action to meet the immediate and personal needs of individuals living within their jurisdiction. City governments provide streets and roads within their boundaries. They provide the water supply and the sewer system for residents. They provide police and fire protection for the community. Also, they license and regulate certain business firms for consumer protection. The elected officials establish laws and ordinances to protect the rights of the citizens of the community. These services are provided by

In most communities, fire protection is provided by the local government. (Romano/Stockmarket, Los Angeles)

almost all units of city or town government. Large cities provide a number of additional services. These may include courts and jails, libraries, parks, swimming pools, auditoriums or civic centers, stadiums, or parking lots. Other examples are health and welfare services, and a variety of other social services. County governments may provide such services as highways, libraries, hospitals, courts and jails, and a number of social services. The local school district, of course, provides the public school system for those who live in the school district. But these are only some examples of the services provided by local governments. The citizens of each city, town, or county decide, through their votes, what specific services should be provided to meet their particular needs.

In addition to the services listed above, what are some particular services provided by your city, town, or county government?

Services of State Governments

There are state governments located in the capitol city of each of the states. The activities of state governments often affect individuals in a direct way. Their services, however, are not as

Of all government services, police protection is perhaps the most visible. (Oregon State Police)

closely connected to immediate personal needs as those provided by local governments. State governments provide services that will benefit all residents of the state. These services are, therefore, much more general in nature than the services of local governments. State governments build and maintain highways and bridges. They provide police officers to patrol the highways. They assist in financing public secondary and elementary schools. They build and operate state colleges and universities as well as other types of institutions for education beyond high school. State parks and other recreational areas are often provided through state government. Courts, prisons, jails, mental hospitals, and institutions for the care of the handicapped are provided by state governments. State governments protect consumers by inspecting goods. They license and regulate certain business firms in the state. Many states provide consumer protection agencies within the state government. State governments operate employment service systems, unemployment benefits systems, and the workmen's compensation systems. These, among others, are some of the services furnished by each of the 50 state governments. Just as the citizens of local units determine their local services, the citizens of the state decide the type and quantity of state government services they desire. As a result, some states provide more than others.

List services provided by your state that are not listed above.

Services of the Federal Government

The activities of the federal or national government are, for most individuals, even further removed than those of the state government. The services provided by the federal government are directed

Government must be prepared to serve our needs not only on a day-to-day basis, but also in times of crises. (Monkmeyer)

more toward national welfare and are designed to be beneficial to all citizens. One of the primary responsibilities of the federal government is to provide for national defense. The federal government assists in financing the operation of the public school systems of the nation. It also helps in the construction of highways—especially the interstate highway system. It constructs and maintains dams to prevent flooding and to produce electric power. It establishes and operates agencies to work on conservation of natural resources and regulates and supervises harbors and waterways. The postal service is provided by the federal government, as are a variety of health care programs, including the social security program. The federal government licenses and regulates a variety of business activities in the fields of finance, banking, transportation, and communication. Finally, the federal government operates a system of courts, prisons, and rehabilitation centers designed to handle criminals who violate federal laws. The preceding discussion is by no means a complete list of the services provided by the federal government. It does, however, give you some idea of the scope of services provided at the national level.

Identify some federal government services, other than those used as examples above, that affect you personally.

PAYING FOR GOVERNMENT SERVICES

All of the government services listed above have a price. They must be paid for in some way. Local, state, and national governments buy raw goods, hire employees, construct buildings, and pay interest on borrowed money. In general, they operate like other business firms while they provide services. Government must receive money in order to pay for the social goods it provides. The money received by a government is called *revenue.* Governments collect or receive revenue from taxes and from the sale of services.

Nontax Revenue

The revenue collected by a government from the sale of services is called *nontax revenue.* All three levels of government collect nontax revenue in varying degrees. The water you use each day at home and at school is not free. There is a charge for its use, based

Road and bridge tolls are a common source of revenue. (Stock, Boston)

on how much water is consumed. The public parking areas in your town or city probably have parking meters. The money collected from these meters is part of the general revenue for the local government. Entrance fees to museums, parks, and zoos are paid by those who visit them. Many cities and metropolitan areas collect revenue from operating mass transit services such as subways, trains, or buses. State governments collect tolls from those using toll roads or bridges. They collect revenue from the sale of hunting and fishing licenses to those who wish to participate in these activities. Tuition and fees are charged students who attend state-owned and -operated colleges and universities. The states also charge entrance fees to various recreational and historical sites. Revenue is also received from the sale of reports and other information published by the state. The federal government collects revenue from those who use the postal service, visit federal recreational or tourist attractions, or purchase any of the vast number of federal publications.

You should notice that in each case this nontax revenue is collected directly from those using the various services listed. This is characteristic of nontax revenue. It is collected from the sale of a good or a service to an individual or business firm. The amounts of nontax revenue are usually small, and the total amount of nontax revenue is uncertain. It depends upon the number of people using the service involved. In many instances the nontax revenue does not even cover the cost of the service provided. Therefore, for a more reliable source of revenue, governments depend on taxes.

What are some examples of nontax revenue you or your family have paid to some level of government during the past year?

Tax Revenue

A *tax* is a compulsory payment to some level of government. You will recall that nontax revenue is collected from those who voluntarily use certain government services. Taxes, on the other hand, are collected from all who earn incomes above a certain level. They are also collected from all who own property, and from all who purchase certain goods and services.

Four taxes provide most of the revenue for the three levels of government. They are income taxes, social security and employment taxes, sales taxes, and property taxes. In the next chapter, you will learn about each of these taxes and a number of other taxes. First, you should be aware of how great a share of government revenue is raised through taxes. Table 11-1 shows that in 1977

TABLE 11-1   SOURCES OF FEDERAL GOVERNMENT REVENUE— 1977 (by percent)

Individual income taxes	43.2
Corporation income taxes	16.0
Employment taxes	30.8
Excise taxes	5.1
Other revenue	4.9

Source: Statistical Abstract of the United States, 1977.

the federal government received more than 90 percent of its revenue from income and employment taxes. Less than 5 percent of the total revenue was raised in the form of nontax revenue. In Table 11-2, notice that state governments received the largest part of their revenue from sales and other taxes. In addition to their own taxes, state governments also receive revenue raised by the federal and local governments. This revenue is called intergovernmental revenue and accounts for about 25 percent of state revenues. Together, these two sources made up 76 percent of all state revenues. In other words, more than three-fourths of the state government revenue came from taxes.

TABLE 11-2   SOURCES OF STATE GOVERNMENT REVENUE—1972 (by percent)

Taxes	53.3
Sales and gross receipts taxes	29.6
Licenses	4.8
Individual income taxes	11.6
Corporation income taxes	3.9
Property taxes	1.1
Other taxes	2.3
Intergovernmental revenue	24.9
From federal government	23.9
From local governments	1.0
Charges and miscellaneous general revenue	9.6
Other revenue	12.2

Source: Statistical Abstract of the United States, *1974, p. 257*

Remember, the benefits of the social goods provided by the federal and state governments are usually shared by all citizens of the nation or state. As you can see from these tables, most of the revenue to pay for these social goods is collected through taxes. And taxes are paid by almost everyone in our society. It is obvious that taxes are the most important source of government revenue.

What are some kinds of taxes you have paid recently?

Borrowing by Government

Along with nontax and tax revenues, all three levels of government borrow money to cover the cost of some expenditures. A school district, for example, borrows money to build new school buildings. State governments also borrow to finance building and other

STREET PAVING CONSTRUCTION
D C REDEVELOPMENT LAND AGENCY
DISTRICT OF COLUMBIA ★★★
FINANCIAL ASSISTANCE FROM THE U S DEPARTMENT OF HOUSING
AND URBAN DEVELOPMENT
FORT LINCOLN NEW TOWN IS AN
OFFICIALLY DESIGNATED BICENTENNIAL PROJECT

Government borrowing is necessary to finance the cost of some expenditures. (HUD)

programs. All three levels of government usually cover any deficits by borrowing. A *deficit* is what results when a government spends more than it receives in revenue in a given period. A *surplus* is what results when a government receives more in revenue than it spends.

Most Americans are aware that there is a federal or national debt. The *national debt* is the amount owed by the federal government. The federal government sells bonds and other debt securities to the public in order to finance budget deficits. Private citizens, banks, corporations, insurance companies, and state and local governments are the major holders of these debt securities. The federal government also sells debt securities to certain agencies within the federal government. These agencies have acquired funds, usually trust funds such as those set up for the social security program. In the late-1970s the national debt was approximately $700 billion. Of this amount, about 70 percent was held by the public and 30 percent by federal government agencies. The net interest payment on national debt securities held by the public amounted to approximately $35 billion. This was about 10 percent of the expenditures of the federal government.

Many people have voiced concern about the size of the national debt. The amount of the national debt is large and growing. Yet, it has steadily declined in relation to the total economic activity of the nation. In 1955, the national debt held by the public equalled 62 percent of gross national product. In 1965, it equalled 42 percent. In 1975, it equalled about 25 percent. The national debt has also grown much more slowly than the debt owed by individuals, corporations, and state and local governments.

What type of expenditure by the federal government over the years has been the major cause of national debt?

GOVERNMENT SERVICES IN THE FUTURE

The role of government in the economy has increased dramatically since the nation was founded. The number of government services has increased steadily over the years. It seems that people generally want government to continue to assume the responsibility for providing more and more services.

Since the 1930s the majority of people have felt that one of government's major roles is to ensure a relatively stable economy. In times of high inflation, high unemployment, or recession, citizens turn to the government for assistance. Likewise, government is expected to assist in solving the so-called social problems— poverty and pollution, for example. Citizens have come to expect government services to be provided in many areas by all three levels of government. If citizens continue to demand more government services, the role of government will probably be expanded. One limiting factor on the expanding role of government will be the ability of taxpayers to finance the services provided. A second limiting factor will be the taxpayers' willingness to give a larger share of their incomes to pay for social goods. It is interesting to try to guess how far the role of government will be expanded and in what areas this expanded role will occur. All citizens will have something to say about that decision.

What are some services that are not currently provided by government that you feel should be provided? Explain why you feel government should provide the services you suggest.

Learning Activities

Increasing Your Business Vocabulary

You should become familiar with each of the terms shown below. On a sheet of paper write the numbers 1 through 7. Then write alongside each number the term that best matches each of the numbered definitions.

deficit / national debt / nontax revenue / revenue / social goods / surplus / tax

1. What results when a government receives more in revenue than it spends in a given period.

2. A compulsory payment to some level of government.

3. Money received by a government.

4. What results when a government spends more than it receives in revenue in a given period.

5. The amount owed by the federal government.

6. Goods and services provided by government on the basis of group choice.

7. Revenue collected by a government from the sale of services.

Understanding Business

1. Why do people look to government to produce social goods?

2. List some services usually provided by a city government?

3. List some services usually provided by state government.

4. Give some services provided by the federal government.

5. List examples of how governments obtain nontax revenue.

6. From whom is the nontax revenue for a service collected?

7. What are some reasons why governments need sources of revenue other than nontax sources?

8. Name the taxes that provide most of the revenue for the three levels of government.

9. Has the national debt grown more rapidly or more slowly than debts of individuals, private corporations, and state and local governments?

10. What are two limiting factors on the expanding role of government?

 # Business Problems and Projects

1. Read the article below and then answer the questions.

CITY COUNCIL APPROVES NEW SPORTS COMPLEX FOR WESTSIDE

The city council approved yesterday the construction of a multi-purpose sports stadium to be built in the Westside Urban Renewal Area.

The stadium would cost an estimated $64.4 million and would be designed to accommodate professional baseball, football, and soccer as well as college football.

The existing stadium on Lake Avenue would be torn down and the land sold. The money from the sale of the land would be used to pay in part for the new stadium.

Downtown business leaders have already pledged to supply the site, worth $15.7 million, at no cost to the city.

The primary method of financing the new stadium, however, would be general obligation bonds to be repaid with stadium revenue. A 3 percent tax on hotels and motels would be available as a backup in case revenue is insufficient to repay the bonds. Stadium income would include parking and concession revenue, rent from the professional and college teams, and rent from others who would want to use the facility.

a. What type of facility does the city plan to build?

b. How much would the facility cost?

c. What kinds of activities would the facility accommodate?

d. What will happen to the old facility?

e. What sources of revenue will be used to finance the facility?

f. How does the city plan to repay the debt incurred in building the facility?

g. What are the sources of income from the facility?

2. On a form similar to the one shown below, list five goods or services that are provided by each of the three levels of government.

	Good or Service	Level of Government
Example	Highway patrol	State

Chapter 12

Taxes and the Economy

Objectives

After completing your study of this chapter, you will be able to do the following:

1. Identify the most important types of taxes.

2. Describe and discuss the major features of these taxes.

3. Name the tax that raises the largest amount of revenues for each of the three levels of government.

4. Distinguish between the benefits received and ability-to-pay principles of taxation.

As our society has grown more complex, government services have expanded to meet new needs. These services are paid for from money raised from taxes. Since the 1930s, both the number of different taxes and the total amount of taxes collected have increased. The increasing burden of taxes raises many questions. For example, which taxes raise most of the government revenues? Should some people pay more taxes than others? Are some taxes more fair than others? These and similar questions are discussed in this chapter.

TYPES OF TAXES

When a tax is placed on an item such as gasoline or an activity such as traveling by airplane, the tax is said to be *levied* on that item or activity. Taxes are levied on what is earned and what is spent. Taxes are also levied on what is owned and what is left to a person's heirs. Americans have been very clever in thinking of ways to tax themselves. In the past, taxes were levied on rare spices and fabrics, the right to vote, and even on other taxes. In the sections that follow, four taxes widely used today will be discussed.

Income Taxes

An *income tax* is a tax on the income of individuals and corporations. Income is the money earned from *all* sources, not just wages. Income taxes are probably the most important taxes in our country. In fact, more federal revenue comes from income taxes than from any other source. Most state governments today also levy income taxes. But state income taxes are usually low. And they are not the main source of income for a state. Some cities also levy individual income taxes. Usually, however, city income taxes apply only to income received from wages or salaries. Therefore, they could be more appropriately called wage or salary taxes.

Two factors are used in figuring income tax. One is the tax rate, and the other is taxable income. The amount of tax is computed by multiplying the tax rate by the taxable income. If the tax rate were 10 percent, a taxpayer who had a taxable income of $6,000 would pay $600 income tax (.10 × $6,000 = $600).

Taxable income has a definite meaning in federal and state tax laws. Not all income is taxable. The government allows each

Most federal revenue comes from individual and corporate income taxes. (Marshall Licht)

taxpayer some tax-free income. Moreover, all taxpayers are allowed to make deductions from their gross income for dependents, medical expenses, gifts, charity, taxes paid to other levels of government, and a number of other items. Taxable income is the income that is left after all of these deductions are made.

Progressive Taxes   As a person's income increases, income taxes take a larger percentage of that income. This is because the tax rate increases as the income increases. The tax rate schedules below show how the rate goes up.

As you can see, the individual with the larger amount of income pays a larger percentage of income tax. A tax that takes a larger percentage of income as income increases is called a *progressive tax*. Progressive taxes place the burden of tax most heavily on those who are most able to pay. The individual income tax is a progressive tax.

TAX RATE SCHEDULES
Single Person or
Separate Return of a Married Person

Taxable income		Tax Rates	
$0 to $2,000		1%	
2,000 to 3,500	$20 plus	2% amount over $ 2,000	
3,500 to 5,000	50 plus	3% amount over 3,500	
5,000 to 6,500	95 plus	4% amount over 5,000	
6,500 to 8,000	155 plus	5% amount over 6,500	
8,000 to 9,500	230 plus	6% amount over 8,000	
9,500 to 11,000	320 plus	7% amount over 9,500	
11,000 to 12,500	425 plus	8% amount over 11,000	
12,500 to 14,000	545 plus	9% amount over 12,500	
14,000 to 15,500	680 plus	10% amount over 14,000	
15,500 and over	830 plus	11% amount over 15,500	

Head of Household

Taxable Income		Tax Rates	
$0 to 4,000		1%	
4,000 to 6,000	$40 plus	2% amount over $4,000	
6,000 to 7,500	80 plus	3% amount over 6,000	
7,500 to 9,000	125 plus	4% amount over 7,500	
9,000 to 10,500	185 plus	5% amount over 9,000	
10,500 to 12,000	260 plus	6% amount over 10,500	
12,000 to 13,500	350 plus	7% amount over 12,000	
13,500 to 15,000	455 plus	8% amount over 13,500	
15,000 to 16,500	575 plus	9% amount over 15,000	
16,500 to 18,000	710 plus	10% amount over 16,500	
18,000 and over	860 plus	11% amount over 18,000	

Source: California Franchise Tax Board

Income Tax Withholding   At one time, taxpayers paid their income tax in one lump sum at the end of each year. This system proved to be too much of a burden for many taxpayers. The federal government then adopted a pay-as-you-go system. Employers became the tax collectors for their employees. Now, on each employee's paycheck, an employer must withhold a certain amount of income tax and send this directly to the government. This system is called *income tax withholding*. The amount of tax

Form **W-4**	**Employee's Withholding Allowance Certificate**
Department of the Treasury Internal Revenue Service	(This certificate is for income tax withholding purposes only; it will remain in effect until you change it.)

NOTE: If you incurred no tax liability for last year and anticipate no liability for this year, you may file Form W–4E to claim exemption from Federal income tax withholding. See Form W–4E for details.

Type or print your full name	Your social security number
FRANCIS Leon Rodda	987 – 04 – 3391

Home address (Number and street or rural route)
1343 N. Revere Street

Marital status
☐ Single ☒ Married
(If married but legally separated, or spouse is a nonresident alien, check the single block.)

City or town, State and ZIP code
Boston, MA   02176

1 Total number of allowances you are claiming . . . .

2 Additional amount, if any, you want deducted from each pay (if your employer agrees) . . . . | $

Under the penalties of perjury, I certify that the number of withholding exemptions and allowances claimed on this certificate does not exceed the number to which I am entitled.

Signature ▶ Francis Leon Rodda   Date ▶ Oct. 15, , 19

The Employee's Withholding Allowance Certificate (Form W-4) indicates to your employer the number of allowances you deserve.

Wage and Tax Statement 19--

For Official Use Only	Type or print EMPLOYER'S name, address, ZIP code and Federal identifying number.	Copy A For Internal Revenue Service Center
52-0123456 Burton, Inc. 200 Main Street Charlestown, Ma. 02178		Employer's State identifying number

Employee's social security number	1 Federal income tax withheld	2 Wages, tips, and other compensation	3 FICA employee tax withheld	4 Total FICA wages
987-04-3391	1,137	11,583.00	701.00	11,583

Type or print Employee's name, address, and ZIP code below. (Name must aline with arrow)	5 Was employee covered by a qualified pension plan, etc.?	6 °	7 °
Francis L. Rodda 1343 N. Revere Street Boston, MA 02176	No		

	8 State or local tax withheld	9 State or local wages	10 State or locality
	579.00	11,583.00	MA

	11 State or local tax withheld	12 State or local wages	13 State or locality

° See instructions on back of Copy D

Form **W-2**   See instructions on Form W–3 and back of Copy D   Department of the Treasury—Internal Revenue Service

A Wage and Tax Statement (Form W-2) must be filed with your tax forms.

withheld is an estimate based on the tax rate that applies to the employee. At the end of the year, an employer prepares a statement for each employee showing the amount of wages paid during the year and the amount of taxes withheld. This statement is called a Wage and Tax Statement and is commonly referred to as Form W-2. A copy of this form is shown below. The employer sends copies of the Form W-2 to the governments (federal, state, or local) that levied the tax, and the employee also receives copies. The employee's copies are used in filing an individual's tax return. Using forms supplied by the government, an individual figures the amount of income tax he or she owes. If this amount is more than the tax withheld, as shown on Form W-2, then the additional tax must be paid when the tax return is filed. If too much tax was withheld, then the taxpayer applies for a refund at the time the tax return is filed.

Both federal and state governments will answer questions regarding income taxes. These questions can be made by phone, by letter, or in person. The state and federal tax agencies also offer free assistance in preparing income tax returns.

Why do you think individual income taxes are used as the major method of raising revenue in our tax system?

Corporate Income Tax   The federal corporate income tax is much simpler to figure out than the federal individual income tax. A corporation is taxed on its profits. Some people feel that corporations are treated unfairly. They point out that not only are the profits of a corporation taxed, but also the shares of profits paid to shareholders as dividends are taxed. They consider this to be double taxation. Sole proprietorships and partnerships, however, pay income taxes in the same manner as individual taxpayers.

Do you feel the federal corporate income tax law should be changed so that profits paid to stockholders are not subject to double taxation? Give reasons for your answer.

Sales and Excise Taxes

The major sources of revenue for state government are sales and excise taxes. A *sales tax* is a tax on the sale of a wide range of goods and services. Sales taxes are paid on clothing, certain food items, meals in restaurants, and numerous other things. In some states, sales taxes must be paid on almost all goods. Some states also use

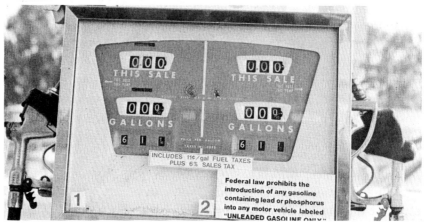

With each purchase of gasoline, you pay both excise and sales taxes. (Marshall Licht)

an excise tax. An *excise tax* is a tax on the sale of a select group of goods or services. These items include tobacco, gasoline, liquor, cosmetics, and jewelry.

Regressive Taxes Sales and excise taxes are based on a percent of the selling price of goods or services. They are both considered to be regressive taxes. A *regressive tax* is a tax that takes a smaller percentage of income as income increases. No matter what income an individual may have, the sales tax on a given item is the same. For example, if two individuals buy $100 worth of goods on which there is a 5 percent sales tax, each would pay $5 in sales taxes. For an individual whose weekly income is $100, that sales tax is 5 percent of income. For an individual whose weekly income is $500, however, that sales tax is only 1 percent of income.

What reasons can you give to justify regressive taxes as part of the tax system? Progressive taxes as part of the tax system?

People with low incomes usually spend most of what they earn, and they save little. They therefore pay sales taxes on almost all their income. People with higher incomes, on the other hand, spend less of their income and are able to save more. They therefore pay sales taxes on only part of their income. Thus, regressive taxes put the burden of taxes most heavily on those with lower incomes.

Some states have attempted to make their sales taxes less regressive. The most common method is to not levy sales taxes on necessities. In this way, low-income people who spend a large percentage of their income on such necessities as unprepared food, medicine, and clothing, pay less sales tax than they otherwise would. Some states also tax services such as hotel rooms and theater or sports tickets. People with higher incomes usually spend more on such services than do people with lower incomes. There-fore adding a tax to some of these services results in a sales tax more suited to an individual's ability to pay.

What percent is the sales tax in your state, if your state has a sales tax? What, if any, goods or services are free of the tax in your state?

Property Taxes

At the turn of the century, property taxes produced more than half of the total tax revenues collected by all levels of government. Although this percentage has decreased, property taxes still are the second most important source of government funds. They are by far the most important source of revenue for local governments, who rely on them for over 80 percent of their revenue.

There are two types of property taxes—the real estate tax and the personal property tax. A *real estate tax* is a tax on land and buildings attached to the land. A home, farmland, resort, factory, and apartment house are examples of real estate. A *personal property tax* is a tax on property that is not permanently attached to land. Automobiles, clothing, appliances, and jewelry are exam-ples of items that may be taxed as personal property.

Today, the real estate tax is used to a much greater extent than the personal property tax. Real estate taxes are based on the assessed value of the property. The *assessed value* is the value placed on the property for taxation purposes by officials of the local government. In some areas, the assessed value may be equal

An important source of revenue for local governments, property taxes have become the center of taxpayer dissatisfaction in recent years. (Maria Karras)

to the full market value of the property. In other areas, it may represent only a portion of the full market value. The amount of tax is determined by multiplying the tax rate by the assessed value. Therefore the amount of tax can be increased or decreased by raising or lowering either the tax rate, the assessed value, or both.

In some states, steps have been taken to either lower or keep at a constant amount the property taxes paid by elderly and low-income homeowners. This is done by freezing the real estate tax on a home if the tax exceeds a percentage of the homeowner's income.

Death and Gift Taxes

To prevent the large accumulation of wealth among a few families or individuals, the federal and state governments use so-called death taxes. These taxes are levied on property, including money, when it passes from a deceased person to the person's heirs. There are two kinds of death taxes. The *estate tax* is a federal tax on the total value of the deceased person's real and personal property. The *inheritance tax* is a state tax on the value of the real or personal property a person receives from someone who has died. The methods and rates of taxation vary from state to state, but both estate and inheritance taxes are considered progressive.

To avoid paying death taxes, some people make gifts of money or property to their heirs before their death. Government created another tax, the gift tax, to counter this practice. The *gift tax* is a tax on the value of gifts from one person to another when the value exceeds a certain amount. Gift taxes, together with estate and inheritance taxes, account for only a small percentage of the total revenues collected by the federal and state governments.

Do you feel that estate, inheritance, and gift taxes should be part of the tax system. Why or why not?

Other Taxes

In addition to the more common types of taxes already discussed, there are many other types of taxes. The federal government places a tax called a *tariff* on goods imported into the country. Governments often levy tariffs in an attempt to discourage imports. By increasing the tariff on a good, the government can raise the price of the good to consumers. This makes the good less competitive with American-made goods. Tariffs are used more to control the amount of imports than to produce revenue.

Among other taxes paid by individuals are licenses or fees to fish, hunt, or operate a motor vehicle. Registration fees for automobiles and trucks are another form of tax. Both individuals and businesses are required to make contributions to the social security program. Because these contributions are compulsory, they are, in effect, taxes.

ESTABLISHING A TAX SYSTEM

Finding fair and productive taxes is not easy. No one is anxious to pay taxes of any type. In fact, some individuals and business firms take illegal means to avoid paying taxes. Most people consider a good tax to be one that must be paid by someone else. The elected officials who plan how much money will be spent for government services must also decide how to collect enough revenue to pay for these services. As you learned in Chapter 11, most of the revenue collected by government comes from taxes. A major task for lawmakers, therefore, is to decide what kinds of taxes to levy and

Tariffs on these imported cars not only provide revenue, but also help protect our own automobile sales. (Stock, Boston)

who will pay them. No matter how equal a tax may be, there will be some people who will not like it. It is impossible to develop a tax system that will please everyone or be acceptable to everyone.

Why do you think people dislike paying taxes?

There are two different ways of looking at the question of who should pay a tax. These two views are the benefits-received principle and the ability-to-pay principle.

Benefits-Received Principle

The *benefits-received principle* holds that individuals and business firms should pay for social goods in the same manner as they pay for other goods and services. This means that those who benefit most from goods and services provided by government should pay the taxes needed to finance them. Some social goods are paid for in this way. For example, gasoline taxes are used to build and repair highways. They are paid by those who get the most benefit from the highways—truckers, bus lines, and individual car owners. The benefits-received principle can't be applied to any great degree, however. For example, how do you identify the benefits received by individuals, households, or business firms from social goods such as national defense, education, and police and fire protection? And, clearly, benefits such as welfare or unemployment payments cannot be paid for by persons who are receiving them. Obviously, transfer payments by government couldn't be made under the benefits-received principle of taxation.

Why is it said that the benefits-received principle is difficult to apply to education? Would a tuition system be a good method of applying this principle? Why or why not?

Ability-to-Pay Principle

With many taxes the ability-to-pay principle is more practical. The *ability-to-pay principle* holds that the amount of taxes paid by individuals and business firms should be related directly to how much they can afford. In the United States this means that individuals and business firms with larger incomes pay more taxes than those with smaller incomes. This principle is based on the idea that the first dollars of income earned by consumers are spent on basic needs. Each additional dollar of income is spent on goods and services that are less urgently needed. Lastly, money is used to buy luxuries. Under this system, one dollar in taxes paid by a person with a very small income would present a greater hardship than a dollar in taxes paid by a rich person. People with the highest incomes, therefore, can afford to pay more taxes. The major problem with the ability-to-pay principle is how to determine accurately what one's ability to pay is. Despite this problem, most of our taxes—and therefore our tax system—are based more on the ability-to-pay principle than on the benefits-received principle.

In addition to deciding how much more ability to pay one person has than another, what are some other problems that may occur in using the ability-to-pay principle of taxation?

Direct and Indirect Taxes

There are so many different types of taxes that it is sometimes difficult to determine who actually bears the burden of a tax. The business firm that pays a tax to government does not always bear the burden of the tax. It may raise its prices to cover the tax and thus shift the burden to the customer. The property tax on a factory, for example, is paid by the owner, but the owner recovers the tax in the prices charged for the goods sold.

The terms *direct tax* and *indirect tax* are used to differentiate between those taxes that cannot be shifted to another person and those taxes that can be shifted. A *direct tax* is a tax that is paid by the person on whom the tax is levied. The property tax paid by a homeowner would be a direct tax. An *indirect tax* is a tax that is paid by someone other than the consumer but whose costs are shifted to the consumer in the form of higher prices. The property tax paid by an apartment owner is an indirect tax. The owner pays the tax to the government, but the cost of the tax is actually borne by the apartment renters in the form of higher rents. Some of the most important taxes in our tax system are indirect taxes. These taxes are sometimes referred to as *hidden taxes,* because those who are bearing the burden of the taxes are not aware of it.

JUDGING TAXES

Table 12-2 summarizes some of the important characteristics of the taxes discussed in this chapter. The table shows whether the tax is regressive or progressive. It shows whether the tax is direct or indirect. And it shows which levels of government use the tax. A review of the table should help you to understand better how each tax operates in our economy.

As a concerned citizen, you should also be aware of ways of telling a "good" tax from a "bad" tax. It is generally agreed that there are four tests of a good tax.

Since the purpose of a tax is to raise revenue, the first test is that it produce a sufficient amount of revenue. The second test is

TABLE 12-2   CLASSIFYING COMMON TYPES OF TAXES

		Type of Tax	Level of Government
	Progressive	Corporation income taxes	Federal and state
		Individual income taxes	Federal, state, and local
		Estate, inheritance, and gift taxes	Federal and state
Direct		Real property taxes	State and local
		Personal property taxes	State and local
		Business licenses and permits	State and local
	Regressive	Motor vehicle licenses	State
		Sales taxes	State and local
Indirect		Excise taxes	Federal and state
		Import taxes	Federal

much more difficult to determine—what is a person's fair share of a tax? Experts tend to feel that a tax should be paid by those who have the most ability to pay. Ability to pay can be judged by income, property ownership, and spending. Those who have the same ability to pay should pay the same amount of tax. The third test of a good tax is that it be easy to administer. Thus, a good tax is easy to collect, difficult to evade, and fairly inexpensive to administer. If the cost of enforcing or collecting a tax is high in relation to the revenue it raises, then the tax is not a good tax. Finally, all taxes have economic effects. A good tax does not discourage people from working or investing. On the contrary, it should make it attractive for business firms to expand and grow. A good tax, then, produces adequate revenue, is fair, is easily administered, and has no harmful economic effects.

Give an example of a tax that may have a harmful economic effect and explain how this would occur.

Learning Activities

Increasing Your Business Vocabulary

You should become familiar with each of the terms shown below. On a sheet of paper write the numbers 1 through 14. Then write alongside each number the term that best matches each of the numbered definitions.

assessed value / direct tax / estate tax / excise tax / gift tax / income tax / indirect tax / personal property tax / progressive tax / real estate tax / regressive tax / sales tax / tariff

1. A tax that is paid by the person on whom it is levied.
2. A tax whose costs are shifted to someone else.
3. A tax that takes a larger percentage of income as income increases.
4. The value placed upon property for the purpose of taxation.
5. A tax that takes a smaller percentage of income as income increases.
6. A tax on land and buildings attached to the land.
7. A federal tax placed on goods imported into the country.
8. A tax on the sale of a wide range of goods and services.
9. A tax on property that is not permanently attached to the land.
10. A tax on the income of individuals and corporations.
11. A tax on gifts that exceed a certain value.
12. A tax on the total value of a deceased person's real and personal property.
13. A tax on the sale of selected goods and services.

Understanding Business

1. Generally, what group of people are affected most by taxes that are progressive?

2. What kinds of taxes are the major source of revenue for state governments in the United States?

3. What is the difference between sales taxes and excise taxes?

4. What people are affected most by regressive taxes.

5. What type of tax is the major source of revenue for local governments?

6. Why are payments made to the social security program called taxes?

7. Explain the benefits-received principle of taxation. What are two problems with using it?

8. Explain the ability-to-pay principle of taxation. What is the major problem with its use?

9. Explain the difference between a direct and an indirect tax.

10. What are the four basic questions that should be asked about a tax to determine if it is a good tax?

Business Problems and Projects

1. The graph below shows the trend in state and local government spending since 1965. Study the graph and then answer the questions that follow it.

STATE AND LOCAL SPENDING TRENDS

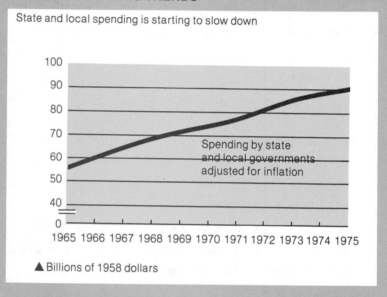

State and local spending is starting to slow down

Spending by state and local governments adjusted for inflation

▲ Billions of 1958 dollars

Source: Business Week: November 17, 1975

a. What was the approximate combined state and local spending for 1974?

b. Do the figures for 1975 reflect the amount of money that was actually spent? Explain your answer.

c. By approximately how much did state and local spending increase between 1970 and 1974?

d. By what percent did state and local spending increase between 1965 and 1970?

2. On a form similar to the one shown below, list six different
   taxes used by the federal, state, or local governments. Indicate whether the tax is regressive or progressive and whether
   it is easy to pay and collect.

	Tax	Regressive or Progressive?	Easy to Collect and Pay?
Example	Sales tax	Regressive	Yes

3. The city of Charleston imposes a sales tax of 6 percent on all
   nonfood items except prescription drugs. If you bought the
   following items, what would be the amount of the sales tax
   and the amount of the total bill?

Item	Price
One head of romaine lettuce	.29
One half-gallon of milk	.64
One box of paper napkins	.29
One can of tomato soup	.18
One box of Alka-Seltzer	1.23
One pound of bacon	1.48
One box of sponges	.45
One *TV Guide*	.35

Part Two

MONEY, BANKING, AND CONSUMER CREDIT

Chapter 13

The Purpose of Money

Objectives

After completing your study of this chapter, you will be able to do the following:

1. Define the term *money* and list the functions it performs.

2. Discuss the important role money plays in a private enterprise economy.

3. Describe the two types of money used in our economy.

4. Discuss inflation and its effect on you and our economy.

5. Explain the need for sound money and what you can do to help keep it sound.

How do you obtain the goods and services that you need and want? How are you going to get that new sweater? That new tape deck? That new record? Most probably you would say that you would go to the store and buy what you want—that is, of course, if you had the money to pay for it.

Without money, you would probably have to do without the sweater, tape deck, or record. And without money, our private enterprise economy would come to a halt. The role and importance of money in our economy is the subject of this chapter.

EXCHANGE OF GOODS IN A MONEYLESS SOCIETY

It has not always been as easy to obtain goods and services as it is today. Imagine that you lived many years ago in a society that had no form of money. In those days, the only way to obtain goods that you did not have or could not produce was through bartering. *Barter* is the direct exchange of one good or service for another. If you wanted or needed something in a barter system, you would have to find someone who had what you wanted. For example, if you wanted iron nails to use in building a house, you would have to find someone who had them. More important, that person would have to be willing to give you the nails in exchange for what you could trade. Very little trade takes place in a society where barter is the only method of exchange because barter clearly has several limitations.

First, exchanges are difficult to arrange. It is hard to find people who own and are willing to exchange their possessions for what is offered in trade.

Second, there is no common unit by which to measure and state the value of goods and services. The value of each item has to be stated in terms of the value of every other item. For example, one cow may be worth 10 goats or 4 pigs or 200 chickens and so on.

Third, many items are not easily divided into parts or smaller portions. Nor is it easy to move them from place to place. For example, a person who has only 20 chickens or 1 pig can not trade with another person for part of a cow. Also, the cow can not be easily transported from one market to another.

A modern version of a barter system is a swap meet. (Stock, Boston)

Fourth, there is no basic unit of value to use in making contracts for future payment of goods. If you owed a debt, its repayment would have to be stated in terms of the value of the goods: so many bushels of wheat, heads of cattle, etc.

Fifth, there is no satisfactory method of storing purchasing power. *Purchasing power* is the amount of goods and services that a means of exchange will buy at any given time. In a barter system, people can store purchasing power for future use only by storing their products for future barter. This is sometimes neither practical nor possible. For example, live animals would have to be carefully tended and fed so that they would be available when needed. And, of course, the animals could die—leaving nothing to use as a means of exchange.

THE NEED FOR MONEY

Barter worked well when people made or grew most of the goods they needed. Even today, people in some countries still use barter. In fact, some forms of barter still exist in our economy. But because of its limitations, barter was quickly replaced in most primitive societies by what is called *commodity currency*. *Commodity currency* is a good such as tobacco, rice, lumber, fish, wool, or cattle that is generally acceptable by most people in a society in exchange for other goods. Many other items have been, and still are, used as commodity currency. These include such objects as elephant tails, wampum, tortoise shells, colored stones, various metals, and even whale teeth.

What are some of the ways in which barter is still used in our private enterprise economy?

MONEY AND ITS FUNCTIONS

What is money? *Money* is anything that is generally accepted and commonly used as a means of payment for goods and services. As such, money performs three very important functions. It serves as a standard of value. It serves as a medium of exchange. And it serves as a store of value.

Standard of Value

The first function of money is as a standard of value. The value of all goods and services is measured in units of money called *monetary units*. Every country has its own monetary unit. In the United States, the monetary unit is the *dollar*. Other countries use different monetary units: Brazil uses the *cruzeiro;* France, the *franc;* England, the *pound;* and Germany, the *mark*.

By using a monetary unit, the value of each good or service can be stated as a price. In a sense a price can be considered as the number of monetary units for which a good or service can be bought. For example, let's say that the average price of a sweater is $15, of a record $5, and of a movie $3. These prices measure the value of these items. They also show the comparative value of various goods and services on the market. Using the example above, we can say that if one sweater is worth $15, it is equivalent to or worth three $5 records or five $3 movies. One has only to compare the value in terms of prices.

Money is a standard of value. (Steven McBradv)

Money not only serves as a standard of value for current purchases. It also serves as the unit in which most future payments are stated. When purchases are to be paid for at a later date, these future payments are specified in money amounts. For example, suppose you buy a car or borrow money on time, your payments will be made in specific money amounts even though the loan may run for several years.

 Different countries use different money units as the base for their monetary systems. Explain how exchange goods and services among countries can still take place.

The second function of money is as a medium of exchange. Money is used as a means of paying for the goods and services you want. Money passes from hand to hand in exchange for goods and services or in payment of a debt.

In a barter system if you wanted to obtain a new sweater, you would have to find someone willing to exchange the sweater for

Money is used as a means of paying for the
goods and services you want.
(Lejeune/Stockmarket, Los Angeles)

something you have to offer, such as three records. By using money
as a medium of exchange, however, you can get the sweater by
exchanging money for it. The seller will accept money because
money can be used to acquire other goods and services.

As a medium of exchange, money is very important in our
private enterprise economy. Without money, business could not be
carried on between individuals and businesses to the extent that it
is today. The ease with which money can be exchanged means that
people can be sure that their money will be readily accepted for
goods and services. As a result, people can work at a job to earn
money and then use the money to purchase goods and services.
The smooth system of money exchange increases the flow of goods
and services, which in turn increases production of more goods and
additional services and improves our standard of living.

Store of Value

The third function of money is as a store of value. By storing—or saving—your money now, you save your purchasing power for the future. By storing your purchasing power, you can spend your money at some future time for the things you will want then. Your money will still be accepted at a later time for the purchase of goods and services.

Give some examples of how people store their purchasing power other than in savings accounts.

CHARACTERISTICS OF MONEY

Money is generally acceptable as a medium of exchange for goods and services. This is a characteristic as well as a function of money. There are certain other characteristics that money must have if it is to carry out its functions effectively.

- Money must be stable in value. This means that the value of money must remain constant over a period of time. While the value of a dollar bill does not change over the years, the values—or prices—of goods and services do change. When prices of goods and services increase, the dollar will not buy as much. Therefore, the value of the dollar remains the same, but the prices of goods and services do change.

- Money must be easy to carry. Can you imagine trying to carry around enough furs, stones, or whale teeth to cover your daily purchases? Money must be in a form that is not only easy and convenient to carry but also that is easy to use in the exchange for goods and services.

- Money must be durable and must wear well. Since money is exchanged and handled many times over, it must be in a form sturdy enough to withstand constant handling. Money that is not durable or long lasting will wear out as it passes from one person to another. If it wears out easily, it will lose its usefulness as a medium of exchange.

- Money must also be easily divided. Different units of money—or denominations—are issued so that money is easy to use. For example, can you imagine trying to divide a fur into smaller parts or units to buy a hamburger, a candy bar, or a magazine?

   And would the total value of the small pieces still equal the value of the original, uncut fur?

Does our money have the characteristics needed for it to carry out its functions effectively? Explain.

FORMS OF MONEY

In the United States, the total supply of money at any given time consists of the coins and paper money in circulation plus the balances in all checking accounts. Coins and paper dollars issued by the federal government are called *currency dollars*. However, the most widely used form of money in the United States is not currency dollars but checkbook dollars. *Checkbook dollars* are money in the form of checks. These checks are written against checking account balances. Individuals and businesses maintain these balances to pay for goods and services by check rather than with cash.

   Currency dollars and checkbook dollars together make up the money supply. They represent dollars that are available on demand that can be used in exchange for goods and services.

   Both coins and paper money are legal tender. *Legal tender* is money that must be accepted as payment for all debts, goods, and services. Checkbook dollars, however, are not legal tender. Although checks are usually accepted by most merchants, a merchant does not have to accept a check and has the right to demand currency dollars. But even though checks are not legal tender, more than 90 percent of all money exchanged in this country is in the form of checks.

Why do you think checkbook dollars are used more frequently than currency dollars?

THE IMPORTANCE OF SOUND MONEY

One of the major problems in our economy is maintaining sound money. *Sound money* is another way of saying money with a constant purchasing power.

Money in and of itself is of little value. Its value, as stated earlier in this chapter, is in its purchasing power. Remember, purchasing power is measured by the amount of goods and services money will buy at any given time. Money itself doesn't change, but the amount of goods and services money will buy does change over a period of time.

When a country goes through a time in which prices of goods and services in the economy are generally rising, the same amount of money will buy less and less. This is referred to as *inflation*. During a period of inflation, the purchasing power of money decreases.

When there is a general decrease in prices of goods and services in the economy, the purchasing power of money increases. This is called *deflation*.

What can you do to help achieve sound money? You can limit your demands on the government for additional services. If government services increase, then the government spends more money. The cost of services is increased further when inflation is a threat. For example, you may have to get along with fewer new roads and highways. Or you may have to get along with fewer police, crowded schools, and less fire protection. If you are old enough to vote, you can use your vote to show your desire that both government and business be run as efficiently as possible.

Also, you can spend your income carefully, save wisely, and produce efficiently.

Why is it so important to the economy to maintain sound money?

Learning Activities

Increasing Your Business Vocabulary

You should become familiar with each of the terms shown below. On a sheet of paper write the numbers 1 through 8. Then write alongside each number the term that best matches each of the numbered definitions.

barter / checkbook dollars / commodity currency / currency dollars / dollar / legal tender / money / purchasing power

1. The amount of goods and services that money will buy at any given time.

2. A good such as tobacco, rice, lumber, fish, wool, or cattle that is generally acceptable to most people in a society in exchange for other goods.

3. Money in the form of checks.

4. The direct exchange of one good for another.

5. Anything that is generally accepted and commonly used as a means of payment for goods and services.

6. The monetary unit of the United States.

7. Money that must be accepted as payment for all debts, goods, and services.

8. The coins and paper money issued by the federal government.

Understanding Business

1. List the limitations of barter as a method for exchanging goods and services.

2. Explain how money serves as a standard of value.

3. Explain how money serves as a medium of exchange.

4. Why is money so important as a medium of exchange in our private enterprise economy?

5. Explain how money serves as a store of value.

6. List the characteristics money must have if it is to carry out its functions effectively.

7. What are two types of money used in the United States?

8. What is the most popular form of money?

9. What happens to the purchasing power of the dollar during a period of inflation? During a period of deflation?

10. What can you do to help achieve sound money?

Business Problems and Projects

1. To determine the percent of increase or decrease in the price of a good or service, divide the *difference* between the current price and the previous price. For example, suppose you had to pay $1.12 today for an item that cost $1 previously. Divide the difference between the two prices (.12) by the previous price ($1). The percent of increase would then be 12%. Compute the missing information on the following form.

	Item	Previous Price	Current Price	Amount of Increase (+) or Decrease (−)	Percent of Increase (+) or Decrease (−)
Example	a.	$1.00	$1.12	+ .12	+ 12%
	b.	.78	.82		
	c.	.43	.68		
	d.	1.14	.98		
	e.	2.98	3.36		
	f.	.50	.41		
	g.	27.50	31.40		
	h.	14.90	13.35		

2. Swap items such as those shown in the ads below often appear in newspapers. Read the ads and answer the questions that follow.

342 SWAPS

WILL SWAP EQUITY IN TRI-PLEX FOR WHAT HAVE YOU—CALL: 442-7800 or 434-5060.

CERAMIC tile job for car, truck, or boat & motor. 825-3020.

TRADE $12,900 Arrowhead lakeshore cabin for motor-home or ? 728-2300.

WILL trade ind. vacuum cleaner w/many att. brand new for upright vacuum w/ shag att. Jean 532-5379.

'72 RUPP snowmobile 1-yr. old for garden tractor or alu-minum boat & motor. Call 789-6434.

'70 MGB OD, $1650 or trade for cycle. Call 540-3232.

a. What term used in the chapter best describes this type of exchange?

b. What must one do or have to take part in this type of exchange?

c. Why do you think people would rather trade in this manner than simply sell their possessions for money?

d. Do you think this would be a good method for everyone to use in transacting business? Explain your answer.

Chapter 14

Banking in Our Economy

Objectives

After completing your study of this chapter, you will be able to do the following:

1. Understand the importance of commercial banks in the economy and describe the major services they provide.

2. Explain the difference between time and demand deposits.

3. Describe the organization of the Federal Reserve System and discuss its major functions.

4. Describe how banks protect their depositors' funds.

You have already studied how important money is to our private enterprise economy. But money alone does not guarantee a high level of business activity. Equally important are the various business firms that deal in money and credit; they are known as *financial institutions*. Some of the most common financial institutions are commercial banks, savings and loan associations, mutual savings banks, credit unions, small-loan companies, and insurance companies. Financial institutions serve as the links between savers and investors. Each type of financial institution differs from the others in several ways. In this chapter you will study about one type of financial institution—the commercial bank.

COMMERCIAL BANKS

Commercial banks are one of the major financial institutions in the United States. A *commercial bank* is a bank that offers a wide variety of financial services. Commercial banks, also called *full-service banks,* provide almost all the banking services offered by each of the more specialized financial institutions such as credit unions. Many people think of commercial banks as financial department stores because these banks offer so many services.

Suppose there were no commercial banks. How would day-to-day economic activities be affected?

Commercial banks are organized for the same reason as any other business enterprise—to make a profit for their owners. Ownership of commercial banks is similar to that of other businesses. They may be owned by an individual, by a partnership, or as a corporation. Because of the large amount of capital needed to start a bank, most are organized as corporations. And the stockholders are, of course, entitled to a share of any profits earned by the bank.

Authority to Carry on Banking Activities

Before a commercial bank can open for business, it must apply for and be granted a charter. Charters are granted by either the state or the federal government. A bank that has been given a charter by the federal government is called a *national bank,* and it must have the word *national* in its name. A *state bank* is a bank that is granted a charter by a state government. However, a state bank may or may not include the word *state* in its name. Since banks can be chartered by either the federal or state governments, the banking system in the United States is a dual banking system.

Why do you think banks are required to obtain a charter before they can open for business?

Approximately one-third of the nation's commercial banks are national banks. But they hold about 85 percent of the total amount of bank deposits. *Deposits* are sums of money left with a bank for safekeeping. In terms of deposits, state banks are generally smaller than national banks.

National banks are supervised by the Comptroller of the Currency in Washington, D.C. State banks, on the other hand, are supervised by the banking department of the state in which the bank is chartered. Additional supervision of banks and banking services is provided by other agencies. These agencies will be identified and discussed later in this chapter.

Major Services of Commercial Banks

Commercial banks offer three major kinds of services. They receive deposits, they transfer money payments made by check, and they make loans.

Receiving Deposits   Suppose you have some extra money that you decide you do not want to spend at this time. You want to put it away so you will have it when you need it. Where will you keep that money? You could put it under your mattress or hide it in a closet. You could even bury it in your backyard. But how safe would your money be if you chose to hide it in one of these places? One reason people deposit their money in banks is that banks provide a safe place to keep money.

In addition to safety, what are some other reasons why you might want to keep your money in a bank?

One of the services of commercial banks is receiving deposits. (Honeywell, Inc.)

Banks receive two kinds of deposits—demand deposits and time deposits. A deposit is called a *demand deposit* if the depositor has the right to withdraw the money at any time without giving prior notice to the bank. Demand deposits are also known as *checking accounts*. Withdrawals from a checking account are made by writing a check against funds in the checking account. (Checking accounts will be discussed in more detail in Chapter 15.)

Time deposits are deposits for which prior notice must be given before withdrawal or that must remain on deposit for a set period of time. Time deposits are also known as *savings accounts*. Although a notice of withdrawal is required for savings accounts, banks usually waive this rule in their day-to-day operations.

Why do you think banks might require that notice be given before the withdrawal of time deposits?

One important difference between demand deposits and time deposits is the ease with which money can be withdrawn from demand deposits. A second important difference is that interest may be paid on time deposits but not on demand deposits. *Interest* is the price paid by the bank to a depositor for the use of the depositor's money for a certain period of time. The rate of interest paid on time deposits usually depends on the period of time the money is on deposit; for example, one year, two years, four years, or more. Banks generally may not pay interest on demand deposits at present.

Transferring Money Payments Made by Check A second major service of commercial banks is transferring money payments made by check. Each day millions of people write millions of checks in payment of goods and services. A *check* is a written order

Commercial banks also make loans. (Chase Manhattan Bank)

for a commercial bank to pay a stated amount of money to a person or business. When the bank pays the amount of the check, it deducts the money from the balance of the checking account. It then transfers the money to the person or company named. For example, suppose you write a check to the Disco Record Center. Your check authorizes your bank to transfer to Disco Record Center the amount of money stated on your check.

Making Loans   A third major service of commercial banks is making loans. A *loan* is money advanced to a borrower based on his or her promise to repay the money plus interest at a later date.

Loans made by commercial banks are important for two reasons. First, banks charge borrowers interest for the use of their money. The interest charged on loans is the major source of income for banks. Second, bank loans help increase the production of goods and services.

Commercial banks make several types of loans. They make consumer loans, real estate loans, business loans, and agriculture loans. They may even make loans to the government. Loans provide additional purchasing power to people. In this way, money that might otherwise be idle—put away under a mattress or buried in a backyard—is put to work in the economy. This money in turn aids in increasing the production of goods and services and improving our standard of living.

What effects would there be on the economy if commercial banks were not allowed to make loans?

Where do banks get the money to make loans? They use the money that has been deposited by their customers in time deposits and demand deposits. This is possible because it is not likely that all deposits in a bank will be withdrawn at the same time. Generally, the total amount of deposits made on a given day will be about equal to the total amount of withdrawals. Therefore, commercial banks are required to keep in reserve an amount of money equal to only a small percentage of a bank's total deposits.

Other Services of Commercial Banks

Commercial banks offer several additional services. Among them are safe deposit boxes, trust services, and financial information.

Safe Deposit Boxes   Almost all commercial banks provide safe deposit boxes. *Safe deposit boxes* are metal containers kept under

Bank customers use safe deposit boxes to safeguard their valuables.
(Chase Manhattan Bank)

lock and key in a section of the bank's vault. These boxes are used by the bank's customers for the safekeeping of such valuable possessions as stocks and bonds, deeds, mortgages, insurance policies, jewelry, and contracts.

Safe deposit boxes are rented to depositors and customers for an annual fee. A safe deposit box may be rented by one person or by two or more persons. Each person must sign the rental agreement, and each one receives a key to the safe deposit box. The bank also has a separate key for each box. The box cannot be opened unless both the bank's key and a customer's key are used. Each time the customer asks for the box, his or her signature is checked with the signature on the rental agreement. Most banks have private rooms where the customer may take the safe deposit box to examine its contents or to add or remove items in complete privacy.

List the advantages for keeping valuable papers and jewelry in a safe deposit box rather than in your home. Would you put cash in a safe deposit box?

Trust Services   Commercial banks also provide trust services. A *trust* is an agreement by which an individual or corporation (known as a *trustee*) holds the title to property for the benefit of one or more persons. This is usually done under the terms of a will or other written agreement. Some of the trust functions performed are those of executor of estates and managers of trust funds. Trust services also include taking care of investments and guardianships for minors. Banks offering trust services can offer many helpful suggestions in handling one's money.

Financial Information   Banks are a valuable source of financial information. They can provide information and guidance on savings and investment plans. They can also advise you whether your financial condition is sound enough to afford making major purchases.

There is probably no one closer to the money problems of the people in the community than a bank. Banks are involved with money problems every day, and their business is to help people work out such problems.

THE FEDERAL RESERVE SYSTEM

It was said earlier that banks must apply for and be granted a charter to operate. The Comptroller of the Currency in Washington, D.C., supervises national banks. State banks are supervised by state banking departments. The regulation of commercial banks is also a concern of the Federal Reserve System. The *Federal Reserve System* serves as the central banking system of the United States. It works with the Treasury Department and other federal agencies to help establish money and banking conditions. The main function of the Federal Reserve System is to maintain the supply of paper money and bank checking deposits at a level that will aid in the economic growth of the country.

The Federal Reserve System consists of a Board of Governors and 12 Federal Reserve Banks. All national banks are automatically members of the Federal Reserve System. State banks may join the system if they meet certain requirements and purchase stock in the Federal Reserve Bank.

The 12 Federal Reserve Banks are different from commercial banks because they do not deal directly with the general public. Federal Reserve Banks are known as "bankers' banks" because they provide services to commercial banks similar to those that commercial banks provide their customers. Federal Reserve Banks assist commercial banks in the transfer of money payments made by check. They are a source of funds when commercial banks need to borrow money. And they are also a source of the coins and currency that commercial banks need to carry on their day-to-day business activities.

FEDERAL RESERVE DISTRICTS

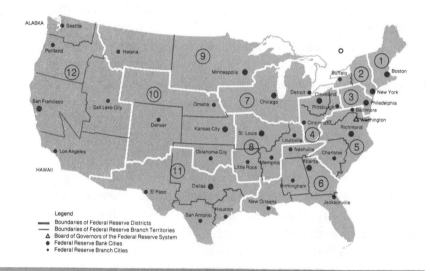

Legend
━━━ Boundaries of Federal Reserve Districts
──── Boundaries of Federal Reserve Branch Territories
△ Board of Governors of the Federal Reserve System
● Federal Reserve Bank Cities
• Federal Reserve Branch Cities

Check Clearing

Have you ever wondered how a check is processed and how it is returned to the person who wrote it? With so many different banks offering checking account services, how are checks actually paid by one bank to another?

When checks are written and remain within the community near the bank on which they are written, banks simply exchange the checks among themselves. However, more than half of all checks leave the local community and are presented for payment in cities or states other than where they are written. For example, suppose someone living in Minneapolis, Minnesota, sends a check drawn on a local bank to pay for a purchase made at a New York department store. The check is sent to the store in New York and is eventually presented to a New York City bank for payment. This sort of thing happens millions of times each day. It would not be practical for representatives of each of the approximately 15,000 commercial banks to meet each day to exchange their checks. Instead, commercial banks use the check-clearing services of the Federal Reserve System to transfer all those money payments that are made by checks.

The Federal Reserve Bank in a particular district accepts checks from the commercial banks in the district. It then sorts the checks according to banks and sends them to the banks upon which they are drawn. Therefore, the Federal Reserve System serves as a clearinghouse for the collection and distribution of checks for member banks.

THE ROUTE OF A CHECK

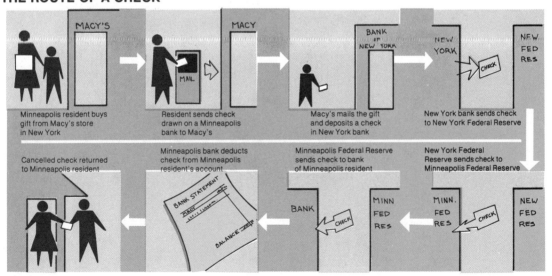

Minneapolis resident buys gift from Macy's store in New York

Resident sends check drawn on a Minneapolis bank to Macy's

Macy's mails the gift and deposits a check in New York bank

New York bank sends check to New York Federal Reserve

Cancelled check returned to Minneapolis resident

Minneapolis bank deducts check from Minneapolis resident's account

Minneapolis Federal Reserve sends check to bank of Minneapolis resident

New York Federal Reserve sends check to Minneapolis Federal Reserve

The illustration shows the route of a check from Minneapolis to New York City through the Federal Reserve Banks. Because clearing checks is one of the most important services provided by the Federal Reserve System, commercial banks and customers who have checking accounts in commercial banks benefit directly from the Federal Reserve System.

Controlling the Money and Credit Supply

The Federal Reserve System regulates both the supply of money and credit in the economy. This is done by changing the cash reserve requirements of member banks. It is also done by changing the interest rate charged on loans to member banks. A guideline that the government uses to regulate the credit and money supply is called a *monetary policy.*

Commercial banks must keep a certain percentage of their deposits on reserve with the Federal Reserve Bank in their district. By changing the amount of reserve required, the Federal Reserve System controls the amount of loans member banks can make. An

Federal Reserve Banks like this one in Minneapolis act as clearing houses for checks. (Federal Reserve System)

increase in the reserve requirements means that a bank must keep more cash reserve on hand. The bank will then not be able to lend so much money. On the other hand, a decrease in the reserve requirement will increase the amount available for loans.

A change in the interest rate paid by commercial banks for loans from the Federal Reserve Banks will also affect the rate that commercial banks charge their customers for loans. This in turn will affect the amount of borrowing that takes place. An increase in interest rates will decrease borrowing; a decrease in interest rates will increase borrowing.

Too much credit and too large a money supply in the economy can lead to inflation. A tightening of credit and too small a money supply, however, can lead to deflation and to a possible decrease in economic activity.

PROTECTING DEPOSITORS' FUNDS

It was mentioned earlier that one reason people deposit their money in banks is because banks are safe. But how safe is money in a bank? One of the major concerns of banks is the safety of their depositors' money. Banks do several things to provide this safety. Officers and employees of banks are chosen with great care. Many banks, especially in large cities, have armed guards on duty during banking hours. Television security systems are also used.

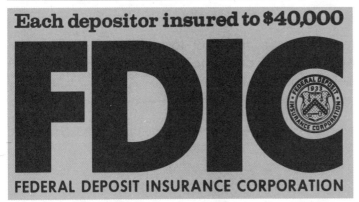

Each depositor insured to $40,000

FDIC

FEDERAL DEPOSIT INSURANCE CORPORATION

This symbol insures that savings in member banks are secure.

In addition to these safety devices, bank deposits are insured. Banks carry several types of insurance. Among them are insurance policies to protect against loss of money from theft, fire, or bookkeeping error. Also, deposits are protected in case a bank can no longer operate. The *Federal Deposit Insurance Corporation* (FDIC) is a government corporation that insures the deposits of member banks. All national banks and state banks that are members of the Federal Reserve System are required by law to be members of the FDIC.

The Federal Deposit Insurance Corporation (FDIC) has three major purposes:

1. It protects depositors, especially small depositors, against loss of money.

2. It protects banks and the economic system against the results of any actual or threatened withdrawals of currency from the banking system.

3. It improves the quality of bank supervision.

Deposits in banks are also protected through regular bank examinations. These examinations may be conducted by the Federal Reserve Bank or by the FDIC. They also may be undertaken by the Comptroller of the Currency, by clearinghouse associations, and by state bank examiners. To save time and effort, these various agencies often work together in carrying out a bank examination.

Why is it important to a depositor to know that deposits are insured? Why do you think commercial banks take so much effort to protect their depositors' funds?

Learning Activities

Increasing Your Business Vocabulary

You should become familiar with each of the terms shown below. On a sheet of paper write the numbers 1 through 15. Then write alongside each number the term that best matches each of the numbered definitions.

check / commercial bank / demand deposit / deposits / Federal Deposit Insurance Corporation (FDIC) / Federal Reserve System / financial institutions / interest / loan / monetary policy / national banks / safe deposit boxes / state banks / time deposits / trust

1. Business firms that deal in money and credit.

2. A bank that offers a wide variety of financial services.

3. Banks chartered by the federal government.

4. Deposits for which prior notice must be given before withdrawal or that must remain on deposit for a set period of time.

5. Money advanced to a borrower based on his or her promise to repay the money plus interest at a later date.

6. A government corporation that insures the deposits of its member banks.

7. Sums of money left with a bank for safekeeping.

8. Commercial banks chartered by state governments.

9. A written order for a commercial bank to pay a stated amount of money to a person or business.

10. Serves as the central banking system of the United States.

11. Deposits which the depositor has the right to withdraw at any time without giving prior notice to the bank.

12. Metal containers kept under lock and key in a section of the bank's vault.

13. An agreement by which the title to property is held for the benefit of others.

14. A guideline that regulates the supply of money and credit.

15. The price paid by the bank for the use of depositor's money.

Understanding Business

1. Why is the United States said to have a dual banking system?

2. What are the three major services of commercial banks?

3. What are some of the differences between time deposits and demand deposits?

4. Explain why the loan services of commercial banks are so important.

5. List the services provided to commercial banks by the Federal Reserve System.

6. Why is check clearing such an important function of the Federal Reserve System?

7. How does a change in the reserve requirement affect the credit and money supply?

8. How does a change in interest rates affect borrowing?

9. How do banks protect their depositors' funds?

10. What are the three major purposes of the Federal Deposit Insurance Corporation?

Business Problems and Projects

1. Mary Wilson was visiting her grandparents in a neighboring town. During the visit, Mary discovered that they kept large sums of money hidden in their home. She asked them why they did not put their money in a bank. Her grandfather replied that he did not trust banks and that he would rather have his money close at hand where he could get it quickly if he needed it. Besides, her grandfather did not see any difference between keeping his money at home or in a bank.

    a. What reasons might Mary's grandfather give for not putting his money in a bank?

    b. What steps have been taken to make banks a safe place to keep money?

    c. Is it true that, other than the safety factor, there is no difference between hiding your money in your home and putting it in a bank?

    d. How might Mary's grandfather be able to get at his money quickly and still have the safety of the bank?

    e. If you were Mary, what arguments would you use to convince your grandparents to put their money in a bank rather than to hide it in the house?

2. In this chapter you studied two ways by which the Federal Reserve System can control the money and credit supply.

    a. How would these tools be used in a period of inflation? What would be the effect?

    b. How would these tools be used in a period of recession? What would be the effect?

3. The table below shows the number of all banks chartered to do business in the United States in 1970 and 1974. Study the table and answer the questions that follow.

COMMERCIAL BANKS BY CLASS OF BANK: 1970 AND 1974
(money figures in billions of dollars)

Class of Bank	Banks		Demand Deposits		Time Deposits	
	1970	1974	1970	1974	1970	1974
All banks	13,686	14,936	247.9	315.8	233.9	432.3
National	4,621	4,710	145.1	180.3	138.6	250.7
State member	1,147	1,072	58.5	68.1	43.0	76.7
Insured						
nonmember	7,735	8,438	42.5	64.3	51.5	101.2
Noninsured	184	237	1.7	3.0	.9	3.7

Source: *Statistical Abstract of the United States.*

a. How many more banks were there in 1974 than in 1970?

b. Were there more national banks or state member banks in 1974? How many more?

c. Which classification of banks had the largest amount of time deposits and demand deposits?

d. Did the number of banks for any classification decrease from 1970 to 1974? If so, which one(s)?

e. Which classification had the fewest banks in 1974? What percent of all banks was this?

Chapter 15

Using a Checking Account

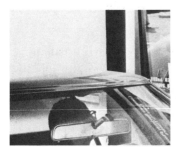

Objectives

After completing your study of this chapter, you will be able to do the following:

1. List the advantages of using a checking account.

2. Describe the steps in opening a checking account.

3. Describe the two types of checking accounts and state under what conditions each should be used.

4. Describe the major kinds of check endorsements and when each should be used.

In this chapter you will learn how to open and use a checking account and how to keep accurate records of the checks you write. You also will learn how to transfer ownership of check through a procedure called endorsing.

Approximately 30 billion checks are issued in the United States each year. This represents a transfer of funds of more than $5 trillion. Clearly, checks represent a major medium of exchange in this country.

ADVANTAGES OF A CHECKING ACCOUNT

A person could carry on daily business activities without using a checking account. However, checking accounts offer many advantages to those who use them. Among these are safety, convenience, recordkeeping, and proof of payment.

Safety for Your Money

Checks eliminate the need for keeping large amounts of currency on hand to cover all expenses. What would happen if you lost your currency or if it was destroyed or stolen? Lost or stolen currency is hardly ever replaced. And destroyed currency is very difficult to replace. When a check is lost, stolen or destroyed, all you have to do is write another.

Convenience in Making Payments

Using checks to pay bills is much more convenient than using cash. One reason is that checks can be sent safely through the mail. If you send cash through the mail, there is a chance it could be lost or stolen. Anyone finding it could use it. If a check is lost in the mail, you simply replace it. Moreover, using checks also saves time. You don't have to go to the place of business to make a payment.

Money Management

A checking account aids money management. It provides a record of where and how money has been spent. It shows how much money is being spent on certain goods and services. And it shows you on what the money is being spent. The use of a checking account can also help save money. Usually, you will stop to consider a purchase more carefully if you have to write a check than if you use credit or pay cash.

Proof of Payment

When you pay a bill, you should always be sure to get a receipt as proof of payment. Checking accounts automatically provide such proof. After a bank makes payment on a check, it returns the canceled check to the person who wrote it. A *canceled check* is a check that has been paid by the bank and charged against the depositor's account. In addition to the information recorded on the check when it was written, a canceled check also shows the date of payment and the bank name or number. It serves, therefore, as a legal receipt.

Why is it important to get a receipt when you pay a bill?

SELECTING A BANK

There is often more than one bank in a community. Each of these banks offers similar checking account services. When you decide to

Drive-in teller services allow customers to bank from their cars. (Maria Karras)

use the checking account services of a commercial bank, which bank should you choose?

The bank you choose should be convenient to get to. Most people select a bank that is located near their homes or their places of work. They want to be able to get to the bank easily and quickly to make deposits or to cash a check.

Some banks, however, provide a service called banking by mail. Using this service, customers can do some of their banking through the mail. There are a number of other services that banks offer which you might consider when you select a bank.

Walk-up or Drive-up Tellers

These services permit customers either to walk up to or drive up to a special teller window outside the bank. This saves time because customers do not have to get out of their cars or go inside the bank.

Banking Hours

Some banks now open early in the morning and stay open later in the day. These hours are more convenient for people who find it difficult to get to a bank during their working hours.

Ready Reserve Accounts

Some banks offer a special checking account service. With this service, the bank will place in a customer's account enough funds to cover checks being written against it. The amount of funds is limited by the bank. In a sense, this is a form of a loan that goes into effect when the balance of a checking account is low. The customer is charged a fee for this service.

Automatic Payment of Bills

Some banks will help customers pay their bills automatically. The bank deducts a certain amount of money from the customer's account each month and pays certain regular bills such as gas, electric, or telephone bills.

Because there may be several commercial banks in a community, it is important that you select a bank that offers the type of service that meets your needs. And for safety, be sure that the bank is insured by the Federal Deposit Insurance Corporation. Whatever bank you choose, take the time to become familiar with its regulations and practices.

Why is it important for a depositor to be familiar with a bank's regulations and practices?

SELECTING A CHECKING ACCOUNT

Commercial banks offer two types of checking accounts: regular checking accounts and special checking accounts. The type you select should depend on how much you keep in the account and how often you use the account.

Regular Checking Account

A regular checking account is best if you expect to write a large number of checks each month. The bank may charge a fee for the checking account services it performs. This fee is called a *service charge*. The amount of the service charge and the way it is determined will vary from bank to bank.

With a regular checking account, some banks charge a minimum service charge each month plus an extra charge for each check written. Some banks may not charge a service charge at all if a certain minimum balance is maintained. And some banks offer checking account services at no cost whatsoever.

Table 15-1 shows how one bank in a large metropolitan area determines the amount of service charges on regular checking accounts.

TABLE 15-1   SERVICE CHARGES ON REGULAR CHECKING ACCOUNTS

If Balance During Month Is	Your Monthly Charge Is
Below $100.00	$3.00
Between $100.00 to $200.00	$2.00
Between $200.00 to $300.00	$1.00
Over $300.00	No charge

Special Checking Account

A special checking account is best if you do not expect to write a large number of checks. This type of checking account is also preferred when you may want to keep only a small balance in your checking account—just enough to cover the few payments to be made each month.

With a special checking account, there is usually no service charge. Instead, the bank charges you for each check that you write. This may be done in one of two ways. You may have to purchase a book of checks for perhaps 10 or 15 cents per check. Or the bank may provide the book of checks free and then charge you each time you use one.

You can see that just as you shop for the best price in other goods and services, you should also shop for the right bank. It is important that the bank you choose offers the services that meet your personal needs.

OPENING A CHECKING ACCOUNT

Once you have decided on a bank, you are ready to open a checking account. Go to the "New Accounts" section of the bank and tell the clerk you want to open a checking account. The clerk will help you decide whether you should choose a special or regular checking account. Perhaps you may want to open a joint checking account. A *joint checking account* is an account in the names of two or more persons. Any of the individuals may write checks on the account and may withdraw money from the account as well. Joint accounts are generally used by husbands and wives, or other members of a family who may want to use the same checking account.

Why might a husband and wife choose to have a joint checking account rather than two individual accounts? What problems might this present?

Completing a Signature Card

When you open a checking account, you sign an agreement with your bank. This agreement, called a *signature card*, serves as the bank's record of the way your checks will be signed. An example of an individual checking account signature card is shown in the illustration. It explains the mutual obligations of both you and the

NAME OF ACCOUNT

Earl F. Storey

Number

TO: FIRST STATE BANK OF LAKEVILLE

THE UNDERSIGNED AGREE(S) TO THE CONDITIONS PRINTED ON THE REVERSE SIDE HEREOF FOR THE TRANSACTION OF BUSINESS WITH YOU FOR THE ACCOUNT NAMED ABOVE.

AUTHORIZED SIGNATURES:

Depositor's Signature *Earl F. Storey*

Signature of Attorney-in-Fact
as per attached Power of Attorney

TYPE OF ACCOUNT:

☑ Personal   Soc. Sec. No.   465-36-7291

☐ Business   Emp. Fed. I.D. No.

☐ _____   Fed. I.D. No.

INDIVIDUAL CHECKING ACCOUNT

A signature card.

bank. The card contains personal information such as your name, home address and telephone number, business address and telephone number, and social security number.

One of the most important items on this card is your signature. It is used for identification. The bank keeps the signature card on hand for easy reference when checking signatures on checks. You should, therefore, always sign each check in the same way you signed your signature card.

Why do you think banks honor only checks on which the signature is exactly as it appears on the signature card?

Making a Deposit

After completing a signature card, you must, of course, make a deposit to the account before you can begin writing checks. The new accounts clerk will assist you in making this first deposit. Each time you deposit money in your checking account the method will be the same.

The first step in making a deposit is to complete a deposit ticket. A *deposit ticket,* also called a *deposit slip,* is a form on which the items to be credited to the account are listed. A deposit ticket should show the date of the deposit; the name, address, and account number of the account holder; the items deposited; and the total amount of the deposit.

Study the deposit ticket shown. Note that this is a personalized deposit ticket. The name, address, and account number of the account holder are preprinted on it. If you do not have a personalized deposit ticket, remember to fill in your account number in the correct space.

Split Deposit   There may be times when you need cash for your day-to-day activities. Instead of depositing everything into your checking account, you may want to keep part of your deposit in cash. To do this, enter the amount of cash you want on the line "Less Cash Received." Subtract this amount of cash from the subtotal to determine the total deposit. You may also have to sign the deposit ticket in the presence of a bank official.

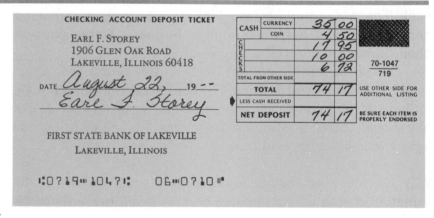

A deposit slip.

Obtaining a Checkbook

When you open a checking account, you will receive a checkbook. A *checkbook* is a book of blank checks used by a depositor to withdraw funds on deposit in his or her checking account. Most banks recommend the use of personalized checks. A *personalized check* is one that has the account holder's name, address, and account number preprinted on it. When you receive your checkbook, make sure that all the preprinted information is correct.

Checkbooks often contain deposit tickets. In addition, there are places in the checkbook to record deposits, amounts of the checks written, and the current balance. These records are kept on check stubs or in a check register.

ENDORSING CHECKS

When you receive a check that is payable to you, you can choose to do one of three things: cash it (receive the money yourself); deposit it to your account; or order it paid to another person. Before taking any of these actions, you must first endorse the check. To *endorse* a check is to sign one's name on the back of a check. When you endorse a check, you become responsible for payment of the check. Suppose you endorse a check and cash it at your bank. Several days later your bank notifies you that the check has been returned because of lack of funds in the account on which it is drawn. You will have to refund the money to your bank. Having endorsed the check, you are responsible for any funds paid on it.

Why do you think you are liable for payment of a check once you endorse it?

There are three major kinds of check endorsements: blank, special, and restrictive. Each has a specific use. Study the descriptions and the examples that explain the differences.

Blank Endorsements

A *blank endorsement* is one that includes only the signature of the endorser. The *endorser* is the person to whom the check is made payable. Sometimes checks are made payable to more than one person. In such cases, each person must endorse the check. A check should not be endorsed until you are actually ready to cash it or deposit it. If a check with a blank endorsement is lost or stolen, anyone can cash it after adding his or her own signature.

Special Endorsement

A *special endorsement* is one that specifies the party to whom the endorser is giving title. Another name for the special endorsement is a *full endorsement.* This type of endorsement is used when a check is made out to you and you, in turn, want to forward it to

Allen B. Bradley

Pay to the order of
Jerry D. Robertson
Allen B. Bradley

Pay to the order of
First State Bank
For deposit only
Allen B. Bradley

Blank endorsement   Special endorsement   Restrictive endorsement

someone else. You write "Pay to the order of (insert the name of person to receive the check)" and sign your name beneath it. The person receiving the check then has to sign the check in order to collect or transfer it.

Restrictive Endorsement

A *restrictive endorsement* specifies the purpose for which the check is being endorsed. It means that the check cannot be further negotiated. The restrictive endorsement is most commonly used when sending checks by mail for deposit. You write "Pay to the order of (name of bank) for deposit only" and sign your name. This guarantees that if the check is lost in the mail it cannot be cashed by anyone else, because it can only be deposited in your account.

Learning Activities

Increasing Your Business Vocabulary

You should become familiar with each of the terms shown below. On a sheet of paper write the numbers 1 through 10. Then write alongside each number the term that best matches each of the numbered definitions.

blank endorsement / canceled checks / checkbook / deposit ticket / endorse / joint checking account / personalized check / restrictive endorsement / signature card / special endorsement

1. An account in the names of two or more persons.
2. An endorsement that includes only the signature of the endorser.
3. An endorsement that specifies the purpose for which the check is being endorsed.
4. To sign one's name on the back of a check.
5. A form on which items to be credited to a checking account are listed.
6. An agreement signed by the depositor and serving as the bank's record of the way the checks will be signed.
7. An endorsement that specifies the party to whom the endorser is giving title.
8. Checks that have been paid by the bank and charged against the depositor's account.
9. A book of blank checks used by a depositor to withdraw funds on deposit in his or her checking account.
10. A check that shows the account holder's name, address, and account number.

Understanding Business

1. List three advantages of using a checking account.
2. List several factors to consider when selecting a bank.
3. When would you choose to use a regular checking account? A special checking account?
4. Why are canceled checks important?
5. What is one purpose of the signature card?
6. What are the most important items of information on a personalized deposit ticket?
7. What responsibility do you accept when you endorse a check?
8. Who can cash a check with a blank endorsement?
9. When is a special endorsement used?
10. When is the restrictive endorsement used.

Business Problems and Projects

1. Read the newspaper article shown below and answer the questions that follow.

CHECKLESS PAYDAY SERVICE OFFERED BY 77 LOCAL BANKS

Seventy-seven banks in the greater Chicago area have joined a system that allows them to offer business customers the opportunity to deposit their payroll checks automatically in employees' checking accounts.

The system, called APEX (Automated Payments Exchange) will be available starting January 1 to businesses that wish to offer "checkless payday" service to their employees.

Employees would be given the choice of whether they wanted to have their payroll checks automatically deposited in their checking accounts or to continue to receive a paycheck.

A company's bank would make deposits for employees who have accounts in that bank, then notify the clearinghouse about money to be deposited in those employees' accounts in other banks. The clearinghouse would tell the other banks about the deposits. Companies would not be required to have accounts in each bank where an employee had an account.

Instead of a check, the employee would get a pay slip showing gross earnings, any deductions and the net or take-home pay deposited to his or her account.

Initially, the only service offered through the APEX system will be automatic payroll deposits, but it is expected that soon banks may offer to participants automatic payments of recurring bills such as utilities, automobile, and mortgage payments.

a. What does the system allow business customers to do?

b. How many banks are taking part in the system?

c. What is the system called?

d. Who will run the system?

e. Will employees of a business firm have a choice as to whether their payroll checks will be deposited automatically? Explain your answer.

f. What will the employees who use the system receive in place of a paycheck?

g. What future services may this system provide?

h. Will the number of personal checks decrease or increase if the system becomes widespread? Explain your answer.

2. Randy Willow has the following checks to deposit in his checking account, 716–14739, in the Irondale National Bank. He wants to keep $20 in cash.

Irondale National Bank, 7–16, $33.00

Newtown Trust Company, 106–27, $21.90

Lewiston State Bank, 21–86, $47.33

First State Bank of Lockport, 73–113, $27.86

Coleman Bank and Trust, 81–67, $41.19

Using a form similar to that on p. 214, prepare a deposit slip for Randy.

3. On forms similar to the ones shown below, write endorsements on checks made out to you for each of the following situations:

a. Blank endorsement

b. Special endorsement to Jeanette Durso

c. Restrictive endorsement for deposit in the Canyon City National Bank

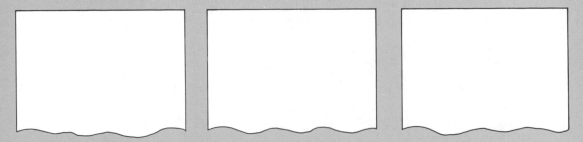

Chapter 16

Making Payments by Check

EARL F. STOREY
1906 GLEN OAK R(D
LAKEVILLE, ILLINO 60418

September 30, 19 —

70-1047
719

PAY TO THE
ORDER OF *Lakeville Bike Shop* — $27 60/100

Twenty-seven and 60/100 —

270

DOLLARS

Objectives

After completing your study of this chapter, you will be able to do the following:

1. Identify the parts of a check and the information contained within each part.

2. Write checks correctly and keep accurate checking account records.

3. Make a stop payment order on a lost or stolen check that you have written.

4. Reconcile a checkbook balance with a bank statement.

When you open a checking account at a commercial bank, you will be joining millions of people all over the United States who use checks as a way of making payments.

In this chapter, you will learn how to write checks correctly and how to keep accurate checking account records. You will also learn to balance your checking account with a bank statement. Knowing how to maintain accurate checking account records will help you become a better manager of your funds.

WRITING CHECKS

Once you have deposited money in your checking account, you can begin writing checks. The correct procedure for writing a check consists of two parts: filling in the check stub or register and filling in the check.

Filling in the Stub or Register

Before writing a check, complete the check stub or register. Enter the check number, the date, the name of the person or company to receive the check, and the amount.

Why should you complete the check stub or check register *before* you write the check?

Most check stubs and registers also provide space to record the reason for writing a check. Recording the reason for writing a check helps you to keep better records and assists you in your money management. You should also keep a running balance of your account by adding the amount of each deposit as it is made and by subtracting the amount of each check as it is written. In this way, you will always know your current checkbook balance. A current balance helps you avoid overdrawing your account.

Filling in the Check

After filling in the check stub or register, you are now ready to write the check. Refer to the illustration of a personalized check as you study the proper procedure for writing checks. Remember, a personalized check is one that has the account holder's name, address, and account number preprinted on it. The account

CHECK NO.	DATE	CHECKS ISSUED TO OR DESCRIPTION OF DEPOSIT	(−) AMOUNT OF CHECK		√ T	(−) CHECK FEE (IF ANY)	(+) AMOUNT OF DEPOSIT	BALANCE	
								507	86
250	2/1	Ed's Auto Repair	34	70	√			473	16
251	2/6	Kelsey Dept. Store	15	60	√			457	56
	2/8	Deposit					100 00	557	56
252	2/13	Town Market	37	23				520	33

PLEASE BE SURE TO **DEDUCT** ANY PER CHECK CHARGES OR SERVICE CHARGES THAT MAY APPLY TO YOUR ACCOUNT

$ 34 70/100 Feb. 2, 19 —

250   Tax Item ✓

To Ed's Auto Repair

BAL. FWD.	507	86
AMT. DEPOSITED	—	00
TOTAL	507	86
AMT. THIS CHECK	34	70
TOTAL	473	16
MISCELLANEOUS DEDUCTION	—	00
BAL. CAR'D. FWD.	473	16

Checks can be recorded either in check stubs or in check registers.

number (lower left corner) is printed with magnetic ink. This speeds up the bank's sorting and clearing procedure. Special machines read the magnetic ink characters and sort them by district and bank branch. In addition to the above information, a personalized check may include such other items as the account holder's phone number, driver's license number, and photograph.

Why might people choose to have personal identification information printed on their checks?

Follow these steps in filling out a check:

1. Date the check the day you write it. Checks are legal even if they are written on a Sunday or a holiday. You should avoid postdating a check. A *postdated check* is a check dated for a future date. Such a check cannot be paid by the bank if it should be presented for payment before the date shown on it.

2. Write the name of the payee. The *payee* is the person or company to whom a check is made out. Write the payee's name after the words "Pay to the order of." Be sure that the name of the person or company is correctly spelled.

3. Write the amount of the check. The amount is written twice, once in figures and once in words. This is to prevent someone from changing the amount of the check. Where the amount is written in figures, start the figures close to the dollar sign.

EARL F. STOREY
1906 GLEN OAK ROAD
LAKEVILLE, ILLINOIS 60418

270

September 30 19 —

70-1047
719

PAY TO THE
ORDER OF *Lakeville Bike Shop* $ 27 60/100

Twenty-seven and 60/100 DOLLARS

THE FIRST STATE BANK OF LAKEVILLE
LAKEVILLE, ILLINOIS

Earl F. Storey

MEMO *for used bike*

⑈0719⑈1047   06⑈0710

A personalized check.

Write the cents as a fraction in somewhat smaller figures than those used for the dollar amounts. Do not leave any space between the dollar sign and the figures or between the dollar figures and the cents figure. If there is too much space, a dishonest person could insert additional figures that would raise the amount of the check.

4. Write the amount in words on the line provided, starting as close to the left edge as possible. Each word in the dollar amount is spelled out. Again, the cents are written as fractions. Draw a line from the fraction to the word "Dollars."

A check may also be written for amounts less than one dollar. In such cases, circle the amount written as a fraction and spell out the amount written on the dollar line. The amount may be written as follows:

19

PAY TO THE
ORDER OF *Coupon Sales, Inc.* $ ⟨72 ¢⟩

Only seventy-two cents DOLLARS

The amount written in figures and the amount written in words must be the same on all checks. If there is a difference, the bank will accept the amount written in words. However, when the difference is large, the bank may refuse the check.

When there is a difference between the amount in figures and the amount written in words, the bank will accept the amount written in words. Why do you think this is so?

5. Sign the check. Be sure to use the same signature you used on the signature card. The person who signs the check is called the *payer*

   When you write a check, always write legibly and in ink. All information on a check may be typewritten except for your signature. You must *write* your name on each check, and it must be written exactly as it appears on the signature card.

Reducing Check Writing Problems

In addition to the suggestions mentioned above, there are other steps you can take to reduce problems in writing checks.

1. Be sure to have enough funds in your checking account to cover the amount of any checks you write.

2. Always use numbered checks, and use the checks in their numbered sequence. This is particularly important with checkbooks that have separate check registers.

3. Record every check. If you tear checks from your checkbook and carry them apart from the check stubs or register, remember to note the check number and amount so that the information can be recorded properly later.

4. Tear up checks on which you make mistakes. Be sure to record the check number and the word "void" in the check stub or register. Do not make erasures on the check. Most often, checks with erasures will be refused.

5. Do not write checks in pencil.

Remember to write your name exactly as it
appears on your signature card.
(Harold M. Lambert)

6. Do not sign an incomplete or blank check.

7. Keep blank checks in a safe place. Notify your bank if they are
    lost or stolen.

8. Do not use someone else's personalized check blanks. Re-
    member that these items are coded with magnetic characters
    which can be read by machines. If, for example, you use
    someone else's personalized deposit tickets, the machine may
    read the preprinted code and deposit your money in the other
    person's account.

9. Make a check payable to cash when you are ready to use it.

INSUFFICIENT FUNDS

Sometimes a depositor writes a check for more than the balance on
deposit. In such cases, it may be returned to the bank from which it
came or to the person to whom it was made out. The returned
check will be marked "Insufficient Funds." *Insufficient funds* is a
term stamped on checks to indicate that there is not enough

money in the checking account to cover the amount of a check. *NSF,* an abbreviation for "Not Sufficient Funds," is sometimes used instead. Most banks charge a fee for any check that is returned due to insufficient funds.

In some instances the bank may choose to pay a check for a good customer rather than to mark it "Insufficient Funds" and return it unpaid. When the bank honors checks for more than the balance on deposit in the account, the account is considered to be an *overdrawn account*. Interest is usually charged on overdrawn accounts. This situation is similar to taking out a loan from the bank for which interest must be paid for the use of someone else's money.

Overdrawn accounts and checks returned because of insufficient funds affect your good credit rating. Therefore, care should be taken to avoid overdrawing a checking account.

Do you think it is fair for a bank to charge interest on an overdrawn account or to charge a fee for checks returned because of insufficient funds? Give reasons for your answer.

STOPPING PAYMENT ON CHECKS

One of the advantages of using a checking account is that checks are safer to carry and use than money. When a check is lost or stolen, it is easier to replace than currency. In the event you lose a check, place a stop payment order on it immediately. A *stop payment order* is a form requesting that your bank not pay a specific check that you have written. You are informing the bank, either in writing or by telephone, that the check was lost or stolen. Nevertheless, you must still go to the bank and sign the stop payment order. When filling out the form you need to know the number of the check, the name of the person or company to whom the check was made payable, and the amount. You will also have to give the reason for stopping payment. If the check is then presented for payment, the bank can refuse to pay it and will return it to the person presenting it for payment.

ACCOUNT NO.		ACCOUNT TITLE				DATE OF THIS ORDER
06-0710		EARL F. STOREY				12/20/--
DESCRIPTION OF ITEM (MUST BE EXACT)	AMOUNT	☑ CHECK ☐ PREAUTHORIZED AUTOMATIC CREDIT ☐ PREARRANGED AUTOMATIC DEBIT				
	CHECK DATE 12/12/--	CHECK NO. 125	CHECK SIGNED BY Earl F. Storey			
	CHECK PAYABLE TO Ann and Fred Soares					
	ENTRY DATE 12/20/-	PREAUTHORIZED ENTRY ORIGINATED BY Main Office				

REASON FOR STOP PAYMENT OR ENTRY

Check lost in mail

☑ NEW ORDER   ☐ RENEWAL

	TELEPHONE
HOME	BUSINESS
395-5292	363-8600

TO: All offices

Please do not pay from or enter to undersigned's account the above item/entry. Undersigned will indemnify and hold harmless said Bank from all costs and liabilities said Bank incurs from honoring this request. **THIS STOP PAYMENT ORDER WILL BE CANCELLED BY THE BANK SIX MONTHS AFTER RECEIPT UNLESS RENEWED IN WRITING.**

SIGNATURE OF DEPOSITOR X   Earl F. Storey

DATE RECEIVED 12/21/--	TIME RECEIVED 9:05 a.m.	SERVICE CHARGE $	☐ RECEIVED CASH ☑ DEBIT CHECKING ACCOUNT	RECEIVED BY C. D. Moore
TELLER'S RECORDS DATE 12/21/--	TIME RECEIVED 3:45 PM	ENTRY NOTICE TO MASTER RECORD PREPARED BY Alicia Mereus DATE 12/22/--		RENEWAL DATE

ORDER TO STOP PAYMENT OR ENTRY
FIRST STATE BANK OF LAKEVILLE

A stop payment order.

The most common reason for stopping payment on a check is that a check has been lost on the way to the payee. Once the stop payment order is in effect, another check can be issued in its place. A small service fee is usually charged by the bank for this service.

Why do you think it is important to stop payment on a check that has been lost or stolen?

YOUR BANK STATEMENT

In using checking account services, it is important that you keep your account up to date, that you record all deposits made, that you record all checks written, and that your account always has sufficient funds to cover the checks that you write.

The bank helps you maintain your checking account records by sending you a report of all activities in your checking account. This report is called a *bank statement*. There are two types of bank statements: a detailed statement and an abbreviated statement.

FIRST STATE BANK OF LAKEVILLE

Checking Account Statement

ACCT 06-0710
DATE 02-12----
PAGE 1

Earl F. Storey
1906 Glen Oak Road
Lakeville, IL 60418

BALANCE FORWARD	NO. OF CHECKS	TOTAL CHECK AMOUNT	NO. OF DEPOSIT	TOTAL DEPOSIT AMOUNT	SERVICE CHARGE	BALANCE THIS STATEMENT
388.98	9	950.13	3	850.00	1.00	287.85

CHECKS AND OTHER DEBITS		DEPOSITS AND OTHER CREDITS	DATE	BALANCE
244	48.00		1/13	340.09
245	142.14		1/15	198.84
246	105.58		1/18	93.26
		500.00	1/26	593.26
247	450.00		1/27	143.26
248	17.13		1/28	126.13
249	30.00		1/29	96.13
250	7.60		1/30	88.53
		50.00	1/30	138.53
251	6.44		2/02	132.09
		300.00	2/05	432.09
252	143.24		2/10	288.85
	1.00 SC		2/11	287.85

PLEASE EXAMINE AT ONCE.
IF NO ERRORS ARE REPORTED
WITHIN 10 DAYS, THE ACCOUNT WILL
BE CONSIDERED CORRECT.
PLEASE ADVISE US
IN WRITING OF ANY CHANGE
IN YOUR ADDRESS.

KEY TO SYMBOLS

AD – AUTOMATIC DEPOSIT
AP – AUTOMATIC PAYMENT
AR – AUTOMATIC REVERSAL
CB – CHARGE BACK
CC – CERTIFIED CHECK
CM – CREDIT MEMO
CO – CHARGE OFF

DM – DEBIT MEMO
EC – ERROR CORRECTED
OD – OVERDRAWN
RC – RETURN CHECK CHARGE
RT – RETURN ITEM
SC – SERVICE CHARGE

A bank statement.

Holders of regular checking accounts usually receive a bank statement each month. With a special checking account, you may receive a bank statement once every three months.

Study the detailed statement shown above. Note that this statement shows every checking account activity for the period of the statement. It indicates the account name and number as well as the date on which the statement was issued. In addition, each check paid is listed by date of payment, and each deposit is listed by date of deposit. Many banks also list the check numbers. Any service or miscellaneous charges are itemized. Note that a new balance is computed at the end of each day on which either checks were paid or deposits were made. At the top, the total number of checks paid and deposits made is recorded. In addition, the account balances at the beginning and end of the period are shown.

An abbreviated, or short, statement includes some of the information stated above. However, each check and deposit is not listed separately. Instead, total amounts of checks and deposits are shown for the period of the statement.

Given a choice, would you choose a bank that provides a detailed bank statement or one that provides an abbreviated bank statement? Why?

RECONCILING YOUR CHECKING ACCOUNT

Usually, the balance in your bank statement will not be equal to the balance in your checkbook. Some of your checks, as well as some deposits sent by mail, may not have been received by the bank at the time the statement was prepared. You may have forgotten to record a service charge. Or either you or the bank may have made an error.

After you receive your bank statement, you should first check the statement and then reconcile it with the balance in your checkbook. The term *reconcile* means to bring into agreement. When you reconcile your checking account, you are bringing the balance on the statement into agreement with the balance in the checkbook.

Checking Your Bank Statement

Along with the bank statement, the bank returns all the canceled checks it has paid during the period. You can determine which of your checks and deposits have been recorded by the bank by following these steps:

1. Examine all canceled checks to see that they belong to you and that you have written them.

2. Arrange the checks in numerical order by check number. This makes it easier for you to work with them.

3. Compare each canceled check with the check stub or register. Check them off as you go through them. Make a note of all outstanding checks. *Outstanding checks* are checks written by you that have not yet been paid by the bank. These checks will not have been returned by the bank.

4. Compare the deposits shown on the statement with those recorded in your checkbook. Make a note of all deposits that have not been recorded by the bank.

Using a Bank Reconciliation Statement

On the back of most statements there is a form, called the *bank reconciliation statement*. This form is used to bring into agreement the balance of your checkbook with the balance of the bank statement. Follow these steps in using it:

1. Record the balance of the statement on the "Statement Balance" line. The balance is shown on the front.

2. Add any deposits made since the date of the statement that do not appear on the statement. Obtain a total and enter that amount.

3. List the outstanding checks that you have noted by check number and amount.

4. Enter the total of the outstanding checks, and subtract this amount from the previous total. This new total is called the adjusted statement balance.

5. Enter your checkbook balance, and subtract any service charge from it. This will give you your adjusted checkbook balance.

6. Compare the adjusted statement balance with the adjusted checkbook balance to see if the two are equal.

Bank Reconciliation Statement

To balance your checkbook with this statement:

1. Sort the enclosed checks by number or date and check them off in your checkbook.
2. Subtract from your checkbook balance any checks you have not already recorded.
3. Subtract the service charge.
4. Complete the forms below.

LIST CHECKS NOT RETURNED WITH THIS OR PRIOR STATEMENTS				
Number	**Amount**		**STATEMENT BALANCE** (See other side)	$ *287* | *85*
253	$ *14* | *29*		Add deposits made since the ending date on statement.	*200* | *00*
254	*7* | *12*			
255	*3* | *87*			
256	*8* | *75*			
257	*21* | *61*			
Total checks not returned.	$ *55* | *64*		**Subtotal**	*487* | *85*
			Subtotal checks not returned	*55* | *64*
			BALANCE	$ *432* | *21*

This should agree with your checkbook balance.

A bank reconciliation form.

If the two adjusted amounts agree, your checking account is in balance. If they do not agree, a mistake has been made by either you or the bank. Usually, it is the account holder who is in error in such cases. The following hints may help you find the errors:

1. Recheck all additions, subtractions, and corrections made while reconciling the bank statement.

2. Check to be sure you have subtracted the service charge, if any, from your checkbook balance. Also check to see if there were any miscellaneous charges to your account that you may not have noticed.

3. Recheck all additions and subtractions and corrections made in the checkbook stubs or register.

4. Check that the correct balances were correctly carried forward from page to page in the register or stubs.

5. Compare the amount of each check with the amount coded by the bank in magnetic ink on the lower right corner of each check.

If after checking the bank statement and your checkbook balance, you find your checkbook balance is correct and the bank statement in error, notify the bank immediately.

Learning Activities

 ## Increasing Your Business Vocabulary

You should become familiar with each of the terms shown below. On a sheet of paper write the numbers 1 through 9. Then write alongside each number the term that best matches each of the numbered definitions.

bank reconciliation statement / bank statement / payer / insufficient funds / outstanding checks / overdrawn account / payee / postdated check / stop payment order

1. A form requesting that your bank not pay a specific check that you have written.
2. A check dated for a future date.
3. The person or company to whom a check is made out.
4. A term used to indicate that there is not enough money in the checking account to cover the amount of the check.
5. An account for which the bank has honored checks for more than the balance on deposit in the account.
6. A monthly report of all activities in a checking account.
7. A form used to bring into agreement the balance of your checkbook with the balance of the bank statement.
8. Checks written by you that have not yet been returned to the bank for payment.
9. The person who signs the check.

Understanding Business

1. Why should a person record the reason for writing a check on a check stub or register?

2. Why should you keep the balance of your checking account up to date?

3. Why should you not use someone else's personalized deposit tickets?

4. Suppose there is a difference in the amount written in words and the amount written in figures on a check. Which amount will the bank accept?

5. Describe the two ways a bank can handle a check that has been written for more than the balance on deposit in a checking account.

6. Why should a person take care to avoid overdrawing a checking account?

7. What should you do if a check you wrote is lost or stolen?

8. List the steps to be followed in checking the bank statement.

9. Describe the steps to be followed in reconciling your checking account.

10. What should you do if your adjusted bank statement balance and your checkbook balance are not equal?

Business Problems and Projects

1. Ann Filipi's bank statement for April showed a balance of $267.84. Her checkbook has a balance of $227.20. Ann found that the following checks were outstanding: No. 123 for $6.73,

235

No. 131 for $11.27, No. 135 for $3.95, and No. 137 for $19.4 . A service charge of 75 cents was recorded on the bank statement. Follow the directions in this chapter to reconcile Ann's checking account.

2. On check stubs similar to the one shown below, record in ink the following checkbook transactions. The beginning checkbook balance is $227.82.

520 $		
	19	
TO		
	DOLLARS	CENTS
BAL. FOR'D		
DEPOSITS		
''		
TOTAL		
THIS CHECK		
OTHER DEDUCTIONS		
BAL. FOR'D		

February 3:	Wrote check 231 to the Disco Shop for stereo tape, $8.95.
February 7:	Deposited $43.
February 10:	Wrote check 233 to Corner Drug for film, $7.23.
February 11:	Wrote check 234 to Neil's Service Station for gas, $11.50.
February 14:	Wrote check 235 to the Sweet Shoppe for Valentine's gift, $3.50.
February 16:	Wrote check 236 to Baer's Market for groceries, $14.55.
February 21:	Deposited $32.
February 22:	Wrote check 237 to Fashionaire Dry Cleaners, $5.25.

3. The check shown below was drawn by Marilyn Hurst to Williams Department store for a purchase of $15.35. Examine the check and then answer the questions that follow.

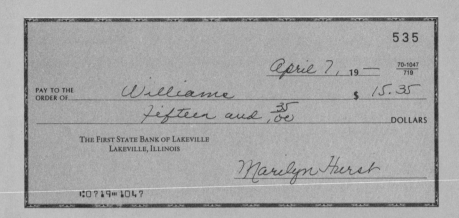

a. What would the bank accept as the correct amount of the check?

b. Could someone other than Williams Department Store cash the check if it were lost? What should Marilyn have done to make sure that only Williams Department Store is able to cash the check?

c. Could the amount of the check be easily changed? What should Marilyn have done to prevent this from happening?

Chapter 17

Other Ways of Making Payments

Objectives

After completing your study of this chapter, you will be able to do the following:

1. Define the term *cashier's check* and state in what situations a cashier's check may be used.

2. Distinguish between a bank draft and a cashier's check and know when to use each.

3. Describe the difference among the various types of money orders and know where each may be purchased.

4. Define the term *traveler's checks* and discuss the advantages of using them.

You have learned the many ways that individuals and businesses use checking account services to make payments. But there are other ways of making money payments besides using checks.

Why are other ways necessary when there are so many advantages to a personal checking account? There are several reasons. First, personal checks, particularly those for large sums of money, may not be accepted because doubt may exist as to whether or not there are sufficient funds in the writer's account to cover the checks. The larger the amount of the check, the greater is the risk to whoever cashes it. Second, if you are not known in a community, you may find it very difficult to cash a personal check. Local merchants, even banks, may not cash your check. Third, some people choose not to have a checking account. Still, they often need to send payments through the mail. In all these cases, other methods of making payments can be used.

In this chapter you will learn of the services that are provided to meet these special situations. These services include certified checks, cashier's checks, bank drafts, money orders, and traveler's checks.

CERTIFIED CHECK
Some businesses will not accept a personal check unless they are guaranteed that there is enough money in the writer's account to

A certified check.

cover the amount of the check. A *certified check* is a personal check that the bank guarantees to be good. A certified check is first written in the usual manner. Then a bank official stamps or writes the word *Certified* across the front. When the bank certifies the check, it takes out of the depositor's account the amount for which the check is written. The bank is therefore certifying to the payee that the check will be covered. Banks charge a small service fee for certifying checks.

CASHIER'S CHECK

A common way of transferring money is by obtaining a cashier's check at a bank. A *cashier's check* is a check that a bank writes on its own funds. Cashier's checks are used when a large amount of

A cashier's check.

money must be paid and a personal check would not be accepted. They are also used when a person does not have a checking account and must make payments by mail. And banks themselves use cashier's checks to pay their own expenses and, sometimes, to make loans to borrowers. Because cashier's checks are drawn on the bank's own funds, there is no question that there are sufficient funds to cover them.

You can obtain a cashier's check by taking the cash to a bank and requesting a cashier's check for the amount desired. A cashier or some other officer of the bank makes out the check and signs it. The bank keeps a file of paid cashier's checks in case a question arises about the receipt or payment of a check. A small fee is charged for the service.

BANK DRAFT

Banks often keep a portion of their funds on deposit in other banks. The depositing bank can then draw bank drafts against these deposits. A *bank draft* is a check drawn by one bank against funds deposited in its account in another bank.

In general, bank drafts are more acceptable than personal checks. They are generally used by business people for making payments out of state or in foreign countries. They are also used when the payee of a check asks that the funds be deposited in the city where the payee's place of business is located.

Bank drafts may be bought at any commercial bank for a small fee. They are considered to be legal receipts because banks keep all paid drafts on file for future reference.

Why would a department store prefer to receive a check written on a bank in the city where it is located?

MONEY ORDER

Many people do not have or want a checking account, yet they realize that sending money through the mail is not safe because lost or stolen money is rarely replaced. An inexpensive and safe way of transferring money is by means of money orders. A *money order* is a form issued by certain agencies that orders the payment of specific sums of money. Money orders generally are used for payments of small amounts because they cost less than bank drafts or cashier's checks. Depending on what agency issues them, money orders vary as to the fee and maximum amount of issue. Among the most popular types of money orders are bank money orders, postal money orders, express money orders, and telegraphic money orders.

Bank Money Order

A *bank money order* is a money order sold by a bank. A bank official stamps the requested amount on the money order blank. The purchaser completes the form, filling in the date, the name of the payee, and the name of the purchaser. The purchaser is given a duplicate of the money order as a receipt. The bank also keeps a copy for its files. When a money order is paid, it is returned to the issuing bank.

Bank money orders are available in larger amounts than are the other kinds of money orders, and they are usually less expensive. However, they are not available in as many places as the other types. Because regulations about bank money orders vary from bank to bank, you should determine your bank's practices before buying one from it.

Why do you think banks are able and willing to issue money orders in larger amounts than are express companies and the postal service?

Express Money Order

Money orders issued by express companies such as the American Express Company are called *express money orders*. The limit on a single express money order is $500, but you can purchase as many as you need. They are relatively inexpensive and are available at many retail stores in addition to the issuing express companies. Like other kinds of money orders, express money orders provide a receipt as proof of purchase.

Postal Money Order

The postal service issues a kind of money order called a *postal money order*. When you buy a postal money order, the postal clerk records the requested amount on the blank, and you complete the rest of the information. A record is kept in the postal service's files. If the money order is lost or stolen, a claim can be filed at the issuing office.

A postal money order may be cashed at a bank or post office by the payee named on it. It may also be transferred to another person or business. Like checks, postal money orders must be endorsed before they are cashed or transferred. Unlike checks, however, postal money orders can only be transferred once.

A postal money order.

The maximum amount for each postal money order is $300. However, if you want to send more than that amount, additional money orders may be purchased. The fee for a postal money order depends on the amount of the money order. It is about the same as the fee charged for express money orders.

Telegraphic Money Order

The fastest way to send money is through a telegraphic money order. A *telegraphic money order* is a message directing a telegraph office to pay a sum of money to a specified person. The name of the person is stated on the telegraph form, and a test question may be used as a means of identifying the payee.

To send money by wire, you complete the telegram form at a telegraph office and pay the clerk the amount to be sent. The clerk will send the telegram to the telegraph office nearest the person who is to receive the money. No cash is actually sent. But the telegrams authorizes direct payment of cash to the person named and identified as payee.

western union ⊔⊔ ⊔
Telegraphic Money Order

A telegraphic money order.

The fee depends on the amount of the money order and the distance it is to be sent. Telegraphic money orders can be sent to any place in the world. Because of the distance these money orders can be sent, they are more expensive than the other types of money orders. However, in an emergency this is the fastest way of sending money and may be worth the extra cost.

Provide some examples of occasions when you or your family have used money orders. What kind did you use? Why?

TRAVELER'S CHECKS

When you travel, you often need a large amount of money to cover expenses. However, it is unwise to carry cash because cash can be easily lost or stolen. And personal checks are of little value because they may be difficult to cash.

For these reasons, people who travel often use traveler's checks. *Traveler's checks* are a form of check especially designed for travelers or persons on vacation trips. They provide a safe and convenient way to carry money when traveling. And they are generally accepted by stores, banks, restaurants, and hotels

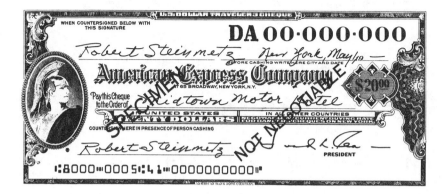

A traveler's check.

throughout the world. Traveler's checks can be bought from banks, savings and loan associations, travel agents, express companies, and telegraph offices. Traveler's checks are issued in convenient amounts of $10, $20, $50, and $100. Usually there is a small service charge for traveler's checks.

Traveler's checks are signed in two places. The purchaser signs each check in the presence of the issuing agent at the time of purchase. Each check is signed again when it is cashed. The two signatures are compared as a means of identification.

The purchaser receives a form on which to record the serial number and amount of each check. This information should be recorded as each check is used. The place and date of use should be noted on the check as well as on the record. This record should be kept in a safe place *separate* from the checks. If the checks are lost or stolen, notify the issuing agency immediately. The agency will then replace them at their full value.

Could a person receiving a traveler's check ask for proof of identity in addition to the signatures on the front of the check? Why?

Learning Activities

Increasing Your Business Vocabulary

You should become familiar with each of the terms shown below. On a sheet of paper write the numbers 1 through 9. Then write alongside each number the term that best matches each of the numbered definitions.

bank draft / bank money order / cashier's check / certified check / express money order / money order / postal money order / telegraphic money order / traveler's checks

1. A personal check that the bank guarantees to be good.

2. A check drawn by one bank against funds deposited in its account in another bank.

3. A form of check especially designed for persons on vacation trips.

4. A check that a bank writes on its own funds.

5. A form issued by a post office, bank, express company, or telegraph office for sending small sums of money.

6. A money order sold by a bank.

7. A money order issued by the American Express Company.

8. A message directing a telegraph office to pay a sum of money to a specified person.

9. A money order issued by a post office.

Understanding Business

1. Why are certified checks usually accepted for payment?

2. For what two reasons do banks use cashier's checks? Why do individuals use them?

3. When are bank drafts used? Why?

4. Why are money orders rather than bank drafts or cashier's checks generally used for making small money payments by people who do not have checking accounts?

5. List the different kinds of money orders and indicate how they differ from each other.

6. What are two advantages of bank money orders over other types of money orders? What is their disadvantage?

7. What should a person do if a postal money order is lost?

8. When are telegraphic money orders used?

9. Why might people who travel carry traveler's checks rather than cash? Rather than personal checks?

10. Why should a person keep a record of his or her traveler's checks in a safe place separate from the checks?

Business Problems and Projects

1. A certified check is shown on the next page. After examining the check, answer the questions that follow it.

EARL F. STOREY
1906 GLEN OAK ROAD
LAKEVILLE, ILLINOIS 60418

201

May 16, 19___

70-1047
719

PAY TO THE
ORDER OF _Summit Ski Shop_____ $ 187 50/100

_One hundred _____ eighty seven and_ 50/100 _____ DOLLARS

CERTIFIED WHEN PROPERLY ENDORSED $187.50 ____ Valley ass... ____ THE FIRST STATE BANK OF LAKEVILLE LAKEVILLE, ILLINOIS

THE FIRST STATE BANK OF LAKEVILLE
LAKEVILLE, ILLINOIS

MEMO _Ski trip_____   _Earl F. Storey_____

⑆07⑈19⑉1047⑆   06⑈0710

---

a. Who is the payee of the check?

b. On whose account is the check written?

c. What is the name of the bank at which the account is held?

d. Who certified the check? What is his position? On what date was the check certified?

e. For what amount has the check been certified?

f. Assume you are the payee of the check. Would you accept it without first checking with the bank to be sure sufficient funds were on deposit in the account to cover the amount? Explain your answer.

2. Assume your family is moving to another city 2,500 miles from where you presently live. Which method of payment discussed in this chapter would you use in each of these cases and why?

a. Rent for your new home, $375, must be sent ahead.

b. You must pay the moving company $900 before they will unload and a personal check is not acceptable.

c. Your family will take a short vacation while traveling to your new home. It is estimated that travel time will take about ten days and you will need $600 to $700 to cover your expenses.

3. Which method of payment discussed in this chapter might you use in each of the following situations?

   a. To pay a bill of $30, owed to a business firm in a distant city, when you do not have a personal checking account.

   b. To make a purchase of $450 in your own city when a personal check is not acceptable.

   c. To send money to a relative in another city to cover an emergency.

   d. To have money available to cover your expenses while on vacation in Hawaii.

   e. To send money to another city in payment of a bill, after withdrawing it from your savings account.

   f. To purchase goods in a foreign country.

Chapter 18

Credit in Our Economy

Objectives

After completing your study of this chapter, you will be able to do the following:

1. Define the term *credit* and identify the two parties to every credit transaction.

2. Distinguish between short-term and long-term credit.

3. Describe the purposes for which governments use credit.

4. Identify the various types of business credit and discuss how each type is used.

5. Identify and discuss the major reasons why consumers use credit.

6. List the various advantages and disadvantages of using credit.

"Buy now, pay later!" "Cash or charge?" You have probably heard these expressions in radio and television commercials or seen them in department store advertisements. These expressions, and others like them, point to the use of credit as a way of increasing a person's purchasing power.

Credit is used by many people many times each day. Credit is used to purchase goods and services in many of the stores or businesses where you shop. In fact, because credit is used so much, it is often said that we live in a credit economy.

In this chapter you will study about credit, learn who uses it, and examine the very important role it plays in our economy. You will also be introduced to some of the general advantages and disadvantages of credit.

WHAT IS CREDIT?

Earlier, you learned that one of the functions of money is to act as a medium of exchange. That is, you can buy goods with money because money is accepted in exchange for goods. Credit also acts as a medium of exchange. *Credit* is a means of obtaining goods, services, or cash in exchange for a promise to pay for them at some future time. Therefore, credit allows a person to use a product or a service now. However, that product or service must still be paid for at a later date.

Credit gives temporary purchasing power to people who might not otherwise have it. However, credit is only a *temporary* increase in purchasing power. It is temporary because the money has to be repaid in the future. In other words, while a person is temporarily increasing his or her present purchasing power, that person is also decreasing his or her future purchasing power.

The word *credit* comes from the Latin word *credere,* which means "to trust." The person who gives credit or lends money is called a *creditor.* The person who borrows money or buys goods and services on credit is called a *debtor.* And a *debt* is an amount owed by one person, business, or government to another. The creditor accepts the promise of the debtor to pay for the goods and services purchased on credit. In other words, the creditor trusts the debtor. Trust, then, is the basis for credit in our economy.

THE THREE Cs OF CREDIT

The trust that a creditor is willing to give to a debtor is based on three factors: the character, capacity, and capital of the debtor. These three factors are commonly referred to as the three Cs of credit. They are used to determine whether or not a person qualifies to receive credit.

Character is the reputation a person has in the community for honesty and dependability in paying debts. It indicates the kind of person a credit applicant is. Character is shown in one's conduct, attitudes, and achievements in relation to money matters. The person who is honest, reliable, and willing to pay his or her debts and who shows a good record of financial responsibility will receive a high character rating when applying for credit.

Capacity is a person's ability to pay a debt. Capacity is based on a person's income—now and in the future. It really represents an individual's ability to earn money and to meet financial obligations when they are due. When people earn enough money to pay their debts as well as their other expenses, they have capacity. People may be honest, dependable, and willing to pay their debts. But if they do not have the ability or capacity to pay, they will not be able to do so. Character is a quality that cannot be easily measured or judged. Capacity, however, can be.

Capital is the total amount of money and property a person owns. Capital includes such things as an automobile, a home, household goods, stocks, bonds, and savings account. Ownership of property indicates that a person will most likely to able to pay any bills. It shows that an individual can manage money wisely and that the person has saved and invested income. Anyone with a temporary lack of capacity but with substantial capital may still be considered a good credit risk.

It is important to note that even though an individual has capacity and capital, it will be difficult—if not impossible—to obtain credit without character.

Based on the three Cs of credit, do you feel you are eligible for credit? Give reasons for your answer.

ADVANTAGES OF CREDIT

From a consumer's point of view, credit has many advantages. Credit allows people to enjoy the use of goods and services immediately while they pay for them over an extended period of time. For example, if you wanted to buy a cassette tape recorder but did not have the cash to pay for it, you could buy it on credit. This allows you to use and enjoy the tape recorder as you make payments on it. Buying on credit is also known as buying "on time," because goods and services purchased on credit are paid for over a period of days, months, or years.

Another advantage of credit is that it increases a person's standard of living. For example, without the use of credit, few people could afford to purchase cars, homes, televisions, and furniture. These major purchases involve large sums of money, and most people do not have enough cash to pay for such costly items at one time. A person is able to live more comfortably and can enjoy a higher standard of living with the use of credit.

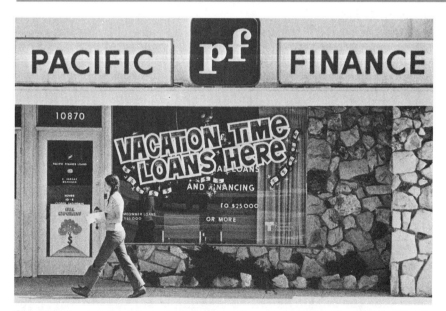

Credit allows you to enjoy goods and services and pay for them later. (Cherkis Stockmarket, Los Angeles)

Credit is used by many consumers because it is convenient. For example, how many times have you gone into a store and seen an item on sale that you wanted but did not have the cash to buy? With credit established at that store, you would be able to purchase the item easily. Also, the use of credit means a shopper does not have to carry a lot of cash when shopping.

From the viewpoint of the economic system, too, credit has important advantages. Credit stimulates business activity. Its use promotes the exchange of goods and services when people do not have ready cash. This results in increased production, greater sales, and more jobs. Businesses are able to produce more, consumers are able to purchase more, and more people are employed. For example, an automobile mechanic may want to purchase additional equipment and tools to expand his repair shop. The mechanic may purchase new equipment and tools on credit. In this way, the repair shop can do more business because of its extra equipment, and the customers of the repair shop will have more services available to them. It is possible that with the additional equipment, the mechanic may need to hire more employees to take care of customers' repairs.

Explain how credit enables individuals and businesses to spread out their goods and services over a period of time.

DISADVANTAGES OF CREDIT

The use of credit has many disadvantages to those who do not manage it wisely. Misuse of credit by individuals, business firms, and governments can lead to financial ruin. It has been said that a person who cannot handle money wisely will not be able to handle credit wisely, either.

One disadvantage is that it costs consumers money to purchase goods on credit. Because payments must be made over a extended period of time, the buyer usually pays a service charge or interest on the unpaid balance. For example, suppose a person buys a $450 refrigerator on a 3-year credit plan. When the refrigerator has been fully paid, the buyer may have actually paid over $550 for it. Those who borrow money or purchase on credit pay billions of dollars each year in interest and service charges.

Credit also costs money for businesses. When a business firm decides to sell on credit, there are costs involved in checking the credit background of credit applicants, in keeping records of amounts owed and payments received from debtors, and in assuming losses when debtors do not pay their bills. All of these costs have to be paid for. Eventually, these costs are paid for by the consumer through higher prices for goods and services.

The convenience of having credit available can also be a disadvantage. A person may be tempted to buy more if he or she has established credit in a store. Also, a person having credit is likely to buy a more expensive item. When a $15.95 sweater is bought on credit, it does not seem to cost as much. However, if a person had only $16 in cash, he or she would think twice about spending that money for the sweater.

Another disadvantage of credit is that it causes people to buy on impulse. For example, a person walks into a store, immediately likes an item, and buys it without a second thought as to whether it is needed or even wanted. A shopper who pays cash for goods is more likely to think about the price of goods than a shopper who uses credit.

Explain how the use of credit may actually decrease the amount of income available for spending.

WHO USES CREDIT?
You will recall that there are three sectors in our economic system: the government sector, the business sector, and the consumer sector. Credit is used by all these sectors for a variety of reasons.

Governments Use Credit
Government agencies at local, state, and federal levels often find it necessary to use credit when their tax receipts are too small to meet current expenses. Rather than raise taxes, governments also

Major government projects like this stadium are often financed with credit. (San Diego Convention and Visitors Bureau)

use credit to borrow money to help balance their budgets. In addition, governments use credit to borrow money to build new facilities. These facilities include schools, public hospitals, public libraries, courthouses, and other similar public buildings. They also include streets, highways, parks, and airports. The funds may also be used for many other projects such as flood control and urban renewal. This type of debt is later paid for out of taxes and other government revenue.

In what ways can your community benefit from your local government borrowing money?

Business Firms Use Credit

Business firms also use credit. Credit provides the money that allows people to start a business. It also provides the money that allows businesses to expand their operations, to start new product lines, and to increase services. But the major reason for which business firms use credit is to increase their profits.

Business firms primarily use three types of credit: investment credit, short-term credit, and commercial credit.

Investment credit is credit used to obtain funds to purchase fixed assets for the business. *Fixed assets* are assets such as buildings and machinery that are a permanent part of the business because they last for many years. Investment credit is considered to be *long-term credit*. It is credit extended over a long period of time, usually five years or more. Many prospective business owners do not have enough capital of their own to purchase land, buildings, machinery, equipment, and other things needed to carry on a business. For that reason, they must use credit.

Short-term credit is credit extended over a short period of time and is used for working capital. Usually the period of time is one to five years. *Working capital* is the money needed for a business firm to carry on a minimum level of business activity from week to week or month to month. This includes money required to purchase merchandise and supplies. It also includes money to pay employee wages, rent, telephone, and other current expenses. For example, a business firm may not be able to sell its products as

Business firms sometimes use credit to expand their operations. (Monkmeyer)

quickly as it would like. Or it may have to carry large stocks of merchandise. In either case, money is being tied up in the merchandise. As a result, it needs more working capital.

Commercial credit is the credit one business firm extends to another when selling goods on time for resale or commercial use. The major purpose of commercial credit is to make goods move through the production and marketing stages easily. When business firms extend credit to one another, merchandise can be sold, exchanged, or returned without the use of cash. Commercial credit does not include credit given by a retailer who sells on credit. It does not include the credit given by manufacturers or middlemen who sell directly to the consumer. This is called *consumer credit*.

Consumers Use Credit

In the United States over 60 percent of all individuals and families owe some type of debt. *Consumer credit* is short- and long-term credit that enables consumers to buy goods and services or to borrow money and pay it back at a later time. There are very few consumers today who do not use credit or who do not have access to it. People who use credit come from all income groups and are in all age groups.

Credit may also be used by consumers as a way of bringing together all their debts into one large debt. This large amount is then owed to only one creditor. Consumers also use credit for paying such things as taxes, moving expenses, insurance expenses, interest on a mortgage, and even a vacation.

Credit can be a valuable tool for consumers if used wisely. To do so, follow these three important guidelines:

1. Use credit only when necessary or when the benefit is worth the costs and the risks involved.

2. Take on no more debt than you can reasonably expect to repay out of your present level of income.

3. Shop for the best credit bargain available.

What do you think would happen to our economy if the use of credit was suddenly stopped?

Learning Activities

Increasing Your Business Vocabulary

You should become familiar with each of the terms shown below. On a sheet of paper write the numbers 1 through 7. Then write alongside each number the term that best matches each of the numbered definitions.

commercial credit / consumer credit / credit / debt / investment credit / short-term credit / working capital

1. Short- and long-term credit that enables consumers to buy goods and services or to borrow money and pay it back at a later time.

2. The credit one business firm extends to another when selling goods on time for resale or commercial use.

3. The money needed for a business firm to carry on a minimum level of business activity from week to week or month to month.

4. Credit used by businesses to purchase fixed assets.

5. A means of obtaining goods, services, or cash in exchange for a promise to pay for them at some future time.

6. An amount owed by one person, business, or government to another.

7. Credit used by businesses to obtain working capital.

Understanding
Business

1. Explain how credit acts as a medium of exchange.
2. Why is credit only a temporary increase in purchasing power?
3. List the three factors used to determine whether or not a person qualifies to receive credit.
4. List three advantages to using credit.
5. List three disadvantages to using credit.
6. What does government use credit for?
7. What is the major reason why business firms use credit?
8. What are the three types of credit used by business firms?
9. For what do consumers use credit?
10. Name three guidelines to follow in using credit.

Business Problems
and Projects

1. Read the article below and then answer the questions that follow.

PUBLIC DEBT WORRISOME

Americans are of two minds about going into debt. When they're confident about what lies ahead, they rarely hesitate to mortgage future income to buy homes, cars, boats, furniture or appliances. But when their government goes heavily into debt—mortgaging future revenues to pay for defense, education, welfare, medical research, or other services— the cries of outrage become a roar.

Consumer debt is considered "good" debt. The decision by consumers to go deeper into debt means retail sales have risen, and that there is greater confidence about the future.

The rising federal debt is considered "bad" debt. As of the end of May, the public debt totaled $528.2 billion. That's an increase of $54.3 billion over the previous year. The debt, of course, is growing as spending outpaces revenues, and the federal government has to borrow to meet expenses.

But there's a worrisome aspect to the debt, one that is far less in the limelight than the size of the debt itself. The federal government, just as you and I, must pay interest on the money it borrows. For the last fiscal year, the interest cost was roughly $33 billion. The Treasury estimates— probably conservatively—that the figure will climb to $36 billion for the current year.

A Treasury analysis shows that interest on the public debt is the third largest item in the federal budget, topped only by outlays for national defense and income security.

Source: Minneapolis Star, August 8, 1975

a. For what reasons are consumers willing to mortgage their future incomes?

b. For what reasons does government go into debt?

c. What is the "worrisome" aspect of public debt that is discussed in the article?

d. What was the interest cost of the federal debt for the last fiscal year?

e. What is the estimated interest cost for the current year?

f. Where does interest on public debt rank in the federal budget? What items ranked higher?

2. On a form similar to one shown below, list four situations where a business might ask for each of the three kinds of credit.

	Investment Credit	Short-Term Credit	Commercial Credit
Example	To purchase equipment	To purchase supplies	To return merchandise

3. On a form similar to the one shown below, list ten items—either goods or services—that your family buys or has bought on credit. After each item briefly state why credit is used rather than cash.

	Item	Reason for Using Credit
Example	Gasoline	More convenient

Chapter 19

Getting and Using Credit

Objectives

After completing your study of this chapter, you will be able to do the following:

1. Define the term *credit rating* and explain its purpose.

2. List the information asked for on credit application forms.

3. Describe the role of a credit bureau in the granting of credit.

4. Identify and discuss the several choices that a debtor with serious credit problems has to better his or her financial situation.

5. Identify and discuss important consumer credit laws.

Learning about credit and how to use it wisely may not seem important to you at this time. However, some type of credit is often available to teenagers. In fact, many retail businesses encourage teenagers to open credit accounts. You should, therefore, know how to apply for it and how to use it. More important, in a few years you will probably be joining the millions of other people who use credit regularly to purchase goods and services.

You will recall that credit is a means of obtaining goods, services, or cash in exchange for a promise to pay for them at some future time. The concept of credit is based on trust. The debtor must trust the business firm to live up to its part of a credit agreement. And, of course, the creditor must rely on the debtor's ability and intention to complete his or her part of the agreement.

In this chapter, you will learn how to apply for credit, how to use it wisely, and what rights you have when you use credit to buy consumer goods.

APPLYING FOR CREDIT

In order to obtain credit at a particular store or financial institution, a credit application must be filled out. A *credit application* is a form used to request credit. Credit application forms generally ask the applicant for such information as full name, current and former addresses, employment record, income, bank accounts, previous credit experiences, and references. Each piece of information may be useful to the creditor when determining whether or not to extend credit.

Applicant's Name

The credit application form always shows the applicant's full name, including middle name or initial. This helps to avoid confusion between persons with similar names.

Current and Former Addresses

The kind of residence an applicant has is important in deciding whether or not credit should be granted. Generally, creditors are more willing to grant credit to people who own their own homes than to people who live in rooming houses or apartments. Also, creditors prefer people who have lived in the same place for several

A credit application form.

years and who have a good record of paying their rent or monthly mortgage payments.

Creditors use the applicant's former address for checking past payment records, employment records, and the length of stay at the former address. A person who has lived in the same place for several years is usually more stable and more dependable than one who has moved frequently.

Employment Record
An applicant's employment record is a major factor in obtaining credit. The creditor wants to know about the place, nature, and

length of time of employment. A record of steady employment is a positive factor. Steady employment is employment at one place for three or more years. The creditor also wants to know whether the applicant is likely to stay in the same job during the period for which credit is granted. Information about an applicant's previous employment, including reasons for leaving, is also requested. This is especially important if the individual has been employed at his or her present job for less than three years.

Why might a creditor be interested in the reasons a person left a previous job?

Income

Since the ability to pay debts is based largely on one's earning power, the applicant's salary is a major consideration. The creditor may want to know if the salary is paid weekly or monthly and if the income varies from one pay period to another. For example, if part of a person's income is in the form of commissions or fees, the income will change from time to time.

Bank Account

How an applicant uses a checking account, whether the account is often overdrawn, and the average account balance can all be determined from the bank. An average account balance of $100 or more is a favorable factor. An account balance of less than $100 is generally an unfavorable credit factor. Having one or more savings accounts usually indicates thrift and is a positive factor in the granting of credit.

Previous Credit Experience

As you might expect, people who have used credit responsibly in the past are usually considered better credit risks than those who have not. For that reason, applicants are asked to list the types of credit they are currently using. They also may be asked about previous credit arrangements that have been paid off. The creditor will try to find out whether these were paid regularly and promptly. Creditors assume that people who have paid regularly and promptly in the past will continue to do so.

In most chain stores, the credit office is located so as to be convenient to all shoppers. (Licht/Stockmarket, Los Angeles)

References

Some creditors also ask for references to help them determine credit rating. *References* are people who know the applicant's character. Merchants with whom credit accounts have been maintained are good references, as well as present and past employers.

List several questions that a credit investigator might ask of the references given by a credit applicant.

CHECKING YOUR CREDIT

The information on the credit application form is checked carefully. The credit check is sometimes done by the company granting the credit. But most of the time, a person's credit rating is checked by a local credit bureau. A *credit bureau* is an agency that collects and maintains files of information on the credit history of individuals.

A credit bureau collects and records any information that may affect one's ability or willingness to pay his or her debts. Their records include information about an applicant's income, employment, residence, assets, and previous use of credit. If a person is late in paying bills, that information is recorded. Most of the information comes from businesses, banks, employers, and newspaper reports. Some of it comes from police and court records. If a person gets a divorce, that is recorded. If a person is arrested by the police, that, too, is recorded.

The credit record begins the first time one makes a request for credit. If a person moves from one city to another, the credit record follows as soon as the person applies for credit in the new city. The credit record is always there for those who have a legitimate interest for using the services of the credit bureau. Your rights in regard to the information included in a credit bureau's files will be discussed later in this chapter.

Do you think it is fair that a credit bureau's file should contain such a variety of information about a credit user? Why or why not? Should all this information be used in making credit decisions? Explain your answer.

Your Credit Rating

The credit record that you have established is used as the basis of your credit rating. A *credit rating* is a measure of one's ability to obtain credit. Credit ratings are given as numbers, ranging from 1 to 10, and are a convenient indication of your credit history. The best credit rating is given the number 1. The worst credit rating is given the number 10.

At times, a good credit rating may be more important to you than cash. Once credit is granted to you, use it wisely whenever you shop or borrow money. Above all, protect your credit rating by making payments regularly and on time.

CREDIT DIFFICULTIES

Occasionally a person may not use credit wisely or may become involved in financial difficulties that prevent the making of payments on a regular basis. People sometimes find that they have purchased too many goods and services on credit or have borrowed too much money on credit. They do not know how to manage their money—or their credit—wisely.

Other people find themselves with credit problems because of sudden illness, injury, or accident. Still others lose their jobs. In any event, there are several things consumers can do to improve their financial situation. First, consumers may use debt consolidation. Second, they may seek credit counseling. And third, in an extreme case they can file for bankruptcy.

Before any action is taken, however, consumers should try to solve the financial difficulty in other ways. First, they should talk to their creditors. Most creditors are willing to help, but they can only help if they are aware of the debtor's problems. Some creditors may be willing to postpone payments. Others may be willing to *refinance* the debt, that is to reschedule payments on the debt so that they are smaller and extend over a longer period of time.

A person should not wait until debts have become long overdue before seeking financial help. Help should be sought as

Individuals with credit difficulties should first discuss the problems with their creditors. (Stock, Boston)

soon as the debtor realizes that each payment deadline is becoming more difficult to meet.

Debt Consolidation

When it is not possible to postpone payments or to refinance a debt, many consumers consolidate their debts. *Debt consolidation* means bringing all debts together as one large debt owed to one source. The consumers arrange a loan that is large enough to pay all other debts. As a result, they have one large debt rather than several small ones.

Repayment of a consolidated debt is extended over a longer period of time. There is a disadvantage for the debtor, however. When a debt is extended, more interest will be paid out over the extended period of the loan. However, debt consolidation is one way to help protect one's credit rating.

Credit Counseling

Some people find themselves in such serious financial difficulties that neither refinancing nor debt consolidation are workable solutions. For these people the best thing to do is to seek professional help of a credit-counseling service. Many communities have nonprofit credit-counseling services sponsored by the National Foundation for Consumer Credit.

The counselor assists the consumer in working out a plan that sets aside a certain amount of money to be applied to the debts. In cases where the consumer's income does not cover full payment of the debts, the counseling service will try to arrange new repayment schedules with creditors. The counseling service works with local merchants, financial institutions, educators, religious leaders, and service organizations to help consumers with financial difficulties. The debtor pays the counseling service a specific amount out of each pay check. The counseling service then distributes this amount among the various creditors. Sometimes there is a small charge for this service.

Financial advice is also available from social service agencies, legal aid societies, clergy, and many financial institutions. Names and addresses of other financial counselors may be obtained from local Better Business Bureaus, Chambers of Commerce, and consumer protection agencies. Before counseling is obtained from any organization, determine whether there is a charge.

Bankruptcy

For some people the final course of action in solving their financial difficulties is bankruptcy. *Bankruptcy* is a legal proceeding in a federal court by which a person unable to pay debts may be freed from the legal obligation to do so. Bankruptcy is a procedure to be taken only if there is no hope of becoming financially sound through other means. There are two types of bankruptcy. *Voluntary bankruptcy* occurs when the debtor asks the court to declare bankruptcy. *Involuntary bankruptcy* occurs when one or more creditors ask the court to declare a debtor bankrupt.

When a person is judged to be bankrupt, all assets and possessions of the debtor are sold except those items excluded by law. The money received from the sale is paid to the creditors in proportion to the amount owed to them.

Does a person who has been judged bankrupt have a moral obligation to repay his or her debts even though there is no legal obligation to do so? Give reasons for your answer.

Bankruptcy proceedings relieve the debtor from those debts claimed by current creditors. Even though the debts may not have been paid in full from the sale of assets and possessions of the debtor, the debtor is legally free of the burden of these debts. However, should the debtor wish to establish credit in the future, it will be very difficult to do so because of the record of bankruptcy. Businesses and financial institutions generally hesitate to extend credit or lend money to a person who has not been able to handle money or credit in the past.

CONSUMER CREDIT RIGHTS

Federal and state goverments have passed laws that regulate credit in the best interests of the consumer. Three of the most important laws on consumer credit passed on the national level are the Truth-in-Lending Act, the Fair Credit Reporting Act, and the Equal Credit Opportunity Act.

Truth-in-Lending Act

The Consumer Credit Protection Act, commonly known as the *Truth-in-Lending Act,* became effective in 1969. Its purpose is to make creditors explain their credit terms clearly and simply so that consumers can understand them. Consumers can also compare the various credit terms available to them. The Truth-in-Lending Act requires that the cost of credit be stated as a dollar amount and an annual percentage rate. With this information, the consumer can make a more intelligent choice as to the best place to obtain credit.

Do you agree that efforts should be made to provide protection for the consumer who uses credit? Give reasons for your answer.

Fair Credit Billing Act

An amendment was made to the Truth-in-Lending Act in 1975. This amendment, called the *Fair Credit Billing Act,* requires that creditors take prompt action in correcting mistakes made in billing customers. Occasionally, a credit user may receive a bill that includes an item that was not bought, that was returned for credit, or that has been paid for. The Fair Credit Billing Act protects the consumer in such situations.

Suppose you think your bill is wrong. Under this law you must write to the creditor describing the error and why you believe it is an error. Ask for evidence of the credit purchase, such as a copy of the charge slip. Include the dollar amount of the suspected error as well as other information that will help the creditor identify you and the reason for your complaint. Be sure to include your name, address, and account number.

In the past, it could sometimes take months or even years to correct such errors. Now the creditor must acknowledge all letters pointing out possible billing errors within 30 days of their receipt. And within 90 days after receiving your letter, the creditor must either correct the error or explain why the bill is correct. During this time, letters requesting payment cannot be sent, and other actions to collect the amount from you may not be taken. You cannot be threatened with damage to your credit rating or sued for the amount in question. The disputed amount cannot be reported to a credit bureau or to other creditors as delinquent until the creditor has answered the inquiry. However, periodic statements may be sent to you, and the disputed amount can be applied against your credit limit. You should be aware that you remain obligated to pay the parts of your bill not in dispute. The creditor who does not follow the rules and time limits is not allowed to collect the first $50 of the disputed amount and finance charges even if the bill is correct.

At times you may have trouble with a product bought with a credit card. Under this act, you may have the right not to pay for it. First you must try in good faith to return the product or give the merchant a chance to correct the problem.

Give examples of incorrect or incomplete information that might be included in one's credit bureau file. Explain how this might affect one's chances for obtaining credit.

Fair Credit Reporting Act

In 1971, the *Fair Credit Reporting Act* was passed by Congress. This act protects consumers against the circulation of inaccurate or out-of-date information that might be found in credit bureau files. It was intended to ensure that consumer reporting agencies operate in a manner that is fair and equitable to consumers. If you as a consumer have been denied credit, insurance, or employment or if you believe that you have had problems because of a credit report, you can now take steps to protect yourself. The Fair Credit Reporting Act includes a long list of consumer rights. Some of the most important are these:

1. The right to be told the name and address of the credit bureau that prepared a consumer report used to deny you credit, insurance, employment, or to increase the cost of credit insurance.

2. The right, at any time and for any reason, to be told the nature and sources of the information collected about you by a credit bureau.

3. The right to have incomplete or incorrect information reex-
    amined, and if the information is found to be inaccurate or
    untrue, to have such information removed from the file.

4. The right to have the bureau notify, at no cost to you, those
    you name who have already received the incorrect or in-
    complete information that the information has been deleted.

5. The right to have your version of the dispute placed in the file
    and included in subsequent reports, when a dispute between
    you and the reporting bureau cannot be resolved. You also
    have the right to request the agency to send your version of
    the dispute to certain businesses for a reasonable fee.

6. The right not to have most adverse information reported after
    seven years. One major exception is bankruptcy, which may
    be reported for 14 years.

Equal Credit Opportunity Act

In 1975, Congress also passed the *Equal Credit Opportunity Act.*
This act prohibits creditors from discriminating on the basis of sex,
marital status, race, color, religion, national origin, or age.

Learning Activities

Increasing Your Business Vocabulary

You should become familiar with each of the terms shown below. On a sheet of paper write the numbers 1 through 10. Then write alongside each number the term that best matches each of the numbered definitions.

bankruptcy / credit application / credit bureau / credit rating / debt consolidation / Equal Credit Opportunity Act / Fair Credit Billing Act / Fair Credit Reporting Act / refinance / Truth-in-Lending Act

1. A measure of one's ability to obtain credit.

2. A proceeding in a federal court whereby persons who are unable to pay their debts in full may be freed from the legal obligation to do so.

3. To reschedule debt payments so that they are smaller and extend over a longer period of time.

4. An agency that collects and maintains files of information on the credit history of individuals.

5. A request to obtain credit.

6. The process of bringing all debts together as one large debt owed to one source.

7. Legislation that requires creditors to explain their credit terms clearly and simply.

8. Legislation that protects consumers against circulation of inaccurate or out-of-date information in their credit files.

9. Legislation that requires creditors to take prompt action in correcting mistakes in billing.

10. Legislation that bans discrimination in the lending of credit.

Understanding
Business

1. Why is the study of credit important to you now?

2. What types of information does a credit bureau keep on file? Where do credit bureaus obtain such information?

3. What are some of the reasons why consumers have credit difficulties?

4. Explain how debt consolidation works.

5. What are three sources of credit counseling?

6. What happens to the property of a person who declares bankruptcy?

7. What was the purpose of the Truth-in-Lending Act?

8. The Truth-in-Lending Act requires that the finance charge be stated in two ways. What are they?

9. In what two ways does the Fair Credit Billing Act help credit users?

10. List the important consumer rights included in the Fair Credit Reporting Act.

Business Problems
and Projects

1. List ten items of information that you might have to supply when applying for credit. After each item, briefly explain why that information may be useful to your prospective creditor.

2. Information similar to the following appears on many credit purchase receipts and statements sent to credit customers. Read it, and then answer the questions that follow.

FINANCE CHARGE EXPLANATION

A **finance charge** will be applied when any part of the previous balance remains unpaid.

Your **finance charge** will be computed on the Average Daily Balance of your account at a monthly periodic rate of 1%, or an **annual percentage rate** of 12%, with a minimum **finance charge** of 50¢.

The **average daily balance** is the total of the daily balances, including charges, in the billing period divided by the number of days in the period. Please note that any payments and credits made during the billing period will be deducted in determining the daily balances. No **finance charge** will be added in a billing period in which there is no previous balance or during which the payments and credits equal or exceed the previous balance.

To avoid **finance charges,** payment of the new balance must be received before your next bill closing date. You may at any time pay any part of your balance to reduce **finance charges**.

a. When is the finance charge applied?

b. On what is the finance charge computed?

c. What is the annual percentage rate?

d. What is the average daily balance?

e. Under what conditions are finance charges not applied?

f. How can a credit customer reduce credit finance charges?

3. Part of a monthly statement from a department store is shown below. Study it, and answer the questions.

REFERENCE	TRANSACTION DATE	STORE	DEPT.	DESCRIPTION	TAX	CHARGES	CREDITS
17370	1-04			PAYMENT-THANK YOU			5.00

ANNUAL PERCENTAGE RATE: 15%   AVERAGE DAILY BALANCE 82.75

ON THIS BILL CLOSING DATE	TO YOUR PREVIOUS BALANCE OF	WE HAVE DEDUCTED		WE HAVE ADDED		TOTAL OR NEW BALANCE	MINIMUM AMT. DUE
		PAYMENTS OF	CREDITS OF	FINANCE CHARGE	CHARGES OF		
1-15	82.75	5.00	.00	1.24	.00	79.02	5.00

PAYMENTS, CREDITS OR CHARGES RECEIVED AFTER THE BILL CLOSING DATE SHOWN ABOVE WILL APPEAR ON NEXT MONTH'S STATEMENT.

ACCOUNT NUMBER

YOUR NEXT BILL CLOSING DATE IS:

Mansfields

STORE CODE:
1 — MINNEAPOLIS
2 — ST. PAUL
3 — SOUTHDALE
4 — BROOKDALE
6 — ROSEDALE
7 — OMAHA

NOTICE: PLEASE SEE REVERSE SIDE FOR IMPORTANT INFORMATION

TO AVOID FINANCE CHARGE, PAY AMOUNT DUE BY 1-30

a. What was the average daily balance on which the finance charge was calculated?

b. What was the amount of the finance charge?

c. Were any payments made during the month?

d. What was the total amount of the purchases made during the month?

e. What was the account balance at the beginning of the month?

f. What was the account balance at the end of the month?

g. What is the minimum payment due?

h. What amount must be paid to avoid a finance charge next month?

i. What is the annual percentage rate on this account?

Chapter 20

Charge Accounts
and Credit Cards

Objectives

After completing your study of this chapter, you will be able to do the following:

1. Define the term *sales credit*.

2. List and describe the various types of charge accounts.

3. List and describe the various types of credit cards.

4. Describe some of the steps that have been taken and can be taken to protect against lost or stolen credit cards.

5. Identify and list the various advantages and disadvantages of using sales credit.

Consumers are big users of credit. In a recent year, consumers had more than $180 billion worth of credit outstanding. Much of this credit was used for the purchase of goods and services. Consumers use credit to purchase expensive items such as a car. They use it to buy inexpensive items such as a restaurant meal. And they use it to borrow money.

There are two types of consumer credit: sales credit and cash credit. *Sales credit* is the credit used by consumers to purchase goods and services. Its most common forms are charge accounts and credit cards. The other major kind of consumer credit, *cash credit,* will be discussed in Chapter 22.

Because purchases are usually paid for in one installment, sales credit is often called *noninstallment credit.* Other types of credit plans are paid for with several payments extending over a period of time. These are called installment credit plans and will be discussed in Chapter 21.

CHARGE ACCOUNTS

The most popular form of sales credit is the charge account. A *charge account* is a credit plan that permits the user to charge any number of purchases and to pay for them according to a particular plan of repayment. When you use charge accounts, you may take the goods with you at the time of purchase but pay for them at a later time. There are several different types of charge accounts. Among the most common are the regular charge account and the revolving charge account.

Regular Charge Account

Regular charge accounts are used most often to meet everyday credit needs at department stores and service stations. Regular charge accounts offer credit to those who are able to pay their statements in full every month. Under the terms of a regular charge account, all purchases made during the month are billed at the end of the month. You are expected to pay the balance owed on your account when you receive your monthly statement.

Most stores allow a credit period of from 25 to 30 days from the date the customer is billed. If payment is not received within the credit period, the store will add a finance charge to the unpaid balance. A *finance charge* is a charge made for the use of credit. Like the interest charged on a loan of money, a finance charge is based on the amount of money owed and the period of time it has been owed.

Although there is no actual stated charge for the use of a charge account, there is a hidden cost in the prices you pay for goods or services. It costs creditors money to extend the convenience of credit to their customers. And it also costs consumers money to use credit. Prices may be a little higher in stores where credit is available. And the consumer who shops in such a store indirectly pays for the credit service. Those consumers who pay cash for their purchases help pay for the convenience of credit for those who use it.

Should cash-paying customers be required to pay the same prices for goods and services as those who use credit? Give reasons for your answer.

The 90-day Plan   A variation of the regular charge account is the 90-day or three-pay plan. This is often referred to as an installment charge account. The 90-day plan is commonly used to purchase large appliances, such as televisions, radios, refrigerators, washers, and dryers. It may also be used to purchase clothes, household items, and other costly goods that could not be paid for in one month.

JOSEPH MAGNIN JMONEY CARD

THIS CARD IDENTIFIES YOU AS A JM CHARGE CUSTOMER NOW ENTITLED TO DELAYED BILLING ON JM PURCHASES MADE BETWEEN OCTOBER 14, 1976, AND DECEMBER 31, 1976, ONLY. PAYMENT FOR JMONEY WILL BEGIN WITH YOUR FEBRUARY, 1977 BILLING.

NO FINANCE CHARGE UNTIL MARCH, 1977

Why do some stores make it so easy for customers to get charge accounts?

With a 90-day or three-pay plan, you may be required to pay one-third of the cost of the item at the time of purchase. The balance is divided into three equal payments to be made over a period of months. If a payment is not required at the time of purchase, one-third of the total purchase price is paid each month over the three-month period. For example, assume you purchased an AM-FM radio that cost $90. To pay for it, you use the three-pay plan. You would make payments of $30 each month over the next three months. This way, you can purchase an expensive item, enjoy it immediately, and pay for it over a short period of time.

In general there is no finance charge on this plan. However, if you do not make a payment on the due date, many stores add a carrying charge to the balance of the account.

Revolving Charge Account

A revolving charge account is similar to a regular charge account except for the way in which it is repaid. The revolving charge account allows the customer to put off payment for a longer period of time. At the time a revolving charge account is opened, a credit limit is set on the amount that can be owed at any one time. For example, the limit might be $500 or $1,000, depending on the credit rating of the customer and the policy of the store. A customer with this type of credit plan can choose to pay the balance of the account in full each month. If the balance is paid, there is no full finance charge. A customer can also choose to pay only a portion of the amount owed. In this case, a finance charge would be added to the amount due in the following month.

The minimum monthly payment is based on the amount of the unpaid balance. For example, if you owed $325, the minimum payment might be $25. This would leave an unpaid balance of $300. Finance charges are often computed at 1, 1½, or 2 percent of the unpaid balance each month. Depending on the percent of the finance charge, you might pay $3.00, $4.50, or $6.00 on the unpaid balance of $300. By law, the actual finance charge must be stated in the credit agreement.

Since any finance charge is made monthly, the annual percentage rate is equal to 12 times the monthly rate. A finance charge of 1½ percent, for example, is equal to 18 percent annually. Also, by law, the annual percentage rate must be clearly stated for the customer so the true cost of credit is known to the customer.

Check with members of your family to see if anyone has a charge account. At what types of businesses do they have these charge accounts? Check whether the accounts are regular charge accounts or revolving charge accounts.

CREDIT CARDS

A *credit card* is an identification card authorizing the holder to charge or obtain goods, services, or money on credit up to a certain amount. A typical example is the credit card used by charge account customers in department stores. The card shows the person's account number, name, and signature. The cardholder uses the credit card to have the charges for goods and services billed to his or her account. Once each month the cardholder receives a statement from the company that issued the card. The cardholder has the option of paying the amount in full or paying only a portion of it. If the account is paid in full, there is no finance charge. If it is not paid in full, a finance charge is added to the unpaid balance.

Credit cards are issued by many different kinds of companies. For some companies, like Diners' Club or Carte Blanche, credit cards are their main business. For other companies such as banks, airlines, oil and gasoline companies, and some hotel chains, credit cards are issued as part of their regular business services.

There are three general kinds of credit cards: single-use credit cards, bank credit cards, and travel and entertainment cards.

Single-Use Credit Cards

Credit cards that can be used only at a particular retail business are called *single-use credit cards.* The most popular types of single-use credit cards are the charge plates issued by department stores. The charge plates authorize the holders to charge purchases made at either the main store or any one of its branches.

Gasoline companies, hotels, and car rental firms also use single-use credit cards. However, some of the credit cards issued by

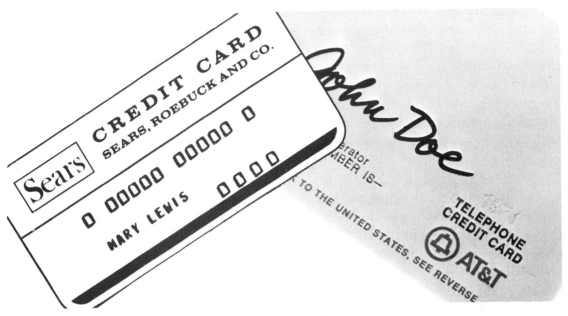

Two examples of single-use credit cards.

these businesses can be also used elsewhere. For example, the Gulf Travel Card, issued by the Gulf Oil Corporation, is honored at Holiday Inns.

What types of single-use credit cards are used by members of your family? For what reasons do they use them?

Bank Credit Cards

Credit cards issued by banks are called *bank credit cards*. **These** cards are also called *multiple-use credit cards*. The purpose of bank credit cards is to help consumers take care of their everyday credit needs with one account. The two best-known examples of bank credit cards are VISA and Master Charge.

Both of these bank credit cards allow you to make purchases at a variety of businesses, not only in your own community but in other cities, states, and countries. You then receive a monthly statement that covers all the purchases made with the credit card.

A bank credit card.

Many department stores, specialty shops, car rental agencies, service stations, restaurants, and airlines accept one or both of these bank credit cards. A person can even use a bank credit card to pay for such school expenses as tuition, books, and supplies. Many department stores, however, do not accept bank credit cards. They prefer to accept charge plates of their own customers. In this way, customers are encouraged to do their shopping only at that particular store.

One major advantage of bank credit cards is that people who have them are considered to be good credit risks. Another advantage is that a business firm is freed from the trouble and expense of checking and approving credit applications. It is also freed of the problems involved in billing and collecting debts. A third advantage is that the plan is attractive to consumers because the card is accepted at so many different businesses. Also, the consumer receives only one bill rather then several.

Travel and Entertainment Cards

Travel and entertainment card plans are offered by American Express, Carte Blanche, and Diners' Club. Airlines, restaurants, and hotels also offer travel and entertainment credit card plans. These cards are similar to bank credit cards, but there are differences. For example, they are harder to obtain. As a result, once you are accepted, your maximum credit limit may be higher. The travel and entertainment cards are usually accepted by fewer types of business firms than are bank credit cards. Such cards are most commonly used for dining and entertainment, travel, and rooms at hotels, motels, and resorts. They are also accepted in some retail businesses. A travel and entertainment cardholder pays an annual fee for using the service. The purchases made are billed in the same manner as those of the bank credit cards.

Travel and entertainment cards like bank credit cards, have certain advantages for the consumer. The consumer does not need to carry large sums of cash. The cardholder receives a single statement each month for many purchases made at many different businesses. The monthly bills are convenient for keeping records of purchases and payments and for keeping records of finance charges paid for income tax purposes.

Who Pays for Credit Cards?

Retailers who participate in the bank credit card plans or travel and entertainment card plans pay a fee. They pay the issuing bank or company a certain percentage of the total amount charged by customers using the cards. For example, if a customer makes a $25 purchase on one of the bank credit cards, the business might have to pay the bank or issuing company $1 out of that transaction.

What, then, do businesses get in return for this payment out of each credit card transaction? The issuing bank or company assumes the burden and expenses of credit investigation, billing,

A travel and entertainment credit card.

record keeping, credit collection, and the risk of bad debts for unpaid accounts. Merchants who accept credit cards have no need for their own credit departments. Also, businesses do not have to maintain customer accounts. Neither do they have have to worry about the expenses of collecting payments. Consumers who use credit cards look for businesses that will accept their cards. Therefore, merchants who accept credit cards encourage customers to charge their purchases. Merchants are therefore willing to pay a commission to the card-issuing bank or business.

As you may guess, the customers also pay for the use of credit. This is done in the way of higher prices charged by merchants for goods and services. You can see in the example above that if a merchant must pay $1 out of a $15 transaction, that merchant

Consumers who use credit cards look for businesses that will accept their cards. (UPI)

might have increased the price of that item by $1 to cover the fee to the bank or issuing company.

Do you think a merchant can operate a successful business by *not* accepting credit cards? Give reasons for your answer.

It has been estimated that more than 150 million new credit cards are issued each year. It has also been estimated that 1½ million credit cards are lost and about 300,000 are stolen each year.

To make it more difficult for someone to use a lost or stolen credit card, federal laws require that all newly issued credit cards include some type of identification. This is usually done in the form of a color photograph or a signature.

Credit cards should be guarded as carefully as cash. All old cards or unwanted cards should be either destroyed or returned to the issuing company. Losing a credit card may be almost as serious as losing a blank check. A dishonest person could use a stolen or lost credit card very easily. Until 1971, a person who lost a credit card was responsible for any bills run up by the finder unless the issuing company was notified of the loss in writing. Today, no credit cardholder can be held responsible for more than $50 of unauthorized purchases by someone using a lost or stolen card. The company issuing the credit card must notify the cardholder of his or her possible liability. And it must provide a self-addressed prestamped notice to be returned if the card is lost or stolen.

If you find that a credit card has been lost or stolen, you should immediately notify the company that issued it. First telephone the issuer, then give the issuer written notice. You might also use a telegram or a letter sent by certified mail.

Certain precautions should be taken to protect against fraudulent use of credit cards. A list of your credit cards and account numbers should be kept in a place separate from the wallet or purse in which you carry them. Many people keep such a list in their safe deposit boxes. If a card is lost or stolen, they can then determine the account number without difficulty.

If you have many credit cards, it may be wise to register them with a credit card registering service. Upon notification by you that your cards have been lost or stolen, the service will contact each of the issuing firms. The registering services do charge a fee, but the time and effort they save you may be well worth it. Individuals with many credit cards also may want to obtain credit card insurance to protect them against financial loss.

Another way to protect against credit card losses is to carefully check your monthly statements against your credit card receipts. Charges could be changed by dishonest establishments to increase amounts. And a dishonest clerk could use the card to imprint additional blank receipts, which could be used later for the clerk's own purchases.

ADVANTAGES OF SALES CREDIT

Some of the advantages of sales credit are as follows:

1. Sales credit is convenient. The customer avoids the bother of paying for small items at the time they are bought. Instead, a check can be written at the end of the month to pay for all of them at one time.

2. Consumers are able to obtain and use the goods and services before they pay for them.

3. Some business firms give more and better service to credit customers who pay their bills promptly. For example, many retail stores send notices of special sales to their credit customers before notice is given to the general public.

4. Consumers who buy on credit frequently find it easier to return goods and to get replacements for faulty products.

5. Consumers who buy on credit do not need to carry large amounts of cash.

Suppose you are opening a clothing store in a small town. Would you make credit available to your customers? If so, for what reasons? What types of accounts would you offer? If you would not make credit available, why not?

DISADVANTAGES OF SALES CREDIT

Although the use of sales credit does have several advantages, the wise consumer is also aware of its possible disadvantages. Some of these follow:

1. Sales credit is easy to get and often leads to overbuying by the consumer. Payment does not have to be made at the time of purchase. Therefore, many consumers buy more goods than they would buy if they had to pay cash.

2. The use of sales credit often leads to careless selection of goods. Business firms that sell on credit are often more liberal in their exchange and return policies. For this reason, many credit customers are not as careful in selecting goods as they would be if it were more difficult to return or exchange goods.

3. Prices at stores that sell on credit are sometimes higher than prices at stores that do not sell on credit. Selling on credit involves the expense of checking the credit records of customers. It also involves a great deal of extra bookkeeping. For example, mailing of monthly statements and recording of payments received is required. The losses due to returned merchandise and unpaid accounts are also added expenses. To make up for these extra expenses, the prices of some or all goods must be increased.

It has been said that "credit leads to extravagance and recklessness." Do you agree with this statement? Why or why not?

Learning Activities

Increasing Your Business Vocabulary

You should become familiar with each of the terms shown below. On a sheet of paper write the numbers 1 through 6. Then write alongside each number the term that best matches each of the numbered definitions.

bank credit card / charge account / credit card / finance charge / sales credit / single-use credit card

1. A charge made for the use of credit.
2. The credit used to purchase goods and services.
3. An identification card authorizing the holder to charge or obtain goods, services, or money on credit up to a set amount.
4. A credit card issued by a bank.
5. A credit plan that permits the user to charge any number of purchases and to pay for them according to a particular plan of repayment.
6. A credit card that can be used only at one retail business.

Understanding Business

1. Explain how a regular charge account works.
2. How does a 90-day or three-pay plan charge account differ from a regular charge account?

3. What convenience does the revolving charge account offer?

4. What are the most popular type of single-use credit cards?

5. What is the purpose of the bank credit card plans?

6. List the advantages to business firms of accepting bank credit cards.

7. What are the advantages to the consumer of using bank credit cards and travel and entertainment cards?

8. What is the maximum amount for which the cardholder is responsible if someone uses his or her lost or stolen credit card for unauthorized purchases?

9. What precautions should be taken to protect against illegal use of one's credit cards?

10. List the advantages of sales credit. The disadvantages.

Business Problems and Projects

1. David Kolb has a revolving charge account at Haynes Department Store. The minimum monthly payment is 1/10th of the new balance up to $500, but not less than $10, or the balance if less. The finance charge is 1½ percent of the previous balance, with a minimum charge of 50 cents. David's latest statement show the following:

A previous balance of $72.75.

A payment of $10.

Purchase of an electric typewriter for $289.95.

Purchase of tennis shoes for $13.95.

Merchandise returned for $8.60.

Purchase of a shirt for $15.90.

a. What is the finance charge on the previous balance?

b. What would be the minimum payment on the previous balance?

c. How much does David now owe Haynes Store?

d. What is the minimum payment he should make?

e. What will be the finance charge on the new balance?

2. This chapter discusses several forms of sales credit. On a form similar to the one shown below, identify the characteristics of each of the four forms.

Form of Credit	Is There a Finance Charge?	Are Payments Made Each Month?	Is the Balance Paid in Full?

3. Allan Soames can choose between two types of credit cards. One type—the Allbank Card—requires neither an annual fee nor payment in full each month; but it does impose a finance charge of 18 percent per year. The other—the Passport Card—requires an annual fee of $25 and the payment in full each month; but it imposes no finance charge. On the average, Allan expects to spend $75 each month with the card.

a. Which of the two cards would cost less in an average year?

b. Which of the two would you prefer? Why?

Chapter 21

Installment Sales Credit

Objectives

After completing your study of this chapter, you will be able to do the following:

1. Explain the difference between installment credit and charge account credit.

2. Describe the types of information that must be included in an installment contract.

3. Identify and describe the various special clauses that are often included in installment sales contracts.

4. Identify the two ways of stating finance charges.

5. Describe the guidelines for using installment sales credit and the obligations of the user.

In Chapter 20, it was pointed out that charge accounts and credit cards are generally used for things that are consumed either right away or, at most, within a short period of time. In this chapter you will study the type of credit used for things that are expected to be used over a relatively long period of time. This credit, called *installment credit,* is a type of credit in which the amount owed is repaid in a series of payments.

Buying on the installment plan has become one of the most popular methods for Americans to buy durable goods such as cars, furniture, and household appliances. *Durable goods* are items that will last a long time. Few people are able to save enough money to pay cash for durable goods. And few merchants are willing to risk selling durable goods on credit unless they have the right to take back the goods if they are not paid for. With large and expensive items, merchants want more than the customer's promise that the item will be paid for as agreed.

Installment credit is used to some extent by consumers of all ages and income levels. Younger households are more likely to have some type of installment credit debt, however, than older households. They have lower incomes, and they need more durable goods to furnish their homes. The older the family gets, the less is its installment credit debt. Older families usually have higher incomes and already own most of the durable goods they need. Thus, they have less need for installment credit.

INSTALLMENT CREDIT VS. CHARGE ACCOUNT CREDIT

There are several ways in which installment sales credit differs from charge account credit.

1. Most purchases made on installment sales credit require a down payment. A *down payment* is a small initial payment made toward the purchase price of an item. Charge account credit does not usually call for a down payment.

2. Finance charges are added to installment purchase prices. Charge account users do not usually pay finance charges for the use of credit.

Installment credit is used to finance expensive purchases such as this tractor. (American Stock)

3. The installment sales credit user signs a contract at the time of each purchase. The consumer who uses a charge account does not sign a contract at the time of purchase.

4. When one buys on the installment plan, title does not pass to the consumer until the final payment is made. *Title* is the legal ownership of goods. Charge account purchasers get immediate title to goods.

INSTALLMENT CONTRACTS

The signing of a contract is an important part of any installment credit purchase. The contract spells out the obligations of both the buyer and the seller. It is a legal document, and both the seller and the buyer are legally bound to its terms. The installment contract must contain the terms of purchase—including the total amount of charges—and the number of payments.

Most installment contracts contain a section called the security agreement. A *security agreement* is a written statement signed by the buyer stating that the seller has the right to take

Seller's Name: _Cook's Department Store_   Contract #_15807A_

3000 W. 63RD, Chicago, Illinois 60629

RETAIL INSTALLMENT CONTRACT AND SECURITY AGREEMENT

The undersigned (herein called Purchaser, whether one or more) purchases from _____Cook's_____ (seller) and grants to _____ a security interest in, subject to the terms and conditions hereof, the following described property.

QUANTITY	DESCRIPTION	AMOUNT	
1	HOTPOINT DRYER	250	00

Description of Trade-in:

	Sales Tax	12	50
	Total	268	50

Insurance Agreement

The purchase of insurance coverage is voluntary and not required for credit. _CREDIT LIFE_ insurance coverage is available at a cost of $ _5.00_ for the term of credit.

I desire insurance coverage
Signed _Donna Pozezinski_ Date _Sept. 1, 19--_

I do not desire insurance coverage

Signed_____ Date_____

PURCHASER'S NAME _Donna Pozezinski_
PURCHASER'S ADDRESS _3509 W. 60th Street_
CITY _Chicago_ STATE _Ill._ ZIP _60629_

1. CASH PRICE		$_250.00_
2. LESS: CASH DOWN PAYMENT	$ _25.00_	
3. TRADE-IN	————	
4. TOTAL DOWN PAYMENT	_25.00_	_225.00_
5. UNPAID BALANCE OF CASH PRICE		$_225.00_
6. OTHER CHARGES:		
SALES TAX		$ _12.50_
		————
7. AMOUNT FINANCED		$_237.50_
8. FINANCE CHARGE		$ _34.77_
9. TOTAL OF PAYMENTS		$_272.27_
10. DEFERRED PAYMENT PRICE (1+6+8)		$_297.27_
11. ANNUAL PERCENTAGE RATE		_26_ %

Purchaser hereby agrees to pay to _Cook's Department Store_ at their offices shown above the "TOTAL OF PAYMENTS" shown above in _12_ monthly installments of $ _24.78_ (final payment to be $ _24.69_) the first installment being payable _Oct. 1, 19--_ 19 _--_, and all subsequent installments on the same day of each consecutive month until paid in full. The finance charge applies from _SEPT. 1, 19--_.

Signed _Donna Pozezinski_

Notice to Buyer: You are entitled to a copy of the contract you sign. You have the right to pay in advance the unpaid balance of this contract and obtain a partial refund of the finance charge based on the "Actuarial Method." [Any other method of computation may be so identified, for example, "Rule of 78's," "Sum of the Digits," etc.]

A retail installment contract.

back goods if they are not paid for. This means that, although the buyer has possession and use of the goods, the seller still has title to the goods until full payment has been made.

To protect the seller's interest in the goods, the seller has the right to repossess goods. To _repossess_ goods means to take the goods back from the buyer if the buyer is unable to meet the payments of the installment contract. After repossessing the item, the seller then has the right to resell it. However, the original buyer may have the right to any money left over after the unpaid balance and any cost of repossession and resale are paid. Costs of repossession may include storage costs, collection fees, and attorney's fees. In some cases, the amount received from the resale may not cover the unpaid balance or the costs of repossession and resale. If so, the original buyer must still pay the difference even though he or she no longer possesses the goods.

Do you think it is fair that the seller has the right to repossess goods? Give reasons for your answer.

There are certain clauses that are often included in installment sales contracts. The clauses are terms of the contract that are used to give the seller a legal advantage over the purchaser. Some of the most common clauses are discussed below. You should always read an installment contract with care before signing it. To avoid future problems, be particularly alert to such clauses.

Wage Assignment Clause

A *wage assignment clause* is a clause under which a debtor's employer may be notified that some of the wages of the debtor are to be paid to the creditor. This clause assures the creditor of receiving payment on the installment contract because the employer automatically deducts a certain amount from each paycheck. There is, however, a limit on the amount that can be collected through wage assignment. No more than 25 percent of the employee's pay may be deducted for repayment of the debt.

The wage assignment clause is a form of wage garnishment. *Garnishment* is a court order directing an employer to withhold part of an employee's wages for payment of a debt. If a wage assignment clause is part of the installment contract, the garnishment is not necessary.

Acceleration Clause

Another clause that is often included in installment sales contracts is the acceleration clause. The *acceleration clause* is a clause making the unpaid balance of the contract amount immediately due if one or more payments are missed. If the buyer is unable to pay the total unpaid balance, the goods can then be repossessed and resold.

Balloon Clause

A *balloon clause* is a clause that makes the final payment much larger than all previous payments. For example, a contract may call for 23 monthly payments of $15 and a final payment of $150. If the buyer is not aware of such a large final payment and has not planned for it, the buyer may be unable to pay it. As a result, the goods may then be repossessed. If an installment contract contains this type of clause, the law requires that the amount of the balloon payment must be stated. A balloon clause is prohibited by law in some states. Elsewhere, anyone signing a sales contract should make sure it does not contain a balloon clause.

Add-On Clause

An *add-on clause* permits the addition of new purchases to an existing installment contract. A new contract does not have to be drawn up for each new purchase. A contract with add-on clause should be avoided if the seller retains title to all items until the last one is paid for. In such cases, the seller can repossess goods that have already been paid for if the buyer fails to make payment for the additional items.

Confession-of-Judgment Clause

In a *confession-of-judgment clause*, the buyer gives up the right to an attorney or to judicial processes. The buyer gives up the right to be notified to appear in court if the seller uses legal action to collect the debt. The buyer also gives up the right to any defense. Court fees and attorney's fees may be added to the amount of the debt. Some states have laws prohibiting the confession-of-judgment clause in sales contracts.

COST OF INSTALLMENT SALES CREDIT

When you are facing a decision to use installment credit, you must keep the cost in mind. The cost of installment credit is high.

Consumers should always check the terms of their contract because some offers of credit may appear better than they are. (Monkmeyer)

Finance charges add up. And over a period of years, they can amount to a lot of money. Unfortunately, many people buying on installment plans do not consider how much they are paying overall to use credit. They are more interested in the amount of the weekly or monthly payments.

The total cost of credit is the total amount that must be paid for all finance charges. Finance charges may be stated in two ways: the dollar cost of credit and the annual percentage rate.

Dollar Cost of Credit

The *dollar cost of credit* is the amount a credit user actually pays for the use of credit. To find the dollar cost of credit, subtract the amount to be financed from the total amount to be repaid. Suppose, for example, that you want to purchase a new color television set. Rather than pay the $400 cash price, you make a down payment of $35 and pay the balance in 12 installments of $34 each. The example below shows how the dollar cost of this installment purchase would be figured.

Total to be repaid ($34 x 12 months)	$408
Less amount to be financed ($400—$35)	—365
Dollar cost of credit	$43

The dollar cost of credit is $43. Therefore, the actual purchase price of the color televison set will be $443. You can see that a larger item repaid over several years would be very costly in terms of the dollar cost of credit.

Annual Percentage Rate

The second way of stating finance charges is as an annual percentage rate. The *annual percentage rate* is the actual rate of interest paid by the credit user for the use of installment credit. Annual percentage rate is also called *true annual interest*.

This is the formula for computing the annual percentage rate:

$$\text{Annual percentage rate} = \frac{2 \times \text{number of payment periods per year} \times \text{dollar cost of credit}}{\text{Amount financed} \times \text{number of installments plus 1}}$$

Let's apply this formula to the purchase of the color television set. In that example there were 12 payments of $34 each. The total amount to be financed was $365. Therefore, the annual percentage rate for the credit used to purchase the set is 21.7 percent.

$$\text{Annual percentage rate} = \frac{2 \times 12 \times \$43}{\$365 \times 13} = 21.7\%$$

When comparing the costs of credit, do you think the dollar cost of credit or the annual percentage rate tells you more?

WHEN TO USE
INSTALLMENT SALES CREDIT

Because the decision to use or not use installment sales credit is a very personal one, only you can make it. Consider all possible sides of the matter. Then, before deciding, ask yourself these questions:

1. Is the good or service a *need* or a *want?*
2. Is the good or service needed now? Could money be saved to pay cash or to make a larger down payment?
3. Are you willing to wait while you save?
4. Is the price of the good or service likely to be higher or lower in the future?
5. Does the good or service have lasting value that will make it worth the extra cost of credit?
6. Will the satisfaction of having the good or service while you are paying for it be worth the extra cost of credit?
7. Will the monthly payments and total payment fit into your spending plans over a period of time?

 What are some of the advantages of waiting to purchase a good or service until you have saved enough to pay cash? What are some of the disadvantages?

RESPONSIBILITIES OF USING INSTALLMENT SALES CREDIT

As they should with all financial transactions, consumers who are considering using installment sales credit must realize their responsibilities. Here are some guidelines for installment buying:

1. Check your ability to repay the obligation.
2. Read the contract carefully before signing it. Determine how much the credit is costing in dollars and cents. Also, determine the annual percentage rate.
3. Be sure all parts of the contract have been filled in before signing it. Do not sign a blank contract or one that is completed in part.
4. Do not sign the contract if there are special clauses that you do not want. Ask that these clauses be crossed out. Do not

accept the contract unless the seller agrees to make these changes.

5. Get everything in writing. Do not accept the seller's verbal agreement about terms of the contract. Have all terms written in the agreement so no questions will arise later.

6. If you do not understand a provision in the contract, ask the seller to explain it to you.

7. Obtain a copy of the signed contract. This agreement is legally binding on the seller as well as the buyer.

Meeting the Terms of a Contract

After signing an installment sales contract, it is important that all terms are met as contained in the contract. Follow these guidelines to protect yourself:

1. Make payments on time to avoid payment of a late penalty charge. Know the grace period. A *grace period* is the number of days after the due date in which payment can be made without a penalty.

2. Know the consequences for late payments. In most cases, the consequence is a late penalty charge. In others, it may involve an acceleration clause.

3. Keep proofs of payment. Keep accurate records when payments are made, how much is paid, and how they are made— whether by check, cash, or money order. Keep receipts of all payments.

4. If you are unable to make a payment on time, call or write to ask for an extension. An *extension* is an extra period of time during which payment may be made.

5. Discuss problems with your creditors. Most creditors are willing to discuss solutions to payment problems. To refuse to meet with creditors only creates a bad credit reputation for you and increases the chances of repossession of goods.

Learning Activities

Increasing Your Business Vocabulary

You should become familar with each of the terms shown below. On a sheet of paper write the numbers 1 through 14. Then write alongside each number the term that best matches each of the numbered definitions.

acceleration clause / add-on clause / annual percentage / balloon clause / confession-of-judgment clause / dollar cost of credit / down payment / garnishment / grace period / installment credit / repossess / security agreement / title / wage assignment clause

1. A written statement signed by the buyer stating that the seller has the right to take back goods if they are not paid for.

2. To reclaim or take back goods from the buyer if the buyer is unable to meet the payments of the installment contract.

3. A clause under which a debtor's employer may be notified that some of the wages of a debtor are to be paid to the creditor.

4. A court order directing an employer to withhold part of an employee's wages for payment of a debt.

5. Legal ownership of goods.

6. A clause making the unpaid balance of the contract amount immediately due if one or more payments are missed.

7. A clause that makes the final payment much larger than all previous payments.

8. A clause that permits the addition of new purchases to an existing installment contract.

9. A clause in which the buyer gives up the right to an attorney.

10. The amount a credit user actually pays for the use of credit.

11. The actual rate of interest paid by the credit user for its use.

12. A small initial payment made toward the purchase price.

13. A type of credit in which the amount owed is repaid in a series of payments.

14. A period of time after the due date in which payment can be made without penalty.

Understanding Business

1. Do younger or older families use more installment credit? Explain your answer.

2. List the major differences between charge account credit and installment sales credit.

3. What types of information must installment sales contracts include?

4. What can a creditor do if a debtor does not make payments on an installment contract?

5. What is the buyer's responsibility if the amount received from the sale of a repossessed item does not cover the amount still owed to the creditor plus the repossession and resale costs?

6. Why does the seller often include clauses such as acceleration or balloon clauses in installment credit contracts?

7. Explain how to compute the dollar cost of credit.

8. What questions should you ask yourself before using installment credit?

9. What are some guidelines for installment buying?

10. What are the responsibilities of the installment credit user?

Business Problems and Projects

1. In this chapter you learned that in many credit purchases, the seller is protected by a security agreement that gives the seller the right to repossess goods. Read this article and then answer the questions that follow.

CRACKDOWN ON CONSUMER-FINANCE REPOSSESSIONS ASKED BY FTC

WASHINGTON, D.C. (UPI)— The Federal Trade Commission (FTC) today proposed a crackdown on the $75 billion-a-year consumer finance industry.

The action was intended to provide borrowers protection from such things as wage attachments and blanket repossession of household goods, the FTC said.

The rule is aimed at provisions commonly found in contracts used for automobile loans and for other consumer credit transactions carried on by financial institutions other than banks.

J. Thomas Rosch, head of the FTC's Bureau of Consumer Protection, told a press conference that a survey shows most people who default on loans are not deadbeats, but are ill, jobless or simply overextended.

He said borrowers simply are not equipped to deal with many provisions currently used in contracts.

Rosch said current contracts often do not identify the household goods that can be repossessed if the borrower defaults. As a result, he said, they "include things such as the baby crib, the nuptial bed, and pots and pans, things which if taken can severely affect the debtors' state of mind."

Under the proposal, the household goods put up as security would have to be clearly spelled out.

The proposal contains two alternatives involving wage assignments—provisions in the contract that allow the creditor to go to an employer and take part or all of the defaulting debtor's paycheck until the loan is paid off.

One proposal would ban such assignments while the second would limit it to loans involving $300 or less.

a. What do the letters *FTC* mean? What is the FTC proposing?

b. What protection would the action give to borrowers?

c. At what kinds of institutions is the action aimed?

d. What types of items may now be repossessed according to the article?

e. What restriction does the proposal put on household goods that are put up as security?

f. What does the wage-assignment provision in the contract allow the creditor to do?

2. Assume that you are purchasing a stereotape player for your car. The cash price for the tape player is $210. You, however, have agreed to make a $15 cash down payment and make $10 monthly payments for a period of 2 years.

a. What is the total amount you will have to pay?

b. What is the dollar cost of credit for this purchase?

c. Compute the annual percentage rate for the use of credit.

Chapter 22

Cash Credit

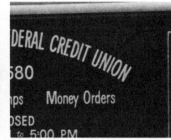

Objectives

After completing your study of this chapter, you will be able to do the following:

1. Discuss the difference between short-term and long-term credit.

2. List and describe the forms of secured loans.

3. Identify and discuss the major sources of cash credit.

4. Describe the method that should be followed when shopping for credit.

Just as consumers have many reasons for using sales credit, they also have many reasons for using cash credit. *Cash credit* is the credit used to borrow money or to obtain a loan. The terms *cash credit* and *loan* mean the same thing. A consumer who applies for cash credit is applying for a loan of money. Cash credit enables consumers to buy goods and services and to pay for them later.

People take out loans to buy homes, automobiles, household appliances, and furniture. They also borrow money to pay medical and dental bills. In emergencies, they may have to borrow to pay unexpected expenses. People also seek loans to pay for education, vacations, and taxes. Some people even borrow to combine small debts or to buy stocks, bonds, or real estate. For whatever reasons people borrow money, it is to their advantage to know about the types of cash credit and where such credit can be obtained.

Do you think it is sensible for someone to borrow money to take a vacation? Give reasons for your answer.

PROMISSORY NOTE

When you borrow money you usually have signed a note promising to repay the loan within a specified period of time. This written promise, which serves as evidence of the loan, is called a *promissory note*. A promissory note can take the form of a letter or, as is most often the case, a preprinted blank. However, it must contain such

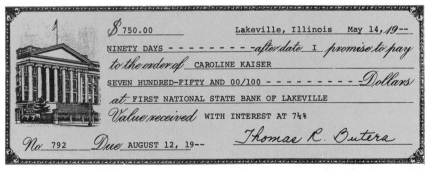

A promissory note.

information as the length of time of the loan, the date, the amount, the interest, the payee's name, and the signature of the maker.

OFFERING SECURITY
FOR LOANS

Cash loans may be either secured or unsecured. A secured loan is one in which the borrower pledges some personal property to the lender to guarantee repayment of the loan. Property that is used as security for a loan is called *collateral.* Stocks, bonds, insurance policies, automobiles, and houses are common forms of collateral. The collateral protects the lender in the event that the borrower fails to repay the loan. If the note has not been repaid by the due date, the lender has the right to sell the collateral. The due date of a promissory note is called the *maturity date.*

Another form of security, called *loan endorsement* or *loan guarantee,* requires the borrower to get another person to assume responsibility for the loan if the borrower is unable to repay it. The other person, called a *cosigner* or *comaker,* signs a promissory note along with the borrower. Thus both the borrower and the cosigner are obligated by the note.

List some factors you would consider before cosigning a loan.

An unsecured loan does not require any type of security. This type of loan, called a *signature loan,* is backed only by the borrower's promise to repay the loan. Signature loans are granted only if the credit investigation shows that the borrower is a very good credit risk. If the loan is not repaid, however, the borrower can be sued by the lender for the amount of the unpaid loan.

DURATION OF LOANS

Loans made to consumers can be either short-term loans or long-term loans. Loans that are repaid within a five-year period are called *short-term loans.* Loans that are repaid during a period of more than five years are called *long-term loans.*

Most of the personal loans that consumers receive from banks are short-term loans. (Chase Manhattan Bank)

Short-Term Credit

Most frequently, consumer credit is short-term credit. This type of credit includes personal loans that consumers receive from banks and other lending institutions. It also includes charge accounts, credit card accounts, and installment contracts—all of which were discussed earlier. But it does not include home mortgages, because they almost always represent long-term debt.

Long-Term Credit

Long-term credit is credit extended for a period of more than five years. The most common form of long-term credit used by consumers is the home mortgage. A *home mortgage* is a secured loan in which the home and the land serve as collateral for the loan. Most home mortgages are repaid over a period of 20 to 30 years, usually in equal monthly installments.

The entire amount of the mortgage, with interest, is paid up on the due date of the final monthly payment. When the final monthly payment is made, the borrower obtains title to the home. Until then, the mortgage lender retains title to the home. The lender has the right to repossess the house if the borrower fails to make payments on time.

LOAN REPAYMENT

There are generally two common kinds of cash credit offered to consumers. These are known as single-payment loans and installment loans. A *single-payment loan* is a type of cash credit in which the amount owed, plus interest, is repaid in one lump sum. Short-term loans are often single-payment loans. This is especially true when the amount of a short-term loan is small, so that repayment can be made in one payment.

What possible problem should a consumer consider when borrowing money with a single-payment loan?

The installment loan is the most common form of cash credit. An *installment loan* is a loan which is repaid in installments over a period of years rather than in a lump sum. This type of credit is similar to installment sales credit except that the borrower receives money instead of goods or services. If the borrower fails to make payments when they are due, the lender has the right to repossess the goods purchased on installment credit.

SOURCES OF CASH CREDIT

Commercial banks, credit unions, small-loan companies, and life insurance policies, are some of the many sources of cash credit that are available to consumers.

Because of the variety of lenders, borrowers will find that terms of borrowing money differ. The charges for the credit services will vary, the amount of money a lender will lend will vary, and the risks that the lenders are willing to assume will vary. The repayment period may be different, the requirements for security or collateral may be different, and the requirements for cosigners or comakers may be different. Some lenders will grant loans on the basis of the borrower's signature. Some will not extend credit to unemployed persons or to those individuals whose incomes fall below a certain level.

Most lenders want to know why the money is needed or for what purpose it is intended. Some lenders will not bother with short-term loans of one or two months. Others are limited in the length of time for which they can lend money.

Explain how the degree of risk a lender will accept affects the cost of credit to the borrower.

Commercial Banks

Commercial banks are the largest single source of cash credit. They account for about one-third of the total of all personal loans outstanding. Generally, commercial banks are able to grant small loans at interest rates similar to those of credit unions, which are lower than the rates charged by small-loan companies.

Commercial banks offer a wide variety of cash credit plans for both small and large loans. Loans may be secured or unsecured, depending on the amount of the loan and the period of repayment. Personal loans can be granted for any number of reasons.

Commercial banks also offer savings account loans. A *savings account* loan is a loan for which the borrower's savings account is used as security or collateral. Money can be borrowed from the bank at a fairly low rate of interest. Any loss to the bank because of an unpaid loan is fully protected by the savings account.

Give some reasons why a person might choose to borrow money rather than to withdraw it from a savings account.

"Checking plus" Account   An increasingly popular type of personal loan service is the "checking plus" account. This is a cash credit service connected with a checking account. A "checking plus" account permits you to write checks in excess of the balance in your checking account. You must, however, have your bank's approval for this type of service. Suppose you write a check for more than you have in your checking account. Enough to cover the

excess amount of the check is transferred automatically into your checking account from your credit reserve. The reserve is available when you need it, and you can draw on it up to a certain limit. As you repay, your credit reserve is rebuilt so that you can use it again. Each month a credit reserve statement is sent. It shows the amount, if any, that has been transferred to your checking account and the amount you have to repay. There is, of course, a charge for this type of credit service just as there is with other types of credit.

 Ask members of your family and friends whether they have a "checking plus" or similar account. Find out why they have it. Ask them what they like and dislike about it. Write a short report on your findings.

Credit Unions

A *credit union* is an association whose members have a common bond and join together for the purpose of saving money and making small loans at low interest rates to members. Credit union rates are among the lowest of all. One reason is that credit unions are not trying to make a profit.

There are several advantages of borrowing from a credit union:

1. Interest rates are relatively low—the lowest available for many people. One percent a month is often the maximum rate that the government regulating credit unions allows to be charged on the unpaid balance of unsecured loans.
2. Secured loans may have monthly interest costs as low as three-fourths of one percent. Interest costs for credit union loans, therefore, are between 9 and 12 percent annually.
3. Collateral and a cosigner are not required on small loans. Because the borrower belongs to the association, security is not necessary.

A major drawback of credit unions is that they lend only to their own members, not to the general public. Credit unions are essentially owned by those who invest money in them.

Because credit unions are not trying to make a profit, they are able to offer low interest rates. (Stock, Boston)

Small-loan Companies

A *small-loan company* is a company that specializes in making small loans to consumers. Small-loan companies are often referred to as *consumer finance companies*. Next to commercial banks, small-loan companies are the largest source of small loans. The maximum limit for unsecured loans is set by each state. It ranges from $1,000 to $5,000. The maximum repayment period is also set by each state. Eighteen months to five years are common limits. Small-loan companies are generally willing to grant loans in smaller amounts than most other lending agencies. However, restrictions on the amount of the loan and the length of time over which the loan may be repaid are disadvantages.

Small-loan companies often lend to people who are considered to be poor risks by other lenders. In fact, if one has a poor credit rating, small-loan companies may be the only source of a loan. Because of the high-risk nature of their loans, small-loan

The interest rates for loans from consumer finance companies are higher because the risk on these loans is generally greater. (Monkmeyer)

companies charge high interest rates. These rates may range from 24 to 36 percent annually, depending on the size of the loan and the length of time for repayment.

Life Insurance Policies

One of the least expensive ways of obtaining a personal loan is to borrow on a life insurance policy. The maximum loan amount available on a life insurance policy is usually limited to 80 to 90 percent of its cash surrender value. The *cash surrender value* is the amount of money that will be paid to a policyholder who stops paying premiums and turns in the policy. There are several advantages to borrowing on the cash surrender value of your policy. First, the interest rate is fixed and generally stated in the policy. The interest rate may be quite low—about 5 or 6 percent. Second, interest is usually charged only on the balance of the loan outstanding, and it may be paid with the regularly scheduled premium payments. A disadvantage is that you decrease your insurance coverage by the amount of the loan. Another disadvantage is that the company will not bill you for repayment. For that reason, you must discipline yourself to make payments. If not, you will be paying interest on the full amount year after year.

Why do you think you are required to pay interest on money borrowed on the cash surrender value of your life insurance when this money could really be considered your money?

Pawnbrokers

Another source of cash loans is the pawnbroker. A *pawnbroker* is a person licensed to lend money in exchange for goods. People usually borrow from pawnbrokers either in emergencies or when their credit is not accepted by other lending agencies. To get a loan from a pawnbroker, one must turn over personal property, such as jewelry, musical instruments, and the like, as security. The borrower will receive about 50 percent of the resale value of the goods pawned. To redeem the article, the borrower must repay the money with interest within a specified period of time. Interest may range from 24 to 120 percent, or higher, on an annual basis.

In some states if the pawned item is not redeemed within a certain time limit, the pawnbroker can sell it. If there is a surplus over the loan amount, it is supposed to be given to the borrower. In

Pawnshops lend money using personal property turned over to them as security. (Tyler Janssen)

other states if the pawned item is not redeemed within a certain period, title passes to the pawnbroker.

Would you consider borrowing money from a pawnbroker? Why or why not?

SHOPPING FOR CASH CREDIT

If you are considering a personal loan, you should do several things. First of all, you should decide the exact amount of money you need. This will help you decide the right loan source to use. Second, you should list the reasons why you want to take out a loan in that amount. You should also note the purpose or purposes for which the money will be used. You should be able to tell the lender about your financial resources, including your net worth and amount of income. You should be prepared to tell the lender about your financial obligations. These include the number of dependents, the amount and repayment schedule for current debts, and your monthly living expenses. As a prospective borrower, you should also review your employment record. You may have to describe any jobs you have held in the previous 10 years in addition to your present job. And finally, you should review your credit record. You will need to accurately describe any debts and installment loans that you paid off on time. Any credit references such as credit cards, charge accounts, and bank loans should be listed. All of the above information presents a good image to lending agencies.

Name reasons why you would want to present a good image to lending agencies.

Once the above information has been gathered, you are ready to shop for a loan. You should talk with several lending agencies in order to find the best offer. Be sure to find out the following:

1. The exact amount of money that will be loaned.
2. The manner in which the finance charges will be figured.
3. The actual annual interest rate.
4. The dollar cost of credit.
5. The repayment schedule.
6. The charges for early payment.
7. The charges for late payment.
8. The collateral required.

With this information, you can easily decide which agency would be your best source for a loan.

Learning Activities

Increasing Your Business Vocabulary

You should become familiar with each of the terms shown below. On a sheet of paper write the numbers 1 through 17. Then write alongside each number the term that best matches each of the numbered definitions.

cash credit / cash surrender value / collateral / credit union / home mortgage / loan endorsement / pawnbroker / promissory note / savings account loan / secured loan / signature loan / single-payment loan / small-loan company / short-term credit / long-term credit / maturity date / installment loan

1. Written evidence of a debt that states the nature and conditions of the promise to repay.

2. A secured loan for which the home and the land serve as collateral.

3. A loan backed only by the borrower's promise to repay.

4. The amount of money that will be paid to a policyholder who stops paying premiums and turns in the policy.

5. A loan for which a savings account is used as security.

6. A company that specializes in making small consumer loans.

7. Property used as security for a loan.

8. A loan in which the borrower pledges some personal property to the lender to guarantee repayment of the loan.

9. A person licensed to lend money in exchange for goods.

10. A type of cash credit in which the amount owed, plus interest, is repaid in one lump sum.

11. An association whose members have a common bond and join together for the purpose of saving money and making small loans at low interest rates to members.

12. Credit used to borrow money or to obtain a loan.

13. Loans repaid within a five-year period.

14. Loans repaid during a period of more than five years.

15. The due date of a promissory note.

16. A loan repaid in a series of payments.

17. A form of security requiring a cosigner.

Understanding Business

1. List the reasons why people use cash credit.

2. What does a loan endorsement or loan guarantee require of the cosigner?

3. On what basis are signature loans granted?

4. What is the most common form of cash credit?

5. List several ways in which the various lending agencies differ.

6. Which type of lending agency is the largest single source of cash credit?

7. Why can credit unions charge such low rates?

8. What are the advantages of borrowing on a life insurance policy? What are the disadvantages?

9. Explain how you obtain a loan from a pawnbroker. How do you repay the loan?

10. What should you check when you are considering taking out a personal loan?

Business Problems and Projects

1. Determine the maturity date for each of the promissory notes listed below.

   a. 1-year note, dated January 15, 1980

   b. 30-day note, dated April 1, 1979

   c. 6-months note, dated June 20, 1981

   d. 90-day note, dated October 3, 1980

   e. 30-day note, dated December 27, 1981

2. For each of the loans shown below, calculate the amount of interest to be paid and the total amount to be paid when the loan is due.

   To calculate interest for full years, use this formula:

   $$\text{Interest} = \text{Amount of Loan} \times \text{Interest Rate} \times \frac{\text{Number}}{\text{of Years}}$$

   To calculate interest for a certain number of months, use this formula:

   $$\text{Interest} = \text{Amount of Loan} \times \text{Rate of Interest} \times \frac{\text{Number of Months}}{12}$$

   To calculate interest for a specific number of days, use this formula:

   $$\text{Interest} = \text{Amount of Loan} \times \text{Rate of Interest} \times \frac{\text{Number of Days}}{360}$$

   a. $600 for 1 year at 6% interest

   b. $350 for 2 years at 5% interest

   c. $150 for 6 months at 7% interest

d. $400 for 30 days at 8% interest

e. $300 for 90 days at 10% interest

f. $1,000 for 3 months at 4% interest

3. The amount of down payment a person can make will affect the total amount of interest as well as the amount of monthly payments. Study the chart below and answer the questions that follow.

EFFECT OF LARGER DOWN PAYMENTS
(purchase of a $20,000 home to be financed at 7½%)

Down Payment	Mortgage Amount Borrowed	Monthly Payment for 25 Years	Total Interest Paid in 25 Years
$3,000	$17,000	$124.85	$20,455
4,000	16,000	117.50	19,250
5,000	15,000	110.16	18,048
6,000	14,000	102.82	16,846
7,000	13,000	95.47	15,641

a. Assume that you make a down payment of $3,000.
   (1) What is the mortgage amount borrowed?
   (2) How much is the monthly payment?
   (3) What is the total amount of interest paid in the 25-year period?
   (4) What is the total amount that must be paid to the mortgage company by the end of the 25-year period?

b. Assume that you make a down payment of $7,000.
   (1) What is the mortgage amount borrowed?
   (2) How much is the monthly payment?
   (3) What is the total amount of interest paid in the 25-year period?
   (4) What is the total amount that must be paid to the mortgage company by the end of the 25-year period?

Part Three

CONSUMER DECISION MAKING AND MONEY MANAGEMENT

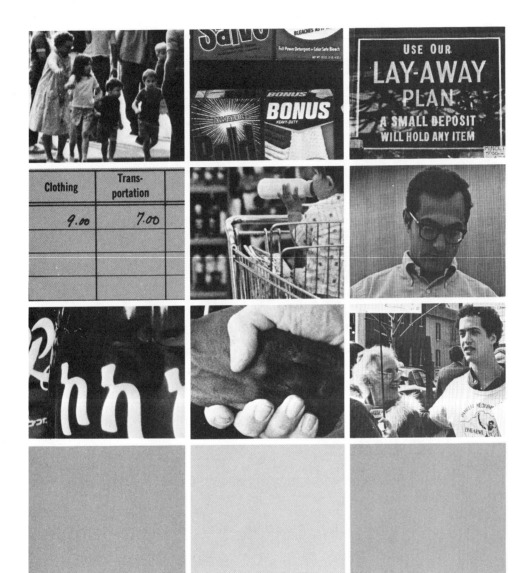

Chapter 23

The Consumer in Our Private Enterprise Economy

Objectives

After completing your study of this chapter, you will be able to do the following:

1. Define the terms *consumer needs* and *consumer wants.*

2. Explain the importance of setting consumer goals and describe how such goals affect the way people live.

3. Describe the difference between initial and secondary demand.

4. Explain how consumer demand directly affects production.

5. Explain how consumer demand affects the job market.

Throughout your lifetime, one of your most important roles will be that of consumer. Whatever your income, you will be making many consumer decisions. These decisions, together with those of millions of other consumers, will have a great effect on our economy. They will determine what our businesses produce, how they produce, and how much they charge for what they produce.

A large part of your earnings will be spent for your basic needs. Some will be spent for things that you may not need, but that you want nevertheless. And some may be set aside in a savings program. In the end, of course, how you use your money and how much satisfaction you receive from it will be up to you.

What is meant by the statement: "How you use your money and how much satisfaction you receive from it is up to you"?

CONSUMER NEEDS AND WANTS

People have all kinds of needs and wants. As consumers, their wants are for goods and services. If a want is for something that is necessary for survival, we call it a *consumer need*. Food, clothing, and shelter are the most obvious consumer needs.

In addition to the needs of food, clothing, and shelter, there are many other things that consumers want. These other wants may not be necessary for survival, but they certainly make life more pleasant and enjoyable. They are called *consumer wants*. You can probably think of many goods and services that make your life more pleasant and a great deal easier. For example, clothes can be washed by hand, but this chore becomes a great deal easier if an automatic washing machine is used. Swimming in a lake or river is fun, but having a canoe or perhaps a motorboat for water-skiing might be even more fun. Simple clothes provide the basic protection you need, but you may be one of those people who get a great deal of pleasure from wearing the newest and most fashionable styles. A beef stew may provide the nourishment you need, but a thick steak may satisfy you more.

Consumer wants are limitless. They are limitless because the moment one want has been satisfied, another want takes its place.

The day never comes when you can say, "Now I have satisfied all my wants." Even those with a lot of money have to face the fact that wants go on forever. If wants, then, are unlimited, how do consumers decide which wants they will try to satisfy? How do they decide which wants are important to them?

 Prepare a list of your most important wants. Is it realistic for you to think you can obtain the items needed to satisfy these wants? Why or why not?

SETTING CONSUMER GOALS

Very often people do not satisfy their wants. This happens because they do not give enough thought to which wants are most important to them. They soon find that they do not have enough money to get all the things they want. Everyone faces this problem. The way to solve the problem is to think ahead. Decide now on the things you really want, and start working toward getting them. The process of sorting out wants and deciding which ones are most important is called *goal setting*. By setting goals, people can get the most satisfaction from their limited incomes. They know what it is they are working for.

All too often, however, people do not know what they are working for, and they spend their money in a rash, unplanned way. Many of their purchases are made on the spur of the moment. Unplanned consumer spending is called *impulse buying*. Buying on impulse is often the same as throwing money away. Later, the buyer may regret having made the purchase.

The selection of the goals can also be a problem. Sometimes people set consumer goals that they cannot reach. When this happens, the goals must be reexamined and weighed against realities. New goals should be set, goals that are both reasonable and attainable.

 Give some examples of your own impulse buying.

Goals Guide Your Way of Life

The goals people set for themselves determine to a great extent how they live. These goals may determine the number of hours they work, the amount of money they save, and of course the things on which they spend their money.

To some people, an expensive car or boat is an important goal. To achieve this goal, they may take a second or even a third job to earn the money to buy it sooner than otherwise possible. Others may be willing to give up one thing completely or spend less for several things so that they can buy what they want sooner. Suppose your family decides to save for a long vacation trip next summer. To achieve this goal, all of you may choose to give up movies, sports events, and eating out. Or your family may choose not to purchase a new car. Or your family may decide to take no vacation this year and save the money for next year's vacation.

Perhaps your spending habits will have to change so that you can satisfy a certain want. You may, for example, look forward to buying an 8-track stereo sound system. You want this stereo so much that you are willing to give up all other unnecessary

The goals people set for themselves help determine how they spend their money. (Betty Medsger; Lejeune/Stockmarket, Los Angeles)

expenses until you get the stereo system. You may decide to spend less for clothing. You may decide to give up daily stops for a hamburger and a soft drink after school. You may give up part of your free time or study time for a part-time job. Goals that are carefully and earnestly thought out determine to a large extent how an individual or a family carries on daily activities. In other words, goals guide your way of life.

Give some examples of how goals set by you or your family have affected your way of life.

CONSUMER ACTIONS AFFECT OUR ECONOMIC SYSTEM

The goals that consumers set and the spending decisions they make have a direct impact on our economy. Consumer demand dictates what goods and services will be produced. In turn, this demand also affects the kinds of jobs that will be available. Before discussing these points, let's examine how the demand for one good or service affects the demand for other goods and services.

When consumers are willing to spend their money for a good or a service, they are expressing *initial demand*. Each consumer is demanding of business a particular good or service. A business firm feels this demand not from just one or two consumers but from hundreds or thousands of consumers. These initial demands are the beginning of a series of business operations that will in turn create secondary demands.

Secondary demand is the demand made by a business firm that is trying to satisfy a consumer's initial demand. For example, suppose you go to the showroom of a local car dealer and order a new car. This is an expression of initial demand. The dealer in turn sends the order to the manufacturer, who may have a great many similar orders that must be met. To fill these orders, the manufacturer orders more steel, paint, rubber, or parts. In this way, the manufacturer creates secondary demand for all the things needed to build a car.

An initial demand for a good or service creates a series of secondary demands for other goods and services. (Stock, Boston; Monkmeyer; Flying Tigers)

List some of the secondary demands created when a school shows initial demand through the purchase of a textbook.

Demand for goods and services sets up a chain reaction in the economy and has two important effects. First, demand gives a clear and direct order to producers to supply certain goods or services. Demand, in other words, directs production. Second, as producers prepare to make the goods or deliver the services being demanded, they hire workers. Demand, therefore, creates jobs.

When you and thousands of other consumers demand, for example, a specific car model, you indirectly create a demand for hundreds of jobs. In order to produce the car, the automaker may have to hire additional assembly-line workers, office workers, and even food service workers. The companies that supply paint, parts, and upholstery may have to hire additional workers. And the retail stores and restaurants serving the areas in which the automaker and its suppliers are located may have to employ additional workers to meet the increased demand on their services.

If you and the other consumers shift your demand to another car model, many of these employees will lose their jobs. However, a new series of jobs may be created by the new demand.

List two examples where a shift in the demand for a product has created either employment or unemployment in your area.

Learning Activities

Increasing Your Business Vocabulary

You should become familiar with each of the terms shown below. On a sheet of paper write the numbers 1 through 6. Then write alongside each number the term that best matches each of the numbered definitions.

consumer needs / consumer wants / goal setting / impulse buying / initial demand / secondary demand

1. Those wants not necessary for survival but that make life more pleasant and enjoyable.

2. The process of sorting out wants and deciding which ones are most important.

3. The demand made by a business firm trying to satisfy consumer demand.

4. Unplanned consumer spending.

5. The demand made by a consumer for a good or service.

6. Something that is necessary for physical survival.

Understanding Business

1. For what purposes do people spend most of their earnings?

2. What are the three basic consumer needs?

3. Explain the difference between a consumer need and a consumer want.

4. Why must consumers make choices as to how many of their wants they can satisfy?

5. What should you do if you find you cannot reach the consumer goals that you have set?

6. Give five examples of ways in which goals affect the way a person lives.

7. What is initial demand?

8. Explain how initial demand creates secondary demand.

9. Explain how consumer demand affects production.

10. Explain how consumer demand creates jobs.

 # Business Problems and Projects

1. On a form similar to the one shown below, list five each of your most important consumer needs and wants. Rank each need or want from 1, the most important, to 5, the least important. Place a check next to those you think you will fulfill within the next year.

	Consumer Needs	Rank	Consumer Wants	Rank
Example	Overcoat	2	Record player	1

2. Prepare a list of your consumer goals, separating them in three groups—short-term, intermediate, and long-term. Short-term goals are those you hope to achieve by the end of the present school year. Intermediate goals are those you hope to achieve by high school graduation, and long-term goals are those things you would expect to achieve by age 30.

Chapter 24

Consumer Decisions

Objectives

After completing your study of this chapter, you will be able to do the following:

1. Explain the difference between the terms *basic consumer decisions* and *discretionary consumer decisions.*

2. Define the term *discretionary income* and show its importance to consumer decisions.

3. Identify the various factors that affect consumer decisions.

4. Explain what is meant by the term *disposable income.*

As a consumer you are faced with a great number of consumer decisions each day. Buying a sandwich rather than the hot lunch at the school cafeteria is a consumer decision. Choosing a chocolate candy bar with almonds instead of one with coconut is a consumer decision. Heating your home with electricity rather than natural gas is a consumer decision. And leaving your money in a savings account rather than spending it is a consumer decision.

Clearly, a list of consumer decisions could go on forever. Anytime you are faced with spending, there are choices. As a consumer you have to decide among these choices. In order to help you make wise choices, this chapter presents several different types of consumer decisions and examines some of the factors that affect those decisions.

What was your most recent consumer decision? How many consumer decisions do you make in an average week?

TYPES OF CONSUMER DECISIONS

Consumer decisions can be divided into two main types: those that relate to spending for the necessities of life and those that relate to all other spending. Most people have to satisfy their basic needs before they can satisfy their other needs. Therefore, basic consumer decisions will be discussed first.

Basic Consumer Decisions

All consumer decisions that involve the purchase of goods and services to satisfy the basic need for food, clothing, and shelter are called *basic consumer decisions*. For some people, particularly those with very low incomes, almost all spending may involve basic consumer decisions. The range of their choices may be limited. They may have to be concerned mainly with getting enough food to survive, enough clothing to keep warm, and enough housing to protect them against the elements.

For other people, only a relatively small percentage of spending will involve basic consumer decisions. And their range of choices may be quite wide. Most people, however, fall somewhere between these two extremes. The major part—but not all—of their spending is related to basic consumer decisions. And their choices are fairly wide.

For example, food is a basic need. But although you must eat everyday, your eating habits will have much to do with how much you spend on food. If you like eating in restaurants or only enjoy fine foods, your food bills will be high. If you are a thrifty shopper or prefer plain meals, your food bills will be low.

Clothing is another basic need. However, the kind of clothing you wear often depends on where you live and on your life-style. A person living in Hawaii, for example, has different needs from a person living in North Dakota. Working people have different clothing needs from children or retired people. Even the type of work a person does affects that person's clothing needs. A bus driver who wears a uniform each day does not have the same needs as a salesclerk in a department store. Factory workers have different clothing needs from office workers. And individual preferences affect clothing bills. Some people will buy only high-cost fashionable clothing, while others prefer low-cost utility clothing.

Shelter, the third basic need, is usually the most costly expense. Most likely, you will spend more of your money on housing than on any other expense. Again, your individual life-style will determine how much you are willing to spend for this particular need.

Discretionary Consumer Decisions

After you have made your basic consumer decisions, you can begin to consider your discretionary consumer decisions. *Discretionary consumer decisions* are those decisions that involve the buying of goods and services from choice rather than from necessity. The money used in this type of spending is *discretionary income*—the income left after meeting the expenses for all the necessities.

Decisions on how to use your discretionary income are made far more often than basic consumer decisions. These decisions usually involve consumer wants, and they are concerned with pleasure, satisfaction, and comfort. You could use your discretionary income in any number of ways. It could be saved. It could be spent on travel, entertainment, or recreation. Or it could be spent on a car, a boat, or a hobby. Even more than basic consumer decisions, discretionary consumer decisions are determined by personal preferences and goals. Learning to manage your discretionary income is essential to effective consumer decision making. If you can make wise decisions, you will probably be able to satisfy the wants that are most important to you.

List five of your most recent discretionary consumer decisions.

FACTORS THAT AFFECT CONSUMER DECISIONS

As you have learned, your basic needs importantly affect your spending decisions. A number of other factors—some of which were mentioned earlier—also influence consumer decision making. Chief among these factors are income, personal goals, social pressures, habit, and advertising. More often than not, a combination of these factors, rather than just one, will determine how you spend your money.

Income

Both basic and discretionary consumer decisions are largely dependent on the amount of disposable income an individual has. *Disposable income* is the amount of money left after all deductions for taxes, insurance, social security, and other similar items have been made. Disposable income is the money available for spending. Disposable income is also called *take-home pay*.

If you have no disposable income, your spending choices are clearly limited. The greater your income, the wider your spending choices. Generally, the larger the income you have, the smaller the percentage of it that has to be spent on satisfying basic needs. Thus the larger the percentage of it that is available for discretionary spending. Therefore, an individual with little disposable income has very little discretionary income and a small selection of goods and services from which to choose.

Which type of consumer decision—basic or discretionary—would most likely be made in a store like this? (Robbins/Stockmarket, Los Angeles)

Equally important, how much you have to spend often determines the kinds of goods and services you can buy. So in addition to having a smaller selection to choose from, the individual with little disposable income may have only items of lower quality within that selection.

STATEMENT OF EARNINGS AND PAYROLL DEDUCTIONS									
PERIOD ENDING	HOURS	EARNINGS		TOTAL EARNINGS	FED. WITH.	STATE TAX	FICA	INSURANCE	NET PAY
		REG.	OT						
4/26	44	200	30	230	36.80	0	14.49	2.25	176.46

Your take home pay is your disposable income.

Provide an example of when you had little disposable income, the selection of goods or services available to you were smaller than they were when you had more disposable income.

Personal Goals

Your consumer decisions will also be affected by your personal goals. If, for example, you want to become a champion swimmer, your discipline and determination in achieving this goal may govern your way of life. And, most likely, it will influence your spending decisions. While your friends and classmates are enjoying a movie or ball game, you may choose to spend your time practicing. Savings that others may have put aside for vacations may be used for swimming camp. And even the food you eat may be determined by your desire to keep in good physical condition.

Social Pressures

The consumer decisions of most people are affected by other people in their social group. Social pressures may exert great

Some consumer decisions are greatly affected by social pressure. (Stock, Boston)

influence on clothing styles, hair styles, the type of housing, and the kind of recreation you choose. Sometimes, social pressures can keep people from buying a particular product. At other times they may cause people to purchase goods and service so that they can be "one of the gang."

List two examples of how social pressure affected your recent consumer decisions.

Habit

Consumer decisions are affected by habit. We do many things automatically, including much of our spending. Habit may cause you to do most of your shopping in just a few stores or to buy only certain brands of merchandise. You may have used one good or service for so long that it has almost become a part of your life. You

Advertising reaches us in many ways. (Beetleboards)

may not be able to remember when or why the habit started. You may see no reason to change and may even not listen to suggestions for change. You are happy with your present habit even though you may not know why.

Give an example of a recent consumer decision that you made largely on the basis of habit.

Advertising

Advertising influences consumer decisions. Advertising reaches us in many ways—through newspapers, magazines, radio, and television. Advertising circulars may be placed in your mailbox or left on the windshield of your car. You may find advertising on the pens and pencils you write with. You see it as you look through the classified section of the telephone directory. You see it in your school newspaper.

Some advertisers urge us to go out and buy their products immediately. Other advertisers try to make a lasting impression on our minds so that when we need a product, a well-known product name comes to mind. Many advertising methods and techniques are used, but they all try to keep the name of a good or service in front of you, the consumer. When you go into a store to make a purchase, you may see some product that is familiar to you from a television ad. You identify the product with the ad. If you liked the ad, the chances are good that you will try the product.

Give an example of a recent purchase you made that was influenced by advertising. Did the good or service live up to your expectations? Why or why not?

Learning Activities

Increasing Your Business Vocabulary

You should become familiar with each of the terms shown below. On a sheet of paper write the numbers 1 through 4. Then write alongside each number the term that best matches each of the numbered definitions.

basic consumer decisions / discretionary consumer decisions / discretionary income / disposable income

1. The amount an employee actually receives after deductions for taxes, insurance, social security, and other similar items.

2. Consumer decisions that involve the purchase of goods to satisfy the need for food, clothing, or shelter.

3. The income you have left after meeting all your necessary obligations.

4. Consumer decisions that involve the purchase of goods or services from choice rather than from necessity.

Understanding Business

1. List some examples of common consumer decisions that people make each day.

2. What are the two main types of consumer decisions?

3. Which of the two kinds of consumer decisions, basic or discretionary, are made more often?

4.   Why should you learn to manage your discretionary income?

5.   List the different factors that influence consumer decisions.

6.   Give some examples of how personal goals affect consumer decisions.

7.   Give some examples of how social pressures affect consumer decisions.

8.   How is habit a force in consumer decision making?

9.   Give examples of how advertising reaches the consumer.

10.   What is the one purpose that all advertisers have in common?

Business Problems and Projects

1.   The purchase of a home is one of the most important consumer decisions made. A common guideline is that the cost of the home should not be more than 2½ times your annual income. Based on this guideline, complete the following table.

	Total Income	Maximum Cost of Home
Example	$5,000	$12,500
	$10,000	?
	$15,000	?
	?	$50,000
	?	$100,000
	$18,000	?

2. Study the table below and answer the questions that follow it.

WEEKLY FOOD COST FOR FAMILIES, BY TYPE OF FAMILY
(in dollars. Based on moderate cost food plan; assumes
all meals are eaten at home or taken from home)

Family Type	1965	1970	1973
Couple, 20–35 years old	20.20	23.20	30.80
Couple, 55–75 years old	17.20	19.40	25.70
Couple with children:			
1 child, 1–5 years old	25.10	28.80	38.20
1 child, 15–18 years old	29.30	33.30	44.40
2 children, 1–5 years old	29.40	33.70	44.70
2 children, 6–11 years old	34.00	39.20	52.00
2 children, 12–18 years old	37.50	42.90	57.10

Source: U.S. Agrcultural Research Service

a. What type of family spends the least money on food?

b. What type of family spends the greatest amount of money on food?

c. On the average, did food expenditures increase more between 1965 and 1970 or between 1970 and 1973?

d. For a couple, 20–35 years old, how much did the cost of food increase from 1965 to 1973? What was the percent of this increase?

e. Did all couples, 55–75 years old, spend $25.70 per week on food in 1973? Explain.

f. How much more did the couple with 2 children, 12–18 years old, pay for food per week than the couple with 1 child, 1–5 years old?

3. Social pressures have a great impact on consumer behavior. On a form similar to the one shown below, list five purchases that you have made within the past month that in one way or another were affected by social pressure. Identify the pressure that led to the purchase.

	Purchase	Social Pressure
Example	Skis	All my friends were skiing

Chapter 25

Planning for Consumer Spending

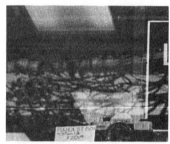

Objectives

After completing your study of this chapter, you will be able to do the following:

1. Name the benefits of planned spending.

2. Define the term *budget* and explain the importance of budgeting in managing money.

3. Discuss the steps to be followed in preparing a budget.

4. Tell the difference between fixed and variable expenses.

Earlier you studied about the differences between consumer needs and consumer wants and about the importance of determining consumer goals. In addition, you studied about the different types of consumer decisions and some of the factors that affect these decisions. In order to make decisions that will help you achieve your goals, you must first do a great deal of planning. In this chapter you will learn about *money management,* the planned control of income and expense.

BUDGETING

Most people never have enough money to satisfy their needs and wants. They find it necessary, therefore, to plan their spending. In

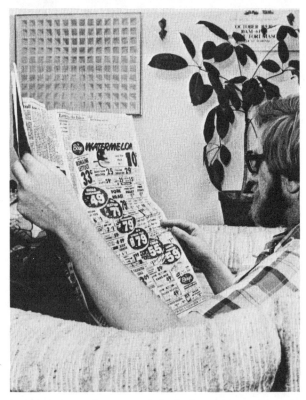

Most people have to plan their spending to satisfy their needs and wants. (Robbins/Stockmarket, Los Angeles; Maria Karras)

order to plan, they make up a *budget,* which is a plan for spending and saving money.

The purpose of budgeting is often misunderstood. Budgeting is not simply the recording of every penny spent. In fact, recording expenditures is only one small part of managing money.

The real purpose of budgeting is to help you get the things you want and to get the most satisfaction from the dollars you spend. A budget helps you select your major goals and to set priorities. It is an organized way to plan your spending so that you can reach your goals. And it helps you consider the available spending choices.

A budget lets you know ahead of time whether or not you have enough income to meet the expenses you expect to have. If you find that you do not, a budget alerts you to look for ways to increase your income or decrease your spending.

List some of the problems that might be faced by individuals and families who do not make budgets.

PREPARING A BUDGET

Although individuals and families may budget for different reasons, the procedure they follow in preparing a budget is the same. Basically, they must know how much money they can expect to have and how much money they can expect to spend. Therefore, the budgeting procedure consists of two steps: estimating income and estimating expenditures.

Estimating Income

The first step in preparing a budget is to estimate income. If you are a student, you should include in this estimate wages from part-time employment, allowance from parents, and any money you might expect to receive as gifts. In estimating the income for a family, you would include income from regular and part-time employment, dividends, interest, and bonuses or gifts. It is important to estimate income as accurately as possible. Include only money that you actually can depend on receiving. As you will see later, your estimated income may not actually cover your estimated expenses. In order to balance income and expenses, you may have to increase your income or cut your expenses. And sometimes you may have to do both.

For example, the Boswell family has a goal—they want to buy their own home. The Boswells want to prepare a budget to help them reach that goal. Table 25–1 shows how average families of four people with different incomes spent their money in a recent year. Although the Boswells' budget will have similar categories for expenses, they must make the budget suit their own family's needs.

TABLE 25-1   SUMMARY OF ANNUAL BUDGETS FOR A FOUR-PERSON FAMILY AT THREE LEVELS OF LIVING, URBAN UNITED STATES

	Lower Income	Intermediate Income	Higher Income
(Income for family)	($9,588)	($15,318)	($22,294)
Expenses for family	7,795	11,725	16,141
Food	2,952	3,827	4,819
Housing	1,857	3,533	5,353
Transportation	702	1,279	1,658
Clothing	771	1,102	1,613
Personal care	248	331	470
Medical care	818	822	857
Other family expenses	447	831	1,371
Other items (savings, gifts, contributions)	436	701	1,182
Taxes and deductions	1,358	2,891	4,971
Social security and disability	577	834	841
Personal income taxes	781	2,057	4,130

Note: Because of rounding, the sums of items may not equal the totals.
Source: U.S. Department of Labor, Bureau of Labor Statistics

Figure 25–1 shows how the Boswells estimated their income. Mark Boswell's take-home pay every month is $1,250. Because Linda and Mark have two small children, Linda and Mark have agreed that she will not work outside of the house for the time being. Although she supplements their income from time to time with jobs she can perform at home, the money she earns from these jobs varies from month to month. Because this is not income they can depend on, they do not list it.

Estimate Income Available for Spending
    Dependable monthly income
        Wages or salary (after deductions) $1,250.00
        Spouse's net earnings (if any)   0
        Other income   20.00
            Total Dependable Income $1,270.00

Figure 25-1. Estimating income.

For the last four years the Boswells have been saving money regularly. They now have $4,000 in their savings account, and it earns 6 percent interest a year. This means that they will be paid $240 in interest this year, so their monthly interest is $20. In Figure 25-1, this amount is entered on line "Other income." As they have no other sources of income, Mark and Linda can now see that they can depend on an estimated monthly income of $1,270.

Does your family have sources of income that are different from those of the Boswell family? If so, what are they? Are they dependable sources of income?

Estimating Expenditures

The next step in preparing a budget is to estimate expenses. There are two types of expenses: fixed and variable. *Fixed expenses* are expenses that occur regularly and remain about the same in amount over a period of time. Rent or mortgage payments, insurance premiums, and installment payments are examples of fixed expenses. *Variable expenses* are expenses that do not occur regularly and that vary a great deal in amount. Clothing, medical, and dental bills are common variable expenses.

Prepare a list of your fixed expenses and of your variable expenses. Which list has more expenses? Why do you think this is so? Explain your answer.

Fixed Monthly Expenses   Mark and Linda began the expense part of the budget by estimating their fixed monthly expenses.

First they entered their monthly rent. Then they entered their insurance expenses. In order to simplify their budget, the Boswells try to group similar types of expenses into descriptive categories. However, they use enough different categories to make sure that each one provides useful information about the actual expenses it covers. Under the insurance category, they listed the cost of their automobile insurance, their group health insurance, and their life insurance. The Boswells also have insurance to protect against the loss of personal property in their apartment. They listed this cost under "other" insurance as shown in Figure 25-2.

```
Estimate Monthly Expenditures
    Fixed monthly expenses
       Rent or mortgage                       $  265.00
       Insurance--auto                            27.00
          Health (medical)                        47.00
          Life                                    14.00
          Other                                    7.00
    Loans                                         95.00
    Installment purchases                         40.00
    Savings                                      100.00
       Total Fixed Expenses                   $  595.00
```

Figure 25-2. Estimating fixed monthly expenses.

When Mark and Linda bought a new car, they took out a loan to pay for it. The monthly payment on that loan is also listed as a fixed expense. They recently bought a new washer and dryer and arranged to pay for them in monthly installments. This amount is listed under "Installment purchases." Because they are determined to save $100 each month towards the purchase of their new home, they listed this amount as a fixed expense. If the amount of their savings were to vary from month to month, savings would be listed as a variable expense. Finally, they added their fixed expenses and entered the total.

Variable Monthly Expenses   Next, Mark and Linda estimated their variable monthly expenses. Figure 25-3 shows the categories they used.

Variable monthly expenses	
Food	
At home	$ 275.00
Away from home	25.00
Housing	
Utilities	50.00
Telephone	15.00
Furnishings or supplies	20.00
Clothing	
Purchases	50.00
Cleaning	10.00
Transportation	
Gasoline	55.00
Maintenance and repair	25.00
Health care	
Doctor	30.00
Dentist	25.00
Personal care	30.00
Education	
Tuition and books	10.00
Recreation	40.00
Contributions	15.00
Total Variable Expenses	$ 675.00

Figure 25-3. Estimating variable monthly expenses.

Notice that food is a major expense for the Boswells, and this is true for most families. Transportation is also a big expense. Under this category, Mark and Linda have included a monthly allowance for upkeep on their car. They do not know, of course, if their car will require any repairs during a given month, but they do want to have some money set aside for auto repairs if they do occur.

The Boswells have found that it is much easier to prepare their budget when they have some idea of how much money they have spent in a category in the past. To do this, they kept a trial record of expenses. For a period of time before they actually began to prepare their budget, they kept a record of what they did with all the money they received. In this way they had a better understanding of how much they should set aside for each of their variable expenses.

After all the amounts in each category were entered, Linda and Mark entered the total. They realize that these amounts are just estimates and that their family's needs will change from time to time. Therefore, after they have used their budget for a while, they may need to change the amounts accordingly.

Balancing the Budget   Finally, the Boswells next added up the estimated fixed and variable monthly expenses and compared the total with the total estimated income. As you can see from Figure 25–4, the Boswells' estimated monthly income equals their estimated monthly expenses. Their budget balances.

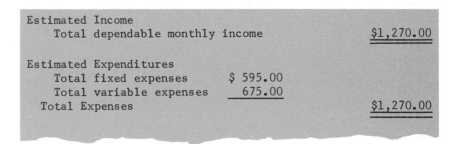

```
Estimated Income
    Total dependable monthly income          $1,270.00

Estimated Expenditures
    Total fixed expenses        $ 595.00
    Total variable expenses        675.00
  Total Expenses                             $1,270.00
```

Figure 25-4.

ADJUSTING THE PLAN

Now the Boswells must find out how well their spending and saving plan works for them. For the next few months, they will have to check actual expenditures in each category to see if they are spending more than the budgeted amounts. In Chapter 26 you will see how they do this. If the Boswells find that they are spending more than the budgeted amounts in some categories, they will need to find ways to cut down their spending in other categories. Or they will have to find other sources of income. If Mark and Linda can do this, they will be able to save $100 each month as planned. This will enable them to reach their goal of buying a house.

If their income did not cover their expenses, the Boswells would have to go over their priorities. They would have to decide where changes could be made. Remember that most families have limited resources, and it may be impossible for them to have everything on their lists of priorities. They may have to give up or postpone getting certain items. They may try to increase income by taking part-time jobs, working overtime, or having additional members of their family go to work. They could also use credit to obtain those things they want now. But whatever course of action they choose, a well-prepared budget should allow them to achieve their major goals.

How much of your spending in the last week was based on a spending plan? Do you think you would benefit if you carefully followed a budget? Explain.

Learning Activities

Increasing Your Business Vocabulary

You should become familiar with each of the terms shown below. On a sheet of paper write the numbers 1 through 4. Then write alongside each number the term that best matches each of the numbered definitions.

budget / fixed expenses / money management / variable expenses

1. The planned control of income and expenses.

2. A plan for spending and saving money.

3. Expenses that occur irregularly and that vary a great deal in amount over a period of time.

4. Expenses that occur regularly and remain about the same in amount over a period of time.

Understanding Business

1. What is the major benefit of planned spending?

2. Why do people find it necessary to plan their spending?

3. List the steps to be followed in budgeting.

4. What are some of the types of income a person might include in a list of estimated income?

5. When you prepare a budget, on what basis do you estimate expenses?

6. What is the difference between fixed and variable expenses?

7. What are some examples of fixed expenses?

8. What are some actions that an individual or family can take if estimated expenses are more than estimated income?

Business Problems and Projects

1. Prepare lists of the probable categories of fixed expenses and of variable expenses that a young married couple in their twenties with two small children would face.

2. The graph below shows the expenditures of an average family of four. Study it and then answer the questions that follow.

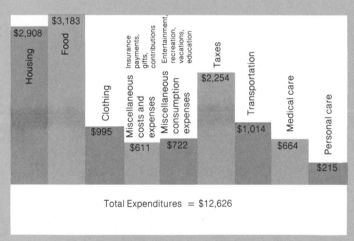

Total Expenditures = $12,626

Source: Bureau of Labor Statistics

a. According to the graph, what are the three largest expenses faced by this family?

b. What single expense requires the greatest amount of money?

c. What percentage of total expenditures is paid in taxes? What type of taxes are likely to be included in this figure?

Chapter 26

Accounting for Consumer Spending

Clothing	Trans-portation	alth re	Personal Care	Education	Recrea on	Contri-butions	Total Expenses
9.00	7.00						281.00
					00		61.20
		11.00	5.00		00		18.00
						3.00	23.00

Objectives

After completing your study of this chapter, you will be able to do the following:

1. Explain the importance of record keeping in money management.

2. Describe the ways in which record keeping benefits the consumer.

3. Explain how to compute an individual's net worth.

4. Explain how a budget can be revised.

An important part of money management is accounting for consumer spending. Unless some type of spending records are kept, there is really no way to keep track of both income and expenditures or to know if your budget has been followed. In addition, personal spending records provide much other useful information. In this chapter you will learn how to keep records of your spending and how records work to your benefit.

Check with your parents to see what kind of spending records they keep. Write a short paragraph describing the general procedures that they use. If they do not keep records at all, list their reasons for not doing so.

WHY KEEP RECORDS?

One of the major reasons for keeping complete and accurate records is to determine how successful your planning has been. Records can also provide almost any kind of information about your personal finances that you might need. They can show how much income was received, from whom the income was received, and when it was received. They can also show how much money was paid, to whom it was paid, and when it was paid. In addition, records can show how much money has been saved, when it was saved, and where it was saved. With accurate records, you are also able to tell how much money is owed, to whom it is owed, and when payments are due. A good record-keeping system, then, provides information about expenditures, information about credit purchases, direction for spending, information for tax returns, and information about economic progress.

Records Provide Information About Expenditures

For a number of reasons, you may want to refer to your records for information about your past expenditures. Depending upon how detailed your records are, you may be able to locate the following kinds of information:

1. The amount paid for a good or service.
2. The amount paid for the same good or service at different

stores or at different times. This information may be valuable in a time of rising prices and will help you revise your budget.

3. The dates on which purchases were made. By comparing the date on which an item was first bought and the date on which it was replaced, you will know how much use you got from it.

From your records, you can analyze your expenses to see if your spending has followed any kind of pattern. You will know if certain expenses have increased greatly. If they have, you should try to learn why. This analysis of your expenses will help you see how successful your budget has been.

Records Provide Information About Credit Purchases

Sometimes you may pay cash or write a check for the things you buy. At other times you may buy on credit and agree to make payments at some time in the future. If you do most of your spending on credit, you will have several credit payments to keep in

Records provide direction for future spending. (Camerique)

mind in your financial planning. You should manage your expenses so that you have no trouble paying large credit payments when due. For example, each month the Boswell family has to make a car payment, a rent payment, and a payment on their new washer and dryer. Rather than have all these payments due at one time, the Boswells arranged to spread them out throughout the month. As a result, the rent payment is due on the first of the month, the car payment on the fifteenth, and the washer and dryer payment on the twenty-second.

Carefully prepared records should provide answers to the following questions about credit purchases:

1. What bills are due in that month?

2. What are the amounts of the bills?

3. What are the specific dates of the payments?

4. How long will these payments be made?

5. How much must be paid in interest or service charges?

When you make credit purchases, keep your charge slips for future reference. By comparing your charge slips with your monthly statement, you can make sure that no mistakes have been made in the billing. Be sure that only items that you have actually charged are included on your statement. Also be sure that all amounts are correct. The skillful consumer pays only for those goods and services actually received.

Ask members of your family who make credit purchases if they have ever received incorrect billing statements for items they purchased. Describe the situation and tell how the problem was settled.

Records Provide Direction for Spending

Budgeting helps people realize that there are limitations on the use of income. Remember, your goal in budgeting is whatever you are working for. Spending records tell you whether you are using money wisely or unwisely—whether your spending habits are sensible and reasonable, or careless and haphazard. You may find that you are spending too much money on snacks at school. As a result, you do not have enough money left to save each week for the camera you want. Clearly, you must change your spending habits if you want to reach your goal. In this way, record keeping helps control impulse buying. It helps give direction to your spending and helps you reach your goals.

Records Provide Information About Economic Progress

It is always good to know where you stand financially—to know exactly how much money you have and to know how much money you owe. If you have money left after paying all your expenses, you may want to buy something special or you may want to add to your savings or investment program. It is also a good feeling to have records that show that you are financially better off this month than last.

Detailed records provide information about an individual's assets, liabilities, and net worth. *Assets* are items of value owned by

Assets	
Savings account	$4,000
Furniture and appliances	2,000
Car	3,800
Total	$9,800

Liabilities	
Unpaid balance for car	$2,600
Unpaid balance for washer/dryer	450
Total	$3,050

Net Worth		
Assets	$9,800	
Liabilities	3,050	
Net worth		$6,750

Figure 26-1. A statement of net worth.

an individual, family, or business firm. Cash, jewels, money in the bank, cars, and clothing are examples of personal assets. *Liabilities* are the amounts owed by an individual, family, or business firm. Home mortgage payments, money owed on installment purchases, and money borrowed from a friend are examples of liabilities. Once you know the amount of your assets and liabilities, it is easy to determine your net worth. *Net worth* is the difference between assets and liabilities of an individual, a family, or a business firm.

As an example of how to figure your net worth, here is the method the Boswell family used to determine their net worth.

Explain how the purchase of a good or service could result in both an asset and a liability.

Records Provide Information for Income Tax Returns

Complete and accurate records are valuable in preparing state and federal income tax returns. Many expenses may be deducted from a taxpayer's total income to determine taxable income. Some deductions a taxpayer may take are medical and dental expenses; interest on loans, mortgages, and installment contracts; gifts to charities; and certain taxes such as gasoline and real estate taxes. When a taxpayer claims any of these expenses as deductions, he or she must be prepared to produce proof of payment. Two ways of providing this proof are canceled checks and receipts. In your study of banking, you learned that one advantage of using checks is that canceled checks serve as legal receipts. If bills are paid in cash, it is important to get a receipt as a proof of payment.

Why do you think taxpayers have to prove payment for items claimed as income tax deductions?

HOW TO KEEP SPENDING RECORDS

Your budget is a plan. It contains only estimates of income and expenses. Spending records, on the other hand, show your actual expenses. Much of the success of your budgeting efforts depends on how well your records are kept. When you keep spending records, you should record expenses often enough so that none are forgotten. There are different forms that can be used to make the recording process easier. The form that you decide to use will depend on your financial goals and the amount of data you need.

Classified Expense Record

A classified expense record has a special column for each expense category included in the budget. Figure 26–2 shows the Boswell family's classified expense record. When they occur, expenses for each day are recorded on a single line. Usually, Mark and Linda enter them each Saturday. Income, however, is recorded as it is received. The total expenses for each day is shown in the last column of the form. At the end of the budget period, all the columns are totaled at the bottom. By using such a method, it is easier and more efficient to determine the total amount of expenses for each budget category.

The Boswell's budget, has a category for recreation. This category is very general and does not provide detailed information. All Mark and Linda know is that a certain amount of money was budgeted for recreation. But if they wanted to know how much was spent for each form of recreation, they could itemize the list.

Date	Savings	Rent	Insurance	Loan	Installment Purchases	Food	Housing
MAY 1		265.00					
2						52.20	
3							
4			14.00			6.00	
7							
8							9.50
9						49.99	
10							
TOTALS	100.00	265.00	61.00	95.00	40.00	300.63	82.00

Figure 26-2. A classified expense record.

HOW DETAILED SHOULD RECORDS BE?

Personal spending records should be as detailed as you want them to be to provide all the information you need. What is necessary information? The answer to this question probably depends on what your financial goals are. Your records should provide you with the information necessary to measure your progress in reaching those goals. Keep in mind, though, that if record keeping is too detailed it may be self-defeating. If keeping your records becomes a tiresome chore, you may give it up. But if you do not mind spending a lot of time on detailed records, your record keeping and money management will be more precise. You must decide how much time and attention you are willing to give to keeping records.

How detailed would you want your records to be? Why?

COMPARING YOUR EXPENDITURES WITH YOUR BUDGET

In Chapter 25 you learned that after you have used your budget for a while, you might have to revise the amounts to make them more accurate. One way of doing this is to use a budget comparison sheet. The budget comparison sheet used by Mark and Linda

Clothing	Trans- portation	Health Care	Personal Care	Education	Recreation	Contri- butions	Total Expenses
9.00	7.00						281.00
					9.00		61.20
		11.00	5.00		2.00		18.00
						3.00	23.00
		21.00					21.00
12.00	11.00			10.00			42.50
			7.50		5.00		62.49
		7.00	2.00				9.00
62.00	81.00	52.00	30.50	10.00	36.00	12.00	1227.13

Figure 26-2. (Continued)

Boswell is shown in Figure 26–3. This sheet indicates the amount budgeted as well as the amount actually spent for each expense category. With this information they can find out if their expense estimates were accurate.

Month	Explanation	Savings	Rent	Insurance	Loan	Installment Purchases	Food
MAY	BUDGETED	100.00	265.00	61.00	95.00	40.00	300.00
	SPENT	100.00	265.00	61.00	95.00	40.00	300.63
	+ OR –	0	0	0	0	0	– .63
JUNE	BUDGETED	100.00	265.00	61.00	95.00	40.00	300.00
	SPENT	100.00	265.00	61.00	95.00	40.00	305.50
	+ OR –	0	0	0	0	0	– 5.50
JULY	BUDGETED	100.00	265.00	61.00	95.00	40.00	300.00
	MONTHLY AVERAGE	100.00	265.00	61.00	95.00	40.00	304.15

Figure 26-3. A budget comparison sheet.

In this budget comparison sheet, Mark and Linda recorded the amount budgeted and the amount spent during each month for four months. They totaled the amount spent for the four months for an expense category. Then they divided by four to get

Month	Explanation	Savings	Rent	Insurance	Loan	Installment Purchases	Food
	REVISED BUDGET	100.00	265.00	61.00	95.00	40.00	305.00

Figure 26-4. A revised budget.

the average monthly expenditure for that expense category and wrote the average at the bottom of the column. They did this for each expense category. Then they compared the average amounts with the budgeted amounts. Mark and Linda can see that in July,

Housing	Clothing	Trans-portation	Health Care	Personal Care	Education	Recreation	Contri-butions
85.00	60.00	80.00	55.00	30.00	10.00	40.00	15.00
82.00	62.00	81.00	52.00	30.50	10.00	36.00	12.00
+ 3.00	− 2.00	− 1.00	+ 3.00	− .50	0	+ 4.00	+ 3.00
85.00	60.00	80.00	55.00	30.00	10.00	40.00	15.00
80.00	53.00	79.00	51.00	27.00	10.00	41.00	15.00
+ 5.00	+ 7.00	+ 1.00	+ 4.00	+ 3.00	0	− 1.00	0
85.00	60.00	80.00	55.00	30.00	10.00	40.00	15.00
79.75	58.25	82.00	48.50	28.75	10.00	40.50	13.50

Figure 26-3. (Continued)

when they went on a trip, they spent more than planned for food, transportation, and recreation and could not save $100.

They believe that their budget is working fairly well for them, but they have decided to allow a little more money each month for

Housing	Clothing	Trans-portation	Health Care	Personal Care	Education	Recreation	Contri-butions
80.00	60.00	85.00	50.00	30.00	10.00	40.00	15.00

Figure 26-4. (Continued)

Records provide information about expenditures.
(Cherkis/Stockmarket, Los Angeles)

food and transportation. In order to keep their budget in balance, similar amounts had to be subtracted from other categories. Because their records indicate that they usually spent less than the budgeted amounts for housing and health care expenses, the estimated expenses for these two categories were reduced. Figure 26–4 shows how they revised their budget. Comparisons between budgeted and actual expenses should be made on a regular basis to determine if budget revisions should be made.

Learning Activities

Increasing Your Business Vocabulary

You should become familiar with each of the terms shown below. On a sheet of paper write the numbers 1 through 5. Then write alongside each number the term that best matches each of the numbered definitions.

assets / discretionary income / disposable income / liabilities / net worth

1. The difference between assets and liabilities of an individual, a family, or a business firm.

2. Items of value owned by an individual, family, or business.

3. Amounts owed by an individual, family, or business firm.

4. The amount an employee actually receives after deductions for taxes, insurance, social security, and other similar items.

5. The income you have left after meeting all your necessary obligations.

Understanding Business

1. Why is it necessary to keep some kind of spending records?

2. List some of the kinds of information that should be available from your records.

3. What kinds of information about past expenditures should be available from detailed records?

4. What kinds of information about credit purchases should be available from your records?

5. Why are complete and accurate spending records valuable when preparing income tax returns?

6. List some common examples of personal assets.

7. Explain how net worth is determined.

8. How detailed should a person's personal spending records be?

9. Why may detailed record keeping be self-defeating?

10. Why would a person keep a classified expense record?

 # Business Problems and Projects

1. Jan and Dennis, a young couple, are making a sincere effort to determine their economic progress from year to year. Last year at this time, they carefully figured their net worth to be $3,487. Using a form similar to the one shown below, help them determine their economic success by measuring their current net worth. They provide you with the following information about their financial transactions:

   • They own all of their own furniture and appliances except a washer and dryer. The furniture is valued at $1,650.

   • They still owe $237 on the installment contract for the washer and dryer purchased during the year for $429.

   • Jan values her wardrobe at $500; Dennis estimates the value of his wardrobe at $350.

   • Various forms of personal property are estimated to be worth $600.

   • A dentist's bill for $195 is still unpaid.

   • They owe a major oil company $23 for gasoline purchases made with a credit card.

- Their new car is being paid off in installments. They still owe $2,250 on the contract but the automobile has a current market value of $3,400.

- Last summer they took a vacation trip which was paid for with a bank loan. After they repay the balance of $210, the loan will be paid in full.

- The couple have a balance of $135 in their joint checking account, $150 in their savings account, and cash on hand totaling $35.

- They owe a total of $431 to department stores which resulted from purchases that were made on credit.

Jan and Dennis
Statement of Net Worth

Assets		Liabilities	
Item	Value	Item	Amount

a. What is the total value of all items owned by Jan and Dennis?

b. What is the total amount owed by Jan and Dennis at this time?

c. What is the amount of the couple's net worth?

d. Has the couple's net worth increased or decreased since last year? How much?

e. What was the percent of increase or decrease in the couple's net worth?

2. Read the following article that appeared in a recent issue of a daily newspaper. Answer the questions that follow.

GIVE BUDGETING A TRY

At a time when inflation is reducing the value of a dollar and the goods and services that dollar can buy, most families ought to consider the use of a budget. A budget gives purpose and direction to one's economic activities. Through budgeting, we know where our dollars are going and to whom. We are also better able to acquire those goods and services we want.

Too often people view a budget as a strict and confining curb on spending. They see a specific amount, for example, set aside for clothing, entertainment, transportation, and food. When this happens, budgeting becomes an ordeal. On the other hand, when a budget recognizes that each day and month is different, that consumer moods are different, that merchants are different, and that flexibility is vitally important in money management; then budgeting is likely to be highly successful.

It is estimated that families who do budget the use of their income, and who modify their budgets as circumstances change, are able to sizably increase the potentials that their dollars of income have to offer. The individual's willingness to become concerned with the way in which financial resources are used in an effort to make these resources more productive is the first step to effective money management.

a. On what does the article blame the reduction of the value of a dollar?

b. Provide a suitable definition for the answer given to the first question.

c. What three benefits does the article credit to budgeting?

d. What is the major precaution that the person using a budget must observe according to the article?

e. What is the first thing an individual must do in order to become a wise and effective money manager?

f. What condition, or characteristics, must exist if a budget is to accomplish its purpose?

Chapter 27

The Consumer in the Marketplace

Objectives

After completing your study of this chapter, you will be able to do the following:

1. List and describe the obstacles to skillful buying.

2. Define the term *dollar voting* and describe how dollar voting affects the marketplace.

3. List and describe the benefits of skillful buying.

4. See the relationship of supply, demand, and price from the viewpoint of the consumer.

The marketplace is often confusing and frustrating for the consumer. Even a simple purchase like the buying of shampoo can be difficult. There are so many brands of shampoo to choose from. There are so many different prices to choose from. And there are so many stores where you can buy it. In short, there are too many choices. In a private enterprise economy like ours, buying almost always involves the following choices:

1. Which product to buy.
2. Where to buy the product.
3. How much to spend for the product.
4. How to pay for the product.

Shampoo, of course, is just one of the hundreds of products that consumers buy. And because the buying of each of these products involves a number of choices, the consumer may have to deal with hundreds of choices each time he or she enters the marketplace.

The problem of choosing from the vast number of goods and services is just one of several obstacles to buying that the skillful consumer has to overcome. This chapter will examine some of these obstacles. It will also point out the benefits consumers receive from skillful buying.

OBSTACLES TO SKILLFUL BUYING

Fifty years ago buying was relatively easy. The marketplace was much smaller, and the relationship of buyer to seller was much closer. If, for example, you wanted a pound of bacon, you usually could have bought it only from your neighborhood butcher. The butcher—like the owners of the local drugstore or vegetable market—probably lived in the same neighborhood. The livelihood of these storeowners depended on their business reputations. And their business reputations depended on how well they satisfied the buying needs of their customers. True, the butcher may have only had one type of bacon to offer. But, because you knew the butcher, the decision to buy or not buy the bacon was simplified.

Today, buying is much more complex and, to some, more overwhelming. There are many more goods and services available, and many of these goods and services are unfamiliar to the consumer. Equally important, the consumer may be also unfamiliar with the seller of these goods and services. Each time consumers enter the marketplace, they face the obstacles of variety of choice, lack of information, conflicting interests, and their own attitudes.

Variety of Goods and Services

The next time you enter a department store, shopping center, or supermarket, stop for a moment and look around. How many different goods do you see? How many different brands of the same product are there? If you are at a supermarket, notice how many choices of breakfast cereals, canned vegetables, and frozen foods

One obstacle to skillful buying is the variety of available goods and services. (Stockmarket, Los Angeles)

there are. You will probably see hundreds of different kinds, in different sizes and shapes. Suppose you want to purchase a new bicycle at a department store. You will find that there are a number of different makes of varying quality. Moreover, you will probably find one-speed, three-speed, five-speed, and ten-speed bicycles. Because of the many choices, choosing the bicycle that is best for you may become difficult.

You also have many choices when you shop for services. You usually have several doctors, dentists, and lawyers from which to select. And there are many local businesses that can repair your television, service you car, or cut your hair.

Because there are so many different stores offering so many similar items, it is almost impossible to become familiar with all of them. As a result, it is also almost impossible to know the sellers' reputations and the quality of the goods and services they sell.

Lack of Consumer Information

Because consumers often lack information about goods and services, they make bad buying decisions. Suppose you want to get a low-priced television set. You go into a store and look at both imported and American-made sets. To help you make your choice, you ask the salesperson for information about the product. Usually, you will find that facts are hard to come by. The little that the salesperson knows or the few brochures that are shown to you may be vague and meaningless. Their purpose may be to sell the product rather than to inform the consumer. More often than not you will walk out of the store knowing little more about the product than you did when you entered. Even so, you may still have bought a television set.

In recent years product labeling for items such as food and clothing have become genuinely useful. This is because the law requires exact, factual information for these products. For example, labels on food products must state nutritional value, contents, unit price, weight, and expiration date. However, the laws regarding many other goods, as well as most services, either may not be clear or may not exist at all.

Conflicting Interests

Another obstacle to skillful buying is the basic difference in the goals of business firms and consumers. Business firms want to get the most profit they can for the goods and services they sell. Consumers want to get the most value for their money from the goods and services they buy. The interests of the buyers and the sellers are, therefore, often at odds.

Sometimes this conflict of interest can lead to serious problems for the consumer. For example, if a dishonest seller deliberately misrepresents goods in order to make a profit, the buyer may not receive full value for the money spent on the goods. By the same token, a dishonest consumer who deliberately damages a good in order to get it at a reduced price may prevent the seller from getting a fair profit. It is important for consumers to understand that business firms are entitled to a fair profit. It is equally important that business firms provide the best goods or services at the lowest possible price.

Consumer Attitudes

Many consumers would like to become more skillful but do not know how. Others, however, show little interest in improving their consumer skills. They seem to think it's just too hard and that they'll never be able to get the knack of it. They may also feel that comparing prices and quality takes too much time. To them, the time and effort aren't worth the amount saved. What they save would be small change, hardly worth the bother. They forget that small change adds up to dollars. For example, a car owner may save 5 cents a gallon at a self-service gas station. For the average driver this could result in a saving of $50 to $100 a year. Over a lifetime the amount could be $2,000 to $4,000.

In some instances, consumers feel that there is little they can do to influence business generally. Business, they believe, is too big and powerful to be affected by the actions of one consumer. There are also people who feel that consumers will never be treated fairly because business has great influence in government. They say that courts will rule in favor of business firms and against the individual consumer in most cases. They also say that the passage of laws to protect the consumer is unlikely for the same reason. Judging from the amount of consumer legislation in the past few years, however, it is apparent that they are wrong.

What suggestions do you have for educating individuals in our society to make them more skillful consumers?

BENEFITS OF SKILLFUL BUYING

In view of all the obstacles mentioned above, is skillful buying really worth all the time and effort it takes? What benefits will you receive from it?

Skillful buyers receive maximum value for their money. They encourage sellers to be responsive to their needs. And they encourage good business practices.

Provides Maximum Value

All of us are interested in receiving maximum value for our money. Of course, each of us decides what is a good value and what is not. Because value is a personal thing, it may differ from consumer to consumer. Remember that price and value are not the same thing. Sometimes, price may be a good indication of value, but this is not always the case. As you learned earlier, *price* is the amount of money exchanged between buyer and seller when goods or services are bought or sold. *Value,* on the other hand, is the amount of money a buyer is willing to pay for a good or service. You may be willing to pay an admission price of $10 to see a live performance of your favorite singer. To you, this may be a good value. To one of your friends, however, this price may be $10 too much. To your friend, then, this is not a good value.

If you are a skillful buyer, you will get maximum value from the dollars you spend. You will know what you want to buy and how much you will be willing to spend for it. If an item does not represent a good value to you, you will not buy it. Instead, you will wait until you find one that does.

What are some factors that affect your values?

Skillful buyers compare price and quality to receive maxium value for their money. (Monkmeyer)

Encourages Responsive Sellers

Dollars spent in the marketplace have much the same effect as votes cast in an election. Instead of voting for candidates, the consumer votes for goods and services. This is often referred to as *dollar voting.* *Dollar voting* is a process that tells business firms what goods and services you want them to produce.

If you do not use your dollar vote intelligently, you may encourage the sale of products that are poorly made or overpriced. If you are a skillful consumer and use your dollar vote wisely, you encourage sellers to respond to your need for well-made products sold at a fair rate of profit. Sellers can only make a profit on what

Skillful consumers use their dollar votes to encourage sellers to respond to consumer needs. (Stock, Boston)

they sell if consumers buy their products. If the sellers cannot make a profit because consumers do not buy their products, they will not continue to make them. They will turn instead to making products that do satisfy the consumers, and thus provide the desired profit.

Influences Prices   Dollar voting may also affect prices. In Chapter 3 you learned how the interaction of the supply of and the demand for goods and services influences prices. In general, when supply is greater than demand, the price of a good or service will be low. If, on the other hand, the demand is greater than the supply, the price will be high. If a seller charges too much, skillful consumers may be unwilling to buy. The demand, then, goes down; and the seller may be left with large amounts of unsold goods. In many instances the seller is forced to lower prices.

The relationship of supply and demand to price is not the same for all goods and services. When demand for certain goods and services is greatly affected by price, the demand is considered to be *elastic*. When the demand for goods and services is not greatly affected by changes in price, the demand is considered to be *inelastic*. Entertainment, for example, has elastic demand. If the price of a movie were to change from $3.50 to $7.00, you would probably not go to the movies as often as you do. Your demand for movies would go down because the price went up. The demand for sugar is generally inelastic. Most consumers will continue to buy sugar at the same rate regardless of price increases or decreases.

Give some examples of dollar votes that you made during the last week. Do you think they were made intelligently? Explain your answer.

Encourages Good Business Practices

When you make a purchase, you often choose from among many different business firms. Most of these are honest and reliable. They sell satisfactory goods and services at a fair price. And they stand behind the products they sell. Other firms, however, may not be as honest. They may be only interested in making a large profit on low-quality products. And they are often not around to listen to consumer complaints.

Skillful consumers only buy goods and services from honest sellers. In refusing to support dishonest practices, skillful consumers prevent these firms from making profits. Usually these firms then either change their practices or get out of the business.

Skillful consumers can also influence the activities of firms that violate health, safety, and environmental standards. Using their dollar votes, they can vote "No" to businesses that do not conform to accepted standards.

How do consumers know which business firms are honest and which are dishonest? Where can consumers go to obtain this information?

Learning Activities

Increasing Your Business Vocabulary

You should become familiar with each of the terms shown below. On a sheet of paper write the numbers 1 through 4. Then write alongside each number the term that best matches each of the numbered definitions.

dollar voting / elastic demand / inelastic demand / value

1. When demand is not greatly affected by price.
2. How much a buyer is willing to pay for a good or service.
3. Tells business firms what goods and services you want them to produce.
4. When demand is greatly affected by price.

Understanding Business

1. How does the marketplace today compare to that of 50 years ago?
2. Why are the number of goods and services in the marketplace an obstacle to skillful consumption?
3. Explain the basic difference in the goals of business firms and consumers.
4. List some examples of consumer attitudes that are obstacles to skillful consumption.

5. How is spending money in the marketplace similar to voting?

6. Explain the difference between price and value.

7. Why should you refuse to buy your goods and services from dishonest business firms?

8. Explain how price is determined.

9. Are prices likely to be high or low when supply is greater than demand? Are they likely to be high or low when there is great demand and only a small supply?

10. Explain what happens if a business firm charges too much for a good or service.

Business Problems and Projects

1. On a form similar to the one shown below, indicate whether the demand for each of the goods or services listed is elastic or not.

	Good or Service	Elastic Demand
Example	Eyeglasses	no
	Magazines	
	Bread	
	Movie admissions	
	Gasoline	
	Shoes	
	Milk	
	Topcoat	
	College tuition	
	Laundry detergent	
	Electricity	

2. List ten prepared food items that you or your family regularly buy that would cost less if the individual ingredients were purchased separately and the item were homemade.

   Example: Angel food cake mix

3. One way that skillful consumers exercise their "dollar votes" is by temporarily boycotting products whose prices are unreasonably high and substituting other items in their place. On a form similar to the one shown below, list ten foodstuffs and their appropriate substitutes.

	Item	Substitute
Example	Butter	Margarine

Chapter 28

Becoming a Skillful Consumer

Objectives

After completing your study of this chapter, you will be able to do the following:

1. Describe how to become a skillful consumer.

2. Define the term *unit price* and compute unit price when given prices and weights or measures.

3. List the basic metric units and demonstrate how to use a metric conversion table.

Some consumers are always in a hurry. They rush through the aisles of the supermarket, barely stopping as they impulsively reach out to grab this item from one shelf and that item from another. They clearly have no plan—not even the barest outline of a shopping list. Yet when their groceries have been totaled at the check-out counter, they are constantly surprised to find that their grocery bill is quite a bit higher than their neighbors'.

How is it, they wonder, that their neighbors always seem to get more value for their money? Why is it that their neighbors' washing machine seemed to cost so little and that when it finally did break down, the manufacturer paid for most of the repairs? In short, why are other people so lucky when it comes to buying?

More often than not, these "other people" are not just lucky buyers. They are, instead, skillful buyers. Skillful buyers understand the basic principles of skillful consumption. And they understand that the time and effort it takes to learn and practice these principles will be repaid each time they enter the marketplace. Skillful buyers plan their shopping. They allow time for shopping, use advertising effectively, and compare goods and services for price and quality.

ALLOW TIME

It takes time to buy wisely. Time spent before the shopping trip in deciding what to buy, when to buy, and where to buy. And time spent during the shopping trip in comparing price and quality. Skillful consumers know this, and they plan their schedules to allow enough time.

Skillful consumers also know that there is a right and a wrong time to buy. They buy only when their budget indicates that they can afford the purchase or, at least, enough of a down payment to avoid paying unnecessarily large monthly payments. And they know how to postpone buying until what they want is on sale. Nevertheless, they do realize that the savings from some sales may be great enough to cause them to consider advancing the date of a planned purchase.

Provide an example where you or your family moved up the date of a purchase in order to take advantage of a good sale.

A shopping list can greatly reduce grocery bills. (Monkmeyer)

USE A SHOPPING LIST

The wise consumer prepares a shopping list before going shopping. While a shopping list will not help you save money, it will help you avoid buying things you do not really need.

Almost everyone buys on impulse at some time or another. As you walk through a store, you may see a product that catches your eye because it is packaged in an attractive way. You do not need the item, but almost without thinking you buy it. Usually, the item is small—an ice cream cake, a magazine, a new shampoo. It could, however, involve much more of an expense—a $60 pants suit, for example. If you use a shopping list to control impulse buying, you will probably save yourself many dollars. These dollars will, in turn, provide you with other things more in line with your goals and priorities.

Another advantage of using a shopping list is that it helps you organize your shopping trip. A shopping list also helps you to remember the things you need. As a result, you will have fewer trips to the store and fewer opportunities for buying on impulse.

MAKE EFFECTIVE USE OF ADVERTISING

The average consumer is exposed to 300 advertising messages a day. For many, the influence of advertising on their spending decisions is great. Just how much your buying habits will be influenced by advertising depends partly on how aware you are of the ways in which you can use advertising to your own advantage.

For example, you can use advertising to become aware of new goods and services. Goods and services offered on the market for the first time must be introduced to the public, and advertising does this job. Advertising can also be used to discover new ways of using a product. And advertising provides useful shopping information. It allows you to compare prices and values of various products. It tells you where to find a particular good or service. And it can help you make specific consumer decisions. By merely comparing ads in a newspaper, you may find that making a choice between products is easier than you thought it would be.

In what other ways does advertising benefit consumers?

Skillful consumers are aware that some advertising may be misleading and that some advertising really says nothing. For these reasons, they study ads carefully. They disregard attention-getting devices and obvious sales pitches. They also realize that much advertising is designed to appeal to their emotions. By ignoring these emotional appeals and picking out only the facts that are most useful to them, skillful consumers use advertising to *their* advantage, not to the seller's.

Choose an ad from your local newspaper. Discuss how helpful the ad is to you in terms of giving information about the product advertised. Also, explain how the ad would or would not influence your decision to buy the product.

WATCH FOR SALES

The skillful consumer watches for clearance sales and promotional sales in order to save money. A *clearance sale* is a price reduction

Some sales may be only advertised at the store. (Maria Karras)

to get rid of merchandise that a retail store no longer wishes to carry in stock. Clearance sales are usually seasonal. For example, after Christmas, when stores want to clear their shelves and make room for new merchandise, they often have a sale. At the end of summer, air conditioners may be reduced in price to sell them. Buying at clearance sales may save quite a bit of money. But before buying a sale item, be sure that you can use it.

A *promotional sale* is a price reduction to get people to purchase regular merchandise or to get people into a store. Promotional sales are often used to get people to try a new product. The merchant hopes that after trying the product the consumer will continue to buy it at the regular price.

A merchant may also use loss leaders. *Loss leaders* are goods sold below cost to draw customers to a store in the hope that they will buy other items. The merchant expects to make up the losses on the goods sold below cost by selling more of the other merchandise at its regular price.

The skillful consumer makes sure that the goods advertised as being on sale actually have been reduced in price. You may find a store that advertises 10 percent off all merchandise; however, the 10 percent decrease in price may not be a true reduction. Some merchants raise the price of the merchandise a few days or weeks before the sale. The sale price then may actually be the same as the original price. Other merchants buy low-quality goods just for the sale.

What sales other than those mentioned are often advertised?

COMPARE PRICES

The skillful consumer is a comparison shopper. *Comparison shopping* is buying in which the prices and quality of similar goods is compared in order to determine the best buy. Sometimes, comparison shopping can be done within one store. At other times, it involves going to several stores. There may be a number of sources for the good or service you want. Moreover, the price of an item may vary greatly from source to source. For example, some specialty shops and department stores regularly sell goods at higher prices than other stores. The higher prices may pay for the cost of such services as personal selling, credit, gift wrapping, and delivery. If you do not use or need these services, you may have no reason to pay the higher prices.

You may choose instead to shop at a discount store. *Discount stores* are self-service retail stores that sell goods at prices lower than many other stores selling the same merchandise. Owners of these stores try to keep their operating costs low. Because of the reduced operating costs, the businesses can sell merchandise at lower prices and, possibly, attract more customers and make more sales. Lower prices, however, may also mean lower quality merchandise. Therefore always carefully compare both price and quality before making a buying decision.

If you choose to shop at one particular store or shopping center, be sure it is to your benefit. If you find a store where a product is offered at a lower price, be careful that the cost of getting there does not use up what you might save in the sale. Remember, your time is worth money. Spending hours and hours to save a few dollars may not be worth your time and effort.

The skillful shopper compares unit prices. (Steven McBrady)

For certain items it is difficult to compare the prices of even similar products. For other items, however, comparison pricing can be made easier if you understand how to compute unit prices and to deal with metric units.

Unit Prices

Because goods are often packaged in different amounts, it may be difficult to make a buying decision simply by comparing the prices stamped on the items. For example, one package of laundry detergent may contain 1 pound, 4 ounces. Another may contain 3 pounds, 1 ounce. To determine the best buy in such a case, you must compare unit prices. *Unit price* is the price per unit of measure. To compute unit price, divide the price by the number of units of measure. For instance, suppose you wanted to know whether a can of fruit juice containing 12 ounces and priced at 48 cents is a better buy than an 18-ounce can priced at 81 cents. By dividing 48 by 12, you find that the unit price of the first can of juice is 4 cents. Dividing 81 by 18 gives a unit price of 4.5 cents for the larger can. Clearly, in this case the smaller can is the better buy of the two.

Most packaged goods are cheaper in larger sizes than in smaller sizes. If this is true, should consumers always purchase the larger size? Give reasons for your answer.

Metric Units

As the United States moves to join the rest of the world in adopting the metric system of measurement, you will see more and more items marked in metric units. Because the old, unhandy system of measurement may disappear in time, it is important for you to become familiar with metric units.

The *metric system* is a system of measurement based on the number 10. It is a decimal system, much like the one we use for our money. Because both the metric system and our monetary system are based on the number 10, computing the unit price of an item will be much easier under the new system than it is at present.

Unlike our present system, the metric system has just a few basic units of measurement. For example, the basic measure of distance is the *meter,* which is a little longer than a yard (about 1.1 yards). The basic measure of weight is the *gram,* which is approximately 1/500 of a pound. And the basic measure of volume is the *liter,* which is a little larger than a quart (about 1.06 quarts).

To obtain larger or smaller measures, one of the following prefixes is added to each of the basic measures:

Milli, which means one-thousandth (0.001)
Centi, which means one-hundredth (0.01)
Kilo, which means one thousand times (1,000)

Therefore, a milligram is 1/1000 of a gram; a centigram is 1/100 of a gram; and a kilogram is 1,000 grams (about 2.2 pounds).

Eventually, you will be able to measure in metric units more easily than you do in standard units. For the present, however, it may be more convenient to convert metric units into units of measurement with which you are more familiar. The chart below shows some of the most frequently used conversions.

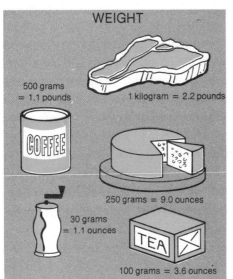

WEIGHT

500 grams = 1.1 pounds

1 kilogram = 2.2 pounds

COFFEE

250 grams = 9.0 ounces

30 grams = 1.1 ounces

TEA

100 grams = 3.6 ounces

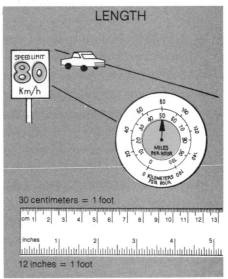

LENGTH

SPEED LIMIT 80 Km/h

30 centimeters = 1 foot

12 inches = 1 foot

VOLUME

5 milliliters = 1 teaspoon

15 milliliters = 1 tablespoon

1 CUP — 250 ml
¾ CUP — 200 ml
½ CUP — 150 ml
— 100 ml
¼ CUP — 50 ml

APPLE JUICE

4 liters = 1.06 gallons

MILK

PoP

500 milliliters = 1.06 pints

1 liter = 1.06 quarts

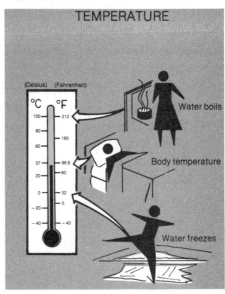

TEMPERATURE

(Celsius)   (Fahrenheit)

°C   °F

100 — 212   Water boils

80 — 160

60

37 — 98.6   Body temperature

20 — 80

0 — 32

−20 — 0

−40 — −40   Water freezes

COMPARE QUALITY

Although it is important to compare prices, it is also necessary to compare the quality of the specific good or service you intend to buy. Take the time to carefully analyze competing products. Study the material from which they are made and the way they are constructed. If a product looks cheap or has flaws, it probably is not the best choice.

When you find it difficult to judge the quality of goods, rely on the experts. A growing number of product-testing and product-rating organizations offer help in comparison shopping. Various consumer publications can be of enormous value. Become familiar with sources of consumer assistance and information, many of which are described in Chapter 29.

When goods cannot be inspected for quality, many consumers rely on brand names. Honda, RCA, Wrigley's, Avon, Ford, and General Electric are examples of brand names with which you may be familiar. The quality of a brand name good is generally the same no matter where or when you buy it.

List several goods that you usually buy by brand name.

USE THE TELEPHONE

Skillful consumers use the telephone and the classified section of the telephone directory to save time and expense. Call rather than visit business firms to see if they have the item for which you are looking and to compare prices. This is a much more efficient and economical way to do comparison shopping than by visiting several different stores. You should be aware, however, that some business firms will not give out the price or tell you whether the goods are in stock over the phone. Remember, too, that sometimes you can actually order merchandise over the phone, especially from large department stores. If you are familiar with the product and the store selling it, telephone ordering may be a convenient way of shopping.

List the disadvantages to using the telephone for shopping?

ASK ABOUT EXTRAS INCLUDED IN THE PRICE

At the time a purchase is made, the skillful consumer asks what extras are included in the price. Does the purchase price include delivery and set up? With certain goods such as furniture this may be very important, and many business firms charge extra for this service. Does the company that made the merchandise or the store that sells it give a warranty? A *warranty* is the statement of a manufacturer or seller to be responsible for the quality and performance of a product or service. The term *guarantee* is often used for warranty. A warranty may be express or implied. An *express warranty* is one made orally or in writing as to specific quality or performance. An example of an express warranty is the label attached to a pair of jeans, stating they will not shrink more than 1 percent. In some instances an express warranty may be simply hand-stamped.

Because it is difficult to prove an oral warranty, get a warranty in writing. Then take the time to read and understand it. Find out specifically what is guaranteed and what period of time is covered. Some warranties apply to the entire item, while others apply to only certain parts of it. A warranty is only as good as the firm that makes it. A warranty given by a firm that is no longer in business has no value. Therefore, find out who is making the guarantee and who will service the product during the period covered by the warranty. If you buy something with a warranty card attached, fill out the card and return it to the manufacturer or dealer to make the warranty effective.

An *implied warranty* is one imposed by law and understood even though it is not stated orally or in writing. In many cases the law requires that sellers provide certain minimum standards of quality and performance for the good being sold. When you buy food from a grocery store, there is an implied warranty that the food is fit to eat. The seller is liable for any illness or injury to the buyer or to the buyer's family that results from eating the food.

Give some examples of implied warranties other than the one mentioned above.

AVOID OVERUSING CREDIT

When considering a purchase, think about the number of dollars you have to spend. Can you pay for it out of your current income? If not, what are your alternatives? You may choose to postpone the purchase or you may select a different good or service (a good used car instead of a new one). You might also consider using credit. You must decide whether you really want to tie up future income to satisfy a present want. You must decide whether your purchase, with the additional credit charges, is still a good buy. If you do not need the item badly, it might be better to save for the item and not pay those credit charges. In addition, you can sometimes obtain a better price by paying cash at the time of purchase. However, if a real bargain comes along and it fits into your financial plans, using credit is appropriate. Just be sure that the "bargain" is still a bargain after you figure the cost of the credit. Skillful consumers know how much money they have to spend and when to use cash and when to use credit.

Suppose a student has a part-time job and just enough money in a savings account so that cash could be paid for a used motorcycle. Should the student pay cash or use credit to make the purchase? Explain the reasons for your answer.

Learning Activities

Increasing Your Business Vocabulary

You should become familiar with each of the terms shown below. On a sheet of paper write the numbers 1 through 11. Then write alongside each number the term that best matches each of the numbered definitions.

clearance sale / comparison shopping / express warranty / gram / implied warranty / loss leaders / liter / metric system / promotional sale / unit price / warranty

1. The statement of a manufacturer or seller to be responsible for the quality and performance of a product or service.

2. Goods sold below cost to draw customers to a store in the hope that they will buy other items.

3. The basic metric measure of weight.

4. A price reduction to get rid of merchandise that a retail store no longer wishes to carry in stock.

5. A warranty that is imposed by law and understood even though it is not stated orally or in writing.

6. The price per unit of weight or measure.

7. The basic metric measure of volume.

8. Comparing the prices and quality of similar goods at more than one store to find the best buy.

9. A price reduction to get people to purchase regular merchandise or to get people into a store.

10. A warranty made orally or in writing as to specific quality of performance.

11. A system of measurement based on the number 10.

Understanding Business

1. Why should consumers carefully analyze advertisements?

2. Give some reasons why a merchant might have a promotional sale.

3. How does a merchant expect to make up losses when goods are sold below cost?

4. What is the major benefit of a shopping list? What are other advantages of using a shopping list?

5. Why are some specialty shops and department stores able to sell their goods at prices higher than other stores?

6. Explain how unit price is determined.

7. Provide the approximate metric equivalents for a yard, a quart, and a pound.

8. Some consumers find it difficult to judge the quality of goods. What should they do?

9. Explain the difference between the terms *express warranty* and *implied warranty*.

10. List the alternatives a consumer might consider if he or she cannot pay for an item out of current income.

Business Problems and Projects

1. List five factors other than price that might enter into your decision as to where to shop.

2. Compute the unit price of each of the following items.

Size	Item	Retail Price	Unit Price
13 ounce	Evaporated milk	$ .35	$____per_____
16 ounce	Salted crackers	.69	____per_____
9¼ ounce	Chunky light tuna	.90	____per_____
24 ounce	Mustard	.57	____per_____
1 gallon	Milk	1.35	____per_____
10 pounds	Idaho potatoes	1.20	____per_____

3. Solve the following problems, using the conversion table shown on page 393 when necessary.

   a. How many meters are there in 100 centimeters?

   b. How many centiliters are there in 4 ounces?

   c. If a bolt of cloth costs $1.29 per yard, how much would 2 meters of it cost?

   d. Two cans of vegetable soup cost 30 cents each. If one can of soup weighs 12 ounces and the other weighs 300 grams, which can has the lowest unit price?

Chapter 29

Sources
of Consumer
Information

Objectives

After completing your study of this chapter, you will be able to do the following:

1. Understand the value of using consumer information in making consumer decisions.

2. Describe the types of consumer information provided by business firms.

3. Describe the types of consumer information provided by the various levels of government.

4. Describe the types of consumer information provided by consumer organizations.

5. Describe the types of consumer information provided by the mass media.

Sometimes even the most skillful consumers have difficulty making intelligent buying decisions because they lack sufficient information about the goods and services they want to buy.

Suppose, for example, that you wanted to buy a fairly expensive winter jacket. You see one in a store that looks good, and the price is about what you wanted to pay. But, because you are a skillful consumer, you know that choosing a product just by its appearance or price is very much like guesswork. You want to know much more about the jacket. You want to know if it will be warm, if it will last, if it can be cleaned easily and inexpensively, if it is inflammable, if it will or will not shrink, and—perhaps—if others have or have not gotten satisfaction from similar jackets.

Where do you go for this information? Like many others, you may go to your family or friends. In fact, they form a valuable source of consumer information. You have surely heard friends and relatives discuss why they liked or disliked a certain local business or a product. Your mother may feel that prices are too high at the local department store. Your uncle may praise the food at the newest restaurant. Perhaps your sister has complained about poor service at the corner gas station. And friends and coworkers may suggest where you should shop.

Sometimes, however, consumer information from relatives and friends may be incorrect or misleading. They may not be skillful consumers, they may have values different from yours, or they may not fully understand your needs. It may be necessary, therefore, to turn to other sources of consumer information. Chief among these other sources are those provided by business, government agencies, consumer organizations, and the mass media.

Do you ask your family or friends for advice and information when buying goods and services? Is this information usually reliable?

INFORMATION PROVIDED BY BUSINESS

The major source of consumer information is business itself. Naturally, the primary concern of business is to persuade consumers to buy their goods and services and to reject those of competing firms. At times, therefore, business's interest may conflict with the consumer's interest, which is to obtain reliable knowledge to use in making buying decisions. Nevertheless, the skillful consumer can find valuable product information in the sources provided by business. These sources of information include advertising, trademarks, labels, seals of approval, warranties, and owner's manuals.

Advertising

Much advertising is simply aimed at getting your attention. It may tell you little more than what is being sold, where it is being sold, and how much it is being sold for. Other advertising, however, does contain enough facts to help you make a buying decision. Advertising for cameras and stereo sets, for example, often describe the product in great detail. They may tell you exactly what it can and cannot do. And they may tell you why the features that it offers are superior to the features provided by competing products.

Many skillful consumers keep a scrapbook of advertisements of products identical or similar to products that they are considering buying. In this way they can compare the features of each item and, as a result, know what to expect when they go shopping.

Trademarks and Brands

Another source of product information are brands and trademarks. A *brand* is a symbol, mark, picture, or name used to identify a good or service. A *trademark* is a brand that has been registered with the government. It can be used only by the business that registered it. Familiar trademarks include *Kleenex, Coca-Cola, Xerox,* and *Jello.*

Brands and trademarks identify one product or line of products and set them apart from many similar products. Consumers learn to recognize a certain product by its brand or trademark. If the consumers find that a brand or trademark is generally satisfactory, they are likely to purchase it again. To them, it represents a standard of expected performance. For this reason, business firms spend a lot of money trying to make you remember their brands and trademarks.

Some trademarks are recognized by consumers throughout the world.
(Coca-Cola Company; Licht/Stockmarket, Los Angeles)

Labels

Intelligent consumers make a point of checking product labels. There are two basic types of labels: descriptive labels and grade labels. *Descriptive labels* provide information about products in the form of specific, itemized facts. These facts include the name and address of the maker, directions for use and care, ingredients or contents, and quantity or size. In addition, there may be something about what the product will do and the precautions that should be taken in using it.

For many products, quality is shown by grade. A *grade* is a classification or rating given to a product on the basis of such characteristics as size, quality, or uniformity. *Grade labels* are labels that indicate a definite standard of quality.

When using grade labels as a source of consumer information, you have to know what each of the grades means. In grading food products, for example, the government uses a system of letters or words. But because the grading systems are not the same for all products, the different systems may create a problem for you. Meat is commonly graded "prime" (highest grade), "choice," and "good." Eggs, on the other hand, are graded for both quality and size. The quality grades are "AA," "A," and "B," and the six sizes of eggs range from "jumbo" (largest) to "peewee" (smallest). As a consumer, you will have to learn the meaning of these and other grades if you are to make use of the information they provide.

Do you think that all food products should carry a grade label?

Tomorrow morning take a good look at the box your favorite breakfast cereal comes in. See how much information there is about the ingredients. Then look for information about its nutritional value. Also look at a milk carton. Many food products such as milk or frozen foods are stamped with a date. These dates tell you when a product should no longer be bought because of loss of nutritional value or spoilage.

While you may not find all the information you want on a label, what there is must be accurate. Mislabeling of goods is a violation of state and federal laws. Skillful consumers know how to read labels and use the information to their best advantage.

Seals of Approval and Certification Marks

Many products carry a special type of label called either a seal of approval or a certification mark. A *seal of approval* is a written statement or symbol indicating that a testing agency has accepted or approved the product. A *certification mark* is a symbol issued by a testing agency that indicates that a product meets specific standards of performance or design. The testing agencies that issue seals of approval and certification marks may be either independent agencies or agencies sponsored by a *trade association,* which is an organization set up to serve the needs of businesses with related interests.

One of the most familiar symbols is that of the Underwriters' Laboratories, Inc. Underwriters' Laboratories (UL) is a nonprofit, independent testing organization. Products that carry its symbol or mark have been tested for fire, casualty, and electrical safety. Underwriters' Laboratories does not judge product quality or performance. The symbol means only that the product design meets recognized safety requirements. If a product is tested for a specified hazard only, the label will indicate this fact. For example, roofing shingles may be tested for fire resistance only. The UL label would state that clearly.

The International Fabricare Institute, composed of members of the cleaning industry, has developed a certification program for clothing, household linens, and other fabrics. Its seal means that an item will stand up under typical professional cleaning techniques. Articles that the institute approves can then use the institute's seal on labels and in advertising.

Certain magazines authorize some of their advertisers to use the magazine's seal in the marketplace. Two of the most common magazine seals are the Good Housekeeping Seal and the Parents' Magazine Seal. These seals are granted when an advertiser meets certain requirements. The magazine may test samples of the

These symbols indicate to consumers specific standards of performance.

product in their own laboratories, or they may use independent testing agencies. These tests are conducted to gather facts about a product and about the reliability of the advertiser's claims. They are not done to compare the quality or value of goods with other goods of the same kind. Because the wording of the seal may vary from magazine to magazine, you should read the wording of the seal itself as well as the magazine's published explanation of its policy in using the seal. The wording of the seal and the policy statement that appears in every issue of the magazine will make clear the benefits the seal brings to the consumer.

Why do you think a testing organization such as Underwriters' Laboratories is independently operated?

Warranties

Another source of consumer information is the warranty. A warranty, remember, is the manufacturer's or seller's statement of responsibility for the quality and performance of a good or service. The warranty tells you what you can expect from a good or service. It may tell you how long you can expect the product to work without repair or service. It may also tell you what to do if the product fails to live up to the manufacturer's promises. And it may explain how the product is made and what materials went into it.

Warranties may be very short and simple, or they may be lengthy and detailed. In any event, you should make use of the warranty information on any good or service you intend buying.

Owner's Manuals

Much useful consumer information is also found in the printed materials that come with merchandise. Automobiles, bicycles, and most appliances are sold with owner's manuals that provide information on use of the product, maintenance, repair, replacement parts, and safety.

Many business firms also publish booklets and other printed materials describing their goods and services. Other firms publish booklets that provide general buying tips. For example, a utilities company may issue a brochure on the merits of gas ranges.

INFORMATION PROVIDED BY GOVERNMENT

Almost all levels of government have agencies that deal with consumer affairs. Some of these agencies are concerned primarily with protecting consumers against unfair or unsafe business practices. Other agencies are concerned chiefly with providing consumers with general product information.

The federal government has been involved with consumer protection and information longer than any other level of government. Of the many federal agencies that issue consumer information, only a few are listed here.

The U.S. Department of Agriculture (USDA) and its branches are a particularly good source of information. Of special interest to consumers are the many USDA booklets on such subjects as food preparation, clothing, gardening, canning and preserving, and homemaking. The Department of Health, Education, and Welfare (HEW) is one of the largest departments of the government. From its numerous agencies, a wealth of consumer information is issued each year. Some of these agencies are the Office of Education, the Public Health Service, the Food and Drug Administration, and the Social Security Administration. Most of this material is available from the Government Printing Office, which also publishes *Consumer Information, Price List 86,* a list of consumer information sources throughout the federal government.

Generally, local and state governments are less active in consumer affairs than the federal government. However, in recent years many many cities and states have set up special consumer agencies. These agencies often focus attention on such consumer-oriented topics as buying a used car, understanding warranties, or hiring a building contractor. They also regularly issue warnings on home repair schemes, illegal door-to-door selling, swindlers, and similar dishonest practices. The names and addresses of these agencies are listed in your local telephone directory.

Why do you think the federal government can and does provide more consumer information than local or state governments?

INFORMATION PROVIDED
BY CONSUMER ORGANIZATIONS

A number of nonprofit organizations exist primarily to serve consumers. Among these, Consumers Union and Consumers' Research, which are supported entirely by consumers, are major sources of consumer information. These groups examine and test consumer products and then report their findings in magazines and newsletters. Both organizations deal almost totally with goods advertised and sold nationally.

Products tested by Consumers Union are rated as "acceptable" or "not acceptable." "Best Buy" ratings are given to products that are not only rated high in overall quality, but are also priced low. Results of the testing are reported in the publication, *Consumer Reports.*

Consumers' Research also tests and rates consumer products. Its ratings are "recommended," "intermediate," or "not recommended." Ratings and price information in relation to quality are reported in *Consumers' Research Magazine.*

INFORMATION PROVIDED
BY BETTER BUSINESS BUREAUS

Better Business Bureaus are another reliable source of consumer information. A *Better Business Bureau* is a nonprofit organization supported by the business firms of a community and operated to promote fair business practices and to inform and protect the consumer. Better Business Bureaus will not tell you which firm to deal with, but they will provide information about a company you intend to do business with. They will tell you the number and types of complaints made by consumers about a specific business firm and whether these complaints have been satisfactorily settled. Consumers may also complain to Better Business Bureaus about misleading information or misrepresentation of goods and services. A second way Better Business Bureaus inform consumers is through their publications. The publications include tip sheets, fact books, and information pamphlets. A listing of current Better Business Bureau publications is available from the Council of Better Business Bureaus, Inc.

INFORMATION PROVIDED
BY MASS MEDIA

Consumer problems interest nearly everyone, and because they do, useful information on these problems regularly appear in the mass media. *Mass media* is a means of communication such as newspapers, magazines, radio, and television that is designed to reach the greater part of the public.

Newspapers have long been a source of consumer information. News stories about consumer activities appear almost daily. Feature stories on such consumer topics as trends in food prices or budgeting hints are quite common. And many newspapers carry regular columns written by experts in such fields as real estate, food buying, money management, and investment.

Many magazines feature at least one or two articles each issue that are of interest to consumers. Some others, such as *Better Homes & Gardens, Good Housekeeping,* and *Family Circle,* are primarily concerned with consumer topics. Still other magazines, such as *Changing Times* and *Money* are devoted entirely to consumer-related topics.

In their news coverage, radio and television stations regularly carry stories that affect consumers. Many stations present feature stories on consumer issues such as rising food prices or food shortages. In addition, some stations now provide programs designed to obtain immediate satisfaction of consumer problems submitted by their listeners.

Many television stations now provide programs that attempt to solve consumer problems resulting from dealings with local business firms. Do you feel that this service is valuable? Why or why not?

Learning Activities

Increasing Your
Business Vocabulary

You should become familiar with each of the terms shown below. On a sheet of paper write the numbers 1 through 9. Then write alongside each number the term that best matches each of the numbered definitions.

Better Business Bureau / brand / certification mark / descriptive label / grade / grade label / seal of approval / trade association / trademark

1. A symbol, mark, picture, or name used to identify a good or service.

2. A written statement or symbol indicating that a testing agency has accepted or approved the product.

3. A classification or rating given to a product based on characteristics such as size, quality, or uniformity.

4. An organization of firms, in similar businesses, set up to promote the interests of the members.

5. A label that indicates a definite standard of quality.

6. A label that gives information about a product in the form of specific, itemized facts.

7. A nonprofit organization supported by business firms of a community and operated to promote fair business practices and to inform and protect the consumer.

8. A symbol issued by a testing agency that indicates that a product meets specific standards of performance or design.

9. A brand that has been registered with the government to show ownership.

Understanding Business

1. What types of consumer information are available from business firms?

2. What type of information is provided by Better Business Bureaus?

3. What kind of information can be found on a descriptive label?

4. How do brand names and trademarks serve as useful shopping guides for consumers?

5. What types of consumer information might be provided in a warranty?

6. Give some examples of the type of information one might find in owner's manuals.

7. What does the seal of the Underwriters' Laboratories, Inc., mean?

8. What is the purpose of the testing of the International Fabricare Institute?

9. Give the names of two major nonprofit consumer organizations that provide much consumer information.

10. What types of consumer information are available to consumers through the mass media?

Business Problems and Projects

1. On a form similar to the one shown below, list five products that you see advertised which are, in your opinion, socially undesirable and probably not in the best interests of the consumer.

	Product	Reason
Example	Cigarettes	Harmful to one's health

2. What type of consumer information would most likely accompany each of the following items?

   a. Dishwasher   d. Pillow

   b. Electric cord   e. Box of cereal

   c. Wool sweater

3. On a form similar to the one shown below, indicate whether a descriptive or grade label would most likely be used for each of the items listed.

	Item	Descriptive Label	Grade Label
Example	Beef		
	Electrical cord		
	Wool sweater		
	Eggs		
	Aspirin		
	Motor oil		
	Cake mix		
	Leather wallet		
	Toothpaste		
	Butter		

Chapter 30

Common
Consumer Contracts

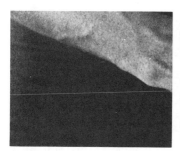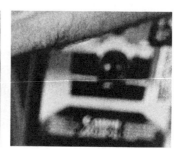

Objectives

After completing your study of this chapter you will be able to do
the following:

1. Define the term *contract* and list the four features of a legal
   contract.

2. Define the term *bailment* and describe the obligations of the
   parties to a bailment.

3. Define the term *negotiable instrument* and name the most
   common types of negotiable instruments.

4. Name and discuss the common sources of legal assistance.

As a consumer, you will take part in a great many business transactions throughout your lifetime. For the most part, these transactions will simply involve the buying of goods and services. Usually, you will have little or no difficulty in handling these transactions. Occasionally, however, things will not go as smoothly as you would like. Perhaps you may feel that you are being treated unfairly. Or you may want to be particularly sure that the terms of an agreement will be met. When this happens, a knowledge of the law that applies to business transactions or of where to seek advice may help you to solve your problems.

You should be aware of your rights in any business dealing. If you are, there is less chance of your getting into legal difficulty or of losing money. Knowing some business law also keeps you aware of your own responsibilities. Keep in mind that our system of business law favors neither the consumer nor the business firm. It assists and directs both parties in any business transaction by providing guidelines.

Because most business transactions involve contract law, every consumer should be familiar with the law of contracts. This chapter takes a look at contracts that have special importance for consumers.

THE NATURE OF CONTRACTS

A contract is a legally enforceable agreement between two or more parties. Many consumers think that contracts apply only to large purchases such as homes or cars where the buyer makes a written promise to pay over an extended period of time. But this is not true. Even the simplest purchases result in contracts. Ordinarily, any time you give someone money in payment for a good or service, you have entered into a contract. When you pay for a ticket to a movie theater, you have made a contract. When you pay for a soft drink and a box of popcorn, you have made a contract. When you get into a taxi cab and tell the driver where you want to go, you have made a contract. All these transactions, though simple everyday acts, involve contracts.

From these examples, you can see that many contracts are implied contracts. *Implied contracts* are contracts in which the

**Conditional Sales Contract to
Pay for Personal Property**

Edward Castell

TO

Vivienne Simmons

Office of..

State of Minnesota,

County of *Hennepin* } ss.

I hereby certify that the within instrument was
filed in this office for record on the *5th*
day of *June*, A. D. 19—, at *10*
o'clock *A.*M., and was duly entered in Book *6.75*
on page *14-63* *Ella Moreno*

Register of Deeds—City Clerk.

By *Alan Ashe* , Deputy.

A conditional sales contract is a
written contract in which the terms
of the agreement are clearly stated.

intent of the contracting parties is understood by their actions
rather than stated in either spoken or written words.

It is also clear that most contracts are oral. However, because
implied and oral contracts are hard to prove, you should have all
important contracts put in writing. In fact, under the Uniform
Commercial Code, the following types of contracts *must* be in
writing:

- Contracts that cannot be completed in one year.
- Contracts that involve the purchase or sale of real property.
- Contracts that involve the purchase or sale of goods for $500 or more.
- Contracts that agree to guarantee the obligations of another person.

Not all contracts must be in writing. For what reasons might you
want to have a contract in writing even though it is not required?

All parties must mutually agree to a contract. (Maria Karras)

A contract must have certain features in order for a court to uphold it as a valid contract. These features are (1) mutual assent, (2) consideration, (3) competent parties, and (4) legal purpose.

Mutual Assent

If a contract is to be binding, there must be mutual assent. *Mutual assent* is agreement by the parties to all the terms of a contract. Mutual assent exists when there is an offer and complete acceptance of that offer. An offer must meet certain requirements to be legally binding. It must be definite, and it must show genuine intent to enter into an agreement. If a friend jokingly offers you a million dollars for a ride to school, it is obvious that there is no real intent. Similarly, an offer made in anger, fear, or stress is not usually one that is serious in intent.

The party making the offer is the *offeror*. The party to whom the offer is made is the *offeree*. Acceptance takes place when the offeree agrees to the offer made by the offeror. The acceptance by the offeree must be without condition. That is, the offeree cannot change the terms of the offer in any way. For example, suppose you offer to sell your bicycle to a friend for $25 and your friend says, "I'll buy it if you put reflectors on first." This is not acceptable because your friend has made a condition.

The acceptance must also be stated directly by the offeree to the offeror. If your friend tells someone else that he or she is planning to buy your bicycle, this is not an acceptance. Once the acceptance has been made to the offeror, the agreement is a contract, and both parties are bound by it.

Why do you think that the terms of the offer cannot be changed in any way?

Consideration

Another feature of a contract is that something must be promised, given, or done by each of the parties to bind the agreement. That something is called *consideration*. Money, services, and goods most frequently serve as consideration in a contract. Promises may also be regarded as consideration. To be valid, promises must meet certain requirements. A promise cannot be a promise to do something that one is already required by law to do. Also, a promise cannot be a promise to do something against the law.

Competent Parties

A third feature of a binding contract is that the parties who enter into it must have the ability to make a contract. Persons who have the ability to make a contract are called *competent parties* Competent parties means those who are able to understand the contract and its consequences. In general, minors are not regarded as being competent parties.

Sometimes business firms do make contracts with minors. This is risky because minors are sometimes able to refuse to carry out the terms of the contract. If the contract is for necessaries, a minor is liable for their reasonable value. *Necessaries* are those things that are needed for life and that are suitable to one's economic and social position. Food, clothing, shelter, medical care, basic education, and tools with which to earn a living are necessaries by law. Goods for recreational use, such as motorcycles, sailboats, and stereo sets, are not necessaries. A merchant who makes a contract with a minor for such goods is taking a risk because the minor can refuse to pay for the goods. The minor cannot keep the goods, but sometimes there may be no goods to give back. Suppose a minor made a contract to buy a sailboat and the boat sank before it was paid for. If the minor refused to pay for the boat, there would be no goods to give back. Even if the merchant gets the goods back, they may be damaged or used. In either event, the merchant will have lost money.

Should minors be allowed to make contracts of any type? Why or why not?

Legal Purpose

A fourth feature of a binding contract is that it cannot in any way violate the law. The contract must be for a legal purpose. In addition, many contracts have been judged by the courts to be against the public good or to be harmful to the health and morals of the general public. Examples of illegal contracts are those involving gambling, crime, or doing business without a license when a license is required by law.

If a contract is not for a legal purpose, it is not considered a valid contract. Why do you think this is so?

BAILMENTS

Consumers enter into a special kind of contract many times each day. Consider, for example, the following kinds of day-to-day consumer activities. Your family car is left with a garage for repairs or service. Clothing is left at the dry cleaners. A fisherman rents a boat at a lakeside resort. You borrow a friend's car to go to the movies. In each of the above examples, a bailment is created. A *bailment* is a contract that involves the transfer of possession, but not ownership, of personal property from one person to another. The transfer is made with the understanding that the property is to be returned at a later date. The owner who gives up possession of

What type of contract is this
customer about to make?
(Maria Karras)

the property expects to get the article back, even though it may
have been changed or modified in some way. As you can see from
the examples above, bailments are very common. Since bailments
are contracts, they must contain all the features of any valid
contract to be legally enforceable.

There are two parties to a bailment, the bailee and the bailor.
The *bailee* is the party who receives possession of the property.
The *bailor* is the party who gives possession of personal property
to another. The bailee must be careful in using the property,
whether clothing, a television, or a car. If he or she is not careful
and the property is damaged, the bailee can be held responsible for
damages. For example, suppose you leave your best winter coat at
the dry cleaners and the dry cleaner loses it. The store is responsible for the lost coat and will have to pay an agreed amount for it.
After the bailee has completed his or her part of the agreement, the
article is then to be returned to the bailor.

Why do people enter into bailments? Because it is to their advantage to do so. That is, in most bailments, both parties stand to gain something from the exchange. When you send clothing out to be cleaned, you benefit by getting back clean clothes, and the cleaner benefits by getting paid. When you rent a floor sander or a carpet cleaner, you benefit from its use, and the owner benefits from the rental fee.

Give several examples of bailments that you and your family have entered into during the past month. Which business firms in your community depend on bailments for their income?

NEGOTIABLE INSTRUMENTS

A special type of contract that is widely used in business transactions is the *negotiable instrument*. It serves as a substitute for money, and like money, it can be passed freely from one person to another. Defined in simple terms, a *negotiable instrument* is a written order or promise to pay money. A check is one kind of negotiable instrument. It is payable on demand when presented to the bank on which it is drawn. Not all negotiable instruments, however, are payable on demand. Some, like promissory notes, are payable at a fixed date in the future. These negotiable instruments are often used to create credit, for the party who accepts the instrument agrees to be paid at a later date.

A negotiable instrument must have all the features of a contract described earlier. It also has its own special rules:

- It must be in writing and it must be signed.

- It must contain a promise or an order to pay a certain sum.

- The promise or order must be unconditional, that is, no conditions attached.

- It must be payable on demand or at a definite future time.

- It must be made payable to order or to bearer.

- The payment required must be in money only.

Frequently, promissory notes and checks are made payable to the bearer. This means that payment is made to whomever has possession of the note or check. A note made payable to the bearer can be transferred to another party simply by delivering it to that party. A check or a note made payable to the order of a specific party cannot be transferred to any person until the payee signs it.

What risks are involved when a person or business accepts a check or a promissory note made payable to bearer?

SOURCES OF
LEGAL ASSISTANCE

It is important that consumers know when they need legal help. It is also important that they know where they can get such help. There are several common situations where consumers may need

People with little money can get legal advice from legal-aid societies.
(Robbins/Stockmarket, Los Angeles)

the advice of a lawyer. A consumer should seek help when buying or selling real estate because such activities are usually very complicated and involve large sums of money. A consumer should also seek legal help when entering into a contract that he or she does not understand or a contract that involves a large sum of money. Most people need legal help when drawing up a will. And they should use a lawyer when entering into or setting up any type of business.

For those who cannot afford a lawyer, many large cities have legal-aid societies. *Legal-aid societies* are organizations that give legal advice to people with little money.

Does your city or county have a legal-aid society? If so, what types of services does it provide? If not, do you think it should have one? Why or why not?

Various levels of government have become increasingly concerned with consumer problems. Government officials, especially the city or county attorney or the state's attorney general, may provide needed legal assistance to the consumer. A growing number of states have small-claims courts. *Small-claims courts* handle claims of small dollar amounts at little cost to the consumer. There are several advantages to using small-claims courts. The court is less formal than a regular court, and you do not have to have a lawyer. Both parties simply tell their stories. In most instances the case is brought before the court without much delay, and the costs are low. In a regular court the legal costs may be greater than the amount won.

Does your city or county have a small-claims court? If so, what are some of the common types of disagreements or cases heard in that court?

Learning Activities

Increasing Your Business Vocabulary

You should become familiar with each of the terms shown below. On a sheet of paper write the numbers 1 through 10. Then write alongside each number the term that best matches each of the numbered definitions.

bailment / competent parties / consideration / contract / implied contract / legal-aid societies / mutual assent / necessaries / negotiable instrument / small-claims courts

1. Persons who have the ability to make a contract.

2. Contracts in which the intent of the contracting parties is understood by their actions rather than stated.

3. A legally enforceable agreement between two or more persons.

4. A written order or promise to pay money.

5. The transfer of possession, but not ownership, of personal property from one person to another.

6. Courts that handle claims of small dollar amounts at little cost to the consumer.

7. Agreement by the parties to all the terms of a contract.

8. Anything promised, given, or done to bind an agreement.

9. Those things that are needed for life and that are suitable to one's economic and social position.

10. Organizations that give legal advice to people with little money.

Understanding Business

1. What types of contracts must be written?
2. What are the four features of a legal contract?
3. List the requirements that must be met for an offer to be legally binding.
4. What four things most often serve as consideration in a contract?
5. What types of people are usually not regarded as being competent parties?
6. Give several examples of illegal contracts.
7. Give some common examples of bailments.
8. List the requirements that a negotiable instrument must meet.
9. When should consumers seek the advice of lawyers?
10. Where is help often available for citizens who cannot afford a lawyer?

Business Problems and Projects

1. Which of the following examples of contracts must be in writing to be legally enforceable?

   a. A contractor is sent to Europe to guide construction of a new office building. He will be in his new job for eighteen months. Rather than sell his home he decides to keep it and earn rental income. He asks you to maintain the property while he is gone in return for $50 a month.

b. You purchase a new bicycle from the local hardware store. The bike sells for $66 and you agree to pay $30 at the time of purchase, $18 in 30 days, and $18 in 60 days.

c. A neighbor has purchased a vacation cabin located on five acres in northern Minnesota. The property will be paid for over a three year period.

d. You wish to purchase a car from a local car dealer. The dealer will allow you to pay for the car over the next twelve months if one of your parents will cosign the note. Your mother agrees to do so.

2. A state attorney general's office asked newspaper publishers to print the following public service message. Read the message and react to the questions that follow it.

When consumers are presented with unfair business practices or feel they have been taken advantage of, they have the right to correct the purported injustice. Consumers may go back to the particular business in an attempt to satisfy their claim. If these efforts fail, a growing number of urban areas provide small claims courts to which the consumer can bring his problems. Businesses have the same opportunity if they feel they have a valid claim against a consumer. The small claims courts are specifically designed to handle civil cases where the amount of money in question is small, usually no more than $150. These legal clearing houses are inexpensive as court costs are usually a fraction of the cost of regular legal channels. Cases that come before such a court are handled quickly and with a minimum of legal procedure. The party bringing the action tells his or her side of the story and the defendant in the action has the same opportunity. In a small claims court no attorneys are required and there are no juries. The judge, who presides over the proceedings, after hearing both sides, rules on the case. The judgment is legally binding, but the parties in the action have the right to appeal. Small claims courts and the speed and efficiency they possess may save the parties in the action several months of waiting for room on the usual court's docket.

a. What can consumers do if a business firm fails to satisfy a claim?

b. What are the two big advantages of using a small claims court to settle a disagreement over a business transaction?

c. What two ingredients that are commonly seen in a court of law are not seen in small claims court?

d. What steps might a consumer want to take before bringing a businessman before a small claims court?

e. Why would you imagine that lately the number of small claims courts has been increasing rapidly?

3. On a sheet of paper list each of the following transactions or business activities. After each item indicate whether it is a contract, a bailment, or negotiable instrument.

a. Clothing is taken to the dry cleaners for spot removal.

b. A piece of paper that promises to pay a certain amount of money to a certain individual at a specific time.

c. An auto is driven to the service station where it is left for an oil change and lubrication.

d. The paycheck that you receive from your employer.

e. You agree to act as a caretaker maintaining a home and its grounds for $20 per weekend.

f. A close friend gives you an I.O.U. for $5 that he borrowed.

g. You pay the bus driver the 40¢ fare for the ride from the suburban area to the downtown shopping area.

Chapter 31

Protecting Consumer Rights

Objectives

After completing your study of this chapter, you will be able to do the following:

1. List and describe your rights as a consumer.

2. Identify some of the agencies protecting consumer rights and discuss the services they provide.

3. Identify and discuss two major weaknesses of federal consumer protection activities.

4. List and describe your responsibilities as a consumer.

Today, consumers are not completely on their own in the marketplace. In recent years, a great deal of emphasis has been placed on consumer's rights, and laws have been passed to protect these rights. These laws have improved the situation of the consumer and have made the seller more responsible and careful.

In this chapter you will learn in some detail about your rights as a consumer. You will also learn about some of the federal agencies that have been formed to protect your rights as a consumer. And, finally, you will learn about some of your responsibilities as a consumer.

CONSUMER RIGHTS

For many years, consumers were at a disadvantage in business dealings. In many cases, consumers were cheated, misled, or mistreated by business firms, and there was little they could do about it. Business interests were able to keep Congress from passing laws that would help the consumer. But in the late 1950s and early 1960s, consumers began to organize in groups to protect their rights. A consumer movement was begun that resulted in laws to guarantee consumers' interests. Consumerism had come of age. *Consumerism* is the movement that seeks to protect the rights of consumers. It is concerned with requiring such practices as honest packaging, labeling, and advertising; fair pricing; and improved safety standards.

In 1962 President John F. Kennedy sent to the Congress a special message on protecting the interests of consumers. In this message, President Kennedy presented what has been called the Consumers' Bill of Rights. These rights are the right to safety, the right to be informed, the right to choose, and the right to be heard. Since 1962, the administrations of the presidents who have followed Kennedy have continued to support these rights.

Name some of the groups in our nation that have been active in working to maintain or increase consumer rights. Are there local branches of these groups in your community?

The Right to Safety

The right to safety refers to the consumers' right to be protected against the marketing of goods that are hazardous to health or life. For example, the right to safety means that consumers have the right to expect that the food they buy is wholesome and fit to eat. They have the right to expect that electrical appliances are safe from electrical shock. It also means that they can expect cars to meet certain standards of safety such as seat belts.

The Right to Be Informed

Consumers have the right to find out the facts they need in order to make informed choices. They also have the right to be protected from fraudulent, deceitful, or grossly misleading information, advertising, or labeling. Consumers have the right to know what ingredients go into canned or frozen food products, for example. They have the right to know credit costs and true interest rates when they buy on credit or borrow money. And, of course, consumers have the right to know whether a product will actually do all the things that an advertisement claims it will do.

The Right to Choose

Consumers have the right to expect competition in the business system. This means they have the right, whenever possible, to choose from a variety of goods and services. For consumers, there should be more than one place to buy a car, a pair of slacks, or a loaf of bread. Services like radio and television repair, travel, and medical and dental care should be available from more than one source. It also means that consumers have the right to have these goods and services available at fair and competitive prices. In some cases, such as public utilities, competition does not work. Then consumers have the right to government regulation to make sure of satisfactory quality and service at fair prices.

Name some industries in which competition has been eliminated by allowing only one producer to supply goods or services to consumers under government regulation.

All consumers have the right to be heard. (Monkmeyer)

The Right to Be Heard

Consumers have the right to be heard in the writing of consumer legislation. Consumers know more about what's wrong with the marketplace than does government. They are the best source of ideas for protecting themselves because they are looking out for their own interests. Consumers also have the right to fair and efficient settlement of claims when they have been unfairly treated.

GOVERNMENT PROTECTION OF CONSUMER RIGHTS

Federal, state, and local governments have taken steps to protect consumers' rights. In recent years a number of state, city, and county governments have passed regulations that protect the rights of consumers. Generally, these regulations are concerned with sanitary methods in food handling, weights and measures, and quality standards. Safety and advertising are other areas of regulation.

As noted in Chapter 29, many cities and counties have set up consumer protection offices. Also, the number of state consumer affairs offices and protection bureaus has increased steadily. Remember that the responsibility and powers given to these consumer protection offices vary greatly. Some can do a great deal to protect the rights of the consumer while others can do little.

The federal government has taken the lead in protecting consumers' rights. Among the agencies it has established for this purpose are the following.

Consumer and Marketing Service

The Consumer and Marketing Service is an agency of the U.S. Department of Agriculture (USDA). One of its major purposes is to help make the marketing of food products as economical, orderly, and fair as possible. A second purpose is to assure the safety and wholesomeness of meat and poultry supplies. The Consumer and Marketing Service inspects meat and poultry products to make sure that those sold in interstate commerce (that is, products shipped outside state boundaries) are wholesome, free of disease, and fully and truthfully labeled. The Consumer and Marketing Service sets grade standards and provides grading services to certify quality, size, and condition of food products. It also inspects plants processing egg products shipped in interstate, intrastate (within a state), and foreign commerce.

National Bureau of Standards

The National Bureau of Standards is a part of the U.S. Department of Commerce. It develops tests for measuring the quality of many goods, including consumer goods. Among the states, it works toward uniform laws governing weights and measures. It provides standards for weights and measures used in the states. These standards directly affect consumers because they are concerned with the accuracy of scales, meter, gas pumps, and other devices that measure consumer goods in the market. In addition, it encourages industry to voluntarily control the number of package sizes of consumer products. The Bureau of Standards sets standards of fire resistance for products made of fabric or related materials. It is also responsible for overseeing America's conversion to the metric system.

Environmental Protection Agency

The Environmental Protection Agency (EPA) seeks to create a cleaner environment. It sets standards and enforces laws passed by

Congress concerning the environment. The EPA is involved with six environmental hazards: air pollution, water pollution, solid waste, pesticides, radiation, and noise. It cooperates with industry and all levels of government to meet environmental quality standards. Some of the major laws administered by the EPA are the Clean Air Act, Solid Waste Disposal Act, and Federal Water Pollution Control Act.

Look up and write down the definition of the terms *pesticide* and *radiation*. Why is the EPA concerned with these things?

Federal Trade Commission

The Federal Trade Commission (FTC) regulates commerce among the states. To do this, the FTC—as far as it is able—keeps the marketplace fair and competitive. It works to prevent deceptive advertising, packaging, and selling. It checks advertisements on television and radio and in print for possible fraud. It also investigates complaints of fake advertising and misrepresentation and misbranding of goods. The FTC conducts education programs through its field offices.

The FTC also looks into complaints of price fixing. *Price fixing* is an agreement among competitors to sell a product at a certain fixed price. In other words, the price is not a result of supply and demand. For example, auto makers could agree among themselves to sell cars at $6,000 each. Since only a few makers produce most of the autos sold, it is possible that this could happen. The FTC tries to prevent this. But if price fixing does occur, the FTC prosecutes those who took part in the price fixing.

Food and Drug Administration

The Food and Drug Administration (FDA) is a division of the Department of Health, Education, and Welfare. The FDA protects consumers by enforcing laws and regulations to prevent distribution of impure or mislabeled foods. It is concerned with making sure that drugs and medical devices are safe and effective and that cosmetics are safe. It approves or disapproves the marketing of new drugs based on evidence of safety and effectiveness. It also makes sure that food, drugs, and cosmetics are labeled and packaged in compliance with the law. It regulates use of consumer products including flammable fabrics and mechanical and electrical products. It can request seizure of products that are in violation of the law. Hazardous items such as flammable toys may be banned from the market. It also makes sure that dangerous chemical products have safety labeling. It sets and enforces standards for food products.

The FDA also informs consumers about protection provided by the law, advises consumers on ways they can protect their health, and listens to what consumers have to say about their problems.

Office of Consumer Affairs

The Office of Consumer Affairs advises the President on matters of consumer interest. It coordinates all federal activities in the consumer field and seeks ways to protect consumers. It also handles consumer complaints. In addition, it pays for and oversees research, consumer education programs, and the development of information of interest to consumers. The office is especially interested in those with limited incomes, the elderly, the disadvantaged, and members of minority groups.

Consumer Product Safety Commission

The Consumer Product Safety Commission has responsibilities in three areas:

1. Protecting the public against unreasonable risks of injury from consumer products.

2. Assisting consumers in judging the safety of products.

3. Developing uniform safety standards for consumer products.

The Consumer Product Safety Commission can set standards of performance, contents, design, construction, or packaging of a consumer product. The commission may ban a product it considers unsafe or dangerous.

U.S. Postal Service

The U.S. Postal Service is also involved in consumer protection. It is against the law to use the mails to cheat or swindle people.

Individuals of all ages have a stake in consumer affairs. (Julie Jensen)

Therefore, postal inspectors investigate and stop illegal activities such as unlawful lotteries, sale of worthless stocks, fraudulent sale of land, and appeals for donations to fake charities when the mails are used for the purpose of promoting these schemes.

List some schemes, other than those given above, that are used to defraud people.

PROBLEMS IN PROTECTING CONSUMER RIGHTS

As you can see, there are many laws and government agencies that protect consumers' rights. The Office of Consumer Affairs constantly looks for areas where more consumer protection is needed and areas where laws are not being enforced.

Because consumer protection activities of the federal government are shared among so many agencies, coordination of their activities is often difficult. Many of these agencies are responsible for enforcing the same legislation. For example, several agencies enforce the Fair Packaging and Labeling Act. The same is true for the Truth-in-Lending Act.

An additional problem is that consumers just do not know where to go for help when it is needed. It has been proposed that a cabinet-level post for consumer protection be added in the President's Cabinet. Whoever held this job would be responsible for enforcing all laws relating to consumers and for looking for areas where new laws are needed. Consumers would then know where to seek help when they need it.

CONSUMER RESPONSIBILITIES

Just as you have certain consumer rights, you also have certain consumer responsibilities. Let's take a look at some of your responsibilities as a consumer.

Responsibility to Be Informed

Consumers should be informed. This is their basic responsibility. Many consumer problems result from a lack of knowledge. Before you make a consumer decision, seek out as many facts about a product as you can find, using the various sources already named. Learn how to judge the quality of goods. Read labels and warranties carefully and make use of this information when you buy goods or services.

Skillful consumers also know their rights. They find out about laws that protect these rights, including those at the federal, state, and local levels. If they are treated unfairly in a business dealing, they know where to go for help.

Responsibility to Be Fair and Honest in Consumer Activities

Consumers have the responsibility to be fair and honest in consumer activities. As a responsible consumer, you should treat business firms in the same manner that you expect to be treated. Remember that business firms are entitled to a fair return on their investments. Honor your contracts, and pay your bills on time. Deal only with honest and efficient business firms. Report all violations of consumer protection laws to the proper authorities.

Do you feel that American consumers in general are fair and honest in their dealings with business firms? Why or why not?

Responsibility to Improve the Status of the Consumer

Responsible consumers work to improve the status of the consumer in the marketplace. As a consumer, you should help educate consumers about their rights and responsibilities. Work for the passage of laws that will cover any gaps in consumer protection. If certain laws are not being enforced, work to improve enforcement. Protection agencies need enough funds to operate effectively. Use your political rights to see that these funds are made available.

Learning Activities

Increasing Your Business Vocabulary

You should become familiar with each of the terms shown below. On a sheet of paper write the numbers 1 through 5. Then write alongside each number the term that best matches each of the numbered definitions.

business sector / consumerism / consumer sector / government sector / price fixing

1. The movement that seeks to protect the rights of consumers.
2. An agreement among competitors to sell a product at a certain fixed price.
3. Supplies productive resources and buys goods and services in the economy.
4. Produces and buys goods and services while it acts as a transfer agent and protective agency in our economy.
5. Produces goods and services and supplies productive resources in the economy.

Understanding Business

1. Give three examples of kinds of product safety that consumers have the right to expect.
2. What is meant by the consumer's right to be informed?
3. What should the right to choose mean to the consumer?

437

4. In what ways do consumers have the right to be heard?

5. What are two major purposes of the Consumer and Marketing Service? How does it meet these purposes?

6. What are six environmental hazards with which the EPA is concerned?

7. How does the FTC work to keep the marketplace fair and competitive?

8. Give several ways in which the FDA protects consumers.

9. What are two problems in protecting consumer rights?

10. What are some of the responsibilities of the consumer?

Business Problems and Projects

1. Read the following article that appeared in a recent issue of a daily newspaper. Answer the questions that follow.

CONSUMERS WARNED OF FRAUD AND DECEPTION POSSIBILITIES

While it is generally agreed that most of the businesses with which we are involved are fair and honest, there are exceptions.

Deceptive and clearly illegal business operations are practiced by a few, and the consumer is wise to be aware of those which appear most frequently. Beware of the following practices:

Bait and switch Consumers are persuaded to go to a particular store because of an advertised low price on a product. Upon arriving at the store, the consumer is told that the advertised product is really not a good buy and is persuaded to buy a more expensive item. Sometimes the advertised product is not available at all; the ad was merely a device to get the customer into the store.

False discounts A product may be reduced in price by 30% but in truth there may be no savings. Perhaps the price before the reduction was extremely high. The new price may be what you have to pay for a competing product anyway, so in truth there is no saving.

Old merchandise Many grocery products bear a date after which they are not to be sold. A few grocers will reduce these products to sell them before the date and the consumer heads home with the bargain which may spoil before it can be eaten.

Giveaways Consumers may be deceived by shady operators who present gifts or prizes. These devices are used merely as a means of getting the consumer's attention and willingness to listen to a sales presentation. Frequently, the prize is delivered only if the individual buys the item being promoted.

Home repair and maintenance schemes Roofing, siding, concrete and blacktop work, and landscaping operations may attempt to saturate a particular area with a "special package" at a very low price. The work is done in a hurry, and the money is collected just as quickly. After the work crew has gone, the consumer notes sloppy work, inferior materials, and a truly second-rate job.

Be aware of these consumer deceptions. If you see any of these consumer deceptions being practiced, report them to the police and the nearest Better Business Bureau.

a. Are most businesses out to "rip-off" the consumer? Explain your answer.

b. Which of the fraud and deception practices are most likely to relate to food sales?

c. Describe an example of a bait-and-switch deception.

d. Which of the fraud and deception practices is probably the most costly to consumers?

e. What action does the article suggest you take if you become aware of any of these fraudulent business activities?

Part Four

BUILDING FINANCIAL SECURITY

Chapter 32

Protecting Against Economic Loss

Objectives

After completing your study of this chapter, you will be able to do the following:

1. Define the term *insurance* and explain when insurance protection is needed.

2. List and describe the risks against which people most commonly need protection.

3. Describe how insurance works and how insurance costs are determined.

4. Explain how to shop for insurance and describe what an insurance agent does.

Each of us constantly chances the possibility of financial loss. Homes may be damaged or destroyed by fire, storm, or vandalism. Automotive accidents may result in loss of life, large medical expenses, or damaged property. A wage earner may no longer be able to earn a living because of illness, injury, or old age. Death may result in unexpected expenses and loss of income for the rest of the family. Situations such as these in which you chance the possibility of financial loss are called *economic risks*.

What would happen if your family lost its home and personal belongings in a fire? What would happen if your family lost the income of its major wage earner? For most individuals or families, such a large financial loss would mean severe hardship.

To avoid financial hardship, many people try to build financial security. They regularly put aside savings to pay for small financial emergencies or to tide them over in case of temporary loss of income. Most people, however, are not able to build up enough savings to cover large or long-term losses. Therefore, they buy insurance as part of their financial security plan. In this chapter you will learn about insurance. In addition, you will learn about some of the more common types of economic risks against which people need to be protected.

What are some large financial losses, other than those listed above, that an individual or family may suffer and not be able to pay for from savings?

WHAT IS INSURANCE

Suppose that you and nine of your friends belong to a bicycle club and that one of the bikes is destroyed in an accident. The person whose bike is destroyed has to buy a new bike in order to continue to participate in the activities of the club. Unfortunately, the cost of a new bike is $100—which is more than that person or any other club member can afford. As a result, your club loses one member.

Imagine, however, that all club members had agreed earlier to share equally in any losses that might occur. In this case, each of you would have to pay only $10 to cover the cost of the new bike.

Your friend could continue to belong to the club. Moreover, you would know that whenever one's bike was lost, neither you nor your friends would suffer a financial loss of more than $10. Thus, by sharing the risk, each of you receives some protection against the possibility of major economic loss.

This type of sharing is a form of insurance. *Insurance* is the protection against economic loss provided by sharing the risk with others. It would be impractical, of course, to use this method of sharing with your friends to protect against all economic losses. The replacement cost of some items might be too much to be economically shared by a small group. And if all the insured items were destroyed at the same time, the cost of replacing them would be more than the group could manage.

For these and other reasons, most people turn to insurance companies. *Insurance companies* are businesses that provide insurance services. Because insurance companies are able to insure many people against a specific risk, the pool of people sharing the risk is large. And so the cost to each member of the pool is small. In addition, insurance companies base their costs on the *theory of*

The possibility of financial loss is a danger we all constantly face.
(U.S. Department of Interior)

probability; that is, an estimate of the likelihood that a particular event will occur. On the basis of past experience, insurance companies can determine with reasonable accuracy how many accidents of a given type will likely occur within a certain period. The greater the chance, the greater the cost of that type of insurance.

You, too, can base your need for insurance on the theory of probability. If you think it is not likely that you will suffer a loss, you may choose to not buy insurance. In the example mentioned earlier, you might have been one of the people whose bike was not damaged. In that case, you would have been financially ahead by not joining in the group's loss-sharing plan. However, if your bike had been damaged, could you afford to repair or replace it? If you had insurance, you would have received some help in paying for repairs or a new bike. Remember, insurance does not eliminate the possibility of a loss. It does, however, spread some of the financial burden so that it is not a hardship on any one family or individual.

Give examples of some types of financial losses for which a high school student may want insurance.

SELF-INSURANCE

Sometimes large companies protect themselves against various kinds of losses by means of self-insurance. *Self-insurance* is setting aside money regularly to provide enough cash to cover possible financial losses. For some large companies, it is cheaper to self-insure than to buy insurance from commercial insurance companies.

Suppose that a large trucking firm has a fleet of 1,000 trucks. In an average year, the accident rate is two accidents for each 100 trucks. If they bought insurance for each of the trucks at, perhaps, $400 per truck per year, their annual insurance costs for the entire fleet would total $400,000. However, from past experience the firm knows that the average cost per accident is $750. With this information, the firm can set aside $15,000 for repair costs (2 × 1,000 ÷ 100 × $750). In this way the firm is insuring itself against financial losses resulting from accidents.

Rather than buy insurance for risks such as glass breakage, some business firms set aside a self-insurance fund. (UPI)

Families that regularly place money in their savings accounts to cover possible financial losses are also practicing a form of self-insurance. But most families find it very difficult to self-insure against such large financial losses as the destruction of their homes or the loss of income because of illness.

What kinds of large companies are most likely to self-insure?

WHAT ECONOMIC RISKS DO PEOPLE PROTECT THEMSELVES AGAINST?

All people face certain kinds of risks that could result in financial loss. Many of these risks are part of daily living. There is the risk of being responsible for damage or destruction to someone else's property. This is especially true if you are a car owner and your car is involved in an accident that damages another car, a building, a fence, or other property. There is also the risk of causing injury or death to another person. You might have to pay hundreds or thousands of dollars to make good the loss. Being responsible for

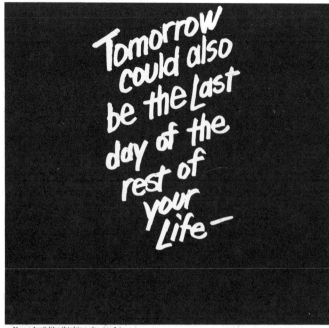

If you don't like thinking about safety, think where you might be without it.

National Safety Council

Insurance can only help lessen the financial loss from a risk. It cannot protect us from risk.
(National Safety Council)

injury to other people or damage to other people's property is called *liability*. The risk of liability is among the most serious risks because it can result in very large financial loss.

Also, there are the risks of sickness or injury that could result in large bills for hospital and doctor care. Related to this is the risk of loss of income because of injury, sickness, death, unemployment, or retirement. There is the risk of theft. Your home or apartment may be burglarized, or your car may be stolen. Finally, there is the risk of fire. Your clothes, furniture, or home may be damaged or destroyed by fire.

The following is a brief explanation of the types of insurance that people most commonly buy. Each of these is examined in greater detail in subsequent chapters.

Auto Insurance

Auto insurance covers the cost of injury to other people or damage to other people's property caused by your car. It also covers the cost of repairing your own car if it is damaged in an accident. And if your car is totally destroyed or stolen, auto insurance pays the cost of replacing it.

Life Insurance

Life insurance pays a specified amount of money upon the death of the insured person. People buy life insurance so that their death will not place a financial burden on their survivors. They buy usually enough insurance to pay funeral expenses and take care of their unpaid debts. The insurance also provides money for a family's living expenses after the death of a parent. Working parents buy life insurance to help make up for the loss of earnings caused by the death of one of the parents.

Health Care Insurance

Health care insurance covers hospital, doctor, and dental bills. There are different kinds of health care insurance that pay for such expenses as room and meals in a hospital, operations, X rays, medicines, surgeons' fees, and visits to a doctor or dentist.

Income Insurance

Income insurance pays you money when you are unable to work. There are different kinds of income insurance to cover different kinds of risks. For example, disability insurance pays you a fixed monthly amount while you are in the hospital or otherwise disabled. Unemployment insurance pays you a fixed weekly amount when you cannot find a job. And retirement insurance pays you a fixed monthly amount after you reach a specified age for retirement.

Home and Property Insurance

Home and property insurance covers the cost of repairing or rebuilding a home after a fire or other disaster. It also covers the cost of replacing damaged or stolen personal property, such as a television set or clothing. Home insurance often includes liability insurance to cover possible injuries to other people while they are on your property. A person injured on your property could sue you for damages suffered because you are responsible for the safety of others while they visit or work in your home.

This carelessly abandoned bicycle could be the cause of a costly law suit. (Maria Karras)

What You Can and Cannot Insure

There are some things that you can insure and some things that you cannot. If you want to insure someone or something, you must have an insurable interest in the person or property insured. An *insurable interest* is a financial interest in an insurable person or property. When you take out insurance on yourself, there is no question about your insurable interest in yourself. If you insure your car or your home, an insurable interest means that an accident or fire might cause you a financial loss. But could you insure your neighbor's car? No. Because the loss of your neighbor's car would not be your financial loss, you have no insurable interest in the car.

If you wish to take out life or health insurance on another person, you must have an insurable interest in that person. For example, parents can buy life and health insurance for their children. Husbands can insure wives, and wives can insure husbands. In life or health insurance, however, insurable interest does not have to involve a possible financial loss. Persons such as a husband or wife or children have an insurable interest because of marriage or a close blood relationship. For example, when parents insure the lives of their children, they do not expect to suffer a financial loss if one of the children should die.

Can you think of any cases in which the lives of people are insured and those who take out the insurance are not related to them? Give some examples.

Are there some things that should not be insured? If there is no chance of financial loss, then there is also no need for insurance. If the financial loss would not create a hardship, then perhaps there is no need for insurance. Finally, if the cost of insurance is equal to the value of what is to be insured, then insurance should not be bought.

What are some things that probably should not be insured?

AN INSURANCE POLICY

When a person insures something, there is always a written agreement or contract between the insurer and the insured. This agreement is called the *insurance policy.* The company selling the insurance is called the *insurer.* The insured, or *policyholder,* is the person on whose life or property an insurance policy is issued. An insurance policy is a legally binding contract. It is important, therefore, that you study it very carefully. You should be familiar with all the benefits as well as the restrictions that might affect your coverage. Many insurance policies have been standardized. But you will find there are differences, especially in health and car insurance.

THE COST OF INSURANCE

When you buy insurance, you make regular payments for the insurance protection you receive. The amount of money paid for insurance protection is called the *premium*. Several factors determine the amount of the premium. Two of these factors are the dollar amount (or dollar value) of the object to be insured and the likelihood of loss. For example, the owner of a $35,000 home probably would pay more for home insurance than the owner of a $20,000 home. This is because the dollar amount of the risk is higher. However, if the $20,000 home were located in an area in which forest fires frequently occurred, the premium may be higher than for a $35,000 home in a fire-safe area. This is because the chance of loss by fire is higher. Similarly, life insurance for a 60-year-old person would cost more than for an equal amount of insurance for a 15-year-old. This is because the 15-year-old can expect to live longer than the 60-year-old.

Give examples of people who might be required to pay more for life or health insurance because of the kind of work they do. Why do you think this is so?

When a policyholder has a loss, he or she asks for payment from the insurance company. This request for payment is called a *claim*. The amount of money the company has paid in claims is another major factor in determining the cost of insurance. Insurance company employees study past losses to help them predict future losses. For example, they study the auto accident record of male and female drivers between the ages of 16 and 24. From this record they determine auto insurance premiums for these age groups. As the total dollar amount of claims increases, so does the cost of insurance.

Insurance companies, like other businesses, have operating costs. Some of these costs are office expenses, selling expenses, and margin. Office expenses are the costs of running the insurance company. They include such things as salaries, office equipment, telephones, and office space. Selling expenses are commissions and salaries paid to sales personnel. Margin is the amount of money above and beyond all expenses that is set aside to be used in case of unusual losses. These expenses also affect the cost of insurance.

HOW TO SHOP FOR INSURANCE

Shop carefully for any insurance you purchase. Although many insurance policies have standard coverage, the cost for the same protection may vary among companies. You should compare the cost and the coverage. For example, if you want to insure a car, check the rates of several companies—don't just settle for the first one.

Some types of insurance can be bought where you work. Most often, however, you will have to rely on the advice of an insurance agent. An *insurance agent* is a person who sells insurance. Some insurance agents may represent only one company or specialize in only one type of insurance. Other agents may represent several different companies or offer many kinds of insurance.

Choosing a knowledgeable insurance agent is an important part of shopping for insurance. Most people do not know what types of insurance are available or what a specific insurance policy includes. A good insurance agent can help you understand the language of an insurance policy. And he or she can help you decide on the best kind of policy for your needs.

As your family grows, it is important to reexamine your insurance needs. (Lambert)

Learning Activities

Increasing Your Business Vocabulary

You should become familiar with each of the terms shown below. On a sheet of paper write the numbers 1 through 11. Then write alongside each number the term that best matches each of the numbered definitions.

claim / economic risk / insurable interest / insurance / insurance agent / insurance policy / insurer / insured (policyholder) / liability / premium / self-insurance /

1. A person who sells insurance.
2. A financial interest in an insurable person or property.
3. The company selling the insurance.
4. The possibility that a financial loss may occur.
5. Protection against economic loss provided by sharing the risk with others.
6. A written agreement or contract between the insurer and the insured.
7. The person on whose life or property an insurance policy is issued.
8. Setting aside enough cash to cover possible financial losses.
9. The amount of money paid for insurance protection.
10. Being responsible for injury to other people or damage to other people's property.
11. The request for payment made by a policyholder when he or she has a loss.

Understanding
Business

1. List several economic risks that people face throughout their lives.

2. Give two ways in which individuals or families can build financial security.

3. Explain how insurance helps people share financial losses.

4. What is self-insurance? Explain why a business firm might choose to use a plan of self-insurance.

5. List five common economic risks against which people protect themselves by buying insurance.

6. List the five most common types of insurance.

7. Under what three conditions would a person probably not purchase insurance?

8. Why should an individual study an insurance policy carefully?

9. What factors determine the cost of insurance?

10. Why should people shop for insurance?

11. Explain how an insurance agent can help you with your insurance problems.

Business Problems
and Projects

1. Cranston Supermarkets is a chain of 40 convenience stores that are open 24 hours a day. Each of the stores in the chain has 2 large plate glass windows that cost $975 apiece to replace. If the annual rate of breakage of the windows is

estimated to be 3 windows for every 10 stores, how much money should be set aside each year by the chain to provide self-insurance against this type of loss?

2. Collect from newspapers and magazines four advertisements for insurance. For each advertisement, answer the following questions.

   a. What is the name of the insurance company that is advertising?

   b. What type of insurance is being advertised?

   c. Is the advertiser a local company or does it have a local agent?

   d. Is it a mail-order insurance company?

3. On a form similar to the one shown below, list four risks that you might face that could result in economic loss. Also briefly explain how that risk would create an economic loss for you.

	Risk	Resulting Economic Loss
Example	Sickness	Loss of income

Chapter 33

Automobile Insurance

  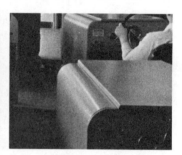

Objectives

After completing your study of this chapter, you will be able to do the following:

1. Explain the need for automobile insurance.

2. List and describe the basic types of automobile insurance coverage.

3. Explain how the cost of automobile insurance is determined.

4. Describe no-fault insurance and explain the major advantage of no-fault insurance plans.

In a recent year there were over 122 million licensed drivers in the United States. In that same year more than 27 million drivers were involved in auto accidents. Those accidents resulted in 67,300 deaths and almost two million personal injuries. The cost to the people involved in these accidents was approximately $19 billion. In addition to dollar costs, there are other costs such as personal suffering that result from death and injury that cannot be measured in dollars.

About one of every four licensed drivers is involved in an auto accident each year. Clearly then, there are many risks involved in driving or owning an auto. One of the most serious risks is the risk of liability. In this chapter you will study about the various types of auto insurance coverage available to help people share the risk of financial loss resulting from auto accidents. Automobile insurance also protects against damage or loss resulting from perils such as theft and fire. A *peril* is a risk that something may be lost, stolen, damaged, or destroyed.

IS AUTO INSURANCE NEEDED?

Insurance is the best way to share the risk and provide protection against the financial loss resulting from auto accidents. In most states, the car owner can decide whether or not to buy insurance. All states, however, have financial responsibility laws. *Financial responsibility laws* make a person responsible for the expenses of an auto accident caused by that person. If you are involved in an auto accident, the financial responsibility law requires that you show proof of your ability to pay for damages. Most people meet this requirement by buying insurance.

Each state sets the minimum amount of insurance a driver must have. If a driver does not carry that amount of insurance, the law requires the driver to settle the claim or deposit security for damages caused by an accident. Otherwise, the driver may lose not only his or her license but the car registration as well.

Some states have laws that make it compulsory for drivers to carry certain kinds of insurance. This insurance covers injury to other people and damage to other people's property. Minimum amounts are set by the state.

Assigned Risk

Some drivers, because of age or driving record, are unable to get auto insurance through regular methods. For that reason, every state has an assigned risk plan. The *assigned risk plan* provides auto insurance coverage to those drivers who cannot purchase insurance through regular methods.

The assigned risk plan works in this way. Each insurance company selling auto liability insurance in a state is assigned a number of high-risk drivers based on the amount of auto liability insurance that company sells in the state. In this way each insurance company has to accept its share of high-risk drivers in that state. Usually the assigned risk plan provides liability coverage up to the limits set in the state's financial responsibility law. Drivers insured under an assigned risk plan have to pay higher premiums than other drivers who are not in high-risk groups.

TYPES OF AUTOMOBILE INSURANCE COVERAGE

Automobile insurance covers a number of different risks. Most people carry coverages to protect against injury to people and damage to property. These coverages may be purchased as a package or separately. Some car owners feel that certain coverages are unnecessary, so they purchase only those they feel they need.

Bodily Injury Liability Coverage

Car owners are responsible for injury they may cause to others. *Bodily injury liability coverage* protects the car owner against financial loss resulting from death or injury to other people. "Other people" includes pedestrians, persons in the insured's car, and persons in other vehicles involved in the accident.

Accidents that cause death or injury to other people can be very costly. For example, a driver could injure someone so badly that the person could never work again. In such a case, the driver could be responsible for all the possible income the injured person might have earned during that person's working life.

All auto policies state the exact amount of bodily injury liability coverage that the insured has. The amounts are given in maximum figures. For example, an insured might have liability coverage of $25,000 for each person injured in an accident and $50,000 maximum liability for any one accident. These figures normally appear in shortened form on the policy. They would be stated as 25/50, 50/100, or 100/300. Many states require at least 25/50 coverage for all drivers.

What is the minimum bodily injury liability amount in your state? Do you think this is too low or too high? Why?

In addition to insuring the car owner, bodily injury liability coverage can be used to cover anyone who operates the car with the owner's permission. And it can cover the insured when operating someone else's car with permission. A further benefit is that the insurance company will furnish legal aid in the event that a lawsuit is brought against the insured as the result of an accident.

It is important to note that bodily injury liability coverage does *not* apply to any injury that the insured or members of the insured's household might suffer in an accident. Injuries of this sort are covered by medical payments coverage, which is discussed later.

What do you suppose could happen if you were the driver of an automobile and caused an accident, but had no bodily injury liability coverage?

Property Damage Liability Coverage

A car owner is responsible for damage he or she might cause to someone's property. *Property damage liability coverage* provides protection when an auto damages property belonging to others. "Property" means both other motor vehicles and any property such as buildings, trees, or fences that might be damaged in an accident. The financial responsibility laws of each state have established minimums for property damage liability coverage, just as they have for bodily injury liability coverage. The minimum amount for most states is $5,000, but in some states, it can be as low as $1,000 or as high as $10,000. When a policy has both property damage liability coverage and bodily injury liability coverage, the amounts of coverage are stated as, say, 25/50/10. The last figure represents property damage liability coverage.

If you are found legally liable for property damage, your insurance company will provide a lawyer to represent you and pay damages up to the amount provided for in the policy.

Is the Minimum Enough?   State laws that set minimum coverages are passed to make certain that drivers are held responsible for losses resulting from accidents which they have caused. Quite often, however, these minimum amounts do not provide enough protection. Financial losses from accidents may go beyond these minimums. Therefore, drivers should consider buying more insurance than the minimum. Table 33–1 lists the premiums set by one major company for bodily injury and property damage liability insurance for a married driver over 25 years of age in a rural and an urban area in one state. Notice how little the premium changes for coverage beyond the minimums. Notice also how much more expensive insurance is in cities than in rural areas.

TABLE 33-1   COMPARISON OF PREMIUM RATES FOR RURAL AND URBAN AREAS FOR SIX MONTHS

Bodily Injury and Property Damage Liability Coverage	Premium (6 months)	
	Rural Area	Urban Area
25/50/10 (minimum)	32.40	42.50
50/100/10	34.30	45.10
50/100/25	36.20	47.50
100/300/10	37.90	49.70
100/300/25	39.80	52.30
100/300/50	42.50	55.70

Source: State Farm Insurance

Which automobile insurance coverage do you feel would be most important for a driver to have—bodily injury liability coverage or property damage liability coverage? Why?

Medical Payments Coverage

When drivers buy bodily injury liability coverage, they can also choose to buy protection for themselves and their families against medical expenses that might result from an accident. This protection is *not* provided by bodily injury liability coverage. *Medical payments coverage* pays the cost of medical, dental, hospital, and funeral expenses for the driver and passengers riding in the policyholder's car. It also covers the policyholder and his or her immediate family as pedestrians or while riding in someone else's car. Medical payments insurance can be purchased in amounts ranging from $500 to $10,000. In case of accident, payment is made up to the limits of the policy, regardless of who is at fault.

Why would a driver want both bodily injury liability coverage and medical payments coverage? What kind of protection does each coverage provide?

Uninsured Motorists Coverage

In spite of compulsory insurance and financial responsibility laws, some drivers still do not carry auto insurance of any kind. When those drivers are involved in accidents, they often cannot pay for the damage they are responsible for. For this reason, many insured drivers buy uninsured motorists coverage. *Uninsured motorists coverage* provides protection in case you are involved in an accident caused by an uninsured driver. It covers the insured and passengers riding in the insured's car. It also protects you should your car be hit by a hit-and-run driver.

In which sections of our nation would automobile insurance cost the most? Where would it cost the least? Why do you think costs would be higher or lower in these areas?

Comprehensive Coverage

Property damage liability coverage, discussed earlier, only covers damage to other people's property. An automobile owner also needs coverage to pay for damage to his or her own car. This is what comprehensive coverage does. *Comprehensive coverage* provides protection against loss from damage to the policyholder's car except damage caused by a collision or when the car turns over. It covers such perils as fire, theft, windstorm, or vandalism. Coverage can also be bought for explosion, earthquake, falling objects, hail, flood, riot, and civil disorders. This coverage also includes damage caused by collision with animals. When you purchase auto insurance, it is important to check the policy carefully to see which kinds of perils are included in the comprehensive coverage.

Collision Coverage. There are two major hazards that are not covered by comprehensive coverage: collision and turning the car over. *Collision coverage* protects against loss resulting from damage to the policyholder's car from a collision or when the car turns over, regardless of who is responsible.

Collision coverage is generally sold with a deductible clause. A *deductible clause* requires the policyholder to pay a part of the loss before the insurance company pays anything. Deductible clauses

Collision coverage greatly reduces your financial loss. (Camerique)

are generally for a specified amount or for a percentage of the loss. For example, suppose Cindy owns her own car. She has collision coverage with a $50 deductible clause. If Cindy is involved in an accident and the damage to her automobile is $500, she is responsible for the first $50 of the repair costs. The insurance company is responsible for the other $450. Sometimes the deductible is a percentage of the repair costs. If Cindy's policy had a 20 percent deductible clause, her share of the repair costs would have been $100. The insurance company would pay $400.

Deductible clauses help reduce insurance premiums. The more financial loss the insured agrees to pay himself or herself, the lower the cost of the coverage. The table below shows how this works. It gives examples of the cost of collision coverage for a late-model automobile. These costs are for an adult driver using the automobile for average use.

TABLE 33-2 COMPARISON OF PREMIUM RATES FOR COLLISION COVERAGE FOR RURAL AND URBAN AREAS FOR SIX MONTHS

| Collision Coverage | Premium (6 months) | |
	Rural Area	Urban Area
20 percent deductible	38.40	40.80
$50 deductible	29.50	31.40
$100 deductible	26.40	28.10
$200 deductible	21.40	22.60

Source: State Farm Insurance

Deductible clauses are also available with other types of insurance such as health insurance and homeowner's insurance. When purchasing insurance, you should ask about the various kinds of deductible clauses that are available.

FACTORS AFFECTING AUTOMOBILE INSURANCE RATES

Auto insurance premiums are often called *rates*. The rate that the consumer must pay for automobile insurance is set by the insurance company. Rates are based on the amount of risk the insurance company must assume to insure a driver. This means that those who have the most losses must pay the highest rates.

To decide who has the most losses, insurance companies study records of the amount of money paid out in claims. They do this for different areas and for different groups of drivers. When a large amount of money is paid out for claims in a certain area or for a certain group of drivers, higher rates are set. Some of the factors that insurance companies use to set rates are discussed below.

Where the Insured Person Lives

The number of auto accidents in an area and the amount of loss due to the accidents affect the rates in that area. Auto insurance rates are lower in rural areas and small towns where there isn't much traffic. Less money is paid out in claims in such areas so the rates are lower. Rates are higher in areas of heavy traffic where there are more accidents and more claims. Rates vary from state to state and in different areas within a state.

Classification of Driver

Automobile drivers are usually classified by age, sex, marital status, and driving record. Then rates are set according to the amount of claims of each group. Unmarried males under the age of 29 who are owners or principal operators of a car usually pay the highest rates. The reason is that drivers in this group have the greatest number of accidents of all groups of drivers. Rates for female drivers under the age of 25 are much lower than for males because females have fewer accidents than males. In most states the rates for insurance decrease as the driver grows older.

Male drivers under age 29 have more accidents and cause insurance companies to pay out more money to settle claims from accidents than any other driver group. Why?

Type of Vehicle

The age, make, and model of your car also affects insurance costs. Rates are higher for newer and more expensive cars because they cost more to repair. Rates are also higher for high-powered cars and sports cars because statistics show that drivers of these kinds of cars usually have more accidents.

Use of Vehicle

The purpose for which you use your car has an effect on insurance costs. If the car is used for daily business purposes, as in door-to-door selling, the costs are greater than if it is used only to drive to and from school. The distance you drive each day also affects the cost of insurance. Farmers and ranchers may qualify for special rates if the vehicle is kept on a farm or ranch and used only for farming or ranching purposes.

FACTORS THAT HELP REDUCE AUTOMOBILE INSURANCE COSTS

There are several factors that may help you reduce your automobile insurance costs. Among them are driver education courses and good student discounts.

Driver Education

In most states insurance companies offer a discount to young drivers who complete driver education courses. Studies have shown that drivers who complete a driver education course have fewer accidents than those who do not. In some states, drivers are eligible for this discount until they reach the age of 24.

Students who complete driver education courses are often allowed special insurance discounts. (National Education Association)

Good Student Discount

Another way for young people to save on insurance costs is with the good student discount. Many companies in most states offer up to a 25 percent discount to students who are on the Dean's List, have a B average, or are in the top 20 percent of their class. To qualify, students must be at least 16 years old and must be juniors or seniors in high school or full-time college students.

Give some reasons why you think insurance companies are willing to sell automobile insurance coverage for less to persons they classify as good students.

Other Factors

There are several other situations in which many insurance companies reduce policy rates. Families with two or more automobiles insured by the same company are usually given a discount. Most companies give discounts for claim-free drivers. Claim-free drivers are those who have not had an accident claim for a certain period of time. Some companies even give discounts to nonsmokers and nondrinkers.

Why do you think insurance companies consider the above factors to be important enough to affect the cost of insurance?

WHAT IS NO-FAULT INSURANCE?

The auto insurance laws that have been discussed so far were based on who is responsible for an accident. This means that a driver who is at fault or causes an auto accident is liable for damage to the other car and for personal injuries to passengers of that car. However, long court trials are often necessary to prove who is at fault in an accident. To try to avoid the long delay of a trial and to make payment of claims faster, many states have passed so-called no-fault insurance laws. *No-fault insurance* is a plan by which victims of an accident are covered and paid by their own insurance companies, regardless of who caused the accident.

With pure no-fault insurance, every motorist would have the same type of policy. However, the states with no-fault automobile insurance laws have what are called modified no-fault systems. In these systems most cases are settled quickly by the companies involved. However, there is a maximum no-fault amount. If the claims go beyond a set maximum amount, the case may go to court for settlement. With these modified systems, drivers get both the benefits of quick claim settlement on smaller amounts and the right to bring suit for greater losses.

SPECIAL INSURANCE FOR MOTORCYCLES

Insurance on motor scooters, motor bikes, and motorcycles is similar to auto insurance in some ways. Costs are determined by age, driving record, cost, and size of the motorcycle.

Because the coverage and restrictions on motorcycle insurance vary so much, you should ask several insurance agents to explain their policies completely before buying such insurance. Compare each policy, and select the one that best fits your needs.

Why do you think insurance companies place special coverage restrictions on motorcycle insurance?

RECREATIONAL VEHICLE INSURANCE

Many people now own recreation vehicles of one type or another. Special insurance is generally needed for these vehicles.

Insurance for recreational vehicles is very much like auto insurance. Coverages can include bodily injury liability insurance, property damage liability insurance, medical payments insurance, physical loss and damage to the vehicle insured, and uninsured motorists insurance. The above coverages can apply to all recreational vehicles except camping trailers. Only physical loss and damage insurance is needed for camping trailers because other coverages are included in one's regular auto insurance. As with auto insurance, deductible clauses are available.

Learning Activities

Increasing Your Business Vocabulary

You should become familiar with each of the terms shown below. On a sheet of paper write the numbers 1 through 11. Then write alongside each number the term that best matches each of the numbered definitions.

assigned risk plan / bodily injury liability coverage / collision coverage / comprehensive coverage / deductible clause / financial responsibility laws / medical payments coverage / no-fault insurance / peril / property damage liability coverage / uninsured motorists coverage

1. Laws that make a person responsible for the expenses of an auto accident caused by that person.

2. A clause in an insurance policy that requires the policyholder to pay a part of the loss before the insurance company pays anything.

3. A way of providing auto insurance coverage to those drivers who cannot purchase insurance through regular methods.

4. Coverage providing protection for the car owner against financial loss resulting from death or injury to other people.

5. Coverage providing protection when an auto damages property belonging to others.

6. Coverage providing protection for medical, dental, hospital, and funeral expenses for the driver and passengers riding in the policyholder's car.

7. Coverage providing protection in case of an accident involving an uninsured driver or a hit-and-run accident.

8. Coverage providing protection against loss from damage to the policyholder's car except damage caused by a collision or when the car turns over.

9. Coverage providing protection against loss resulting from damage to the policyholder's car from a collision or when the car turns over, regardless of who is responsible.

10. A plan by which victims of an accident are covered and paid by their own insurance no matter who caused the accident.

11. A risk or danger that something may be lost, stolen, damaged, or destroyed.

Understanding Business

1. Explain why automobile insurance is needed.

2. List the six basic types of auto coverage.

3. Explain the coverage provided when the following figures are shown on an auto insurance policy: 100/300/50.

4. Why should a driver consider purchasing bodily injury liability and property damage liability coverage beyond the minimum amount required by state law?

5. Explain why a car owner might choose to include uninsured motorists coverage in an overall auto insurance policy.

6. List the perils usually covered under comprehensive coverage.

7. What two major hazards are not covered by comprehensive coverage?

8. What factors affect insurance rates?

9. How can young people get reduced auto insurance rates?

10. What are the major benefits of the modified no-fault insurance system?

Business Problems and Projects

1. The table below is from the National Safety Council. It shows information related to the age of drivers involved in motor vehicle accidents in a recent year. After studying the table, answer the questions that follow it.

AGE OF DRIVERS—TOTAL NUMBER AND NUMBER IN ACCIDENTS

Age Group	All Drivers Number	%	Fatal Number	%	Drivers in Accidents All Number	%
Total	122,400,000	100.0%	67,300	100.0%	27,700,000	100.0%
Under 20	12,600,000	10.3	11,300	16.8	5,700,000	20.6
20–24	13,900,000	11.4	13,100	19.5	5,200,000	18.8
25–29	13,400,000	11.0	7,900	11.7	3,300,000	11.9
30–34	12,500,000	10.2	6,900	10.2	2,600,000	9.4
35–39	11,400,000	9.3	4,700	7.0	2,100,000	7.6
40–44	11,400,000	9.3	4,700	7.0	1,800,000	6.5
45–49	11,500,000	9.4	4,600	6.8	1,800,000	6.5
50–54	10,700,000	8.7	3,500	5.2	1,500,000	5.4
55–59	8,100,000	6.6	2,900	4.3	1,300,000	4.7
60–64	6,400,000	5.2	2,500	3.7	900,000	3.2
65–69	4,900,000	4.0	2,000	3.0	800,000	2.9
70–74	3,300,000	2.7	1,400	2.1	300,000	1.1
75 and over	2,300,000	1.9	1,800	2.7	400,000	1.4

Source: National Safety Council

    a. What was the total number of drivers in the United States for the year given? How many of these drivers were in fatal accidents? What was the total number of all accidents?

b. Which age group had the highest number of drivers? How many drivers were there in the age group?

c. Which age group had the second highest number of drivers in that year? How many?

d. Which age group had the highest number of fatal accidents? How many? What percentage of fatal accidents did this age group have?

e. Which age group had the highest number of all accidents? How many? What percentage of all accidents did this age group have? Was this age group the same as the one given for your answer to the preceding question?

f. Which age group had the lowest number of drivers? Did this age group have the lowest number of fatal accidents? If not, which age group did have the lowest number of fatal accidents?

g. Suppose insurance rates are based on the number of all accidents. Which age group would you expect to pay the highest insurance rates? The lowest insurance rates?

2. Alfred was driving his car when a tire blew out. The car ran off the road, struck a light post, and then hit a pedestrian. Frank, who was riding with Alfred, suffered a cut on his head when he struck the windshield. After Alfred got out of the car to inspect the damages, his car was sideswiped by a hit-and-run driver.

What kinds of insurance would be required to protect against loss from each of these damages:

a. Damage to the light post.

b. Damage to the automobile when it hit the lamp post.

c. Injury to the pedestrian.

d. Injury to the passenger.

e. Damage caused by the hit-and-run car.

Chapter 34

Life Insurance

Objectives

After completing your study of this chapter, you will be able to do the following:

1. Explain why people purchase life insurance.

2. Explain the difference between term and permanent life insurance.

3. List the main kinds of permanent life insurance and give the purpose of each.

4. Describe how benefits from life insurance can be paid.

5. Discuss how to select the right kind of life insurance protection.

Life insurance is the most common form of insurance in America today. Six out of every seven Americans have life insurance policies. The average family with life insurance has $25,000 of protection in its policies. Over $16.5 billion in life insurance benefits are paid out each year.

WHY BUY LIFE INSURANCE?

Wage earners buy life insurance for two important reasons. The chief reason is to protect their families from financial hardship. If the major wage earner in a family dies suddenly, the family is faced with serious financial hardships. The primary source of income is cut off. There are funeral expenses and perhaps medical expenses. And regular living expenses for such things as the rent or mortgage, food, and utilities continue. The loss of the wage earner's salary leaves the family without the money to meet these expenses. Life insurance provides money payments to help the family cover these expenses and, also, to continue to fulfill its financial goals.

Do you think every wage earner should have life insurance? Why?

The money payments that life insurance companies pay to the insured or to survivors of the insured are called *benefits*. Life insurance benefits are used to meet the following types of needs:

- To provide money to meet expenses caused by a person's death.
- To provide money on which to live while adjusting to the loss of the wage earner.
- To provide money for children while they are attending school.
- To provide an income for the surviving parent after the children have left home.
- To provide money to care for the children in case both mother and father die.

These benefits are called *death benefits* because they are paid only after the death of the insured. About 44 percent of all insurance benefits are paid in the form of death benefits.

A second important reason why people buy life insurance is that it provides a means of regular saving. The real purpose some people buy this kind of life insurance may be to build up savings for long-range goals such as a college education for the children or retirement income for the insured. The benefits paid in this case are called *living benefits,* because death does not have to occur for the benefits to be paid. About 56 percent of all insurance benefits are paid in the form of living benefits.

From what has been said so far, you might think that life insurance is for married adults only. Why might junior and senior high school students consider purchasing life insurance?

KINDS OF LIFE INSURANCE POLICIES

There are two major kinds of life insurance policies: term insurance and permanent insurance. *Term insurance* provides protection for a limited period of time. *Permanent insurance* provides protection for as long as the policyholder continues to pay the premium. Both of these kinds of life insurance policies have a *face value,* which is the dollar amount printed on the front of the insurance policy. This is the amount that the insurance company will pay when the policyholder dies.

Term Insurance

Term insurance provides protection for a limited period of time, usually 1, 5, or 10 years. If the policyholder dies during the term of the policy, the face value of the policy is paid to the beneficiary. The *beneficiary* is the person the policyholder names to receive the payment of benefits. When the term is up, the insurance protection ends. Some term insurance policies include a renewable clause. The *renewable clause* allows the policyholder to renew a policy at the end of a term. The cost of term insurance is based on the age of the policyholder when the insurance is purchased. As the policyholder gets older, the premium goes up each time the insurance is renewed. Term policies may also contain a conversion privilege.

A *conversion privilege* allows the policyholder to exchange the term policy for permanent insurance without a physical examination. Usually, this must be done before the policyholder reaches a certain age.

There are several reasons why people buy term insurance. First, it costs less than permanent insurance. Another reason is that the purchaser may need protection for only a short period of time. Term insurance is often used to guarantee the repayment of a loan in case the policyholder dies before the loan is repaid.

Permanent Insurance

Permanent insurance differs from term insurance in several ways. First, permanent insurance gives lifetime protection. As long as the premiums are paid, the policyholder is protected. Second, the premiums for permanent insurance do not change as they do with term insurance. Third, permanent insurance builds a cash surrender value, while term insurance does not. The *cash surrender value* is the amount of money that will be paid to a policyholder if he or she stops paying premiums and turns in the policy. The cash surrender value is not the same as the face value of the policy. The longer a permanent insurance policy is kept by the policyholder, the more cash surrender value it has.

Because of the cash surrender value feature, premiums for permanent insurance are usually much higher than for term insurance. Permanent life insurance policies also contain a loan provision. The policyholder may borrow money from the insurance company against the policy at a relatively low interest rate. The loan value of the policy depends on how much has been paid in premiums at the time the loan is taken out.

Permanent life insurance policies can be classified as either participating or nonparticipating. A *participating policy* allows the insured person to receive a dividend from the insurance company at the end of the policy year. This dividend is really a refund. The policyholder pays more money in premiums than the insurance company needs to meet its expenses. Then at the end of the year, the extra money is paid back to the policyholder as a dividend. Dividends may be paid in cash, applied to reduce the

Shop around for the insurance plan that best fits your needs. (Maria Karras)

premiums, left with the insurance company to earn interest for the insured, or used to purchase additional insurance. A *nonparticipating policy* does not allow the insured to receive a dividend. Therefore, premium costs for participating policies are usually higher than for nonparticipating policies. When dividends are figured into the insurance costs, however, the total costs of participating and nonparticipating policies are usually similar.

Forms of Permanent Insurance Permanent insurance is bought in one of three forms: straight life, limited-payment life, and endowment.

In a *straight life policy,* premiums are paid for the entire lifetime of the insured. It is also known as *ordinary life insurance* or *whole life insurance*. Straight life is one of the most widely used types of life insurance. The premium for straight life is less than that of the other permanent life insurance plans. This is so because it is paid as long as the policyholder is living. As with all permanent life insurance plans, straight life builds a cash surrender value and has a loan provision.

Why would the premium for a straight life insurance policy be less for a 17-year-old person than for a 35-year-old person?

With a *limited-payment life policy,* the insured is covered for life although the premiums are payable only for a limited number of years. There are a number of different limited-payment plans, such as 10-, 20-, or 30-year payment plans. With a 20-year payment life policy, premium payments are made only for a period of 20 years. After that time, the policy is paid up and the coverage continues.

Because payments are completed in a shorter period of time, the premiums for limited-payment life insurance are larger than for straight life insurance. However, this plan is popular because it allows people to complete premium payments during the years when their income is at its highest level. With higher premiums, the cash surrender value and loan value of limited-payment policies increase faster than with straight life insurance policies.

An *endowment policy* is really a savings plan that also provides life insurance protection. It is available in various amounts of face value. At the end of a certain period, the face value of the endowment policy is paid to the insured person and the insurance protection stops. When this happens, the policy is said to *mature.* An endowment policy can mature in different periods of time, such as 10 or 15 or 20 years, or at a certain age, such as 60 or 65. If the insured person dies before the policy matures, the face value of the policy is paid to the beneficiary at the time of the insured's death.

People who buy an endowment policy are usually saving for a long-range goal. Some people use an endowment policy to provide retirement income, and others use it to cover future educational expenses of their children.

Endowment policies are often bought to meet future educational costs. (UCLA)

The cost for this kind of policy is greater than for other permanent life insurance. However, the cash surrender value builds much faster. At maturity, the cash surrender value and the face value are equal.

Why are endowment insurance policies like savings plans?

SPECIAL OPTIONS WITH LIFE INSURANCE

An *accidental death benefit clause* provides that the insurance company pay double the face amount of the policy if the insured person should die by accidental means. This clause is often called *double indemnity*. The insurance company defines what is accidental. Therefore, when purchasing insurance, the policyholder should check the insurer's definition of "accidental." Most life policies offer this option with an increase in premium.

Under a *waiver of premium clause*, the insurance company will pay all premiums if the insured person becomes permanently disabled. The insured person must be disabled for a period of six months before the disability is considered permanent. The person must also become disabled before a certain age, usually 60, and before the maturity date of the policy. This benefit option may be included in most policies at a small increase in the premium.

Check with your parents to see if they have an accidental death benefit clause or waiver of premium clause in any of their life insurance policies. Why do they have these clauses, if they do? Why don't they have the clauses, if they do not?

INDIVIDUAL AND GROUP POLICIES

There are two main ways to buy life insurance. The most common way is to buy an individual policy through an insurance agent. Premiums may be paid monthly, quarterly, semi-annually, or annually. People applying for insurance are usually required to show proof of insurability by taking a physical examination. *Proof of insurability* is evidence that a person's health and occupation are such that he or she would not be a high risk to the insurance company. A person with poor health or with a hazardous occupation would probably not be insurable.

What are some health conditions and kinds of occupations that might limit a person's insurability?

A policy that covers a group of people is known as a *group life insurance policy*. Very often a group is made up of all the employees working for one employer. This type of insurance is usually issued as term insurance and does not require proof of insurability as an individual policy does. The cost of a group policy is less than the cost of the same protection through an individual policy. Costs are usually shared by the employer and the employees. Some business firms, however, furnish group life insurance at no cost to their employees as part of their fringe benefits. When employees share the costs of group insurance, each employee usually pays the same premium regardless of age. The employee's share of the premium is deducted from his or her wages.

When employees leave a company, their coverage under the group plan stops. Most group plans, however, include a conversion privilege like that of some term insurance policies. This conversion privilege allows those who leave the company to convert their term insurance to a permanent plan. When a person converts to permanent insurance, the premium costs go up according to the kind of insurance the person purchases. When an employee retires, the employer may keep the employee under the group plan as part of the employee's retirement benefits.

Talk with someone who is currently covered by a group policy—your parents, other relatives, neighbors, teachers. Find out the amount of group life insurance this person has, the cost to the person, and the advantages of the program.

SELECTING THE RIGHT KIND OF INSURANCE

At the beginning of this chapter, some of the reasons for buying life insurance were discussed. That discussion and the one above on the various kinds of life insurance may lead you to think that life insurance is only for older people with families. This is not the case, however. Young people and people without families also buy life insurance.

Regardless of your age or family situation, your need for insurance is the major factor that determines the type of policy you select. Are your needs long-term or short-term? Are you interested in forced saving as well as protection for your family? Will your needs be different in 10 or 20 years than they are at the present time?

For example, young married couples often have limited incomes. At the same time, their insurance needs at this age may be very great. They may have a number of small children. And they may have a large mortgage. If such is the case, they will want to get as much insurance as they can at the lowest price. They will most

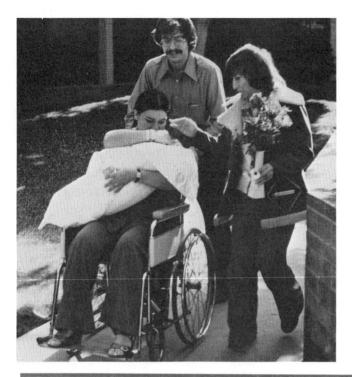

At this stage in their life, this couple's insurance needs may be quite different from what they will be later.
(Steven McBrady)

likely decide to purchase term insurance. In order to provide for more permanent protection at a later date, they will also select a policy that includes the conversion privilege. In this way, their large temporary insurance needs can be met. As incomes increase and insurance needs decrease, they can then convert to permanent coverage.

Suppose the parent of a young child wants to make sure that there will be enough money available to send the child to college. This parent has more money to spend on insurance than did the couple in the previous example. The parent might choose to buy an endowment policy that matures when the child reaches age 18. If the parent dies before the policy matures, the face value will be paid. If the parent lives, the policy will mature and the face value will be paid. In either case, the money needed for the college education is available.

The insurance needs of no two people may be exactly the same. Their incomes, ages, living styles, and family obligations may be very different. For that reason, the right kind of insurance in each situation may be different. You have to review your needs and goals as well as your financial situation and family obligations. Based on that review you select the insurance that is best for you.

Regardless of the type of policy selected, there are two advantages of purchasing life insurance at a young age. The earlier in life a person starts a life insurance program, the lower the premium will be for that insurance. Also, if people start insurance programs when they are young, they may be able to protect their insurability. Many insurance companies allow a person who has bought life insurance at a young age to buy additional insurance as the need arises without additional proof of insurability.

HOW LIFE INSURANCE BENEFITS CAN BE PAID

Most people take care in selecting a policy and its options. However, they often fail to consider how benefits can be paid to beneficiaries. There are four ways in which benefits are paid. The choices are these:

1. Take the benefits of the policy in one cash payment. This is known as a *lump-sum settlement*.

2. Leave the benefits with the insurance company to draw interest. Then the benefits will be available when the beneficiary needs them in the future. This is called an *interest option*.

3. Take the benefits of the policy in the form of a monthly income, with the payments covering a specified period of time. The amount of each payment will depend on the face value of the policy, the period of time, and the interest rate. This is called a *time option*.

4. Take the benefits of the policy in the form of income, with the payments for a specified amount. The payments are continued until the funds and interest are used up. This is called an *amount option*.

Describe situations where each of the above settlement options might be best.

Learning Activities

Increasing Your Business Vocabulary

You should become familiar with each of the terms shown below. On a sheet of paper write the numbers 1 through 12. Then write alongside each number the term that best matches each of the numbered definitions.

accidental death benefit clause / beneficiary / benefits / cash surrender value / endowment policy / face value / group life insurance policy / limited-payment life policy / permanent insurance / straight life policy / term insurance / waiver of premium clause

1. A policy that combines a savings plan with life insurance protection.

2. Insurance that provides protection for as long as the policyholder continues to pay the premium.

3. A requirement that the insurance company pay double the face amount of the policy if the insured person should die by accidental means.

4. The dollar amount printed on the front of the insurance policy.

5. The person the policyholder names to receive the benefits.

6. An insurance policy that covers a group of people under one policy.

7. Insurance that provides protection for a limited period of time.

8. The amount of money that will be paid to a policyholder if he or she stops paying premiums and turns in the policy.

9. A requirement that the insurance company pay all premiums if the insured person becomes permanently disabled.

10. A policy that covers the insured for life although the premiums are payable only for a limited number of years.

11. A policy for which premiums are paid for the entire lifetime of the insured.

12. The payments made to the insured or to his or her survivors.

Understanding Business

1. What are the two types of life insurance benefits? Explain the difference between them.

2. What are the two most important reasons for buying life insurance?

3. Why do many people buy term insurance rather than permanent life insurance?

4. List three ways permanent life insurance differs from term life insurance.

5. What is the main difference between a straight life policy and a limited payment life policy?

6. Why do people buy an endowment policy?

7. Who usually pays the premiums on most group life insurance plans?

8. What does it mean whan a group term insurance policy contains a conversion privilege?

9. What is the major factor that determines the type of policy you select?

10. List the different ways in which the benefits from life insurance can be paid to beneficiaries.

Business Problems
and Projects

1. Some kinds of life insurance are better for certain situations than for others. Which kind of insurance would be the best for each situation given below?

    a. A person needs the least expensive protection for a limited period of time.

    b. A person wishes to have limited protection while saving for a specific purpose.

    c. A person wishes to finish making insurance payments after a certain period of time.

    d. A person wishes to accumulate cash value while making payments for life insurance.

2. The cash values of different insurance policies grow at different rates. The graph below compares the increase in cash value of three kinds of life insurance policies. Study the graph and then answer the questions that follow.

COMPARISON OF BASIC POLICIES

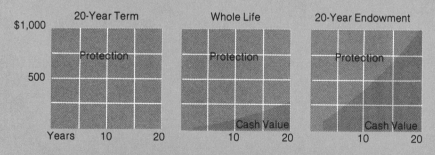

    a. What is the cash value of a 2-year term policy of $1,000 at the end of 10 years?

    b.   Approximately how much cash value does a $1,000 whole life policy have at the end of 10 years? At the end of 20 years?

    c.   What is the cash value of a 20-year endowment policy of $1,000 at the end of 15 years? At the end of 20 years?

    d.   After 20 years how much more cash value will a 20-year endowment policy have than a whole life policy?

    e.   Which of these policies would probably have the highest premiums? Which would probably have the lowest premiums? Explain your answer.

3.   Eric Kelso took out a $15,000 life insurance policy for which he has to pay an annual premium of $46.50 for each $1,000 of insurance. Eric has the choice of paying on a semiannual, quarterly, or monthly basis using the rates shown in the following table.

Payment Basis	Percentage of Annual Rate
Semiannually	51.0%
Quarterly	26.0%
Monthly	8.7%

    a.   How much does Eric pay on an annual basis?

    b.   If payments were made on a quarterly basis, how much would Eric have to pay each year?

    c.   If payments were made on a semiannually basis, how much would Eric have to pay each year?

    d.   If payments were made on a monthly basis, how much would Eric have to pay each year?

Chapter 35

Health Insurance

Objectives

After completing your study of this chapter, you will be able to do the following:

1. Give several reasons why people buy health insurance.

2. Identify the types of health insurance coverage.

3. Identify three private sources of health insurance.

4. List the benefits and purpose of government plans such as workmen's compensation and medicare.

5. Explain how the costs of health insurance are determined.

Medical technology has advanced greatly in the past 20 years. The need for more equipment, more training, more personnel, and more care have made health costs rise at a very fast rate. Because of these increased costs, the total operating expenses of some hospitals are more than 10 times greater today than 20 years ago. People are also demanding more in the way of medical treatment. And they are spending more money on health care than they once did.

With the rising costs of medical treatment, the American public has realized the increasing need for health insurance. Today, 9 out of every 10 people are protected by at least one form of health insurance. Billions of dollars are paid in health insurance premiums each year.

Although 9 out of every 10 Americans are covered by some form of health insurance, people still have to pay billions of dollars for health care in addition to what insurance companies pay. Why do you think this is so?

HEALTH CARE EXPENSES COVERED BY INSURANCE

Health insurance is not a single policy covering all areas of health care. Rather, there are six basic types of health coverage. They are (1) hospital expense coverage; (2) surgical expense coverage; (3) medical expense coverage; (4) major medical expense coverage; (5) comprehensive medical expense coverage; and (6) dental expense coverage.

Hospital Expense Coverage

All or part of the cost of hospital care resulting from illness or injury is paid by a type of insurance called *hospital expense coverage*. Over 180 million people had this type of insurance in the mid-1970s. The cost of room and meals in the hospital, as well as other in-hospital expenses, come under hospital expense coverage. There are usually limits on the payments made under this coverage. These limits are for the number of days spent in the hospital and the costs of room and meals. Other hospital expenses for

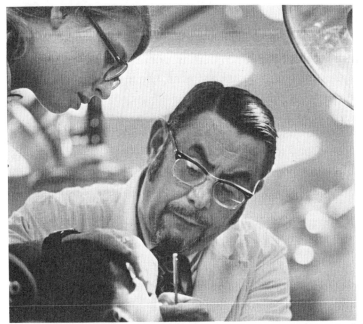

Health care insurance has become almost a necessity for all individuals.

which payments are made include X-ray costs, operating room costs, laboratory tests, and medicines. Because the average daily cost of providing care in the community hospitals is over $110, the need for hospital expense coverage is obvious.

One of the reasons that hospital expense coverage is such a common type of health insurance is the high cost of hospital care. What are some other reasons that hospital expense coverage is so common?

Surgical Expense Coverage

All or part of the cost of surgical fees is paid by a type of insurance known as *surgical expense coverage*. Most insurance policies contain a surgical schedule like the one in Table 35–1. This schedule lists the maximum amount the insurance company will pay for the more common kinds of operations. Some insurance policies, however, state that the "usual and customary" charges of the surgeon will be paid. These policies are much more expensive than policies with surgical schedules. When a policy has a surgical schedule, the insurance company will pay the maximum amount shown in the schedule for a particular operation. If the surgeon charges more than the maximum amount, the insured person must pay the difference.

How do you suppose insurance companies determine the amounts they will pay for the operations they list in their surgical expense schedules?

TABLE 35-1   SURGICAL SCHEDULE

Kind of Operation	Fee
Tonsillectomy and Adenoidectomy	$ 60.00
Maternity/Delivery	100.00
Hemorrhoidectomy, Internal and External	150.00
Appendectomy	180.00
Operation for Hernia, Single	180.00
Suture, Septal Defect of Heart	600.00

Medical Expense Coverage

All or part of a doctor's fees for care other than surgery are covered by *medical expense coverage*. Such fees include visits to the doctor's office and care given at home or in the hospital. Some medical expense policies also cover special X rays and laboratory tests. All policies set limits on their coverage for medical expenses. They usually limit the amount paid for each doctor's visit. There is also a maximum number of visits per illness or injury. In general, medical expense insurance is not offered as a separate policy. It is sold along with a hospital-surgical expense policy.

Why do you think insurance companies set limits on the amount they will pay per physician's visit and the maximum number of visits?

Major Medical Expense Coverage

The kinds of coverage discussed so far are designed to meet the expenses of most illnesses and injuries. But they are not meant to cover the cost of an expensive, long-term illness or disabling injury. For this reason, there is a coverage that takes over where most other medical plans end. *Major medical expense coverage* protects against unusually large expenses resulting from prolonged illness or severe injury. It covers all kinds of health care expenses, including hospital room and meals, doctors' bills, medicines, nursing care, laboratory charges, wheelchairs and crutches, and ambulance service. Major medical expense coverage will help pay for expenses in and out of the hospital. Many major medical plans also provide for expenses of treating mentally ill patients. Some major medical policies still limit the amount to be paid for hospital room charges and surgeons' fees.

Why do you suppose major medical plans cover almost everything, yet they limit hospital room charges and surgeons' fees?

There are several factors that make major medical expense coverage different from other types of health insurance coverage. First, all major medical plans have a deductible. The deductible is similar to the deductible in auto insurance. That is, the insured pays a set amount first and the insurance company pays the rest of the bill. The deductible may range anywhere from $50 to $500. Because major medical coverage has a deductible, the number of small claims is kept low. Fewer claims means that the premiums are kept as low as possible.

Another feature of major medical expense coverage is the coinsurance clause. The *coinsurance clause* requires the policyholder to pay a share of the expenses beyond the deductible amount. With most policies, the insurance company pays 75 or 80 percent of the expenses beyond the deductible amount and the policyholder pays the rest. This provision keeps most major medical claims at a reasonable level.

Finally, there are maximum limits on major medical coverage, but they are usually high. Maximum benefits may range from $10,000 to $60,000, with some as high as $250,000. These maximums may apply to one illness or injury, or they may apply to all expenses during a single year.

Comprehensive Medical Expense Coverage

In the past major medical coverage was separate from hospital, surgical, and medical coverage. Under many group insurance plans, they are now combined into one policy giving the same coverage as separate policies. The combined coverage is known as *comprehensive medical expense coverage*. This coverage still has a deductible like major medical, and it also has a coinsurance clause. However, the deductible is usually low, usually from $50 to $100. Because comprehensive coverage is normally offered under group plans, the premium the individual pays is reasonable.

Dental Expense Coverage

As the name implies, *dental expense coverage,* provides coverage for the expenses of dental care. More insurance companies are offering dental care coverage each year. However, this kind of insurance is still being offered mainly to groups. Dental care coverage will become popular in the future as it becomes more available and as dental treatment costs continue to rise.

Most families have a combination of many or all of the basic types of health coverage. What types of health coverage does your family have?

PRIVATE SOURCES OF HEALTH INSURANCE

Health insurance is available from different private sources. These sources include insurance companies; service plans such as Blue Cross and Blue Shield; and independent group plans sponsored by social, industrial, union, consumer, community, and other groups. Because there are so many sources from which to choose, it is difficult to decide which source has the insurance that best meets your needs. A look at each source may help you to make a choice.

Insurance Companies

Health insurance plans for both individuals and groups are available from insurance companies. You can obtain an individual health insurance policy from an insurance agent. In many instances, the policy may cover only one area of health care needs. However, it can be adapted to meet your particular requirements. A physical examination may not be required, but there is often a waiting period for people with certain health conditions or in certain age groups.

Like other kinds of insurance, health insurance is usually less expensive when it is purchased through a group. Insurance companies issue group policies to employees, trade associations, labor unions, and other organizations. If you belong to one of these, you may be eligible for protection under its group policy.

Benefits from health insurance policies issued by insurance companies can be paid to either the insured, the hospital, or the physician.

Hospital Service Plans

Individuals and groups can also obtain health insurance through prepaid plans organized and administered by hospital and medical societies. Of these plans, those operated by Blue Cross and Blue Shield are the largest and best known. Blue Cross plans provide hospital expense insurance, and Blue Shield plans cover medical and surgical expenses.

Although these plans are run by nonprofit organizations, there is no single national Blue Cross plan or Blue Shield plan. Instead, there are many different Blue Cross and Blue Shield plans throughout the country, and each offers many different benefits. Generally, payments for benefits under these plans are made directly to the hospital or doctors, and not to the individual insured members.

Independent Group Plans

A third major source of private health insurance are the plans offered by organizations such as labor unions, religious groups, trade associations, and private-citizen groups. Generally, members of these organizations pay an annual fee that entitles them to participate in the plan and benefit from all of its services. Some of these plans require members to use their own medical staff,

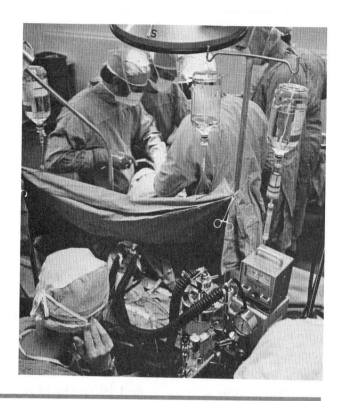

Prepaid hospital plans such as Blue Shield
help many meet surgical expenses.
(Hollywood-Presbyterian Hospital)

treatment centers, and hospitals. Others permit members to use
any doctor or medical facility.

From what source does your family buy its health insurance? Is
the source different from the sources described above?

GOVERNMENT SOURCES OF HEALTH INSURANCE

The private sources of health insurance are voluntary. People can
decide whether they want coverage and what kind of coverage they
will buy. There is another type of health insurance that is provided
for by state law. All states have laws providing workmen's compensation. Under these laws most employers must provide insurance
for their employees. *Workmen's compensation* is a type of insurance that covers workers for injury and loss of income caused by

accidents occurring on the job. Benefits vary from state to state. In some states the employer or the employer's insurer is liable for all reasonable medical and hospital expenses, including medicine and treatment. In other states the benefits are limited to specific amounts. Some states also require rehabilitation training for those who cannot return to the same kind of work.

In all states, income is provided in case an employee is unable to return to work. Usually the amount of income is a percentage of the employee's wages. A common amount is two-thirds of the employee's wages, but most states specify maximum and minimum limits. Also, most states specify maximum periods of payments for nonpermanent injury or illness. They also make sure that people who are permanently disabled receive disability payments for life. In case of death resulting from employment, most states provide that benefits be paid to the survivors.

Workmen's compensation laws are state laws, passed by the various states. Therefore, although these laws may be very similar in some ways, they may also have major differences. Furthermore, not everyone is covered under workmen's compensation. Your state labor department can tell you about the workmen's compensation laws in your state.

If workmen's compensation is such a good form of health protection, why do families still have other forms?

Medicare

Another government source of health insurance coverage is a program called Medicare. *Medicare* is a health insurance plan for people 65 and over operated under the social security system. It was set up under the Social Security Act to provide coverage for older people on fixed incomes who cannot afford enough health insurance coverage. Medicare is partially paid for out of money the government receives in taxes. There are two parts to the Medicare program. The first part is a basic coverage program under which nearly all persons 65 years or older are provided with hospital insurance. The other part provides medical insurance.

One advantage of hospital insurance under Medicare is that it is available to nearly everyone at age 65. Another is that those insured under Medicare hospital insurance are entitled to as many benefits as they would receive if they were insured under the best policies of private companies. Medicare pays for the major part of the costs of hospital care. It may also cover care in a nursing home and in the patient's home for a certain amount of time. However, it does not pay for all services while the insured person is in a hospital or nursing-care facility. It pays for the cost of semiprivate (2 to 4 beds) rooms, meals, and regular nursing care. It also pays for medicines and regular equipment needed when the insured person is in the hospital. Hospital insurance does not pay for doctors' bills, private nurses, or conveniences such as telephones or televisions.

Medical insurance under Medicare pays doctor bills, regardless of whether the treatment is in the hospital, the office, or the home. It also pays for other medical services such as physical therapy, X rays, dressings, splints, and casts. Under special conditions, it also provides for a number of home health visits each year.

Since medical insurance is voluntary, anyone at age 65 who wants it must register for it. Those who sign up for medical insurance under Medicare must pay premiums just as with most other kinds of insurance. The premiums are small because the federal government shares equally in the cost of medical insurance. Premiums have been climbing steadily, however, to meet rising health care costs.

Do you think Medicare should be extended to people of all ages? Why or why not?

COST OF HEALTH INSURANCE

Four factors determine the cost of health insurance. They are the extent of coverage, the number of claims, the age of the policyholder, and the number of dependents. If your health insurance coverage has all of the major benefits, the cost will be high. The limits of the policy also directly affect its cost. For instance, hospital coverage that pays $20 per day for a hospital room will be less expensive than coverage that pays $50 per day.

As with auto insurance, the cost of health insurance is affected by the amount of money paid out in claims by the insurance company. The more claims that are paid, the higher the cost will be to the policyholder. Also, as people get older, they need more health care. Therefore, the older the policyholder is, the higher the premiums are.

The final major factor in determining health insurance costs is the number of dependents included under a policy. A single policyholder pays much less than a married policyholder. With individual policies, the premium is raised a fixed amount for each child. With group policies there are usually three rates: single persons, married couples, and married couples with children. All members of the last group pay the same rate, regardless of how many children they have. The couple with one child pays the same rate as the couple with five children.

Do you think it is fair that under a group plan the cost is the same for all couples with children regardless of the number? Why?

Learning Activities

Increasing Your Business Vocabulary

You should become familiar with each of the terms shown below. On a sheet of paper write the numbers 1 through 8. Then write alongside each number the term that best matches each of the numbered definitions.

coinsurance clause / comprehensive medical expense coverage / hospital expense coverage / major medical expense coverage / medical expense coverage / Medicare / surgical expense coverage / workmen's compensation

1. Coverage that protects against unusually large expenses resulting from prolonged illness or severe injury.

2. Coverage that pays all or part of the cost of surgical fees.

3. A combination of hospital, surgical, medical, and major medical expense insurance.

4. Coverage that pays part or all of a doctor's fees for care other than surgery.

5. Coverage for injury and loss of income caused by accidents occurring on the job.

6. A health insurance plan for people 65 and over operated under the social security system.

7. Coverage that pays all or part of the cost of hospital care resulting from illness or injury.

8. A provision that requires the policyholder to pay a share of the expenses beyond the deductible amount.

Understanding Business

1. Why have health care costs increased so much during the past 20 years? How has this affected health insurance costs?

2. In addition to room and board, what costs may be covered under hospital expense coverage?

3. Who pays the additional cost when surgeons' fees are higher than the maximum amount stated in the surgical schedule of payments?

4. Medical expense coverage pays for doctors' fees other than surgery. Name some expenses for which this would pay.

5. What are the common types of expenses covered by major medical expense coverage?

6. List the three major factors that make major medical expense coverage different from other types of health coverage.

7. What is comprehensive medical expense coverage?

8. What kinds of benefits are available under workmen's compensation insurance?

9. Why was the Medicare program set up?

10. What are the four major factors that determine the cost of health insurance?

Business Problems and Projects

1. The table below shows how much was spent for medical care in recent selected years. Study the table and then answer the questions that follow it.

PERSONAL EXPENDITURES FOR MEDICAL CARE
(billions of dollars)

Year	Total medical care	Hospital services	Physicians' services	Medicines and appliances	Dentists	All other medical care
1962	21.4	6.1	6.0	4.9	2.3	1.1
1963	22.8	6.8	6.4	5.1	2.3	1.2
1964	25.2	7.7	7.1	5.4	2.6	1.2
1965	27.4	8.3	7.7	5.9	2.8	1.4
1966	30.4	9.3	8.4	6.7	3.0	1.6
1967	33.6	10.7	9.3	7.0	3.3	1.7
1968	36.8	12.3	10.0	7.6	3.5	1.9
1969	41.6	14.6	11.5	8.2	3.9	1.9
1970	46.3	16.9	12.9	8.7	4.3	2.1
1971	50.7	19.0	14.3	8.9	4.3	2.2
1972	55.8	21.3	15.4	9.7	4.6	2.3

Source: U.S. Department of Commerce and the Health Insurance Institute.

a. What was the percent of increase in total medical care from 1962 to 1972?

b. What was the percent of increase of hospital services from 1962 to 1972?

c. How much greater was the percent of increase for physicians' services than for dentists' services from 1962 to 1972?

d. In what one-year period did the total cost of medical care show the greatest dollar increase?

2. Vito Benedetto broke his leg in a motorcycle accident and had to be hospitalized for eight days. His medical expenses for this period were as follows:

Hospital room	$93 per day
Laboratory tests	$52
X rays	$115
Miscellaneous hospital costs	$37
Surgeon's fees	$517

Vito's hospitalization plan allowed $76 per day for room fees. It also covered 80 percent of all other hospital costs—excluding surgeon's fees—after a $50 deduction. His surgical plan allowed no more than $490 for the surgical procedure performed by his doctor.

a. What was the total medical expense?

b. How much was covered by hospitalization insurance?

c. How much was covered by surgical insurance?

d. How much of the total medical expense did Vito have to pay?

3. The Ansonia Machine Company offers its employees two different hospitalization plans. Plan A is free and provides the payment of 80 percent of all hospitalization expenses with $75 deductible. Plan B costs each employee $3.50 per month and offers 100 percent of all hospitalization expenses with $50 deductible.

The company estimates that the average yearly hospitalization bill for each employee is $475.

a. What would be the total yearly hospitalization expense for each employee who chooses Plan A?

b. What would be the total yearly hospitalization expense for each employee who chooses Plan B?

Chapter 36

Income Security Insurance

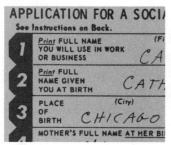

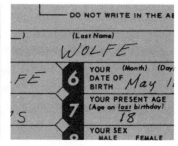

Objectives

After completing your study of this chapter, you will be able to do the following:

1. Identify and describe the different kinds of benefits provided by social security.

2. Explain how an individual or family qualifies for social security benefits.

3. List several reasons why the unemployment insurance program was established.

4. Describe how people can provide disability and retirement income for themselves and their families.

Most people are constantly concerned about the possibility of losing all or part of their income. Perhaps people are so worried because of the many ways in which income can be lost. Wage earners may become sick or have an accident. They may die or become disabled. They may become unemployed. Or they may retire with little or no income to meet their everyday expenses.

As protection against the risk of loss of income, individuals and families need some form of income security insurance. This chapter describes several types of protection available to most people. Among these are social security benefits, unemployment insurance, and retirement and pension plans.

THE SOCIAL SECURITY SYSTEM

In the past, many workers were not able to provide themselves with enough income protection. Therefore, in 1935 Congress passed the Social Security Act, thus creating the social security system. The original purpose of the system was to make sure that retired, unemployed, and needy people received a regular income. In 1956 the act was amended to include benefits for disabled workers, and in 1965 Medicare was added to the social security program.

Who Is Eligible?

Anyone who works in a job covered by the Social Security Act is eligible to receive social security benefits. At present, more than 90 percent of all workers in the United States are protected by the provisions of the law. This includes not only workers in business and industry, but also most farmworkers, most self-employed workers, many local and state employees, and members of the armed forces.

Whether you are an employee or self-employed, you must obtain a social security number if your job is covered by social security. A *social security number* is the account number used throughout a worker's life for recording payments into the system, for collecting benefits, and for tax records. You can apply for a social security number by filling out a form obtained from your employer, your post office, or your local social security office. A card bearing the number will be issued to you. Because this card is the chief means of identification within the system, keep it in a safe

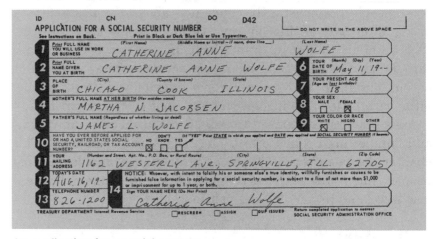

An application for a social security card.

A social security card.

place. If you happen to lose your social security card, apply for a replacement. However, make sure that the number on the replacement card is the same as the number on your original card.

Do you have a social security number and card? Have you ever used the number for identification? When?

Who Pays for It?

The social security program is financed by taxes on workers. Employed workers share the tax equally with their employers. A percentage of the workers' wages is deducted from their paychecks, and this amount is matched by their employers. The employers then forward the total taxes to the social security fund. Self-employed workers must pay all of the tax themselves. But their payments are somewhat less than the combined payments of employers and employees. The self-employed make their payments each year when they file their federal income tax returns.

There is a maximum amount of earnings on which social security taxes are paid. But this amount, as well as the percentage of earnings paid as tax, has risen sharply in recent years. This rise has become necessary because of the great increase in demands on the social security system. The reasons for this increase is twofold. Congress has raised the amount of benefits paid to individuals. And more people are receiving benefits than ever before.

What Benefits Are Available?

Almost one out of every seven persons in the United States receives some kind of social security benefit. The benefits include income for retired people, aid to disabled workers, and assistance for survivors.

TABLE 36-1   EXAMPLES OF MONTHLY SOCIAL SECURITY PAYMENTS (effective June 1975)

AVERAGE YEARLY EARNINGS AFTER 1950

Benefits can be paid to:	$923 or less	$3,000	$4,000	$5,000	$6,000	$8,000	$10,000
You, the worker							
Retired at 65	101.40	209.70	246.80	286.10	323.40	402.00	445.40
Under 65 and disabled	101.40	209.70	246.80	286.10	323.40	402.00	445.40
Retired at 62	81.20	167.80	197.50	228.90	258.80	321.60	356.40
Your wife							
at 65	50.70	104.90	123.40	143.10	161.70	201.00	222.70
at 62, with no child	38.10	78.70	92.60	107.40	121.30	150.80	167.10
Under 65 and one child in her care	50.80	111.00	175.00	242.00	270.00	301.60	334.20
Your widow							
At 65 (if worker never received reduced retirement benefits)	101,40	209.70	246.80	286.10	323.40	402.00	445.40
at 60 (if sole survivor)	74.90	150.00	176.50	204.60	231.30	287.50	318.50
at 50 and disabled (if sole survivor)	56.80	105.00	123.50	143.10	161.80	201.10	222.80
Widowed mother (or father) caring for one child	152.20	314.60	370.20	429.20	485.20	603.00	668.20
Maximum family payment	152.20	320.60	421.80	528.10	593.30	703.60	779.60

Retirement Benefits   The major benefit of social security is retirement income. In order to receive retirement income, you must work a certain length of time in a job covered by social security. The amount of your benefits depends on the money you have earned during your working life. Table 36-1 shows how benefits change according to your average yearly earnings. For example, a person who retires at age 65 and who has had average earnings of $500 per month since 1950 would receive $323.40 a month in retirement benefits. A similar worker who has average monthly earnings of $750 would receive $402 a month.

In the social security program, full benefits are paid when a person retires at age 65. Those who wish to retire earlier may do so, but the earliest you can retire is age 62. However, the monthly benefits are reduced for those who retire early.

How do you think you could provide for your retirement if there were no social security?

Disability Benefits   Workers who become disabled before the age of 65 may receive disability benefits. A person is considered disabled if he or she has a serious mental or physical problem that is expected to last or has lasted at least 12 months and keeps the person from working. In some cases, a person with a very serious medical condition can be eligible for disability payments even if he or she works a little. In order to qualify for disability benefits, a person must have worked a certain length of time in a job covered by social security.

The amount of disability benefits a worker receives is usually the same as the amount the person would receive in retirement benefits at age 65. These amounts are based on the worker's average earnings. Disability payments begin about six months after disability is determined. Social security also pays some of the costs of retraining disabled people. The actual retraining is carried on by state agencies.

Why do you suppose the government is willing to pay for retraining those who have been disabled?

You can determine what your benefits are by visiting your social security office. (Social Security Administration)

Survivors' Benefits   Social security provides not only retirement and disability benefits for the worker but also benefits to the worker's dependents in case the worker dies. Those dependents are called *survivors*. Survivors who may be eligible for benefits include widows, dependent children, and some widowers.

The amount of survivors' benefits for dependents is based on the amount of retirement benefits earned by the worker. The bottom half of Table 36-1 lists benefits for widows.

Survivors are also entitled to a small lump-sum payment on the death of the insured. This payment is often used to help pay funeral expenses.

Do you know anyone who receives social security benefits? What kind of benefits do they receive?

UNEMPLOYMENT INSURANCE
Over 50 million people in the nation are covered by unemployment insurance. *Unemployment insurance* provides money to people

who lose their jobs through no fault of their own and who are able and willing to work. This program started with the passage of the Social Security Act. It is carried jointly by the state and federal governments. Each state has developed its own unemployment insurance laws, but the programs must meet certain minimum requirements set up by the federal Social Security Act. In almost every state, the cost of operating the unemployment insurance program is financed by the tax paid by employers.

Restrictions and Eligibility

Most states require that a person must have worked about a year to be eligible to collect unemployment insurance. Most states also require that a certain minimum amount be earned during this period. Workers are not eligible if they quit a job without good

For those eligible to receive it, unemployment insurance provides welcome income security.
(Becky Roller)

reason or are let go because of misconduct. Those who refuse work and those unemployed because of labor disputes normally are ineligible for unemployment insurance.

Under all state laws, the amount a person can receive in unemployment insurance benefits is based on his or her past earnings. The maximums vary but most states have minimum payments of $10 to $20 a week. All states have also set a time limit on benefits, usually 26 weeks. However, in periods of high unemployment, benefits may be extended an additional 13 weeks. Most states require a one-week waiting period after a person becomes unemployed before he or she becomes eligible.

Why do you think states place a maximum amount on the benefits an unemployed worker can receive?

PRIVATE SOURCES OF INCOME INSURANCE

In addition to government income insurance, there are private sources of income insurance. For example, people can protect themselves from loss of income by buying insurance through an insurance company. This kind of policy is called disability income insurance. *Disability income insurance* is coverage designed to provide wage earners with a regular income if their wages are stopped as a result of illness or accident. There are many different kinds of disability income insurance policies available for people to choose from. The maximum benefits paid by most insurance companies are from 40 to 60 percent of the person's wages or salary. However, a few companies pay as much as 75 percent of a person's wages or salary. Before benefits begin, there is usually a waiting period of from one week to 90 days after the person is disabled. Short-term disability policies may provide benefits for up to two years. Long-term policies provide maximum benefits from 10 years to life, if necessary, depending on the type of illness or injury. As with other forms of insurance, the more benefits a policy provides, the higher the premiums will be.

INCOME FOR RETIREMENT

As a student, you may feel that retirement is for old people, so why bother learning about it now? Although retirement is for older people, planning for retirement should begin at an early age. Ask your parents or grandparents, and they will tell you how important it is to prepare early in life for retirement. Therefore it is useful to gain an understanding of such forms of retirement income as annuities, pension plans, and individual retirement accounts.

Annuities

An *annuity* is a guaranteed retirement income purchased from an insurance company. Many people make regular payments into annuity plans during their working years, just as they pay premiums on their insurance. Then, when they reach a certain age, the insurance company pays them a regular guaranteed income that continues for life or for a certain number of years. Individual annuities are usually bought from an insurance company, and payments are made directly to the insurance company. Annuities may also be purchased by a group of people, such as the employees of a business firm. Employers and employees often share the cost of group annuities, although in some cases the employer pays the entire cost.

A special type of annuity is the *tax-sheltered annuity*. People purchase tax-sheltered annuities because of the tax advantage. Money paid into an annuity is not taxed as income until the insured begins to receive annuity payments. Normally, payments start after the person has retired—when the person's earnings are far less than during working years. The person's taxable income is usually lower then, and therefore the income tax rate is lower.

What are some reasons, other than retirement, that people might want to purchase annuities?

Pension Plans

Many business firms have retirement plans, called *pensions,* for their employees. A *pension* is a sum of money paid regularly as a retirement benefit. Both employer and employee contribute to the pension fund. The funds are invested in government securities, stocks, bonds, real estate, and other forms of investment. Benefits are paid regularly to retired employees.

Why do you think employers are willing to have retirement plans for their employees?

Individual Retirement Accounts

A new federal law allows qualified people to create their own retirement plans. These plans are often called *individual retirement accounts*. An *individual retirement account (IRA)* is a personal tax-deferred retirement savings program. To qualify for an IRA, you can work for yourself or for someone else. But you cannot be already covered by an employer-sponsored retirement plan or by a qualified retirement plan for self-employed individuals. As with tax-sheltered annuities, people participate in IRAs because of the tax advantage. The money paid into the plan is not taxed until it is withdrawn. Since this does not usually occur until retirement, the person's earnings are usually lower than while he or she was working. Because the taxable income is lower, the tax rate is lower.

Why do you think the federal government would encourage people to create their own retirement programs?

Learning Activities

Increasing Your Business Vocabulary

You should become familiar with each of the terms shown below. On a sheet of paper write the numbers 1 through 5. Then write alongside each number the term that best matches each of the numbered definitions.

annuity / disability income insurance / individual retirement account (IRA) / pension / unemployment insurance

1. Insurance purchased from an insurance company designed to provide wage earners with a regular income if their wages are stopped because of illness or accident.

2. A sum of money paid regularly as a retirement benefit.

3. A personal tax-deferred retirement savings program.

4. Insurance that provides money to people who lose their jobs involuntarily and who are able and willing to work.

5. A guaranteed retirement income plan purchased from an insurance company.

Understanding Business

1. Name the income insurance benefits available from the social security system.

2. If you are an employee, who pays your social security taxes? Who pays your social security taxes if you are self-employed?

3. Why is your social security number and card important?

4. Give two reasons why the costs of the social security program have increased steadily over the years.

5. How is the amount of social security retirement benefits determined?

6. How do people qualify for disability benefits? When does payment of disability benefits usually begin?

7. What determines the amount of survivor's benefits that dependents will receive?

8. How does a person become eligible to collect unemployment insurance?

9. How is a pension plan paid for? What is done with pension plans?

10. Who is eligible for individual retirement accounts?

Business Problems and Projects

1. A number of different kinds of benefits under social security are discussed in this chapter: retirement, disability, death, hospitalization and medical. Read each of the following situations and determine which benefit(s) might apply.

   a. A person retires at age 65.

   b. A person becomes permanently disabled at age 40.

   c. A widow who is 63 years old.

   d. A 65-year-old retired person is hospitalized for two weeks.

2. List seven kinds of income security insurance that individuals and families can use to safeguard against the loss of income from illness, retirement, or death. Indicate whether the kind of protection listed is available through social security or through private sources.

Chapter 37

Insurance for the Home

Objectives

After completing your study of this chapter, you will be able to do the following:

1. List the reasons why homeowners and renters need insurance coverage.

2. Identify the three forms of homeowner's policies and indicate the differences among them.

3. Identify the types of coverage available under homeowner's and tenant's insurance policies.

Suppose a friend of yours returns home from school today and finds that the family house and all its contents have been destroyed by fire. Or suppose that someone broke into another friend's apartment and stole furniture and personal belongings. Would the families of these friends have enough savings to replace what was destroyed or stolen? Most would not. To most families losses such as these would be a serious setback—a setback from which they might never recover. In order to protect against such a setback, people buy insurance.

Insurance can be bought to provide coverage for every kind of real and personal property. But because most people are primarily concerned with protecting their homes and personal belongings, this chapter chiefly examines home insurance.

HOMEOWNER'S POLICIES

Many different perils could destroy or damage a home. Fire, for example, poses a constant threat. Your home or personal property could also be endangered by such other perils as lightning, smoke,

Without adequate insurance most families would suffer serious financial losses from a fire such as this. (UPI)

explosion, hail, wind, vehicles, riot, burglary, and theft. In addition, there is always the possibility that someone could be hurt on your property. Although you can buy individual policies to cover each peril, most people buy a single policy, called a *homeowner's policy,* to protect themselves against loss from all or several of these perils.

Homeowner's policies can only be bought by people who own and live in one- or two-family homes. The policy protects against loss resulting from damage to or destruction of a house, including such permanent attachments as garages and porches. It does not, however, cover land.

A homeowner's policy also provides coverage for personal property, including all household contents as well as personal belongings owned, used, worn, or carried by any member of the household. The loss of personal property is usually covered whether it occurs at home or at some other place. There may be a limit to the dollar amount of coverage for such valuables as antiques, furs, and jewelry. However, separate policies can be bought for such objects.

Why may a dollar limit be placed on the coverage of such valuables as antiques, furs, and jewelry?

Homeowner's policies also can be used to provide protection against additional living expenses if your home is so badly damaged that it cannot be lived in. If you have to live elsewhere while your home is being repaired, the insurance company will pay for costs that go beyond everyday living expenses at home. Food, laundry service, and transportation are typical examples.

Tenant's Form Policy

If you rent a house or an apartment, you can buy protection similar to a homeowner's policy. A *tenant's form policy* provides coverage designed to protect renters from the loss of personal property. This policy covers household goods and personal property. And it protects against the same kinds of perils as those that are covered by homeowner's policies.

Forms of Homeowner's Policies

There are three forms of homeowner's insurance policies. The difference between the forms is in the number and kinds of perils that each insures against. The more protection you buy, the more your homeowner's policy will cost.

The *standard form,* sometimes called the *basic form,* insures against these eleven perils:

- Fire or lightning
- Windstorm or hail
- Explosion
- Riot or civil disorder
- Aircraft
- Vehicles
- Smoke
- Vandalism
- Theft
- Glass breakage
- Loss of property removed from premises endangered by fire or other perils

The standard form provides basic coverage, and it is usually the least costly homeowner's policy. However, specific coverages within the basic form will differ from one insurance company to another.

"Since so few homes are ever destroyed by many of these perils, it does not make much sense to purchase this kind of protection." What is wrong with this kind of argument?

The *broad form* of the homeowner's policy protects against all the perils in the standard form (see above) and against the following perils:

- Falling objects
- Weight of ice and snow
- Collapse of buildings
- Accidental bursting of steam or hot water heating systems
- Accidental leakage or overflow of water or steam from plumbing, heating, or other devices
- Freezing of plumbing, heating, and other devices

Landslide damage is not covered by most homeowner's policies. (UPI)

- Accidental damage from electrical currents to electrical appliances, devices, fixtures, and so forth

The broad form of homeowner's insurance is the most popular. Because of the added coverage, the broad form is more expensive than the standard form.

Why would aircraft, vehicles, and falling objects be thought of as perils? List some real life examples in which these perils have caused loss of property.

The form of homeowner's policy that protects against the largest number of perils is called the *comprehensive form*. This form is sometimes called an all-risks policy. It includes all the perils covered by the broad form, as well as many others. As might be expected, this is the most expensive of the three forms of homeowner's insurance. In general, the comprehensive form lists those perils that will *not* be covered rather than those perils that will be covered. These exceptions usually include flood, earth-quake, landslide, surface water, waves, tidal waves, the backing up of sewers, war, and nuclear radiation.

If the comprehensive form is so complete, why do you think it is not the most popular of all the homeowner's insurance forms?

Liability Coverage

All homeowner's and tenant's forms policies include liability coverage, which comes in three forms: personal liability, medical payments liability, and supplementary coverages liability.

Personal Liability Coverage   Suppose someone trips over a toy on your sidewalk and is injured. Or suppose you are cutting down a tree on your property and it accidentally falls on your neighbor's car. If you have homeowner's insurance, *personal liability coverage* would protect you against financial loss caused by an accident for which you are held to be legally responsible. In either case, your insurance company will pay for legal defense and for damages that might be charged against you in a lawsuit. This coverage also applies to accidents that happen away from the home. For example, on a golf course you might hit a golf ball that accidentally hits a spectator. If you failed to give proper warning, you might be held liable. However, your personal liability coverage would protect you against loss of money in this kind of accident.

Each form of homeowner's policy has a standard limit of $25,000 personal liability. This limit can be increased if the policyholder wishes to pay a higher premium.

Give some examples of actual cases in which personal liability coverage was needed. Ask your parents, neighbors, or friends if they can give you some examples.

Medical Payments Liability Coverage   Under a homeowner's policy, *medical payments liability coverage* pays medical expenses for people injured on your property under any circumstances. The main benefit of this coverage is that it pays for the cost of injuries, regardless of who is at fault. The basic protection for each person is limited to $500. As with personal liability coverage, you may buy more protection if you wish at an additional cost.

Supplementary Coverage Liability   Another form of coverage, *supplementary coverage liability,* protects against minor damages that you, a member of your family, or your pets might cause to someone else's property. It is similar to medical payments liability coverage, except that it covers damage to property, while medical payments coverage covers injury to people. Damage caused by children 12 years or younger, whether accidental or on purpose, is covered. The basic protection for any one accident is $250.

COST OF INSURANCE FOR THE HOME

The cost of property insurance is determined by the amount of money insurance companies have had to pay out in claims. Insurance companies estimate the probability of loss in certain situations, based on their past experience. For example, if a house is located in an area of frequent tornadoes, the premium will be higher. Or if it is located where there are frequent burglaries, the cost will be higher. Some of the factors that affect costs of insuring a home include the following:

- Value of property insured.
- Number of perils covered.
- Types of materials used in building a home.
- Availability of fire-fighting equipment, efficiency of fire-fighting personnel, and availability of a good water supply.

The more your property is worth and the more perils it is insured against, the greater the cost of insurance will be. Wooden homes have higher insurance costs than those constructed of brick or other fireproof materials. And homeowners in rural areas often pay higher insurance rates because fire-fighting equipment and a good water supply are not close by.

Most losses that occur to homes are small. Therefore, to cut down on the cost of insurance and the cost of processing small claims, most homeowner's policies have a deductible, usually $50. Many policies also contain a *disappearing deductible clause,* which means that as the amount of loss increases, the amount that the policyholder is required to pay decreases. When the loss is large, the policyholder pays no part of the loss.

It is wise to take an inventory of the personal property in your home. An *inventory* is a list of all personal property with the approximate value of each item. A copy of this inventory should be kept in a safe place outside the home in case the home is destroyed. If you have an inventory when a loss occurs, it is easier to put in an accurate claim for payment quickly.

If you were to make up an inventory of the valuables in your home, what would you put on your list?

Learning Activities

Increasing Your Business Vocabulary

You should become familiar with each of the terms shown below. On a sheet of paper write the numbers 1 through 5. Then write alongside each number the term that best matches each of the numbered definitions.

inventory / medical payments liability / personal liability coverage / supplementary coverage liability / tenant's form policy

1. Protection against financial loss caused by an accident for which you are held to be legally responsible.

2. Coverage designed to protect renters from loss of personal property.

3. Coverage under a homeowner's policy to pay medical expenses for people injured on your property under any circumstances.

4. Protection against minor damages that you, a member of your family, or your pets might cause to someone else's property.

5. A list of all personal property with the approximate value of each item.

Understanding Business

1. What is a homeowner's insurance policy?

2. List some perils against which a home should be insured.

3. What expenses are covered in the additional living expense feature of a homeowner's policy?

4. What types of coverage are provided in a tenant's form policy?

5. Explain the difference between standard form and broad form of homeowner's policy.

6. Which type of homeowner's policy provides the most complete protection?

7. What is the major difference between personal liability coverage and medical payments coverage?

8. How does supplementary coverage liability differ from medical payments coverage?

9. List some factors that affect the cost of home insurance.

10. Why is it important for a homeowner to have an inventory of all personal property?

Business Problems and Projects

1. Harold Kohner raises Great Danes. His neighbor, Craig Owens, raises rare tropical flowers. One day, one of Mr. Kohner's dogs broke loose and trampled forty of Mr. Owens' prize-winning orchids. Mr. Kohner's homeowner's policy provides him protection against such an accident, but only up to $250 for any one accident. Mr. Owens, however, claims that $635 damage has been done and receives a court judgment for that amount.

   a. What type of coverage does Mr. Kohner most likely have?

   b. How much will his insurance cover?

   c. How much will Mr. Kohner have to pay out of his own pocket?

2. On a form similar to the one shown below, prepare an inventory of ten items of personal property that you would least like to lose through fire or theft. Indicate the original cost of the item and the approximate cost of its replacement.

	Item	Original Cost	Replacement Cost
Example	CB Radio	$119	$139

3. Suppose you own a $30,000 home that is insured for $24,000, or 80 percent of its value. Your policy has a $50 deductible. You would pay approximately the following amounts for the different forms of homeowner's insurance:

Coverage	Cost Per Year
Standard Form (11 perils)	$55
Broad Form (18 perils)	$85
Comprehensive (all risks)	$150

a. How much does each of the forms of coverage cost the policyholder per month?

b. If one were paying for insurance by the peril covered, how much would the standard form cost per peril? The broad form?

c. Suppose an individual suffers a loss of $180. How much will the insurance company pay? How much must the policyholder pay?

Chapter 38

Saving
and Investing

Objectives

After completing your study of this chapter, you will be able to do the following:

1. Define the term *saving* and list examples of ways to save.

2. Define the term *investing* and list examples of ways to invest.

3. Identify some reasons why people save and invest.

4. Explain why investing is important in our private enterprise economy.

Although the words *saving* and *investing* are often used in the same way, they do not mean the same thing. They are, however, closely related. Saving takes many forms. When a squirrel puts away acorns for the winter season, it is saving. When a farmer stores seed grain for the spring planting, he is saving. When you put money in a cookie jar, you are saving. When you put money aside and don't spend it, you are actually storing purchasing power. *Saving,* then, is storing purchasing power.

If you took the money you stored in the cookie jar and deposited it in a savings account, you would be investing. *Investing* is putting stored purchasing power, or savings, to work. For example, if you stored $100 in that cookie jar, at the end of a year you would still have only $100. But if you put that $100 in a savings account at 5 percent annual interest, at the end of a year you would have $105. The $5 in interest you would receive is called a *return,* which means the amount earned from an investment.

What are some reasons why a person who has saved money might not want to invest it?

WHY DO PEOPLE SAVE?

Saving money is a habit that is worth developing. Since money is purchasing power, saved money represents purchasing power that can be used in the future.

People save money for different reasons. Often there is a certain item they want to buy—a pair of shoes, a new record, or a bike—and they don't have the amount of money needed to make the purchase. By setting aside some money on a regular basis, they gradually accumulate enough to make their purchase. In general, however, people save for financial security, for retirement, or for special purposes.

Financial Security

Having some money stored away takes some of the uncertainties and worries out of daily life. When you have savings you are better prepared to meet emergencies or unexpected events that require money. A sudden illness, an accident, a theft of personal belongings, or the loss of your job are all risks that could weaken your finances. Saving helps people prepare for such events.

Retirement

Many people save money to help them meet living expenses after they stop working. Most retired people have some income through a pension or social security. But their income is often not large enough to permit them to live the way they would like.

Special Purposes

People save money to buy things they want in the future but cannot afford now. Expensive things, like a car, a refrigerator, a television set, or a motorcycle, cannot be bought by most people from their regular income. Even if an item is bought on credit, it is often necessary for the buyer to save money for the down payment. It may take one month, one year, or several years, to save money for a special purchase. For a young couple planning to buy a home, it may take several years to save enough for a down payment.

Do you or your family save money? For what purposes?

Saving provides you with future purchasing power. (Maria Karras)

People save money for a variety of different reasons. (Colorado Department of Public Relations)

WHERE SHOULD YOU KEEP YOUR SAVINGS?

You have probably read stories about people who kept all their savings at home in a metal box. Suddenly it was stolen, and they had nothing. The most important factor in choosing a place to keep your savings is safety. You want your savings to be safe from theft, fire, and other loss. Some people may have safes in their homes. Most people, however, rely on banks and other financial institutions to provide a place to keep their savings and other valuables safe. When a person puts money in a savings account in a bank or other financial institution, that person is investing.

INVESTING

People invest because they want their savings to show growth. *Growth* is the increase in dollar value of an investment over a period of time. Suppose you buy 5 acres of land for $500 an acre and at a later date its value goes up to $700 an acre. The land has increased in value, so your investment has provided growth.

An investment that provides growth, however, always involves risk, because there is always the possibility that the dollar value of the investment may decrease instead of increase. To see how this happens, let's again use the example of owning land. Suppose that when you wanted to sell the 5 acres of land, you could get only $300 an acre. The dollar value of your land has decreased.

Some people will not put their savings into high-risk investments. They do not want to risk the chance that the dollar value of their investment will decrease. Other people, however, prefer this kind of investment. They seek a much greater return on their money in the form of capital gain. When an investment is sold for more than was paid for it, the difference is called *capital gain* Usually, an investment with more growth potential is also a higher risk investment.

List some reasons why high school students might want to invest.

Common Types of Investments

Investing can be done in several ways. The most common ways are savings accounts, savings bonds, stocks and corporate bonds, real estate, and objects of value such as rare coins.

Savings Accounts   By far the most popular form of investing is the savings account. The reasons for its popularity are clear. The money in a savings account is safe. There is little risk that the dollar value of your savings account will decrease. The savings can be converted to cash quickly, therefore, it can be used easily in case of an emergency in which you might need cash. Also, since there are many financial institutions that offer savings accounts, it is usually easy to find one that is nearby and convenient.

U.S. Government Savings Bonds   Another popular form of saving is buying U.S. Government Savings Bonds. These bonds are safe, they can be easily converted into cash, and they involve a low risk. There are two different kinds of savings bonds—Series E and Series H. Each provides a way of saving for specific savings goals.

Stocks and Bonds   Buying stocks and bonds is another way of investing and a more direct way of investing in the economy. When you buy stocks, you are actually buying shares of ownership in a corporation. When you buy bonds, you are loaning your money to a corporation or government. However, investing in stocks and bonds involves more risk than some other forms of investing.

Real Estate   Many people invest in real estate because land and buildings can bring a large return on an investment. The real estate owner exercises direct control over the management of his or her property. But real estate is a high-risk investment. Real estate prices do not remain constant. They increase or decrease, depending on demand.

Rare Objects   Many people invest in rare objects. They buy coins, stamps, art, or antiques in the hope of showing a return on their investment. Like real estate, rare objects can be a risky investment. Values of objects can change rapidly. Therefore, knowledge about the investment is important.

Identify some ways of saving and investing that have not been discussed in this chapter.

Some Considerations Before Investing

As you have learned, savings can be invested in banks and other financial institutions, or directly in stocks, bonds, and real estate. Before you invest, there are several things to keep in mind. First of all, should you invest? And then, what investment should you choose? Most savers are also investors because they want their savings to grow. Because savings accounts and savings bonds are fairly safe, they are good choices for people with small amounts of money to invest. Also, these investments can be converted to cash easily in emergencies. With stocks, bonds, and real estate, there is greater risk that the investor can lose money. In fact, there is sometimes the chance that the investor could lose most or all of the investment. Further, these types of investments cannot be converted to cash as quickly. For these reasons, the investor should ask the following questions:

1. If I make this investment, do I have enough money available to meet any emergency that might arise?

2. If I make this investment, can I still cover normal living expenses such as food, clothing, and shelter?

3. If I make this investment, can I afford to lose all I invest and still maintain my level of living?

If the investor can answer yes to all these questions, then he or she might consider investing money in more risky investments.

No single type of investment suits everyone. You must consider the growth possibilities and the risks of any investment carefully. But unless you can make more than just one type of investment, it is best to put your savings in the safest investment.

What investments do you or members of your family have? Why did you or your family choose that type of investment?

Investing and the Economy

Investing serves an important economic purpose. Both business and government put invested money to work in many ways. Business, for example, meets operating expenses and plans growth with invested money. Business must have capital in order to build new plants, buy expensive machinery, hire additional workers. It gets the capital from investors. Government uses investments to meet its operating expenses, to help finance public works such as highways and dams, and to meet its long-term needs.

Give some examples of how government is using borrowed money to finance public works in your community.

Learning Activities

Increasing Your Business Vocabulary

You should become familiar with each of the terms shown below. On a sheet of paper write the numbers 1 through 5. Then write alongside each number the term that best matches each of the numbered definitions.

capital gain / growth / investing / return / saving

1. Storing purchasing power.
2. The amount earned from an investment.
3. Putting stored purchasing power to work.
4. The increase in dollar value of an investment over a period of time.
5. The dollar difference when an investment is sold for more than was paid for it.

Understanding Business

1. Explain how savings become an investment.
2. What are some important reasons why individuals save?
3. What is the most important factor to consider when looking for a place to keep your savings?
4. What are some common types of investments?
5. Why are some people willing to put their savings into an investment that has high risk?

6.   Why do most people choose to invest in savings accounts?

7.   Why is investing in real estate considered to be a high-risk investment?

8.   Is buying coins, stamps, art, and antiques considered high-risk investing? Why?

9.   What questions should the investor ask himself or herself before investing?

10. Why is investing important to the economy?

Business Problems and Projects

1.   On a form similar to the one shown below, rank each of the seven situations according to its risk. Assign the number 1 to the situation with the least risk and the number 7 to the situation with the greatest risk. Follow the same procedure to rank each situation according to its potential return.

Situation	Rank by Risk	Rank by Return
A young couple buying a home		
A young career person buying art.		
A farmer buying land, tools, and seed to grow corn.		
A business person buying shares of stock.		
A high school student buying Series E Savings Bonds.		
A young person placing money in a savings account.		
A person burying money in the yard.		

2. Some people have the idea that only the wealthy invest in stocks. Study the figures below that show the income of those who own shares of stock in large corporations. Then answer the questions that follow.

SHAREHOLDERS OF MAJOR CORPORATIONS BY INCOME AND PERCENT OF HOLDINGS

Income	Percent
$15,000 and over	41.6
$10,000 to $14,999	29.5
$8,000 to $9,999	10.3
$5,000 to $7,999	10.1
Under $5,000	8.5

Source: *You and the Investment World,* New York Stock Exchange

a. What percentage of those who own shares of corporations have incomes less than $5,000? Less than $8,000? Less than $10,000?

b. What percentage of those who own shares of corporations earn more than $10,000 per year? More than $15,000?

c. What is the total percentage of ownership for people who make $9,999 or less a year?

3. Elise Evans bought a home five years ago for $62,000. She has since spent $2,400 in improvements on it.

Elise recently sold the house for $75,000. From this amount she had to pay a real estate agent's fee of 6 percent of the selling price and a total of $1,300 in other selling costs.

a. How much did she actually receive from the sale of the house?

b. What was her total profit from the sale of the house?

c. If Elise had put her original investment in a savings account at 7 percent annual interest, how much would she have had after 5 years?

Chapter 39

Savings Accounts and Savings Bonds

Objectives

After completing your study of this chapter, you will be able to do the following:

1. Identify the different types of savings accounts.

2. Describe the advantages of investing in a savings account.

3. List the advantages of saving in each of the major types of savings institutions.

4. Compare the features of Series E and Series H savings bonds.

In Chapter 38, you learned that there are many ways to invest your savings. Some investments, however, are more risky than others. Investments such as stocks and real estate, for example, may offer the pleasant possibility of considerable growth. But at the same time, they also raise the much less pleasant possibility of considerable loss.

Most people want to see their savings grow—even if the growth is relatively small. Accordingly, they prefer to begin their investment programs with safe investments. Perhaps because they are the safest types of investment, savings accounts and savings bonds are the most popular for beginning investors.

SAVINGS ACCOUNTS

When people think of investing, they usually first think of savings accounts. Indeed, savings accounts are the basis of almost all investment programs. And for some people, they are the only form of investment. There are four major reasons why people choose to put their money in a savings account: safety, income, liquidity, and convenience.

Safety

The most obvious advantage of a savings account is safety. Each savings account in most commercial banks is insured up to $40,000 by the Federal Deposit Insurance Corporation (FDIC), an agency of the U.S. government. Banks insured under the FDIC pay the cost of this insurance. Savings and loan associations have a similar insurance program under the Federal Savings and Loan Insurance Corporation (FSLIC). The coverage under both types of insurance is identical.

Credit union savings accounts are protected under the Federal Share Insurance Act. Just as with bank and savings and loan association insurance, each account is insured up to $40,000 under this act. Although these insurance programs give excellent protection for your savings, they are not the only means of protection. All savings institutions are subject to strict regulations established under both federal and state laws. And frequent audits make certain that these regulations are being met.

Income

If you were interested only in safety, you could simply bury your money in a tin can. Or you could place your money in a safe deposit box. But most people are interested in something more than safety for their savings. They want these savings to work for them—in other words, to earn income. Money deposited in savings accounts earns income. The amount of income earned by savings, however, depends on the savings institution and the type of account.

Liquidity

Another advantage of a savings account is that you can withdraw your money quickly and easily in case of an emergency. Because you can do this, a savings account is said to be a liquid investment. *Liquidity* is the ease and speed with which an investment can be converted to cash. Other types of investments are not always liquid. For example, if you wanted to sell an investment in real estate, you would have to wait till you found a buyer. It might take time to find a buyer who would pay the price you wanted. However, with a liquid investment like a savings account, you can be sure of getting your money when you need it.

Buying government bonds through a payroll savings plan is an easy, painless way of investing. (Becky Roller)

Convenience

Savings accounts are convenient. It is usually easy to find a place to open an account in your neighborhood. You can make deposits of any amount whenever you want to. And it is easy to make a deposit or a withdrawal. Depositors just fill out the proper forms and either take them to the bank or mail them in special envelopes.

If a person has only a small amount of money to invest, do you think it should be invested in a savings account? Why?

TYPES OF SAVINGS ACCOUNTS

When a person starts a savings program, he or she usually has a goal in mind. Whether that goal is short-term or long-term, there are saving accounts to suit each kind of goal. Therefore, when you are considering a savings account, you should first determine what kind of saving goal you want to set for yourself. Then you should choose the saving plan that best meets your goals.

What are some short-term goals for which people might save? Some long-term goals?

Passbook Savings Accounts

Most individuals and families save in a passbook savings account. When you open a passbook savings account, you are issued a passbook. A *passbook* is the record of savings account transactions that the bank prepares for a depositor. The passbook shows the deposits, the withdrawals, the interest payments made by the bank, and the new balance after each transaction. It also shows the date of all transactions as well as the teller's initial or number.

You can make a deposit to a passbook savings account at any time. Also, banks usually allow you to withdraw your savings whenever you want to do so. Some banks permit making deposits and withdrawals by mail and supply special envelopes for this purpose.

Passbook accounts pay interest for as long as there is a minimum amount on deposit in the account. The rates of interest

DEPOSITOR'S NAME ON PAGE 1

14-0122

DATE	WITHDRAWALS	INTEREST	DEPOSIT	BALANCE
OCT 02				784.21
OCT 02			102.02	886.23
OCT 08			120.00	1,006.23
OCT 10			200.00	1,206.23
OCT 15	25.00			1,181.23
OCT 20			100.00	1,281.23
OCT 24			200.00	1,481.23
OCT 30	200.00			1,281.23
OCT 31	31.26			1,249.97
NOV 07			160.00	1,409.97
NOV 13	60.00			1,349.97
NOV 21			185.05	1,535.02

THE FIRST STATE BANK OF LAKEVILLE

ALWAYS VERIFY ENTRY BEFORE LEAVING WINDOW

A savings account passbook.

may vary. Interest is usually paid—that is, added to the passbook—quarterly. However, it may be paid semiannually or annually. The interest can be left in the account or it can be withdrawn. If it is left in the account, the interest is compounded. *Compound interest* is interest computed on both the principal and the previously earned interest. Interest may be compounded daily, quarterly, semiannually, or at other time periods. Table 39-1 shows how interest can make your savings grow.

TABLE 39-1   WATCH YOUR SAVINGS GROW WITH COMPOUND INTEREST

Number of Years	Savings without Compound Interest	Savings with Compound Interest	Savings Increase Represented by Compound Interest	
1	$ 260	$ 265.35	$ 5.35	(2.1%)
2	520	541.35	21.35	(4.1%)
3	780	828.55	48.55	(6.2%)
5	1,300	1,438.25	138.25	(10.6%)
10	2,600	3,191.45	591.45	(22.7%)
15	3,900	5,328.60	1,428.60	(36.6%)
20	5,200	7,933.80	2,733.80	(52.6%)

Source: Personal Money Management, *American Bankers Association*

Suppose you have a choice between a savings account that pays 5¼ percent interest computed annually or one that pays 5 percent interest computed quarterly. Which of the two would you choose? Why?

Certificates of Deposit

Certificates of deposit are used by the long-term saver and by the saver who has a large amount of money. A *certificate of deposit* is a receipt for money deposited with a bank in a special account. To open such a special account, a certain minimum amount of money must be deposited. The money must be left on deposit for a specified period of time. The shortest period of time is 30 days. It may, however, be for longer periods of time—one, two, three, and even six years or more.

The rate of interest on a certificate of deposit remains fixed during the time of the deposit. The rate may be as much as 2 to 3 percent higher than on a passbook savings account. Generally, the larger the amount deposited and the longer the specified time of deposit, the higher the interest rate paid.

Holders of certificates of deposit are expected to keep them for the full term. If the funds are withdrawn before the period is over, the depositor will have to pay a penalty in the form of a loss of

A certificate of deposit.

interest. In such cases, the bank will pay only the regular passbook interest rate and, moreover, deduct three months' interest.

Why do you think interest rates paid on certificates of deposit are higher than on passbook savings accounts?

Other Types of Savings Accounts

There are other types of savings accounts and plans that help people achieve their savings objectives. Many banks offer a club savings account. A *club savings account* is a method of saving small amounts regularly for a definite purpose. The most popular such account is the Christmas Club account. Other common club accounts are the Vacation Club, the Travel Club, and the All-Purpose Club. These accounts are temporary accounts into which you place a certain amount weekly or monthly until the money is needed. When all payments have been made, a check is sent to the club member for the total amount saved as well as any interest that might have been earned.

Another popular plan is the payroll savings plan. Under this plan an employer withholds part of an employee's earnings and deposits it in a savings account. Many banks have a similar plan, called an *automatic savings service*. At a depositor's request, a certain amount of money is automatically transferred from a person's checking account to his or her savings account on a regular basis. Both these plans are convenient ways to save, and they encourage saving by people who might not otherwise do so.

Commercial banks also provide check-a-month service. A person deposits a specified amount of money in a savings account. Interest is paid on the account balance just as with any other savings account. Each month the bank sends the account owner a check. The amount of the check is subtracted from the principal and any interest earned to date. Check-a-month is popular with retired people, who use it to supplement their retirement income.

Do you or members of your family have a savings account? What type of account do you have?

WHERE TO OPEN A SAVINGS ACCOUNT

Several different kinds of financial institutions offer savings accounts. The main difference among these institutions is the rate of interest they pay on your savings. In making your choice you should consider the rate of interest paid as well as such factors as the other services the institution offers, the convenience of its location, and its banking hours.

The savings account is one of the most important services that banks offer to individuals and families. Both commercial banks and mutual savings banks offer savings accounts. *Commercial banks,* which are chartered by the state or federal government, offer a variety of other services such as checking accounts, loans, and trust departments. Because they can do all their banking business in one place, some people find commercial banks the most convenient.

Mutual savings banks are owned by their depositors and accept only time deposits. Unlike commercial banks they have no stockholders. All the earnings of a mutual savings bank are paid to their depositors. Mutual savings banks invest their funds in home loans and personal loans. They pay a higher interest rate on savings than commercial banks. Although they also offer some other services, including money orders, traveler's checks, and safe deposit boxes, the higher interest is the main advantage of keeping your money in a mutual savings bank.

What are the names of some commercial banks in your community? Some mutual savings banks? What kinds of savings account services do they offer?

Like commercial banks, savings and loan associations are chartered by the state or federal government. Those chartered by the federal government are called *savings and loan associations.* Those chartered by the state are often called *building and loan associations.* These associations are registered by the Federal Home Loan Bank System, which serves the same purpose as the Federal Reserve System does for commercial banks. All federal and most state associations are owned by their depositors.

Besides offering savings account services, these associations lend money to people to build or buy homes. To secure these loans, the borrowers must pledge their property. When the loan is not repaid, the savings and loan association becomes the owner of the property pledged as security. Savings and loan associations also make unsecured loans for such things as home improvements and college education. Like mutual savings banks, savings and loans pay a higher interest rate on savings than commercial banks.

Suppose you are a loan officer at a savings and loan association. What factors would you consider when deciding whether to grant an unsecured loan to someone?

A *credit union,* you will recall, is a cooperative association whose members have a common bond and join together for the purpose of saving money and making small loans at low interest rates to members. Usually all members are from the same company, fraternal group, labor union, religious organization, or have some other close tie. Most credit unions in the United States are operated by employee groups. Credit unions get their funds by selling ownership shares to members. Their main functions are to receive savings from members and to make personal loans to members. Credit unions make more small personal loans to members than do commercial banks. This is so because their cost of handling these loans is less. Credit unions are run with volunteer help and often have very low overhead costs. The maximum rate of interest they pay on savings is often higher than banks and savings and loans. Since the depositors are also owners of the credit union, the interest they receive is really a dividend.

Are there any credit unions in your city? If yes, give their names and the common bond that each has.

U.S. SAVINGS BONDS

A *bond* is a written promise to pay a definite sum of money, plus interest, at a future date. Bonds are issued as a means for borrowing money. Government savings bonds as we know them today were first sold in 1935. Since that time they have become very popular. The money that people invest in savings bonds has helped the government pay for the expenses of running the government. When you invest in government savings bonds, your money is as safe as the government itself.

U.S. Savings Bonds may be bought at banks, savings and loan associations, and other agencies of the federal government, such as Federal Reserve Banks and their branches. You may also arrange to buy bonds through a payroll savings plan or through a bond-a-month plan. In a payroll savings plan, your employer withholds part of your earnings each pay period and buys savings bonds for you. Under the bond-a-month plan, a commercial bank takes funds from your checking account each month to purchase savings bonds for you.

What would be the advantages of purchasing U.S. Savings Bonds through a payroll savings or bond-a-month plan?

There are two advantages to owning U.S. Savings Bonds. First, they are registered with the federal government in the name of the owner or owners. They will be replaced free—as of the original issue

A United States savings bond.

date—if they are lost, stolen, or destroyed. Second, owners of U.S. Savings Bonds need not pay the same income taxes on the interest earned from their bonds as they do for interest earned on other investments. They must pay federal income tax on the interest, but they do not pay state or local income taxes on it.

Since 1935, different kinds of savings bonds have been issued. Today, however, there are only two: Series E and Series H.

Series E Savings Bonds

Series E savings bonds may be purchased in several amounts. The face value and actual cost of Series E bonds are shown in the following table.

TABLE 39-2   FACE VALUE AND COST OF SERIES E U.S. SAVINGS BONDS

Face Value	Cost
$ 25.00	$ 18.75
50.00	37.50
75.00	56.25
100.00	75.00
200.00	150.00
500.00	375.00
1,000.00	750.00

Face value, remember, is the value payable at the time the bond matures. Series E bonds currently mature in five years. The difference between the cost and the face value is the amount of interest that has been earned. The interest rate is presently 6 percent, if bonds are held until maturity. U.S. Savings Bonds may be redeemed before the maturity date at a lower interest rate, but only if they have been held for two months.

Redemption value is the value at which the U.S. Savings Bonds can be sold back to the federal government. Series E bonds are redeemable at government agencies. This can only be done at the beginning of each half-year period after issue date. The interest rate is lower if bonds are redeemed before the maturity date. However, it is possible to continue holding bonds after the maturity date. If you do, they will continue to earn interest at 6 percent per year.

Series H Savings Bonds

Series H savings bonds include many of the same features as Series E bonds, but there are some major differences between the two. First, Series H bonds come only in amounts of $500, $1,000, and $5,000. Unlike Series E bonds, the purchase price of Series H bonds is the same as the face value. And Series H bonds mature in ten years rather than in five years. As with Series E bonds, Series H bonds can be redeemed before the maturity date. However, you must wait six months after date of issue before you can receive the full face value plus any earned interest.

Interest is paid differently for Series H bonds. Interest checks are mailed to holders of Series H bonds every six months from date of issue. Currently, if held to maturity of ten years, Series H bonds have an interest rate of about 6 percent.

Which do you suppose is the most popular U.S. Savings Bond, Series E or Series H? Why?

Learning Activities

Increasing Your Business Vocabulary

You should become familiar with each of the terms shown below. On a sheet of paper write the numbers 1 through 6. Then write alongside each number the term that best matches each of the numbered definitions.

bond / certificate of deposit / compound interest / liquidity / passbook / redemption value

1. A written promise to pay a definite sum of money, plus interest, at a future date.
2. A record of savings account transactions prepared by a bank for a depositor.
3. Interest computed on both the principal and the previously earned interest.
4. The ease and speed with which an investment can be converted to cash.
5. A receipt for money deposited in a special bank account.
6. The value at which U.S. Savings Bonds can be sold back to the federal government.

Understanding Business

1. What is the major difference between a passbook savings account and a certificate of deposit?

2. What is compound interest?

3. What are some other types of savings account services? Why do people use each of these kinds of services?

4. What are the main reasons why people invest in a savings account?

5. Why is it important to have some of your money in liquid investments?

6. Why are savings accounts considered to be safe investments?

7. What do commercial banks offer that other savings institutions do not?

8. What is the main advantage of saving in a mutual savings bank?

9. What happens if a U.S. Savings Bond is lost, stolen, or destroyed?

10. What are the three major differences between the two types of government savings bonds?

Business Problems and Projects

1. Imagine that you made a pact with yourself. Every month you were going to save double the amount you saved the month before. If you saved five cents the first month, how much would you have saved after one year? After 18 months?

2. Ann Croyden belongs to a payroll savings plan where she works. Under the plan, her employer withholds 5 percent of her weekly salary. If Ann works 35 hours a week and receives $3.15 per hour, how much would be deducted for savings in one year?

3. The regular purchase of U.S. Savings Bonds is one way to save. Many people use Savings Bonds as a means of paying for

the education of their children. This table shows how investments in Savings Bonds grow.

HOW "DOLLARS FOR EDUCATION" GROW IN SERIES E BONDS

If your child's age is:	Value* of E Bonds at age 18 through monthly investments of:			
	$18.75	$37.50	$56.25	$75.00
At birth	$6,767	$13,534	$20,301	$27,068
1 year	6,191	12,381	18,572	24,762
2 years	5,645	11,289	16,934	22,579
4 years	4,638	9,276	13,914	18,552
6 years	3,735	7,469	11,204	14,938
8 years	2,924	5,848	8,772	11,696
10 years	2,197	4,394	6,591	8,788
12 years	1,545	3,089	4,634	6,179

Source: U.S. Government Printing Office

a. If your parents had started a U.S. Savings Bond investment program of $18.75 a month when you were born, what would the bonds be worth when you reach age 18?

b. If they had invested $56.25 each month, how much would the bonds be worth?

c. In Question *a* above, how much of this amount would your parents have paid in? How much would be earned interest?

d. If they had invested $37.50 per month starting at age 6, what would be the value of the bonds?

e. According to the table, what is the interest rate on U.S. Savings Bonds if held for 5 years and 10 months?

f. How is interest computed on U.S. Savings Bonds that have matured (5 years and 10 months) but have not been cashed in?

Chapter 40

Stocks and Bonds

Objectives

After completing your study of this chapter, you will be able to do the following:

1. Describe the features of bonds.

2. Explain how bonds differ from stocks.

3. List and describe the two types of stock.

4. Describe how securities are bought and sold.

5. Discuss the factors that affect stock and bond prices.

6. List some things that should be considered before investing in securities.

Some people are content to limit their investment programs to such safe investments as savings accounts and savings bonds. They take comfort in knowing that while the return from such investments may be small, it is steady and sure. Other people seek investments that involve higher risks. They understand that the amount of money an investment returns is frequently related to the amount of risk it involves. Because they want to obtain the greatest possible return on each dollar invested, they are willing to take certain chances. Still another group of people want both the comfort of safe investments and the greater dollar return of high-risk investments. Accordingly, they prefer a program that has a balance of both safe and high-risk investments.

For the last two groups, the most popular types of high-risk investments are those that involve securities. *Securities,* which is a general term for stocks and bonds, are sold by governments and corporations in order to raise large amounts of money.

There are three ways in which businesses that need a great deal of money for a long period of time can obtain that money. They can go to a bank and apply for a long-term loan. They can use the profits of the business. Or they can sell stocks and bonds. But banks are often reluctant to lend large amounts for periods longer than one or two years. And profits are ordinarily not large enough to finance anything very expensive. Therefore whenever businesses or governments need financing for major projects or for growth, they must raise the money through the sale of securities.

BONDS

A bond is like a promissory note, except that it is issued either by a business or by a government unit such as a city, county, or state. When you buy a bond, you are really lending money to the government or business from which you buy it. In return, you receive from the seller a written promise to pay you a definite sum of money, plus interest, at a future date.

There are two types of bonds. *Government bonds* are issued by state and local governments to help pay for improvements such as streets, schools, and public buildings. *Corporate bonds* are issued by businesses to raise money for expansion and growth.

Features of Bonds

Bonds are usually issued in $1,000 denominations. The *denomination* is the sum of money that the bond represents. This sum is printed on the bond. The interest rate is set at the time a bond is issued. It remains the same until the bond matures. The maturity date of a bond is also fixed. Bonds may be issued for such periods as 10, 20, or 30 years.

Suppose you bought a $1,000 bond at 6 percent interest for 20 years. Each year you would receive $60 in interest (6 percent of $1,000). The interest would probably be paid to you in two payments, $30 every six months. After 20 years, the bond would mature, and you would receive $1,000—the price you paid when you first bought the bond.

Bonds may be either registered or bearer bonds. A *registered bond* is a bond that has the name of the owner recorded with the

Government and business firms can raise money to finance major projects through the sale of securities.
(New York Stock Exchange)

issuer of the bond. Interest is mailed directly to the person registered as the owner. A *bearer bond* is a bond whose owner is presumed to be the person who has possession of the bond. Bearer bonds are not registered. When interest payments are due on a bearer bond, its possessor clips a coupon from the bond and sends the coupon to the issuer for payment.

Bonds are also classified according to the type of security that backs them up. A *mortgage bond* is backed by the issuer's pledge of buildings, land, and equipment as security. A *debenture bond* is backed only by the issuer's promise to pay when the interest and principal are due.

Would you prefer to invest in mortgage or debenture bonds? Explain your answer.

STOCKS

As a bondholder you are a creditor of, or lender to, a business firm or government unit. As a stockholder, however, you are one of the owners of a corporation. *Stock* represents a share of ownership in a corporation. A stockholder may own one share or many shares of a corporation's stock, and each share may cost several dollars or several hundred dollars.

Upon purchase of a stock, a stockholder receives a stock certificate, a printed form that states the number of shares a person owns in a corporation. You can buy either common or preferred stock.

Common stock is stock that permits owners to vote for directors at the annual meeting of the corporation and to share any profits or losses. Holders of common stock share indirectly in the management of the corporation by voting for the directors, who in turn appoint the people who manage the corporation. Although there is greater risk in owning common stock than in owning preferred stock or bonds, there is also the chance of a greater return on your investment. Dividends for common stock are set by the directors of the corporation according to the amount of profit. If profits are high, dividends for common stock can be

Most investors buy and sell securities through stockbrokers.
(Cherkis/Stockmarket, Los Angeles)

much higher than for preferred stock. If profits are low, dividends may not be paid to holders of common stock. For this reason the price of shares of common stock changes more rapidly than the price of preferred stock.

Preferred stock is stock with first claim on the corporation's earnings and assets after the claims of bondholders. Preferred stockholders do not have voting rights in the corporation. Preferred stock dividends are usually set when the stock is first sold and remain the same thereafter. This means that if the dividend is set at $6 per share, preferred stockholders will usually receive this same amount each year. Preferred stock dividends must be paid before common stock dividends can be paid. Since the dividend remains the same from year to year, preferred stock is usually more stable in price than common stock.

Bonds are a more secure investment than stocks because a bondholder has first claim on the assets of a corporation. This means that a corporation must first pay interest to bondholders. Then stockholders are paid their interest. It also means that if a corporation goes bankrupt, the bondholders have first claim on the assets. Should a company fail, its net assets are divided first among the bondholders, then among the preferred stockholders, and finally among the common stockholders.

If you were interested in a safe investment, would you prefer bonds or stocks? Preferred stock or common stock? Why?

BUYING AND SELLING SECURITIES

Securities are generally bought and sold through investment brokers. The *investment broker* is the agent who processes orders for investors who want to buy or sell securities. Brokers usually buy and sell stocks through a *stock exchange,* which is the central market for securities. There are about 20 of these exchanges throughout the United States. The two major exchanges are the New York Stock Exchange and the American Stock Exchange, both located in New York.

Only brokers whose firms are members of an exchange may buy or sell through that exchange. The broker receives a commission for his or her services. This commission is a percentage of the amount of the sale. When securities are first issued, they are sold at a fixed price. Once they are sold, however, the price changes greatly. Sometimes the prices change from day to day, depending on supply and demand.

The Stock Market

Corporations issue only a limited number of shares of stock. After those shares are purchased, they may be traded. This means that people buy and sell the shares. When you buy stock, you can never be sure you will get back what you paid for it. The price of a stock, like the price of most other goods and services, depends on how much buyers are willing to pay. The price a buyer is willing to pay depends on a number of factors. Among them are these:

- The general economic outlook will influence the price of stock. When the outlook is good more people will want to buy stock. This means there is more demand for stock, and stock prices will go up. When the economic outlook is poor, then the demand for stock drops, and prices will go down.

- A corporation's earnings will affect the price of its stock. Usually, the greater the earnings, the greater the dividends a corporation will pay. When corporate earnings are high, the stock is in demand, and prices go up.

- Buyers often borrow money to buy stocks. If interest rates for borrowing are high, people do not borrow and do not buy stock. Because the demand is low, stock prices go down.

Each day's transactions for stocks listed on the major stock exchanges are recorded and published in the daily newspapers. If you want to know the price of a stock, you can look in the financial section of your local newspaper. The illustration on the facing page shows you how to read stock prices in the newspaper.

Each day millions of shares of stock are traded at the New York Stock Exchange. (New York Stock Exchange)

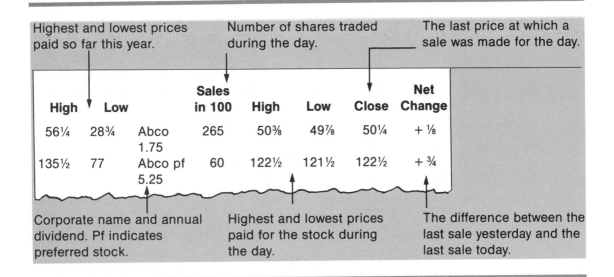

Highest and lowest prices paid so far this year.			Number of shares traded during the day.			The last price at which a sale was made for the day.	
High	Low		Sales in 100	High	Low	Close	Net Change
56¼	28¾	Abco 1.75	265	50⅜	49⅞	50¼	+ ⅛
135½	77	Abco pf 5.25	60	122½	121½	122½	+ ¾

Corporate name and annual dividend. Pf indicates preferred stock.

Highest and lowest prices paid for the stock during the day.

The difference between the last sale yesterday and the last sale today.

The Bond Market

A bondholder may sell a bond before its maturity date. Bond prices, like stock prices, depend on how much people are willing to pay. However, bond prices do not change as much from day to day as stock prices. One of the factors that influence bond prices is the change of interest rates in the economy. For example, suppose you bought a $1,000 bond five years ago at a fixed rate of 5 percent interest. Your bond would pay $50 a year in interest. However, suppose that this year the interest rate on loaned money is 8 percent. A $1,000 bond purchased this year would have a fixed interest rate of 8 percent and would pay $80 a year in interest. If you wanted to sell your bond this year, no buyer would be willing to pay $1,000 for it. With a current earning interest rate of 8 percent, the buyer would lose money in buying your bond for $1,000. To sell your bond on the bond market, you would have to sell for less than $1,000. On the other hand, if interest rates in the economy had dropped below 5 percent, buyers might be willing to pay more than $1,000 for it because it has a fixed rate of interest of 5 percent.

Another factor that affects the price of bonds is the credit rating of the company or government unit issuing the bond. If the credit rating of the company changes during the life of the bond, the price of the bond will change. When the credit rating goes down, the price of the bond may go down also.

557

Corporate and government bond prices are quoted in the financial pages of newspapers, like stock prices. The quotes show the maturity date and the interest rate of the bond and give the market price of the bond that day. Bond prices are given in value per $100. A price quoted as "95" means, then, that you could get $950 for a $1,000 bond.

Why might a person choose to sell a bond before its maturity date?

CONSIDERATIONS BEFORE INVESTING IN SECURITIES

Securities are not for amateurs. The securities market is full of risks for the small investor because knowing what stock to buy, when to buy, and when to sell are difficult decisions. Most investors do not have time to do the necessary research to make wise decisions. They rely on guesswork and are often wrong. However, there are several things to keep in mind if you are interested in buying securities.

- *Be sure you can afford the risk.* Ask yourself three questions: If I make the investment, will I have enough money to meet any emergency that may arise? Can I still cover normal living expenses? Can I afford to lose all I invest? Once you buy securities, you should not have to sell them to cover your day-to-day living expenses or to meet unexpected emergencies.

- *Limit the risks you take.* Don't invest on the basis of tips or rumors. All too often they are wrong. Remember, there is risk in any investment, and only you can decide how much risk you should assume. For every person who has made money on a rumor, there are probably ten persons who have lost money.

- *Get expert advice.* A qualified investment broker can help you decide which securities might be best for you. The broker will also be glad to help you learn more about the operation of the stock market. Brokerage firms sometimes have research departments and libraries to aid the investor. If not, the broker can tell you where you can get information about the market. Study the materials from your broker as well as financial magazines and the financial section of your daily newspaper. When you are ready to buy, place your order through your broker.

What is at least one important reason why you should be wary of tips or rumors when making investments?

MUTUAL FUNDS

You may want to consider either mutual funds or some other method of investing in various stocks to decrease the risk of losing all you invest. When you invest your money, the saying "Don't put all your eggs in one basket" has merit. By investing in the stock of several companies, there is less chance of losing all the funds you have invested. One way of doing this is to buy mutual fund shares.

A *mutual fund* is a corporation that sells its own stocks and uses the money to invest in other corporations. You buy shares in a mutual fund, and your money is used by the mutual fund company to invest in several securities. Because they are large, mutual fund companies can employ investment analysts who study the market carefully. For this reason, mutual funds are preferred by many small investors who are not able to manage their own investments effectively. The mutual fund investor receives dividends on mutual fund shares. Most mutual funds charge a fee for their services.

If you had money to invest, would you buy common stock, preferred stock, or mutual fund stock? Why?

Learning Activities

Increasing Your Business Vocabulary

You should become familiar with each of the terms shown below. On a sheet of paper write the numbers 1 through 11. Then write alongside each number the term that best matches each of the numbered definitions.

bearer bond / common stock / debenture bond / investment broker / mortgage bond / mutual fund / preferred stock / registered bond / securities / stock / stock exchange

1. A share of ownership in a corporation.

2. An agent who processes orders for investors in securities.

3. A bond that has the name of the owner recorded with the issuer of the bond.

4. Stock with first claims on the corporation after the claims of bondholders.

5. A bond backed by the issuer's pledge of buildings, land, or equipment as security.

6. A central market for the buying and selling of securities.

7. A bond whose owner is presumed to be the possessor of it.

8. A general term for stocks and bonds.

9. Stock with voting rights and a share of any profits or losses.

10. A bond backed only by the issuer's promise to pay.

11. A corporation that sells its own stock and uses the money to invest in other corporations.

Understanding Business

1. How do business firms raise the money they need?
2. Why do state and local governments issue bonds?
3. How do owners of registered bonds receive their interest? Owners of bearer bonds?
4. Explain the difference between owning stock in a corporation and owning a bond of a corporation.
5. What are some advantages of owning preferred stock rather than common stock?
6. Why are investors willing to accept the higher risk involved in owning common stock?
7. How are securities usually bought and sold?
8. What are some of the factors that affect the prices of stock?
9. What are some factors affecting the market value of bonds?
10. List some things to keep in mind when investing in securities.

Business Problems and Projects

1. Assume that you have been given $1,000, which you are to invest in stocks of your own choosing. Choose your stocks carefully, because once you have made your selections you will not be allowed to change. Keep a record of your stocks for a two-week period and determine how much you have gained or lost from your investment.

2. Use the table below to figure the broker's commission for each of the transactions that follow it.

Money Value of Transaction	Commission
$100 to $399	2% plus $3
$400 to $2,399	1% plus $7
$2,400 to $4,999	½% plus $19
$5,000 or more	1/10% plus $39

   a. You buy 100 shares of stock at $30 per share.

   b. You sell 50 shares of stock at $36 per share.

   c. You buy 500 shares of stock at $10 per share.

   d. You sell 500 shares of stock at $12 per share.

3. One of the most frequently used indicators of stock market trends is the Dow Jones average of selected stocks. Study the table below and then answer the questions that follow it.

DOW JONES WEEKLY STOCK AVERAGES

Year			Net Change				
High	Low		High	Low	Close	Points	Percent
999.75	910.45	30 Indus	941.91	930.46	930.46	+2.12	+0.22%
246.64	221.81	20 Trans	246.64	243.04	245.03	+4.77	+1.98%
111.81	104.94	15 Utils	111.93	111.07	111.74	+1.28	+1.15%
324.86	302.89	65 Stocks	318.41	314.98	315.59	+2.64	+0.84%

SALES:	30 Industrials	8,466,100	20 trnsp.	2,207,100
	15 Utilities	1,730,800	65 Stocks	12,404,000

   a. Which group of stocks closed for the week nearest to its yearly high?

   b. Which group of stocks has shown the most stability during the year?

   c. Which group of stocks were traded the least during the week covered in the table?

   d. Which group of stocks showed the greatest net change during the week covered in the table?

Chapter 41

Other Types of Investments

  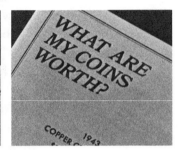

Objectives

After completing your study of this chapter, you will be able to do the following:

1. Explain why real estate investing is different from other types of investing.

2. Recognize the points to consider when buying a home.

3. Recognize the advantages and disadvantages of investing in rare objects.

563

You have probably heard people say, "I like to see what I'm getting for my money." Like these people, you may prefer to see just what you are investing your money in. You may also want to have some degree of direct control over your investments.

The investments previously discussed involve things that cannot be seen or touched. For example, you cannot really see or touch the money you have invested in a savings account. Nor do you have any control over it. You trust that it will be there when you need it, even though you know that the bank has invested it elsewhere. And you have no voice in determining where and how the bank uses it.

This chapter treats two types of investments that you can see, touch, and control: real estate and rare objects.

INVESTING IN REAL ESTATE

Several major differences separate investments in real estate from investments in savings accounts, stocks, and bonds. First, land is fixed and cannot be moved. Its value can change because of what happens to it and to the property around it. For example, the value of land can increase as a result of such improvements as buildings, landscaping, or a swimming pool. However, if the land is allowed to become rundown, its value can decrease sharply.

Second, real estate is usually a long-term investment. Most people who buy real estate expect to keep it for at least several years. Real estate investment involves a lot of money. Houses, commercial buildings, and large tracts of land are all expensive. Therefore, much of the cost of the investment is usually financed.

Third, investments in real estate are usually made within the local community. There is no national market for real estate as there is for securities. Even within a local area each piece of real estate is different, so it is impossible to set standard prices. An investor who is not familiar with the local real estate market stands a good chance of making a poor investment.

What are some other things that cause the value of land to increase or decrease?

Buying a Home

Although the major reason for buying a home is to provide shelter, many people think of a home as an investment. They have something to show for their money. And the value of the home usually grows over a number of years.

There are several points to consider when you make the decision to buy a home. First, you must consider the cost of buying a home. How much can you afford to pay for a home? How much down payment is required? How much of a down payment can you afford? Remember that the cost of buying and owning a home involves more than just the purchase price. It also involves such other costs as yearly real estate taxes, insurance, interest, and maintenance. Will you have enough income to pay these costs as well as your mortgage and other living costs?

Next, you must be willing to accept all the obligations and responsibilities of home ownership. For example, you must make your monthly mortgage payments on time. Also, you must properly maintain your property, or it may decrease in value. And finally, will you live in the house long enough to make home ownership worthwhile? Real estate is not a liquid investment. You may not be able to sell your house quickly for the price you want. As the value of a home increases over a number of years, your investment in a home will be more valuable if you plan to live there for several years.

Many real estate mortgage contracts include a clause obligating a home owner to keep the property in good condition. Why do you think that is so?

Once the decision to buy is made, you have several types of homes from which to choose. You might, for example, buy a single-family home. Or you might choose a condominium.

Suppose you choose to buy a condominium. A *condominium* is an individually owned unit in a multiple-unit housing development. In acquiring a condominium, you receive title to the specific unit you buy. You also get joint ownership of common areas in the buildings and grounds. You must arrange your own mortgage and pay the real estate taxes on your unit. You also make separate payments for maintenance and operating expenses. You can usually sell your unit without approval. If you want to remodel, however, you usually must have the approval of the group of owners that manages the property.

The main advantage to a condominium over a single-family home is economy. There are large savings on the cost of land and construction. However, upkeep of the building and the land must be paid for. To cover these expenses, owners pay a maintenance fee, usually monthly. This can be a disadvantage. Another disadvantage is that remodeling a condominium may require approval of the other owners in the building. Finally, selling the condominium may require the approval of the management.

Many people choose to buy a single-family home because it does not have these disadvantages. A single-family home usually provides more privacy than a condominium. If you want to sell, you and you alone decide when and to whom you sell.

Selecting a Location Regardless of the type of home chosen, a great deal of thought should be given to its location. Are the homes in the neighborhood well maintained? Are the schools good and conveniently located? How far is it from the home to where you and other family members work? How far is it to shopping centers, churches, and parks? Is public transportation available and convenient? What local taxes will you have to pay? How much are they and how are they figured? Is the police and fire protection good? Is there good garbage and rubbish removal service? Do you have to pay extra for these services? What are the local rates for gas, electricity, water, and sewer? Are utilities such as water and sewers in? Or will these be an added expense?

Give several reasons why people want to own their homes.
Give reasons why people might choose not to own a home.

Other Real Estate Investments

There are many other kinds of real estate investments available. Land is one kind of investment property, and it can be in the form

For most people, buying a home is their single largest investment. (M. Licht)

of lots, farms, ranches, and so forth. In addition to land, investment real estate includes industrial and commercial properties such as office buildings, restaurants, and shopping centers. There are also recreational properties that are good investment possibilities. Finally, there are income-producing residential properties such as hotels, motels, apartment buildings, and mobile-home parks. Each of these is an excellent investment possibility.

What are some other things that could be used as real estate investment opportunities?

Advantages and Disadvantages

Owning real estate gives an investor the opportunity to control his or her investment directly. It also provides a return on the money invested. And it gives you the opportunity for growth in the value of your investment. Over the years the value of almost all types of real estate has increased. It seems likely that the value of real estate generally will continue to increase.

But the person investing in real estate should know about some of the disadvantages. While the value of real estate generally increases, real estate other than land loses value over time as it is used. This could result in a decrease in the value of an investment. Making money on a real estate investment requires good management. The investor may not have the time or the skill to manage the investment properly. An investor may choose to use a professional management service, but this costs money and reduces the return on the investment. Another disadvantage is that real estate is not a liquid investment. It is much more difficult to convert to cash than a savings account or securities. And finally, real estate is in a permanent location, so its value can change rapidly as a result of what happens to the property around it. The disadvantage here is that you have no control over the property that surrounds yours.

What factors might cause an increase in the value of real estate? What might decrease the value of real estate?

INVESTING IN RARE OBJECTS

Many people collect rare objects such as antiques, art, coins, and stamps. Some people collect these things as a hobby and have fun doing it. Others, however, buy the items because they feel their value will increase. To these people, rare objects are a form of investment. If the value of the objects does increase, they can be sold at the higher price, thus providing a return for the seller.

Some people consider investing in coins, stamps, art, and antiques a form of speculation. *Speculation* is the process of buying goods or property in the hope of getting a substantial return as a result of a change in the market price. People sometimes also speculate when they buy stocks or land. Speculation often is not a very safe way of investing. There is the chance that the market value of your investment may go down instead of up.

Because rare objects do not yield a return in the form of interest or dividends, their value is in their growth potential. They are, therefore, a long-term investment. Certain rare objects, like some metals that are becoming scarce, have already grown in value for a number of years. But there is no guarantee that a specific rare object has growth potential. The object may also decrease in value. Therefore it is a good idea to have some knowledge of coins, stamps, or other rare objects before making an investment.

What things do you think could determine the value of coins and stamps? How do you suppose a collector decides how much to pay for a coin or a stamp?

Antiques like this Tiffany lamp and these rare coins have become increasingly popular investments.
(Sotheby Parke Bernet; Robbins/Stockmarket, Los Angeles)

Learning Activities

Increasing Your Business Vocabulary

You should become familiar with each of the terms shown below. On a sheet of paper write the numbers 1 through 7. Then write alongside each number the term that best matches each of the numbered definitions.

assessed value / condominium / liquidity / mortgage / real estate tax / return / speculation

1. A written agreement that uses real estate as security for payment of a debt.

2. A tax on land and the buildings attached to the land.

3. Buying goods or property in the hope of getting a substantial return as a result of an upward change in market price.

4. The estimate of worth placed upon a property for the purpose of taxation.

5. The ease and speed with which an investment can be converted into cash.

6. An individually owned unit in a multiple-unit development.

7. The dollar difference when an investment is sold for more than was paid for it.

Understanding Business

1. What things can be done to improve land?

2. Why is investing in real estate considered to be a long-term rather than a short-term investment?

3. Why do people think of buying a home as an investment?

4. What are the important costs of owning a home?

5. Why is real estate not considered a liquid investment?

6. What is the main advantage of buying a condominium over a single-family home?

7. List the various things to think about when choosing a location for a home or condominium.

8. List some of the disadvantages of investing in real estate.

9. Explain the difference between collecting rare objects and investing in them.

10. Is investing in rare objects considered a short-term or long-term investment? Why?

Business Problems and Projects

1. Franklin Chen owns an apartment house consisting of twelve units. Each of the units is a one-bedroom apartment and rents for the same price. What monthly rent should he charge for each of the apartments if he wishes to make forty percent more than his expenses? His monthly expenses are as follows:

Mortgage payments	$1,230
Maintenance	270
Taxes	500

2. The liquidity of an asset is determined by how easily it can be converted into cash. Listed below are six assets. Reorder these assets, ranking them from the most liquid down to the least.

a. Large factory   c. Farm   e. Municipal bond

b. U.S. savings bond   d. Used car   f. House

Part Five

PLANNING YOUR CAREER

Chapter 42

Careers Today

Objectives

After completing your study of this chapter, you will be able to do the following:

1. Define the term *career* and list the questions that should be asked when selecting a career.

2. Explain how your choice of work affects your life-style.

3. List the job clusters classified by the federal government.

4. Name some of the major trends in employment.

Whether we like it or not, most of us have to work. We have to work in order to produce the goods and services that all of us need and want. And we have to work in order to earn the money to pay for these goods and services. In fact, the likelihood is that you will have almost forty years of work ahead of you. Clearly, then, some of the most important and long-reaching decisions you will ever make are those that concern your choice of a *career*—that is the kind of work you choose to pursue for a lifetime.

You may have already made some of these decisions, particularly those that relate to education and training. And soon you will be making many more. This chapter, as well as the remaining chapters in the book, is designed to help you choose wisely. It examines how the work you do affects your life-style. It explores the major categories of jobs. And it presents some of the more important current trends in employment.

HOW WORK AFFECTS YOUR LIFE-STYLE

When choosing a career, you should first determine what things in life are important to you. Is income important? Is satisfaction important? Is social status important? Or is there something else that means more to you? In simpler terms, exactly what do you want out of life?

Remember that almost every aspect of your life is affected by your career choice. Not only does your work provide income, but it may also control almost all your activities. It may influence your choice of friends. It may determine your social status. And it may give meaning to your life.

Work Provides Income

In our economic system, a person's income is generally based on what he or she can produce. The more one can produce, the more money that person should receive. Your job should provide you at least enough income to cover the cost of such basic necessities as food, clothing, and housing. But how much income you need is up to you. Your preferred life-style can affect your career choice. If, for example, your life-style requires no more than the basic necessities, you may not need much of an income. If, on the other hand, your life-style requires a number of luxuries, you should choose a career that will provide you enough income to obtain them.

At the same time, it is important to remember how your life-style can be affected by your choice of work. If you choose a career that provides little income, you may not be able to afford luxuries—no matter how much you want them.

Work Controls Activities

The work that you do affects all of your other activities. Some careers, like those in retailing, may require work in the evenings or on weekends. If you like getting together with your friends in the evening or enjoy Saturday football games, you may prefer work that does not interfere with these pleasures. If your interests center around the home, you may prefer a job that allows you to be home often. On the other hand, if you like to explore new places, you may want to choose a career that either involves travel or allows enough time for travel.

While some may find a television camera operator's work glamorous, others may dislike the irregular working hours. (Lejeune/Stockmarket, Los Angeles)

Skilled craftspersons often get great satisfaction from their work. (Maria Karras)

Work Influences Your Choice of Friends

People usually make friends with those who share common interests. Business people generally associate with other business people. Entertainers generally mingle with other entertainers. And government workers generally mix with other government workers. In all likelihood, then, many of your friends will be people with whom you work. If you prefer outgoing people, you may want to choose a job where you are likely to find outgoing coworkers. But if you feel more comfortable with quieter people, you may want to seek a career that tends to appeal to quieter types.

Work Determines Social Status

A person's social standing within a community is frequently affected by the type of work he or she does. If social status is important to you, perhaps you should consider whether or not your career choice is consistent with this personal value. Remember, however, that social status is not determined by income alone.

Some people earn a great deal of money and yet may be very low on the social scale. Others—members of the clergy, for example—earn very little but still have a high social status.

Work Adds Meaning to One's Life

Some people get much of their satisfaction in life from their work. This satisfaction or fulfillment is called *meaning*. A teacher may find it in helping others to learn. A farmer may find it in working with the soil. A cabinetmaker may find it in crafting a particularly fine piece of furniture. For many people, this sense of meaning is the central purpose of their life. In choosing a career, you, too, should seek a career field that will add meaning to your life.

Is your career choice consistent with the things in life that are important to you? How?

JOB CLUSTERS

Today there are more than 25,000 different kinds of jobs to choose from. With so many jobs available, how do you begin to narrow the choice?

A good way to start is by picking a general field of work rather than a specific job. This task is made easier because of a job classification system established by the U.S. Department of Labor. This system classifies all the jobs in a general field into seven major groups, called *job clusters*. A brief description of each of these job clusters follows.

Professional and Management

Almost all jobs in the professional and managerial cluster require some college education. Many require four years of college or more. This cluster includes such jobs as doctor, lawyer, teacher, accountant, mathematician, and engineer.

Clerical and Sales

Most of the jobs in business and in retailing are included in this cluster. Among these are secretary, bookkeeper, salesperson, business machine operator, and typist. Despite increased automation, the outlook for jobs in this cluster remains good.

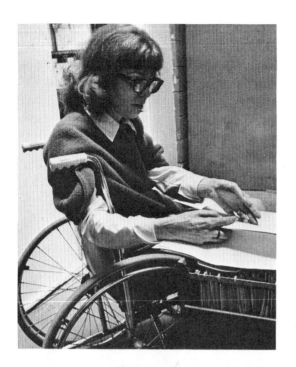

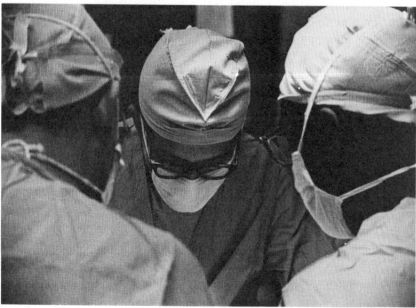

Which of these jobs would appeal to you the most?
(Betty Medsger; ERDA; Lejeune/Stockmarket, Los Angeles)

Service

The service cluster includes jobs in hotels, resorts, restaurants, airlines, and other businesses that provide services. Because service industries are growing at a faster rate than almost all other types of industries, the outlook for jobs in this cluster is quite good.

Fishing, Forestry, and Agriculture

If you prefer working outdoors, you may want to consider one of the jobs in the fishing, forestry, and agriculture cluster. This cluster includes jobs on farms, in forests and parks, and in commercial fishing.

Skilled

Craftspeople are almost always in demand. The skilled cluster includes jobs in such trades as plumbing, mechanics, carpentry, bricklaying, and electrical work. Many of these jobs call for some form of apprenticeship as a requirement for hiring.

Semiskilled

Jobs in the semiskilled cluster require less skill than those in the skilled cluster, and this skill can be generally learned in a relatively short time through on-the-job training. Examples of jobs in the semiskilled cluster are the "helper" jobs found in the various skilled trades.

Unskilled

Workers in unskilled jobs generally perform tasks that require little knowledge or skill. Frequently these jobs can be learned in a few days. And sometimes they can be learned in just a few hours. This cluster includes construction day laborers and porters.

Which of the job clusters is of most interest to you as a possibility for your career? Why?

TRENDS IN EMPLOYMENT

Intelligent career choices depend on careful planning. And planning requires some understanding of the future. While it may be useful to know what jobs are available today, it is clearly far more important to have some idea of what the job market will be like in the years to come. After all, no matter how much training you undergo in preparation for a job, that training will be almost useless if that job does not exist when you need it.

No one knows, of course, exactly what will happen in the future. A major technological breakthrough could eliminate present jobs and require the creation of new ones in their place. A major catastrophe could return us to a nontechnological, agricultural society. Nevertheless, we can get some sense of what is likely to occur if we examine the general direction, or *trend,* that the employment market is taking.

More White-Collar Workers

One of the major trends that has been taking place for a number of years is the shift from blue- to white-collar occupations. *Blue-collar workers* are those in such jobs as factory workers, mechanics, and laborers. *White-collar workers* are those working in professional, administrative, managerial, clerical, and sales jobs.

White-collar workers now outnumber all other workers. There are several reasons for this trend. The main reason is the growth of automation. Many jobs formerly done by blue-collar workers are now done by machines. For example, one bulldozer can do the work of several dozen laborers. And it can do this work in a fraction of the time. Improved machines and farming techniques have also reduced the need for farm workers.

Another reason is that Americans have been using more and more services. Thus, the need for some blue-collar workers has been reduced, while the need for white-collar workers has increased. As a result, professional, technical, and clerical fields will continue to show remarkable growth.

More Women in the Labor Market

Another important trend is the growing percentage of females in the labor market. This trend began during World War II, when women took over jobs formerly held by men. In 1940 only one-fourth of the labor force was women. Today well over one-third of the labor force is made up of women. This trend is expected to continue into the 1980s.

582   PLANNING YOUR CAREER

Women now make up over one-third of our labor force. (Lejeune/Stockmarket, Los Angeles)

There are a number of reasons why women remain in the labor force and continue to enter it in increasing numbers. Income is an important reason. Working wives bring needed income into the household. Also, many women are heads of households. They must work to support the household. Since the average family has fewer children, it is now easier for a married woman to work outside the home.

Not only are more women working outside the home, but they are being paid more money for their work. Equal pay for women has gained wider acceptance in recent years. And there is less prejudice in hiring practices than there once was. As a result, more occupations are opening up to women. In medicine, in law, and in many areas of business, women have successfully gained acceptance and equality with men.

List some occupations where there are still far fewer women employed than men. Why do you think this is so?

Shorter Working Life

There appears to be a trend toward a shorter working life for most people. Several reasons account for this. First, people enter the labor market at an older age than in the past. This is because most young people stay in school for a longer period of time than they once did. Second, the workweek is getting shorter. The forty-hour week is standard in most industries. In many instances, however, the workweek has been reduced to thirty-five or fewer hours. And some businesses have reduced the workweek to four days. Finally, people are retiring at a younger age than in the past. In fact, some employers encourage their employees to take an early retirement. Not too many years ago retirement was unheard of. People worked until they were unable to continue or until they died. Now most people retire at age 65 or younger.

SHORT-TERM EMPLOYMENT TRENDS

The trends noted above have been taking place over a period of time. Job opportunities can also be affected by seasons and by the regular supply and demand of the job market. For example, jobs may be seasonal. Farm workers are needed during the growing seasons of the spring, summer, and fall. Retail workers are in particularly high demand during certain times of the year, such as the December holiday season. In many parts of the country, building trades are more active in the summer than in the winter.

Labor-management relations can also affect short-range job opportunities in some fields. For instance, a coal strike may result in layoffs in the steel industry. This could, in turn, mean cutbacks in the auto industry, as well as in other related industries. Other factors may have more long lasting effects on job opportunities. For example, government programs may change, causing change in demand for certain occupations. Suppose, for example, that the government decides to place more money in social services programs than in space research programs. This would reduce the demand for space workers and increase the need for social workers.

Give some conditions in the United States today that might have an influence on the number of job opportunities in certain fields.

Learning Activities

Increasing Your Business Vocabulary

You should become familiar with each of the terms shown below. On a sheet of paper write the numbers 1 through 6. Then write alongside each number the term that best matches each of the numbered definitions.

blue-collar workers / career / job cluster / meaning / trend / white-collar workers

1. The kind of work one chooses to pursue for a lifetime.
2. All of the jobs in a general field of work.
3. Factory workers, mechanics, and laborers.
4. Workers in professional, managerial, and sales jobs.
5. A direction of movement.
6. A sense of satisfaction or fulfillment in life.

Understanding Business

1. In selecting a career, what things should you consider?
2. Explain how work affects your life-style.
3. What should you do if your work does not add meaning to your life?
4. List the seven job clusters used by the United States Department of Labor.

5. List three employment trends that are evident in the job market today.

6. Why are there fewer blue-collar workers and more white-collar workers?

7. Give three reasons why there are more women entering the labor force.

8. List three reasons why the average working life of Americans is getting shorter.

9. List several jobs that are affected by seasonal supply and demand changes.

10. Give some examples of factors that affect job opportunities.

Business Problems and Projects

1. On a form similar to the one shown below, indicate into which of the seven job clusters mentioned in the text each of the listed jobs would fall.

	Job	Occupational Cluster
Example	Teacher	Professional and Managerial
	Plumber	
	Salesperson	
	Farmer	
	Restaurant cashier	
	Auto mechanic	
	Lawyer	
	Dietician	
	Office receptionist	
	Electrician's helper	
	Park ranger	

2. The chart shown below identifies changes in major occupational groups. Study the chart and then answer the questions that follow it.

PROJECTED PERCENT CHANGE, 1972–85

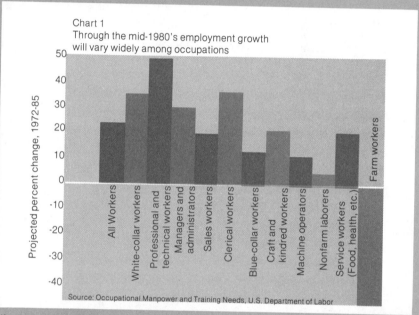

Chart 1
Through the mid-1980's employment growth will vary widely among occupations

Source: Occupational Manpower and Training Needs, U.S. Department of Labor

[1]Includes the 1970 Census classifications "operatives except transport" and "transport equipment operatives."
Source: Occupational Manpower and Training Needs, U.S. Department of Labor

a. Which major occupational groups are projected to decrease?

b. Which major occupational groups are projected to increase?

c. Which major occupational group is projected to increase the most? By what percent?

d. Which major occupational group is projected to decrease the most? By what percent?

Chapter 43

Your Career Potential

Objectives

After completing your study of this chapter, you will be able to do the following:

1. Identify abilities needed for employment.

2. Define the term *aptitudes* and list personal aptitudes.

3. List personal interests and relate them to employment.

4. Define the term *values* and relate personal values to employment.

5. Understand the value of knowing one's abilities, aptitudes, interests, and values when seeking employment.

6. Name some of the advantages and disadvantages of going into business for yourself.

7. Name some of the advantages and disadvantages of working for someone else.

Your career choice will affect many things about your life. It will affect where you live and how you live. It will affect the amount of money you earn and the education you will need. Therefore, in choosing a career, you should carefully look at all the factors that you can bring to bear on this choice. These factors include your abilities, aptitudes, interests, and values. They also include your desire to work for yourself or for someone else.

ABILITIES

A natural or acquired skill or talent is called an *ability*. An ability is not a result of only one thing. Rather, it is the result of a combination of several things. For example, as a person grows older and receives more training, a basic skill such as communication may be developed to the point where he or she becomes an able professional writer.

Basic Skills

The skills that one uses to gain other skills are called *basic skills* Basic skills include manual dexterity, computational skill, communication skill, and compatibility. Everyone has some amount of each of these skills. And most jobs require some degree of each. Furthermore, the amount of each of these skills a person has will determine how easily learning new skills will be.

Manual dexterity is a quickness and skill in using one's hands. Manual dexterity is required for many jobs in offices, factories and on farms. Dentists, lab technicians, and surgeons need manual dexterity as do plumbers, typists, and electricians. In fact, nearly all jobs require some degree of this skill.

In addition to those mentioned, what are some other jobs that require a high degree of manual dexterity?

Computational skill is the ability to work well with numbers. Many jobs require some amount of computational skill. Mathematicians, engineers, and scientists constantly use computational skills. Accountants and computer programmers also require computational skills. Most jobs require a basic knowledge of arithmetic or some basic computational skills.

Most jobs require some degree of each of these basic skills. (Maria Karras; Maria Karras; A.T.&T.; Jacqueline Marsall)

589

Communication skill is the ability to read, write, listen, and speak effectively. Sales people, managers, lawyers, counselors, secretaries, teachers—all these people must communicate effectively with others. Nearly all jobs require some degree of at least one communication skill.

Compatibility is the ability to work with and get along with other people. Some jobs require a higher degree of compatibility than others. However, in most situations the ability to work with and get along with other people is required to keep a job. Indeed, the single most common reason why people lose their jobs is because they are unable to get along with others.

List some jobs that you think require the ability to work well with other people. Why do these jobs require a high degree of compatibility?

PREVIOUS TRAINING

In choosing a career, you should consider your previous work experience. As a result of this experience, you may have had some job training that will aid you in finding a more permanent job. At the same time, take into account other kinds of training and other skills that would also make you better qualified for employment. Do you drive an automobile? This skill makes you more qualified for many jobs than someone who does not drive. Do you type, operate a calculator, operate shop equipment such as a lathe, drive a tractor, cook, or sew? These and other skills can be of help when seeking employment.

Make a list of the skills that you now have that would be of help when seeking employment.

You will learn more about education and employment in another chapter. It should be clear, however, that education can improve your basic skills and that training can help develop additional skills. Therefore, keep in mind the kind of education and training you will need to reach your career goals.

AGE

By itself, age is certainly not an ability. However, basic skills and training are usually gained over a period of time. Therefore, age is a consideration when seeking employment. In fact, some jobs require that you be a certain age. Many states have laws which require that you be at least 16 years of age for most employment. Other laws may require that you be 17 years of age or older for certain kinds of jobs. Some jobs require that you be of legal voting age.

Why do you think that most jobs require a minimum age?

APTITUDES

You have learned that ability is a natural or acquired skill or talent. Ability may be developed through hard work and practice. Sometimes a person has a natural skill or talent. Take, for instance, the person who learns to play a guitar with little effort. That person is said to have an aptitude for music. *Aptitude* is a natural or potential capacity for learning. It is much easier to learn those things for which you have an aptitude.

There are two different kinds of aptitudes—mental and physical. Mental aptitude is often shown by the grades you earn in your school work. If you earn good grades in a certain subject with ease, you probably have an aptitude for that subject. If you do well in all subjects, you probably have high overall mental aptitude. Mental aptitude, or mental ability, as it is often called, is usually measured with a general intelligence test. There are also aptitude tests that measure specific aptitudes. And other tests measure both your mental and physical aptitudes. Physical aptitude includes such things as manual dexterity, finger dexterity, speed, and the like. If you are good at sports, you probably have good physical aptitude.

An awareness of your own aptitudes will help you in making a career choice. An aptitude may be helpful in learning certain job skills. For example, an aptitude for mechanical work could lead to a career as a car or airplane mechanic.

What jobs are you qualified for because of your aptitudes?

INTERESTS

In addition to considering your abilities and aptitudes, when choosing a career, you should also take into account your interests. *Interests* are those types of activities that concern persons so much that they pay special attention to them. One of the best ways to find out about your interests is to ask yourself the following:

- How do I like to spend my spare time?
- What subjects do I like best in school? Why?
- What subjects do I like least in school? Why?
- Do I participate in school activities or clubs? If so, which ones?
- What social activities outside of school interest me?
- Do I like to take mechanical things apart and repair them?
- What kinds of activities are most exciting to me?
- Do I like to work outdoors?
- Do I like to work alone or with others?
- Do I like creative work?

The answers to these questions can help you learn more about your interests. And recognizing your interests can help you to make some decisions about possible career choices. These questions, however, are only an informal way of evaluating your interests. If you want a more formal measure of your interests, ask your school counselor to let you complete an interest inventory. An *interest inventory* is a form similar to a test and is used to identify a person's interests. There are a number of interest inventories, but one of the most commonly used is the Kuder Preference Record. Items in the Kuder Preference Record reflect 10 basic interest areas. These basic interests are:

1. Outdoor
2. Mechanical
3. Computational
4. Scientific
5. Persuasive

6. Artistic
7. Literary
8. Musical
9. Social Service
10. Clerical

The results of an interest inventory are shown in scores for each basic interest. The results of your interest inventory, for example, might show a high degree of interest in the mechanical and scientific areas, and a low degree of interest in the artistic and musical areas. Thus, you might decide to pursue a career that involves mechanical or scientific activities.

List some reasons why a formal interest inventory might be better than asking yourself the questions listed above.

VALUES

After having examined your abilities, aptitudes, and interests, it would seem that you are ready to make a career decision. There is one other area, however, that you should also consider. This area deals with the values you possess. *Values* are attitudes that individuals have regarding the importance of objects, activities, or

---

Here are several pairs of activities or occupations. Show which one of each pair you like better: if you prefer the one on the left, mark in the space labeled "L" on the answer sheet; if you prefer the one on the right, mark in the space labeled "R"; if you like both the same or if you can't decide, mark in the space labeled "=." Work rapidly. Make one mark for each pair.

Airline pilot	282	Airline ticket agent
Taxicab driver	283	Police officer
Headwaiter/Hostess	284	Lighthouse keeper
Selling things house to house	285	Gardening
Developing plans	286	Carrying out plans
Doing a job yourself	287	Telling somebody else to do the job
Dealing with things	288	Dealing with people
Taking a chance	289	Playing safe
Drawing a definite salary	290	Receiving a commission on what is done
Outside work	291	Inside work
Work for yourself	292	Carrying out the program of a superior whom you respect
Superintendent of a hospital	293	Warden of a prison
Vocational counselor	294	Public health officer
Physical activity	295	Mental activity

One of the several types of questions provided in the Strong-Campbell Interest Inventory. (Stanford University Press)

other things. They are developed as a result of where and how you have lived. Many individuals have values similar to those of their parents.

In order to know more about your values, ask yourself the following questions:

- Is being helpful to others important to me?
- Is doing a job well important to me?
- Is spending time on things that help others important to me?
- Is earning a lot of money important to me?
- Is becoming famous important to me?
- Is being active in religion important to me?
- Is security important to me?
- Is having power over other people important to me?
- Is personal appearance important to me?
- Is having many friends important to me?

What jobs would your personal values prevent you from taking?

WORKING FOR YOURSELF OR FOR SOMEONE ELSE

There is still one more important factor to consider before you decide on a career choice. Do you want to work for yourself or for someone else?

In our economic system most people earn their living by working for someone else. In fact, about 90 percent of the American labor force work as employees of business organizations and government. An *employee* is a person who earns income by working for someone else. Employees are paid wages and salaries for the services they provide. As employees, their work is subject to the direction of their employers. Employers have the authority to tell their employees what to do and how to do it.

Being *self-employed* is earning an income directly from one's own business, trade, or profession rather than from a salary or wage paid by an employer. Self-employed people have special skills, talents, or knowledge that enable them to work independently. They are their own bosses and direct their own activities. They sell their services to others and are paid a fee for these services.

Why do you think most people in America earn their living by working for someone else?

Working for Yourself

Self-employed people fall into two broad groups. There are those who are self-employed because of the nature of their work. Writing, singing, painting, dentistry, are all examples of occupations that lend themselves to self-employment. A second group of self-employed people are those who own and operate business firms. You may recall that there are about 10 million single proprietorships in America, most of them small businesses. They sell a wide variety of goods and services in almost all industries. In your community, businesses such as drugstores, laundries, and car dealers are owned and operated by self-employed people. Some of these businesses are one-person businesses that provide a service of some kind. Barbers, beauticians, plumbers, electricians, insurance agents, and lawyers are all common examples. These people have chosen to be self-employed because of the advantages self-employment offers.

Name some business firms in your neighborhood that are run by self-employed persons.

Advantages One of the advantages of being self-employed is that the profit the business makes belongs to the owner. If the self-employed person is successful in business, he or she has the chance to earn a great deal of money and even become wealthy. The profit earned by a self-employed person is the reward for his or her effort, ability, and creativity. Thus, a second advantage of being self-employed is that a person's talents and abilities have a direct

Individuals who work for themselves can be directly rewarded for their efforts. (Maria Karras)

effect on his or her earnings. People who have outstanding abilities or talents often find they can earn far more through self-employment than they can through working as an employee. A third advantage of being self-employed is that a person can control both the number of hours worked and the hours of work. While not all self-employed people are completely free to choose whatever hours they want to work, most of them have more control over this area than do the people who work for salaries or wages.

What are some advantages, other than the ones listed above, to being self-employed?

Disadvantages   As with most things in life, being self-employed is not without problems. First, being one's own boss places the responsibility for success squarely on that individual's shoulders.

Abilities and talents will be put to the test. Everyone has some weaknesses and is less capable in some things than in others. These weaknesses will affect how successful a self-employed person is. Second, though the self-employed can earn substantial profits with a successful business, losses can force them out of business and, in some instances, place them in debt. A third disadvantage concerns income security. Self-employed people have no guaranteed annual wage. Their earnings can vary greatly from year to year, depending on business conditions. Salaried people, on the other hand, can generally count on continued earnings from year to year. In addition, salaried people often enjoy fringe benefits that mean greater peace of mind. *Fringe benefits* are all of the benefits provided for employees in addition to wages and salaries. One of these benefits may be insurance paid for by the employer that continues the employee's salary in the event of sickness or accident. Many self-employed people do not have such protection, unless they put money aside themselves.

What are some other disadvantages to being self-employed?

Working for Someone Else

Most people are content to work as employees because it provides them with enough income to live comfortably. While it may not hold out the opportunity to build a great fortune, working for someone else does offer many advantages.

Advantages   First, an employee does not usually bear all the responsibility for managing a business firm. An employee is usually responsible for only a portion of the overall activities of the business firm. A second advantage is that the employee usually works on a salary basis. This means the person can be relatively certain of the amount of income that will be earned during a certain period of time. Third, an employee does not have to take economic risks. If the business firm is not successful, the employee may lose the job and be forced to seek another source of income. But usually this would be the only personal loss suffered by the individual.

Many business firms provide a variety of recreational activities for their employees. (Stock, Boston)

Disadvantages   An employee does not exercise complete control over his or her activities. In short, the employed person is not the boss. The employed individual is told what to do, at least in part, by someone else. A second disadvantage, somewhat related to the first, is that the employed person usually must work during specified times. Hours of work are normally quite rigidly set. Employees working in assembly line jobs, in stores, and in offices, for example, have little or nothing to say about their hours. A third disadvantage is that income may not be directly related to one's performance on the job. Every person doing a certain type of job may be paid at the same rate no matter how productive each person is. In other words, one person may work very hard and accomplish much more than other employees. That person would, however, still earn the same amount of income as another person employed in the same type of job but contributing much less.

WHY ARE SO FEW PEOPLE SELF-EMPLOYED?

Only about 10 percent of the American labor force is self-employed. The advantages and disadvantages discussed above should provide some clues as to why there are more employees than self-employed. Perhaps the major reason is that only some occupations—for example, small businesses—lend themselves to self-employment. However, there are other reasons.

Lack of Needed Personal Qualities

Many people lack the necessary personal qualities for self-employment. Self-employed persons must possess energy, take the initiative, and have a real desire to succeed. They must have self-discipline and the ability to organize themselves. In order to get along well with customers, they must be even-tempered and possess good common sense. A person who becomes easily rattled and worried by setbacks is not suited for self-employment. The self-employed must be able to accept the responsibility and the pressure that accompany independence.

Lack of Financial Resources

Starting a business requires money capital. But most people simply do not have enough. Therefore, if they want to be self-employed, they have to either borrow the money or go into partnership. Frequently, however, banks and other lending agencies are reluctant to extend credit. And because one of the main advantages of self-employment is independence, many people are unwilling to risk the loss of independence by taking on a partner.

Why might people who lend money to someone starting a business want a share in the ownership of the business in addition to interest on the loan?

Lack of Managerial Ability

Another major problem faced by the self-employed is the lack of managerial ability. Lack of managerial skills is the most frequently given reason for the failure of small business firms. In fact, a person may have all the talent needed to produce a good or service. Yet he or she may lack the skills necessary to manage the business firm successfully. Sometimes the self-employed person has the managerial skills but is too pressed with day-to-day problems to use them properly. To solve this problem, managerial help can be hired. But this may not be a good solution to the owner. Or the income of the business firm may not be large enough to pay for expensive expert help.

What kinds of skills would be considered part of the overall managerial skills needed to run a business firm?

SELECTING A CAREER

Once you are aware of your abilities, aptitudes, interests, and values, you are in a better position to decide on a career. For instance, if you like to work alone, work outdoors, have a high physical aptitude, and are interested in things that help other people, you might decide to pursue one type of career. However, if you like to work with others, work indoors, have a high mental aptitude, and wish to become famous, then obviously a different type of career should be considered.

As you prepare to select your career, consider this warning: Do not be *too* rigid in pursuing your career choice. You may overlook other equally good or better opportunities. And you may so narrow your training and outside interests that you may be unable to take advantage of other opportunities.

After analyzing yourself, what kinds of careers do you think you should study? How did you come to this conclusion?

Learning Activities

Increasing Your Business Vocabulary

You should become familiar with each of the terms shown below. On a sheet of paper write the numbers 1 through 12. Then write alongside each number the term that best matches each of the numbered definitions.

ability / aptitude / basic skills / communication skill / computational skill / employee / fringe benefits / interests / manual dexterity / self-employed / values / compatibility

1. Attitudes that individuals have regarding the importance of objects, activities, or other things.

2. Those skills that one uses to gain other skills.

3. The ability to work well with numbers.

4. Earning an income directly from one's own business, trade, or profession rather than at a specified salary or wage from an employer.

5. A natural or potential capacity for learning.

6. A quickness and skill in using one's hands.

7. The ability to read, write, listen, and speak effectively.

8. Benefits provided for employees in addition to wages and salaries.

9. A natural or acquired skill or talent.

10. The ability to work with and get along with other people.

11. Those types of activities that concern people so much that they pay special attention to them.

12. A person who earns income by working for someone else.

Understanding Business

1. List some of the personal factors that should be considered in career selection.

2. How are abilities gained?

3. List four basic skills discussed in this chapter.

4. What do many studies find is the major reason for people losing their jobs?

5. Give several examples of some kinds of skills and training that may make you better qualified for employment.

6. What are two different kinds of aptitudes?

7. What is one of the most commonly used interest inventories? List the ten basic interest areas it measures.

8. What questions should you ask yourself to learn more about your values?

9. List three advantages and three disadvantages of working for yourself.

10. List three advantages and three disadvantages of working for someone else.

Business Problems and Projects

1. On the facing page are listed the abilities that everyone has in varying degrees. For each of these abilities, suggest a job that would require a high degree of the ability.

a. Academic learning ability

b. Ear for music

c. Ability to recognize and match various forms

d. Manual dexterity

e. Ability to comprehend three-dimensional forms

f. Memory

g. Coordination of hands and eyes

h. Color discrimination

i. Ability to understand and use words

j. Ability to solve problems and use figures

2. On a form similar to the one shown below, indicate the amount of physical and mental skill that you think is required for each of the ten jobs listed. Use the terms *little, some,* and *much* to describe the level of skill.

Job	Physical Ability Needed	Mental Ability Needed
Accountant		
Automobile mechanic		
Cashier		
Cosmetologist		
Nurse		
Plumber		
Secretary		
Surgeon		
Teacher		
Truck driver		

Chapter 44

Preparing for a Career

Objectives

After completing your study of this chapter, you will be able to do the following:

1. Identify sources of career information.

2. Describe how the various educational programs can help one prepare for a career.

3. Describe how the various work experience programs can help one prepare for a career.

4. Explain the differences among apprenticeship, on-the-job training, and cooperative vocational training programs.

By now you should have some notion of what kinds of careers interest you. Or, at least, you should have strong feelings against certain careers. Most likely, though, you may feel that you need more information about careers in general. You may want a better understanding of the requirements and possibilities of specific careers. And you may want to know how to prepare for one.

This chapter identifies sources of career information that are readily available to you in your school, in your community, or elsewhere. It also describes how educational programs can prepare you for a career. And, finally, it examines some of the programs that can provide you with valuable work experience.

SOURCES OF CAREER INFORMATION

You can get career information almost everywhere. Your family and friends, for example, may be useful sources. Just by listening to their telling of work experiences, you may be able to determine whether or not their careers appeal to you. Remember, however, that what they want from life may be quite different from what you want. Moreover, the situations they describe may not be typical. Personal likes and dislikes often flavor the description. It is wise to compare these sources with other sources, including schools, business and industry, labor unions, and government.

Schools

One of the best places to begin your search for career information is your school. The school library, for example, usually has a number of books on specific jobs. If it does not, your school librarian should be able to direct you to books and magazines on business, agriculture, home economics and other career fields.

Another excellent source of career information is the school teaching staff. Teachers usually have backgrounds in many different occupational areas. If, for instance, you are interested in a career in science, visit one of the science teachers. If you are interested in industry, an industrial education teacher could help you. And, of course, teachers can also tell you about teaching and other careers related to education.

Many of the courses offered in your school also provide career information. A class in office procedures will help you explore job

Your school counselor is an excellent source of career information.
(Betty Medsger)

opportunities in the business office. A chemistry or biology course will make you aware of science careers.

Finally, consult your school counselor. Your guidance office is one of the chief sources of career information. It has a wealth of up-to-date materials on job descriptions and opportunities. Moreover, your counselor has a variety of tests that can be used to help determine your aptitudes and interests. Using the data obtained from these tests, your counselor can advise you on career choices.

Make a list of teachers in different departments in your school and then indicate careers about which each might have specific information.

Business and Industry

If you are interested in a career in business and industry, the best source of information is the particular business or industry that appeals to you. Therefore, get in contact with it somehow. If a firm

A visit to a local business firm may help you determine a career choice.
(Aerospace Corporation)

is located near you, go directly to its personnel office. Personnel workers there can tell you what skills are needed and whether job openings exist in that field. If a firm is not located near you, write it. Or write to a related trade association. For instance, the Insurance Information Institute can tell you about careers in insurance. The American Bankers Association has information about careers in banking. And many major companies, such as the General Motors Corporation, have information about a variety of careers.

Labor Unions

Another source of career information is labor unions. Many of these publish material on job opportunities within their own trades. And some actively assist in the training of their members. If a certain trade interests you, check to see if there is a local union office for that trade near you. Or write directly to the union's national headquarters. Trade union members are also good sources of information. A carpenter, for instance, could tell you how to get started in carpentry.

State Employment Services

Information about the availability of jobs and the qualifications needed to fill them can be provided by a state employment service. Career counselors in these offices will help you find jobs that are best suited to your abilities and interests. These offices generally also have printed materials about careers that you can obtain for the asking.

Federal Government

The U.S. government employs more people than any other single employer. Therefore, it should not be overlooked as a source of career information. Remember that the federal government offers employment in all seven major job clusters. Whatever your career interest, the federal government probably has jobs in that field. In addition, through the Small Business Administration and other agencies, the government can also provide advice to those who wish to be self-employed.

The U.S. Department of Labor provides a variety of books and pamphlets on careers. Of particular importance is the *Occupational Outlook Handbook*. This book contains information about the work activities, qualifications and training needs, chances for promotion, working conditions, and job outlook for over 700 occupations. It also tells where you can find further information about any occupation that interests you. Copies of the book are usually available in your school guidance office or library.

The federal government employs several million people. List as many different jobs as you can think about that are available in government.

EDUCATION AS CAREER PREPARATION

Education is a very important key to getting and keeping a job. Regardless of what kind of job you apply for, most employers want to know what kind of education you have. The amount of school ing is *not* always the most important thing. What is important is what you learned while you were in school. You should know, then, the type of education that will best prepare you for the kind of career you want.

High School

As preparation for almost any kind of job, a high school education is desirable. In fact, many employers require it for all jobs. A high school diploma indicates several things about you to a prospective employer. It indicates that you have acquired basic skills in reading, writing, and arithmetic. And it indicates that you have the character and motivation necessary to complete the program.

High school prepares students for careers in two ways. It offers courses that will be required of them if they elect to pursue further education. And it offers courses that provide specific job training in such vocational areas as agriculture, business education, distributive education, health education, home economics, and industrial education. A student who completes a course in automotive repair, for example, may be fully prepared to take a job as an auto mechanic upon graduation from high school.

Make a list of jobs for which only a high school education is required. Indicate why a high school education is needed for each of the jobs on your list.

Colleges and Universities

Some of you may choose careers that require a college or university education. Careers that usually require college preparation include accounting, teaching, dentistry, medicine, business management, and publishing. Certain colleges and universities have better programs for a specific profession than others. Therefore, if you are interested in a profession, ask your school counselor which college is best for your career interest.

Other Schools

Many careers do not require a college education. However, they do require special training beyond high school. Among the schools

Specialized job training is available from proprietary schools.

that do offer this type of training are vocational-technical schools, community colleges, and proprietary schools. Vocational-technical schools offer specialized training for students preparing to enter the labor market in specific jobs. This training includes courses in such fields as auto mechanics, metal work, health occupations, and electronics. Community colleges—which, like vocational-technical schools, are two-year schools—provide general education courses in addition to vocational courses. In some cases, community college students can transfer to four-year colleges, if they so desire. *Proprietary schools* are privately owned trade or vocational schools organized to make a profit. They include private business schools, barber colleges, beauty schools, and aviation schools.

Continuing Education
Many young people take full-time jobs before or just after completing high school. But for some, their education does not end with high school. Employers often consider continuing education so important that they will pay for its cost. Some employers will increase an employee's salary if he or she gets additional education.

Continuing education takes many forms and is available in many places. It may be as simple as a tax accountant studying a tax manual at home. Or it may be more formal, such as attending a college or university at night to complete a degree. It may be studying American history or shorthand. Or it may be a short course in self-defense or speed-reading. There are educational programs to meet almost everyone's needs. Universities, colleges, high schools, private schools, home study programs, television educational programs—all of these offer continuing education courses.

Is anyone you know now taking a course that would fall into the category of continuing education? If so, what type of a course? Where is it offered?

WORK EXPERIENCE AS CAREER PREPARATION

In addition to knowing what kind of an educational background you have, most employers also want to know whether or not you have actual work experience. Of course, you can gain work experience if you finish your educational program and then go to work full time. However, there are several other ways in which you can obtain it. Among them are apprenticeship programs, on-the-job training, and cooperative vocational education programs.

Apprenticeship Programs

An *apprentice* is a person bound by a legal agreement to work for another for a certain period of time in return for instruction in a craft or trade. The legal agreement is a written contract between the apprentice and the employer. Labor unions, businesses, government, and schools work together in conducting apprenticeship programs. A committee composed of members from labor and management supervises the program. It tests and selects each apprentice and then supervises and evaluates his or her work. After the apprenticeship program is completed the committee certifies the apprentice as a journeyman. A *journeyman* is a qualified worker who has fully served apprenticeship in a trade or craft.

There are about 350 apprenticeship trades in the United States. They include plumbing, bricklaying, printing, and film editing.

On-the-Job Training

Unlike apprenticeship programs, on-the-job training programs require no written agreement between the employer and employee. They generally do not require tests for entry into the program. Nor is there a formal committee to oversee training. On-the-job training programs are often run by the employer in a rather informal way. Because the worker learns by performing specific job tasks, these programs are particularly useful for certain types of training. Office clerical jobs and personal selling jobs are often taught by on-the-job training methods.

Cooperative Vocational Education Programs

An excellent way to gain education and work experience at the same time is through a cooperative vocational education program. *Cooperative vocational education programs* are programs in which students alternate study in school with a job in a field related to their school study. Your school may have a different name for these programs. They may be called work experience, cooperative education, or work study.

In these programs, you study about a job in the classroom and then spend part of the day on the job. For example, you might study retailing in class and then work part of the day in a boutique. While on the job, you are supervised by both your employer and by your teacher. The student is usually paid by the employer for working. Therefore, not only do you gain practical work experience, but you also are able to earn some money. Many schools have programs like these in office education, trade and industrial education, distributive education, and other vocational areas.

Learning Activities

Increasing Your Business Vocabulary

You should become familiar with each of the terms shown below. On a sheet of paper write the numbers 1 through 6. Then write alongside each number the term that best matches each of the numbered definitions.

apprentice / cooperative vocational education program / job cluster / journeyman / proprietary schools / trade associations

1. An organization of business firms with related interests.
2. A qualified worker who has fully served as an apprentice in a trade or craft.
3. Privately owned, profit-making, trade or vocational schools.
4. Vocational education programs in which students alternate study in school with jobs in a vocational field.
5. A person bound by a legal agreement to work for another for a certain period of time in return for instruction in a craft or trade.
6. All the jobs in a general field of work.

Understanding Business

1. Briefly describe the various sources of career information available in your school.
2. List several of the ways that you can get information about careers in business.

3. How do many labor unions provide information on the trades they represent?

4. List some of the services that state employment service offices have available.

5. Why do most employers prefer that their employees have a high school education?

6. How do community colleges differ from vocational technical schools?

7. Why might an individual choose to enroll in a proprietary school?

8. Who conducts apprenticeship programs?

9. Explain how on-the-job training programs differ from apprenticeship training programs.

10. What are the two major benefits of cooperative vocational education programs?

Business Problems and Projects

1. For each of the jobs listed below, give five sources of career information. Wherever possible, use sources *not* specifically mentioned in the text.

   a. Professional accountant   d. Court reporter

   b. Farmer   e. Health care

   c. Electronics

2. Many employers require work experience before they will employ a person. Study the want ads section of your local newspaper. Find at least five ads that call for work experience. Give the amount and type of work experience required.

Chapter 45

Finding and Keeping a Job

 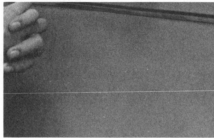 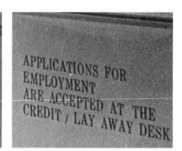

Objectives

After completing your study of this chapter, you will be able to do the following:

1. Name sources of information about employment opportunities.

2. Describe the kinds of information that application letters and data sheets should contain.

3. Identify the points to remember when interviewing for a job.

4. Describe the characteristics employers look for in their employees.

As you learned earlier, only about ten percent of the labor force is self-employed. Chances are, then, that you—like most other people—will be working for someone else. But how do you go about this? Where should you look for job openings? How do you apply for a job once you find one that interests you? Is there a way to prepare for the job interview? And, equally important, how can you work at keeping a job once you have been hired? This chapter presents some answers to these questions that should make your job search easier and more rewarding.

SOURCES OF INFORMATION

Many job seekers mistakenly limit their job search to the want-ad columns of local newspapers. While this is an excellent source, other equally good sources are available. In not investigating these other sources, the job seeker may be overlooking a number of potential opportunities.

Newspaper Advertising

For most purposes, newspaper advertisements are the primary source of job information. Indeed, even if you are not actively seeking a job, the help-wanted section is a good place to learn what kinds of employment opportunities are available, what kinds of qualifications are required for specific positions, and what salaries are being offered. But don't be misled by the wording of the ads. For example, an ad that states the salary as "to $750" is only indicating the maximum salary for the job. Upon investigating, you may find that the starting salary is actually only $350. Also, learn to understand the language that advertisers use. For example, the term "Skls req" in an ad for a secretarial position usually means that the applicant will be expected to demonstrate the necessary typing, shorthand, filing, and communication skills. If you do not have these skills, it probably is not worth either your or the advertiser's time to answer the ad. You should also learn to distinguish between those ads that are genuinely offering employment and those that are really trying to sell you training.

If you are seeking work, make a list of all ads in which you are interested and for which you are qualified. Then set out to follow up on them. Again, carefully follow the wording of each ad. If it

State employment offices offer
free employment services.
(Michael D. Sullivan)

specifies that telephone inquiries are not desired, do not call. If it
says that applications will be taken only at certain times, make
sure that you meet those time requirements.

Employment Agencies

An employment agency is a firm that specializes in finding
employment for people looking for jobs. In a sense, it is a clearing
house for jobs. Businesses supply the agency with their personnel
needs, and the agency tries to match these needs with the
qualifications of its list of job seekers.

There are basically two types of employment agencies—public
and private. Public employment agencies are run and paid for by
the government. Your state employment service office, which
probably has offices in a number of cities throughout your state, is

a public employment agency. In addition to the services described in Chapter 43, state employment offices serve as free placement agencies.

If you are looking for employment, go to the state employment service office nearest you and fill out an application form. An employment counselor will interview you to determine your interests and qualifications. The counselor may even ask you to take a series of placement tests. If you meet the requested qualifications, you are sent to the employer for an interview. On the basis of the interview, the employer will decide whether or not to hire you.

Private employment agencies are owned and operated by people who are in business to make a profit. These agencies are run like any other business, and charge for their services. This charge, called an *employment fee,* is a percentage of your first month's salary. The fee may be paid by the employee, the employer, or both. Private employment agencies often specialize in certain job areas. For instance, some agencies place only office employees, while others place only industrial workers. Private agencies generally will not accept your application unless they are quite sure they can place you. Because they often know about jobs that are not listed with the state employment service, they may be a good source of employment opportunities.

Government Agencies

City, county, and state government agencies hire a large number of employees in many fields. Working conditions are quite good, and retirement and other benefits are usually as good as those for employees in private industry. You can find out more about working for one of these agencies by visiting your local city hall, court house, or state employment service office. Most states and many large cities have civil service commissions.

List some of the kinds of jobs that city, county, and state government agencies might have.

A *civil service commission* is a commission (city, state, or federal) that sets qualifications for and administers civil service exams for government jobs. *Civil service exams* are tests admin-

istered to determine if applicants qualify for government employment. If you are interested in working in a government position,
either at the city, state, or federal level, contact a civil service office
for more information.

Personnel Departments

Many large businesses have personnel departments that hire,
train, and handle all personnel within the company. These departments maintain job descriptions for each job. *Job descriptions* are
guidelines that give the duties, skills, and educational requirements for positions within a business firm.

When there are job openings, the personnel department
generally uses newspaper ads and employment agencies to get
applicants to fill vacant positions. However, jobs are sometimes
found by going directly to a company's personnel office. This is
called a *walk-in,* and it is a method you can try. Don't go to just
any firm, however. Make certain that you know something about
the company. What does it make? Would you like to work there?
Do they offer jobs that would suit your interests and abilities? If
the answer to these questions is yes, then visit the company
personnel office.

What are some reasons why you would want to know something
about a company before applying for a job with it?

Personal Contacts

Another source of job opportunities is personal contacts. Often
your friends, family, relatives, and teachers know about job
openings. In fact, many employers regularly consider their current
employees as excellent sources of new employees. In seeking a job
opening, check with your friends and relatives to find out if their
employer is looking for help. Be sure that anyone who helps you
knows your abilities and qualifications.

Check with your parents and your working friends to see how
many learned of their present jobs through a personal contact.

LETTER OF APPLICATION

Many positions may be secured by going directly to a personnel office or an employment agency. Often when applying for a job, you may have to write a letter of application. A *letter of application* is a letter (usually typewritten) from an individual stating an interest in a particular position in a business firm. Application letters may be needed when answering a newspaper ad or applying for a position out of town. Some employers ask applicants to write a letter of application just to see how well they can write and how well they use the English language. Regardless of why you write a letter of application, it is one of the most important letters you will write.

A letter of application is a form of sales letter. The product you are selling is you. The letter should convince the employer that the business firm needs you. Here are some suggestions that will help you write the kind of letter that employers like to receive from job applicants.

1. If at all possible, your letter should be typewritten on plain 8½ × 11 inch paper. If you cannot have it typed, write it in ink. Remember, this letter is your "foot in the door," and will determine whether you are called for an interview.

2. In the first paragraph, indicate exactly why you are writing. For example, you might say "Your advertisement in this morning's *Journal Star* for a clerk-trainee in the credit department was of great interest to me. Please consider me as an applicant for the position." In this way you come directly to the point and leave no doubt why you are writing. This is sometimes called the contact paragraph because it explains why you are writing.

3. In the second paragraph, indicate why you think you are qualified for the position. Some people enclose a personal data sheet with a letter of application. A *personal data sheet* is a listing of personal information, education, work experience, and references. If you do not enclose a personal data sheet, you should list such things as age, education, work experience, and so forth, in the second paragraph. If you do enclose a personal data sheet, your second paragraph should

9627 West Burnett Street
Omaha, NE 68101
May 20, 19--

Brooks and Browning, Inc.
Personnel Director
1934 Cheyenne Plaza
Omaha, NE 68131

Gentlemen:

Ms. Jean Alexander, who works in your Accounting Department, has
told me that you have an opening for an accounting clerk. Please
consider my application for that position.

In December I completed an accounting program at Metropolitan
Community College. My courses included accounting, management,
finance, and office management. As a student at Fairmont High
School I completed courses in typing, accounting, and clerical
practice. I was a member of our high school business club, serving
as president during my senior year. A personal data sheet giving a
complete picture of my qualifications is attached for your information.

Ms. Alexander told me about the qualifications needed for the
position that is open. I would like to explain to you personally
how I meet these qualifications. Please call me at your convenience so that we can arrange an appointment. My home phone number
is 469-2748.

Yours truly,

Kris Butler

Kris Butler (Ms.)

Enclosure

A letter of application

mention other information that highlights your special qualifications for the job. These things might include special
classes you have taken, clubs in which you have been involved,
and special honors you have earned.

4. The last paragraph should be the action paragraph. It should
   give the employer a way to react. For instance, it might say
   "Please call me at your convenience for a personal interview,"
   or "Please call me so that I can explain to you personally why
   I feel I am qualified to work for you."

5. Make a rough draft of your letter and then check it over very
   carefully for correct spelling and grammar. Ask someone else
   to read it to make sure it makes sense to them. Then type or
   write it for mailing. If it is typed, be sure to proofread it
   carefully for typing errors.

PERSONAL DATA SHEET

The purpose of a personal data sheet is to provide the reader with an easily read clear summary of your experience, training, and possible qualifications. Accordingly, the data sheet should be well thought out and carefully organized. It should not include information that has been presented in the application. But it should contain these four sections: personal information, education, experience, and references.

In the personal information section, you should list your address, phone, age, height, weight, health, and marital status. In

```
                        Personal Data Sheet
                           Kris Butler

     Personal

     Address:          9627 West Burnett Street
                       Omaha, NE 68101

     Phone:            (402) 469-2748

     Age:              21

     Height:           5'3"

     Weight:           110 lbs.

     Health:           Excellent

     Marital Status:   Single


     Education

          Graduate of Fairmont High School, Omaha, Nebraska, (1978)

          Graduate of Metropolitan Community College, Accounting Program,
          (1980)


     Work Experience

          Car hop for Burger Meal for two summers while attending
          high school (summers of 1976 and 1977).

          Accounting clerk (part-time) for two years with Parker and
          Ervine, Inc. (1978-1979).

     References (with permission)

          Mrs. Richard Swanson          Mr. Gordon Ervine
          Burger Meal                   Parker and Ervine, Inc.
          8440 West Burnett Street      4624 North 60th Street
          Omaha, NE 68137               Omaha, NE 68141

                       Ms. Joan Felson
                       Accounting Instructor
                       Metropolitan Community College
                       Omaha, NE 68135
```

A personal data sheet.

the education section, you should list all training that may be relevant to the job for which you are applying, as well as general educational information. For example, if you are applying for a job as a general clerk in a photographic supply house and have taken correspondence courses in photography, it would be useful to list these courses.

If you have had very little work experience, you should list all of it. As you gain additional work experience, you should list only that which makes you more qualified for the position for which you are applying.

The references section of your data sheet is very important. A *reference* is a person who can be contacted for information regarding you. Three references are usually enough but select the ones who will be most beneficial to you. If you have work experience, make sure to list former employers. You might also choose to list those teachers who are aware of your special qualifications. It is a good idea to get permission from those listed before including them as references. Be sure to provide complete addresses of each reference and the phone number, if known.

What are some reasons why references are so important on a data sheet? Why would you want to get permission from a person before using his or her name as a reference?

In addition to the four basic sections, you may want to include information on hobbies, employment objective, and military experience—anything you think will help you get the job. Once you have written a data sheet, you should keep a copy of it. Then, if you ever need to seek employment in the future, you can update the data and use it again.

THE JOB INTERVIEW

An application letter and a well-written personal data sheet get you off to a good start. If effective, they will result in an interview. But as most employers point out, it is the personal interview that often determines who gets the job.

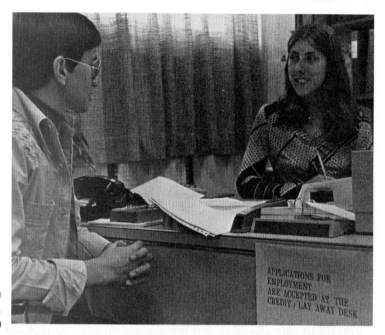

The personal interview often determines who gets the job.
(Robbins/Stockmarket, Los Angeles)

Selling yourself in the job interview is very important. Good sales persons prepare before they try to make a sale. They know their product and they know their customer. You should also prepare before going to an interview, and these points should be kept in mind:

1. Be neatly groomed and properly dressed. Remember, if you want a job you may have to conform to someone else's grooming standards.

2. Learn as much about the prospective employer as possible.

3. Put together any papers that you should take with you to the interview. These might include school transcripts, military discharge papers, social security card, and drivers license.

4. Have facts about your education, experience, training, and so forth, at your fingertips.

5. Know what kind of job you are looking for and the salary range that you expect.

6. Be on time or a few minutes early, and come alone.

7. If offered a position, ask what your duties will include and what salary you are to receive.

8. Thank the prospective employer for the interview, whether or not you get the job.

9. Be completely honest in the interview as well as in your application letter and personal data sheet.

Give some reasons why honesty is so important when applying for a job.

JOB APPLICATION FORMS

Job application forms are required for most positions. You may be asked to complete this form when you arrive for your interview, before you go for the interview, or after the interview. In any case, you should fill out the form completely and accurately. If some questions are not applicable, draw a line through them or print the letters N/A (not applicable) to show you did not forget that part. Either print neatly in ink or use a typewriter. Make sure to sign the form if told to do so.

SUCCEEDING ON THE JOB

Getting a job is an important first step in career development. What you do after getting a job, however, will determine your future success. There are a number of positive characteristics employers look for in their employees. If you have these things, you should have no trouble keeping a job. Chief among these are attitude, loyalty, dependability, willingness to learn and change, honesty, and initiation.

Attitude is your feeling toward an object, person, job, or other thing that causes you to behave in a certain manner. A person with a positive attitude toward a job willingly accepts responsibility, respects the opinion of others, tries to get along, and doesn't make excuses.

Loyalty is being faithful to a person, ideal, or custom. If you can't say something good about your employer, then perhaps you should look for another job. You may not like everything your employer does, but you should not complain to people outside the company. Part of what you are being paid for is loyalty.

The worker who is *dependable* is willing and able to accomplish assigned tasks to meet deadlines set by others. You are expected to be at work and finish assigned duties on time. If you must be absent or late, be sure to inform your supervisor. Whatever you do, do not make a habit of arriving late each day.

Your goal when employed should be to learn and grow on the job. Be willing to study on your own time if necessary. Develop the ability to accept criticism, for with criticism comes new learning. The more you learn and the more you are willing to change, the more likely are the chances that you will be promoted to jobs of greater responsibility by your employer.

Being *honest* is being truthful and trustworthy; not lying, cheating, stealing, or taking unfair advantage. You can be dishonest in a number of ways. Showing a lack of loyalty is a form of

How you succeed on a job depends on you. (Steelcase)

dishonesty. Taking care of personal business on company time is another form of dishonesty. To your employer time is money. Each time you misuse company time, you are wasting company money. Finally, when you use company supplies and equipment for personal use, you are stealing from your employer. Dishonesty is one of the surest ways of losing a job.

A major criticism from employers is that employees have to be told what to do all the time. When you finish all your assigned duties, take a look around you to see what needs to be done. Don't wait for someone to tell you what to do next. In this way you are showing initiative. *Initiative* is the ability to begin or to follow through with a plan or task without constant supervision. It is one of the characteristics held in high regard by an employer. An employee who demonstrates initiative on the job is often rewarded by promotion or an increase in salary.

The six items listed above are some of the most important qualities expected of employees. What are some other qualities which you think would help you to be successful on the job?

Two other characteristics—neatness and speech—are also highly sought by many employers. Neatness, in personal appearance, in your own work, and in the way you maintain your work area, is a trait that can be developed and improved upon with a small amount of effort. And while it may be difficult to change the way your voice sounds, you can change the way you say things. Speak clearly and avoid mumbling. Use appropriate grammar, and try to add a friendly tone to your voice.

Why do you suppose that tone of voice and speaking clearly are so important when speaking on the telephone?

Some personal characteristics are more important than others in certain jobs. For instance, if your speech is poor, you probably would not be good in retail sales. If you are a very shy person, you should seek employment where you do not have to meet a lot of new people. Ideally, you should try to find a job that makes maximum use of your desirable personal characteristics and minimal use of your undesirable characteristics.

MOBILITY

Much of this chapter has been devoted to keeping a job once you've found it. But what if you want to advance in your work? What if you don't like the career you have chosen and need more education and training to make a change? Or what if your job is phased out because of technological advances?

To be prepared to meet the challenge of occupational change, people in today's labor force must have mobility. *Mobility* is the ability to move from one place or situation to another. Without mobility, job opportunities or advancement may be limited. Job mobility, however, is more than just the ability to move from one place to another. It may also mean moving from one firm to another or from one job level to another. Job mobility may even mean changing careers altogether.

Why is job mobility so important to one's career? First, the career for which you are best qualified may require you to relocate. For example, a person might desire to become a computer programmer. That career choice may mean leaving one's hometown and moving to a larger town or city. Second, the higher the level of employment, the greater the need for job mobility. For example, a chemical engineer needs more mobility than a factory worker, because this specialty may lead one anywhere in the world. Third, many large corporations promote from within. If one is unwilling to move from one city to another, he or she may not be promoted. Finally, if there are no jobs in a certain location, the choice may be between changing location or becoming unemployed.

List three occupations for which mobility is essential.

Learning Activities

Increasing Your Business Vocabulary

You should become familiar with each of the terms shown below. On a sheet of paper write the numbers 1 through 9. Then write alongside each number the term that best matches each of the numbered definitions.

civil service commission / civil service examinations / employment agency / employment fee / job description / job mobility / letter of application / personal data sheet / reference

1. A letter (usually typewritten) from an individual stating an interest in a particular position in a business firm.

2. A listing of personal information, education, work experience, and references.

3. A percentage of your first month's salary paid to a private employment agency for job placement services.

4. The name of a person who can be contacted for information regarding you.

5. A commission (city, state or federal) that sets qualifications for and administers civil service exams for government jobs.

6. Test administered to determine if applicants qualify for government employment.

7. Guidelines that give the duties, skills, and educational requirements for positions within a business firm.

8. A firm that finds employment for people looking for jobs.

9. The ability to move from one place to another.

Understanding Business

1. What types of information can you learn from the help-wanted section of a newspaper?

2. What is the major difference between a public employment agency and a private employment agency?

3. What steps should you take if you are interested in getting a job with the government?

4. List the ways that a personnel department in a large firm gets applicants to fill vacant positions.

5. List several personal contacts one might use to find out about job openings.

6. Why do some employers ask for a letter of application?

7. List the four basic sections of the personal data sheet.

8. List the points one should keep in mind when interviewing for a job.

9. List the positive characteristics employers look for in their employees.

10. Why is job mobility important to one's career?

Business Problems and Projects

1. The more education a person has, the more that person is likely to earn in a lifetime. Study the chart shown below and then answer the questions that follow it.

PERCENT OF CIVILIAN LABOR FORCE (AGE 25–34) WITH 4 YEARS OF HIGH SCHOOL OR MORE

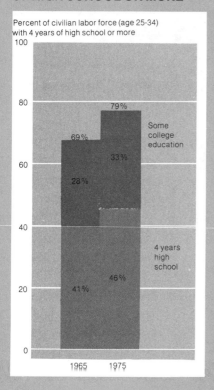

Percent of civilian labor force (age 25-34) with 4 years of high school or more

Source: U.S. Department of Labor

a.   What percentage of the civilian labor force between the ages of 25 and 34 had four years of high school or more in 1965? In 1975?

b.   What was the percent of increase for those with four years of high school between 1965 and 1975?

c.   If twelve million members of the labor force were in this age group in 1975, how many of them had four years of high school?

2.   Using a format similar to the one shown in the text, prepare an up-to-date personal data sheet. Provide at least three personal references.

Chapter 46

Labor Unions and Collective Bargaining

Objectives

After completing your study of this chapter, you will be able to do the following:

1. State the general purpose of all labor unions.

2. List some reasons why labor unions have formed and why workers have joined labor unions.

3. Describe the general organization and status of today's labor unions.

4. Name the purposes of collective bargaining.

5. Identify and discuss the major issues that are usually settled through the collective bargaining process.

Labor unions have existed in the United States since the early 1790s. In those days, shoemakers, carpenters, printers, and other skilled craftsmen formed small but fairly permanent unions. A *labor union* is an organization of employees formed and operated to promote and protect the welfare, interest, and rights of the members. Today, there are over 23 million labor union members in the United States. But the growth of labor unions has not been without problems. Up to the mid-1800s, labor unions and union activities were declared illegal by the courts. It was ruled that joining together for the purpose of improving the status of workers was a criminal conspiracy against the free market system. Later, injunctions were used to prevent strikes and other labor activities. An *injunction* is a court order banning some action because it will cause serious harm or loss to those affected by the action.

Depending on the job you take, you may be asked to join a labor union. Before making such a decision, you should have some idea about their purposes and what they can do for you. This chapter will review briefly the types of labor unions and why they have developed.

THE PURPOSES OF UNIONS

During the industrial expansion of the nineteenth and early twentieth centuries, the pace of business increased and the size of business firms grew in America. But decent working conditions and fair wages were denied to employees. Employees found that as individuals they had little power to improve their working conditions or their pay. A manufacturer could refuse a demand of any type from an individual employee. If an employee did not like the working conditions or the pay, the only choice was to quit and find another job. The unskilled employee, who could be replaced easily, was at a great disadvantage. During these years of industrial expansion, the employee was, in fact, no better off than a person living in a dictatorship.

To match the power held by management, employees formed labor unions. In numbers, employees sought greater bargaining strength. They felt that collectively they could force employers to give them what was denied them as individuals. As an organized group, the employees could ask for certain working conditions and wages or salaries. They could threaten to walk off the job if management refused to listen and did not attempt to meet their demands. Thus, employees had more power in dealing with management if they were organized and stood together as a group. One of the major purposes of labor unions now as then is to help employees deal with management on more equal terms.

Labor unions promote and protect the welfare, interests, and rights of their members. *Collective bargaining* is the process in which management and employee representatives meet and reach agreement on all types of job-related issues and concerns. Employment issues and concerns include such things as wages, working conditions, and hours. Other issues are fringe benefits and seniority rights. You will learn more about the collective bargaining process later in this chapter.

THE DEVELOPMENT OF LABOR UNIONS

Labor unions have existed in our nation for about 175 years. The earliest labor unions, such as the Philadelphia Cordwainers, organized in 1794, were local and consisted of members of a single craft. Today, some labor unions have a large number of members. They are international and include all employees in an industry regardless of the type of job they perform.

Trade Unions

The first attempts to organize employees into labor unions were directed toward craftsmen. These early unions were the forerunners of today's trade unions. A *trade union* is a labor union consisting of skilled workers who are all employed in a particular trade or profession. To make the unions more effective, the American Federation of Labor (AFL) was formed in 1886 under the leadership of Samuel Gompers. In the beginning, the AFL was interested in organizing only skilled workers. Under Gomper's leadership the AFL pursued basic economic goals for its members. The goals then were similar to those today—shorter hours, better working conditions, and higher pay.

Industrial Unions

The AFL grew to almost 4 million members by 1920. Membership then began to level off. One reason was that most leaders of the AFL refused to make attempts to organize semiskilled or unskilled workers. Some of the leaders felt that labor unions should be organized in the mass-production industries. All workers, skilled and unskilled, needed to be able to deal more equally with management.

John L. Lewis organized the United Mine Workers in the coal industry as one of the first industrial unions. An *industrial union* is a labor union consisting of all the employees in a particular plant or industry regardless of their skills or occupations. In 1938, under the leadership of Lewis, the Congress of Industrial Organizations (CIO) was established. The CIO quickly organized the large number of workers in the automobile and steel industries. In view of this success, the AFL also began organizing industrial labor unions. During the period from 1938 to 1950 the two rival labor union groups, the AFL and the CIO, had many bitter disputes.

Why do you think union leaders such as John L. Lewis felt that some labor unions should be organized as industrial unions?

AFL-CIO

In 1955, the two rival union groups merged into one organization. It was called the American Federation of Labor–Congress of Industrial Organizations (AFL-CIO). Today, the AFL-CIO is the major labor union group in the United States. It consists of local unions, national unions, and the parent federation of national unions.

Local Labor Unions   The individual employee is a member of a local labor union. If it is a trade union, the members will all be skilled workers of a particular trade. A local industrial union, on the other hand, will be made up of employees of various skills and occupations from a single large business firm. The officers of local labor unions are elected by the members. They seldom are paid for their services. Decisions of the local labor unions are made democratically by the members who vote on all issues.

What are some reasons why a person would want to become an officer in a local labor union?

___

National Labor Unions   Most labor unions in the United States are organized nationwide with affiliated local branches. If the national labor union includes locals from outside the United States, it is called an international labor union. Each national labor union has an executive board or council. The board sets policy for the labor union. The presidents of the national labor unions carry out the policy of the executive board or council. Business agents provide a link between the local labor unions and the parent national labor union. The business agents are full-time employees of the labor union. Their responsibilities are to do the following:

1. Attempt to organize new locals and gain new members for existing locals.
2. See that the contract terms are being properly met.
3. See that the national policy is being carried out by the local.
4. Ensure that dues are being collected and the proper amount forwarded to the national labor union.

Local labor unions may or may not be affiliated with a national labor union. What are some reasons why a local labor union may not want to be affiliated with a national labor union?

___

AFL-CIO Federation   Approximately 110 national and international labor unions and their local labor unions are affiliated with the AFL-CIO. Each union affiliated with the AFL-CIO determines for itself how it will deal with the employers of its members. Therefore, the AFL-CIO officials do not discuss issues directly with employers.

All AFL-CIO affiliates send delegates to the AFL-CIO national convention held once every two years. This convention is the governing body of the AFL-CIO. Officers are elected and major policy decisions are made by delegates at the convention. The president and executive council of the AFL-CIO deal with major policy decisions between conventions. In addition, a number of standing committees work on special problems such as legislation, political education, and other areas.

National and international labor unions may or may not be affiliated with the AFL-CIO. What are some reasons why a national or international labor union would want to be affiliated with the AFL-CIO?

LABOR UNIONS TODAY

There is no doubt that labor unions have affected and are affecting working conditions and wages for employees in the United States. Labor unions also affect a variety of other areas. By learning about the present status of labor unions, you may be better able to understand why labor unions and their members have played and continue to play important roles in our society.

Labor Union Membership

In the late-1970s membership in labor unions was approximately 23 million. The number of labor union members has increased steadily for the past two decades. However, the percent of non-agricultural employees who are members of labor unions has been decreasing at the same time. Labor union members today belong to about 65,000 local labor unions and about 180 national and international labor unions.

In the early 1970s about one-half of the employees in manufacturing industries were unionized. At that time, about one-fourth of the employees in the private manufacturing industries were unionized. About 91 percent—the highest of any industry—of the transportation industry employees were members of labor unions in the early 1970s. At the same time, more than 75 percent of the contract construction employees were labor union members.

As indicated above, total membership in labor unions has been increasing. However, the percentage of nonagricultural employees who are labor union members has been decreasing. What are some reasons for this decrease?

TRENDS IN LABOR UNION MEMBERSHIP

Labor union membership has been increasing at a faster pace in nonmanufacturing industries than it has in manufacturing industries. The largest increases in labor union membership in recent years have been with government employees and white-collar workers. Union growth among these workers has increased steadily

Labor unions protect the welfare, interests, and rights of their members. (Stock, Boston)

since collective bargaining was allowed for government employees in 1962. Today over one-third of all government employees are unionized; over half of all federal government workers are members of labor unions. In addition, unions have been accepted by teachers, retail clerks, and communication workers in recent years. There are still more blue-collar workers in labor unions. However, office workers and professionals have been joining the ranks of labor unions in increasing numbers. White-collar workers now make up about one-fifth of the labor union and employee association memberships. With the increase in the number of women in the labor force, the percentage of women union members has increased greatly over the same period. Recent surveys show that about one-fourth of all the unionized jobholders are women.

What are some reasons why labor union membership is growing at a faster pace among white-collar workers than it is among blue-collar workers?

THE COLLECTIVE BARGAINING PROCESS

Earlier in this chapter *collective* bargaining was defined as the process in which management and employee representatives meet and reach agreement on such job-related issues as fair pay, a fair day's work, and fair fringe benefits. Of course, both employees and employers have strong opinions on what is fair, and these opinions may differ considerably. Through collective bargaining the representatives of each faction reach a compromise, or middle-of-the-road, agreement. Generally, the bargaining process consists of three steps: the election of a bargaining agent, the negotiation of an agreement, and the ratification of that agreement.

Election of a Bargaining Agent

In companies with few employees, each employee may bargain individually for the amount of wages and benefits he or she will receive. In large companies with many employees, individual bargaining becomes harder or is impossible. On an individual basis, employees are less able to bargain as equals with management. In such cases, employees may choose collective bargaining as the best approach. The first step is for employees to decide to bargain as a group rather than as individuals.

Once this step is taken, the next step is to elect a bargaining agent. A *bargaining agent* is an elected employee group that represents employees in collective bargaining. All employees should take part in the election of the bargaining agent. An official bargaining agent must get the vote of more than 50 percent of all employees. This means 50 percent of those affected by collective bargaining, not just 50 percent of those voting. Usually the bargaining agent is associated with some labor union or employee association.

What are some reasons why an employee group must get the votes of more than 50 percent of the total employee group in order to become the bargaining agent?

Employee and Management Representatives Negotiate

Once a bargaining agent has been elected by employees, representatives are chosen by the agent to speak for the employee group. The employer must bargain only through these representatives. It is illegal for the employer to deal with members of the employee group on an individual basis.

The meetings between employee representatives and management representatives are the crucial part of the bargaining process. Employee representatives begin by presenting a list of demands relating to wages, working conditions, and other employee benefits. Then the two groups negotiate the issues. The end result is generally a compromise—both groups give some ground on their first offer.

The collective bargaining process has proven to be very effective in resolving employee-management differences. Over 95 percent of the collective bargaining contracts are signed without any work stoppage. In recent years less than one-half of 1 percent of all lost working time has been the result of work stoppages resulting from employee-management disputes. Much more work

Through collective bargaining, labor and management generally reach acceptable compromise agreements. (Michael Paynter)

time is lost in sick days and in coffee breaks than in employee-management disagreements.

Briefly describe a work stoppage resulting from employee-management disagreements that you have heard or read about (include the company, employee group, and issues involved).

Employees Ratify the Agreement

At the end of the collective bargaining session, a contract containing the terms of the agreement is drawn up. Printed copies are distributed, and the terms are explained to employees by the bargaining agent. Most times, the agent recommends approval of the contract as negotiated. But the employees themselves accept or reject the contract, with approval or disapproval decided by a majority vote.

Collective Bargaining Issues

Certain issues are almost always dealt with in collective bargaining agreements. Chief among these are those concerning the recognition and status of bargaining agents, wages, working hours and conditions, fringe benefits, and seniority.

Bargaining Agent Recognition and Status   The first part of the collective agreement names the business firm and the bargaining agent. It also states that management recognizes the employee group named as the bargaining agent for the employees. This simply means that management will deal with employees only through the bargaining agent.

Where labor unions are the bargaining agent, they negotiate, if possible, an agreement requiring employees to join the labor union. The most common method of doing this is to set up what is called a union shop. A *union shop* is an arrangement under which an employer can hire nonunion employees but requires that these employees join the union after a specified period of time or give up their jobs. The so-called *closed shop,* whereby an employer could hire only employees who were members of a union, was used prior to 1947. It was held to be illegal by the Labor-Management Relations (Taft-Hartley) Act in 1947. Another type of agreement is the *open shop,* under which an employer can hire union or nonunion employees but no employees are required to join a union in order to retain their jobs.

Under Section 14(b) of the Taft-Hartley Act, the union shop is legal *unless* prohibited by state law. Therefore, if a state passes a law prohibiting the union shop agreement, employees do not have to belong to a union to keep their job. Since 1947, nineteen states have passed such laws, often called right-to-work laws.

Right-to-work laws are state laws that make compulsory union membership and the union shop illegal. These laws have been the subject of disagreement. The labor unions oppose them because they allow nonunion employees to gain all the benefits of contract agreements gained by the union. Nonunion employees are viewed by the unions as "free riders" because they do not have to pay dues to a union. It is also claimed that such laws weaken labor

Some business people say that labor laws deny them the freedom to run their own businesses.
(Wide World Photos)

unions in general by splitting employees into members and non-members. Supporters of these laws have one basic argument. They believe all employees should have the right or freedom to decide whether or not they want to join a union. They contend that no one should be forced to join a labor union in order to have a job. Because there seems to be no easy or clear answer, this debate will probably continue for some time.

Do you oppose or support the so-called right-to-work laws? What are some reasons for your position?

Wages, Working Conditions, and Hours   The most important and most-publicized section of the employee-management contract concerns wages. Wages are usually set at an hourly rate or at a rate per piece of production. Sometimes a combination of these two approaches is used. Closely tied to the wage agreement is the agreement on working conditions and the hours of work. Most agreements today call for a 40-hour workweek and overtime pay for time worked over 8 hours per day or 40 hours each week.

A contract may include a cost-of-living escalator clause or a deferred wage increase plan. The *cost-of-living escalator clause* provides that employee wages will be automatically increased by a certain percent at certain times to keep pace with price increases. The Consumer Price Index is used to determine the percentage of increase in prices in the economy from one period to another.

The *deferred wage increase* plan provides that employee wages will be increased by a specified amount at certain times during the life of the contract. For example, a three-year contract may call for an increase of twenty cents an hour at the end of the first year and another 25 cents an hour at the end of the second year.

Cost-of-living and deferred wage increase clauses have been used effectively in many employment contracts. They have done away with the need to negotiate a new agreement each year. The trend in the major industries in recent years has been to go to three- or five-year contracts.

What are some reasons why both employees and management may favor the long-term agreements of recent years?

Fringe Benefits   The costs of employee benefits other than wages continue to increase. Remember, *fringe benefits* are all benefits provided for employees in addition to wages and salaries. Fringe benefits include paid holidays, paid vacation time, health and accident insurance, dental insurance, pension plans, supplemental unemployment benefits, and other welfare plans. The cost of fringe benefits is paid by the employer.

Give some reasons why bargaining agents have sought more fringe benefits in work contracts in recent years.

Seniority   Almost all employee bargaining groups, labor unions, and employee associations make an issue of seniority. They insist on using it as a factor in situations involving layoffs, promotions, and call back of workers. *Seniority* is the status an employee gets based on his or her length of service with an employer. In layoffs, the person with the least seniority is let go first. In promotions, the person with the most seniority is considered first. Long-term employees support the seniority system. New employees prefer to see layoffs and promotions based on all qualifications including seniority.

Grievance Procedure   The handling of grievances is generally a part of an employment contract. A *grievance* is a complaint by one side or the other that the terms of an employment agreement are not being met. Specific steps must be followed to settle such disputes, which occur frequently.

Working under a contract may be much more difficult than agreeing to its terms. In view of this, both employee and management representatives make sure that a clear and concise method of settling grievances is written into the contract. The first step is the discussion of the grievance between the shop steward and the foreman. A *shop steward* is a union member chosen by a group of employees to represent them in their dealings with management. A *foreman* is an employee selected by management to supervise a group of employees. About 95 percent of all grievances are settled at this first step of the grievance procedure.

Why do you think most grievances can be settled by the shop steward and the foreman?

Collective Bargaining Tactics

Almost all collective bargaining agreements are reached without a work stoppage of any kind. This is so partly because both sides can use the work stoppage as an ultimate threat to obtain agreement on various issues. But both employee groups and management have a number of other tactics they can use to apply pressure to the other side. Work stoppages are costly to both sides. Employees lose wages and business firms lose income. While this tactic isn't used often, the threat is always there. If one side or the other feels strongly enough about its position on an issue, the threat can become real.

A work stoppage is one of the strongest measures that labor unions can use to apply pressure. (Cliff Kallick)

Both employee groups and management attempt to win public support in their disputes. Propaganda is often used. Newspapers, leaflets, and other media emphasize one or the other side of the story. Both sides also work hard to get state and federal laws passed that favor their position. In general, the public isn't concerned with the cause of these disputes. And it doesn't care how they are settled. The only time the public shows any concern is when a work stoppage directly affects many people.

Government's Role in Collective Bargaining

Occasionally, government becomes involved in collective bargaining. It does so as a referee. Some people believe government should take a more active role in such bargaining. There are, on the other hand, people who believe government should be less active in this area. At the present time, government sets and enforces standards of safety and health in work areas. It has set minimum wages and maximum hours of work. It has brought an end to widespread use of child labor. In addition, government prohibits discrimination in employment based on race, religion, sex, age, or nationality.

There has been little direct intervention by government in employee-management relations—even in disputes where work stoppages have occurred. There are times when the two sides cannot reach agreement. At such times, a state or federal mediator is sent to meet with the parties. A *mediator* is a neutral person who meets with employee and management representatives to help settle employment disputes. The mediator, usually a government agent, is an expert in collective bargaining. The mediator has no power to force either side to do anything. Mediators simply try to provide a neutral viewpoint while helping both sides reach agreement.

If the two parties cannot reach agreement through negotiation or mediation, the government usually supervises a process called arbitration. Under *arbitration,* the two sides agree on a neutral person to resolve the issues involved in the dispute. This person is called the arbitrator. An *arbitrator* is a person chosen by the two parties to listen to both sides of a labor dispute and make a decision which must be accepted by both parties. Arbitration may be used in original employment agreements or to settle a grievance arising out of the original agreement. In contrast to a mediator, the arbitrator has the power to make a binding decision. Arbitration is used only when all other means of reaching agreement have failed.

At times when the two sides in a labor dispute cannot reach agreement, mediation may have to be tried. (Licht/Stockmarket, Los Angeles)

Learning Activities

Increasing Your Business Vocabulary

You should become familiar with each of the terms shown below. On a sheet of paper write the numbers 1 through 9. Then write alongside each number the term that best matches each of the numbered definitions.

arbitrator / bargaining agent / collective bargaining / grievance / labor union / mediator / right-to-work laws / seniority / union shops

1. An elected employee group that represents employees in collective bargaining.

2. An agreement under which an employer can hire nonunion employees but requires that these employees must join the union after a specified period of time or give up their jobs.

3. State laws that make compulsory union membership and the union shop illegal.

4. The status an employee gets based on his or her length of service with an employer.

5. A complaint by one side or the other that the terms of an employment agreement are not being met.

6. An organization of employees formed and operated to promote and protect the welfare, interest, and rights of the members.

7. The process in which management and employee representatives meet and reach agreement on all types of job-related issues and concerns.

8. A neutral person who meets with employee and management representatives to help settle employment disputes.

9. A person chosen by the two parties to listen to both sides of an employment dispute and make a decision that must be accepted by both parties.

Understanding Business

1. What is one of the major purposes of labor unions?

2. Identify several employment issues and concerns.

3. How does an industrial union differ from a trade union?

4. Describe the general trends in labor union membership at the present time.

5. What is the purpose of collective bargaining?

6. How does a bargaining agent get the rights to act for a group of employees?

7. What are some reasons why labor unions oppose right-to-work laws?

8. Where cost-of-living clauses are in force, what is used to determine the percentage increase in prices in the economy?

9. Why is seniority so important to employees?

10. What role does government play in collective bargaining?

Business Problems and Projects

1. On a form similar to the one shown below, list at least five business firms in your community where employees bargain collectively with the employer to determine wages, hours,

working conditions, etc. Also list the name of the local union or employee association.

	Employer	Collective Bargaining Agent
Example	Salesclerks	Retail Clerks of America

2. Seniority is a major issue in many employment situations.

   a. List three advantages of using the seniority system as a basis for determining promotions, layoffs, and call backs of workers who have been laid off.

   b. List three disadvantages of using seniority as basis for promotions, layoffs, and call backs.

   c. Why do labor unions and employee associations generally favor the seniority system?

   d. Why do employers and members of management generally dislike the strict application of the seniority system?

   e. Do young employees generally favor or oppose the seniority system? Why?

3. One of the ways in which unions attempt to serve their members is by supporting the reduction of working hours. Read the article below and then answer the questions that follow it.

LABOR LEADERS URGE SHORTENED WORK WEEK

Representatives of several local labor organizations will meet this week to organize a rally for the shortened work week. The rally signals the first real local effort to reduce the work week since labor's 40-hour week campaign of the 1930s. One of the organizers of the rally, Tom Burns, says that the basic purpose of the shorter week is to promote full employment by spreading jobs to more individuals. According to Burns, most of the labor leaders are well aware of the economic predictions that indicate unemployment will remain well above 6 percent for the next ten years. They believe that a shorter work week will hold the rate down to manageable levels. An announcement of the specifics of the rally will be made by next Monday.

Announcement of the proposed rally has several management people taking a very strong position against the proposed cut in the work week. Selma Webster, an executive at United Business, Inc. says that a shorter work week, especially without a cut in pay, is impossible. According to Webster, her main objections to the shorter week are the increased costs to the firm. She indicated that a cut in hours is equivalent to a raise in pay, and that these costs will eventually have to be passed on to the consumers. Mrs. Webster is not confident that the demands will be dropped during the next round of negotiations, however, because the shorter work week has such widespread support among the rank and file employees. When asked whether her firm would move to block the shorter work week, Mrs. Webster replied, "We'll just have to wait and see what develops."

a. What is the purpose of the proposed rally?

b. Why do unions want to shorten the work week?

c. Why is management opposed to a shorter work week?

d. Who is likely to pay the costs of a shorter work week in this case?

e. When is the interest usually highest for a shorter work week?

f. Why is Mrs. Webster not confident that the demands for a shorter work week will be dropped?

g. Does United Business, Inc. have any plans to deal with the demands for a shorter work week?

h. What unemployment trends are predicted by economists in the article?

Index